BERLIN

ABOUT THE CITY GUIDES

Louis Vuitton has selected its favourite places in destination cities around the world. The aim is to offer a good balance of addresses, from time-honoured classics to fashionable new establishments. Well known or offbeat, exclusive or unassuming, they are invariably fascinating, each conveying in its own way something of the essence of the city. Given the speed at which cities evolve, between the time when the guide was researched and its publication some addresses may have closed, others may have emerged and prices may have changed. A renowned chef may have taken his talents to another restaurant, a fashion store may have moved or a museum closed temporarily for renovation. Such changes will be incorporated in the next edition of the Louis Vuitton City Guide.

LOUIS VUITTON AND TRAVEL

Travel is a multifaceted art.
It is something that is imagined,
envisioned and savoured. As for
the journey itself, it cannot be totally
improvised. It requires planning
and organization.

Louis Vuitton and the history of luggage

Right from its foundation in 1854, Maison Louis Vuitton
stood out for its creativity, highlighted by a series of inventions
and innovations that revolutionized the art of travelling.
Representing three generations, Louis, Georges and Gaston were
the three men who, at the turn of the 20th century, built the
reputation of a house whose savoir-faire went well beyond simple
luggage. Each had his own way of meeting travellers' expectations,
ranging from the manufacturing of trunks to the design of
lightweight, refined bags, as the craftsman's skill and the styling
of the object came together in the service of the idea. Witness the
unpickable lock invented in 1890 and still valuable today, and
the famous Keepall, the first duffel-type (*polochon*) bag, which
inaugurated the era of supple bags.

Extraordinary luggage for unique travellers

Travellers and explorers demanded the impossible. A bed-trunk
to withstand the humid heat of the jungle for Pierre Savorgnan
de Brazza, a trunk-cum-secretaire to house his precious scores
for the conductor Leopold Stokowski and a luxurious chest for
the Maharajah of Baroda's tea service. The famous wardrobe,
designed so that travellers would never have to unpack, was followed
by a host of creations, from the supremely surprising to the last word

in luxury. Witness the "driver bag", designed when the motor car was in its infancy, capable of holding spare tyres and inner tubes, as well as the driver's effects, but also usable as a shower tub! Also extraordinary is the extreme refinement of the toiletry set in crocodile, tortoiseshell and cut crystal designed for the opera singer Marthe Chenal. Over the years, Louis Vuitton has continued to invent the most beautiful luggage for the most fabulous journeys.

Moving on: the spirit of travel

Beautiful luggage plays its part in departure reverie. But, ultimately, travellers' dreams are born of encounters. Encounters with cities, to which those other travel essentials, the Louis Vuitton City Guides, hold the key. Redesigned as individual volumes, the Louis Vuitton City Guides know no bounds. Revisited and transformed in 2013 (to mark their fifteenth birthday), the guides explore destination cities the world over. Today, twenty-nine cities covering all continents are celebrated by the Louis Vuitton City Guides. Discovering these cities has been made even simpler thanks to the digital version of the City Guides. Available for iPhone and iPad, the app offers a compact vision of all these exciting destinations, which look to the future while cherishing their past.

A mirror and setter of trends

Readers will discover the subtle cocktail of offbeat finds, classics and dependable addresses that have made the Louis Vuitton City Guides such a success. The guides are served by a team of talented journalists and writers from various countries and backgrounds. Sharp-eyed and informed chroniclers of the transformations at work in the heart of the city, they offer unexpected perspectives on fashion, well-being, interior design, contemporary art, gastronomy and culture, capturing the essence of each metropolis. Always open-minded, they are prepared when necessary to omit the obvious address in favour of some little-known new find, following a discerning trail from the finest hotels to the best chocolatiers and from the hippest fashion addresses to spaces showcasing art. Their contributions, combined with those of renowned artists, designers, business people and gallerists, make the City Guides unique mirrors and setters of trends, astute witnesses to urban vitality. The original photographs illustrating the Louis Vuitton City Guides complement the vision that these unique books offer of each destination.

CONTENTS

BARRIE KOSKY, GUEST

PORTRAIT

<u>Barrie Kosky, who was born in Australia but has Mitteleuropa roots, has been the artistic director of the Komische Oper Berlin since 2012.</u>

A unique institution

Comic opera, which incorporates both song and speech, is the cheeky second cousin of grand opera. When he was appointed artistic director of the Komische Oper Berlin in 2012, nine years after first being hired as a director, Barrie Kosky became the first non-German to occupy this prestigious post. This brilliant, energetic, cosmopolitan, cultured man is an unconventional, fearless director who has brought a unique iconoclasm and vibrancy to the task, ensuring that this institution remains both traditional and innovative. Through his remarkable creative drive, he has propelled the Komische Oper Berlin, formerly one of the most important East German opera houses, to the front rank of international opera houses.

An Australian childhood

Australian-born Barrie Kosky has been a shameless dreamer since early childhood, when he was brought up on bedtime tales featuring frightening creatures and happenings told by his grandmothers and aunts, who had all fled World War II and the Nazis. These are almost certainly the distant source of his flamboyant predilection for phantasmagorical, grotesque, fabled and haunted productions. Barrie Kosky was still a teenager when he staged a version of Büchner's *Woyzeck* for his school to music by Mahler. A world away from the local surf beaches and easy Aussie optimism, which for him were oppressive. He was later to write about all this in his book *On Ecstasy*, a guide to stimulating olfactory, culinary, sexual and musical sensations, which provides a key to understanding how he managed to break out of his past Down Under. As an Aussie who feels like a foreigner when he goes home, Barrie Kosky defines himself somewhat provocatively as a gay Jewish Australian hybrid. He openly refers to this personal chemistry when explaining his work and his vision of things, and also how he lives his life. And lurking in the shadows, there is always the powerful influence of circus, vaudeville, film and the fairy stories told to him by his grandmothers.

A brilliant career

Fascinated by German Expressionism, the dreamy longings of Romanticism and the hysteria of modernism, Barrie Kosky reinvents but does not betray the works of Wagner, Janáček, Weill, Berg and Mahler. There have been soaring attendance figures, critical acclaim and enthusiastic audiences. His productions of Monteverdi's *L'Orfeo*, *The Return of Ulysses* and *The Coronation of Poppea* – played one after another in a twelve-hour marathon – was *the* event of the 2012 season. His programmes each season are built around a mixture of light entertainment and high opera. The operetta *Clivia* played to full houses, Gluck's *Iphigenia in Tauris* was a major hit and Mozart's *Die Zauberflöte* brought the house down – all three were played in German – while Prokofiev's opera *The Fiery Angel* was sung in Russian. Kosky believes in doing a work in the original language when the work demands it, but with subtitles.

A public man

Kosky doesn't have an office and hates sitting behind a desk, so he uses a low wooden structure piled up with such books as a biography of Gogol, a collection of six Yiddish plays and an essay entitled "Messiahs of 1933", sitting alongside the visiting card of the Hungarian ambassador. It feels more like a lounge, with a large sofa and black leather armchairs. A black suitcase lies nearby ready for a sudden trip out of town – it actually got lost once and had to be sent from Amsterdam. It bears witness to the endless travels of this voluble maestro with his horn-rimmed glasses and his wicked sense of humour, which he directs mainly at himself. As the clever alchemist of his own excesses, Barrie Kosky proves that beneath the gilded 19th-century neo-Baroque theatre, set inside a post-socialist bunker, the fusion of tradition and innovation produces miraculous results. Berlin suits him perfectly – and he speaks German so fluently that visitors never hear the slightest accent.

"I love this very open city which ... is simply a collection of villages – 'shtetls', as they say in Yiddish." Barrie Kosky

Melbourne-Berlin, one-way easy street

I was born and grew up in Melbourne, in Australia. My parents were furriers. My father's family originally fled the pogroms in Russia just before the 1917 Revolution. My mother's side was a mix of Hungarian and Polish origins, and the exodus took place after 1945, when my family was liberated from the camps. My grandmothers and great-aunts, all coiffed and dyed with henna, wore jewellery that was as heavy as their accent in several languages. And they would tell me hair-raising stories. I was lucky enough to have a particularly cultivated education. I took my first trip outside Australia to Europe and the United States in the mid-1980s with my father, who wanted to find new types of fur, such as possum or fox. I was fifteen at the time, and chose the cities of our trip based on the fame of their operas: Milan, Vienna and Berlin, where at the time the Wall was still standing. It was actually pretty scary. We only stayed four days and never left West Berlin, but I managed to get two tickets for the New Year Philharmonic concert in the Hans Scharoun building, near the Wall. It was conducted by Herbert von Karajan, who was half packed in plaster after a skiing accident. He led the orchestra with one hand, his only free arm moving as if he was made of rubber. It was a miracle. Unforgettable!

Berlin story

As I travel a lot for work, I have returned to Berlin several times, once right after my studies when I finally went over to the East side. I felt an immediate sense of connection. I'm not the first, nor the last person to experience this. I also came back as an established director at the invitation of the Goethe Institute when I was living in Vienna. I was later invited to become director of the Komische Oper Berlin. I love this very open city which has always been a free place, at least when it was not systematically sliced up, bled to death, decimated and divided. For me, Berlin is simply a collection of villages – shtetls, as they say in Yiddish. I speak German because it was the language of culture for my maternal grandmother. She also spoke Italian and French, the languages of love and good food. I studied German in Düsseldorf and Heidelberg.

Berlin, a home from home

I have no sense of patriotism. I have no roots, no village, town or district that gives me the sort of anchor that many Lebanese, Greeks or Italians have who emigrated to Australia. I have no particular place to go back to. In my case, time and war have wiped out everything from the Warsaw ghetto to Budapest. I have no home, which is probably why I love travelling in trains: I love these real-time, almost romantic trips across Europe, watching the landscapes, sleeping, reading, being alone and waking up in another country. I can't think of anything more exotic. When I think of the many origins of my family, it is strange to realize that I am the first to live in Berlin. And more specifically in Schöneberg. I chose this place and I am happy about the idea of growing old here, after spending half my time travelling across Europe.

My life in Berlin

I do not have a car, so I walk with my dog. I am a workaholic, even if creating stage works is not really a job but a privilege. However exhausting and difficult rehearsals, dialogues and music can be, I really enjoy them. Berlin gives me the energy to unleash my creativity, but also jacks up the complexity of things by the almost tectonic intermixing of culture, music, memory and nostalgia. Berlin was the 20th century's most iconic city, constantly exposed to both superficial and terrible historical events ranging from Bismarck to the Wall. By coming to live here, I have probably come full circle.

THE CITY AND ITS NEIGHBOURHOODS

Following the creation of Greater Berlin in 1920, the city had twenty boroughs (*Verwaltungsbezirke*). When the capital was split in two after the Second World War, half of these became part of the East, where three new ones were created, bringing the figure to twenty-three. Following the reform of 2001, these boroughs were reorganized into the twelve current boroughs. In this latest reshuffling, Mitte (Centre) absorbed Tiergarten and Wedding, and Pankow swallowed up Prenzlauer Berg and Weißensee. Several other old boroughs, such as Charlottenburg-Wilmersdorf and Tempelhof-Schöneberg, were merged. A few remained unchanged, such as Spandau, Reinickendorf and Neukölln.

Berliners are often very attached to their home districts, where in many cases they've lived for a long time, if not all their lives. Above all, they continue to talk about west and east Berlin as separate entities with their own personalities. This is even true of the youngest among them, who never knew the Wall. The inhabitants of Charlottenburg – a huge swanky district in the west – who know how to watch the pennies, rarely see the point of straying beyond the Tiergarten to see what's going on in the east. Conversely, the good folk of Prenzlauer Berg carry their passports with them when they venture into west Berlin, which is enjoying an artistic, retailing and hotel boom that promises to return it to the centre of a city that has always had two centres.

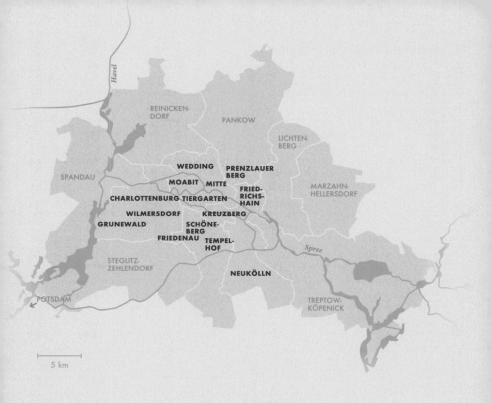

5 km

MITTE
City centre & major museums

TIERGARTEN
Peaceful parkland & new architecture

CHARLOTTENBURG
Smart residential & chic shopping

WILMERSDORF, GRUNEWALD
Affluent districts & woodland lakes

PRENZLAUER BERG
Gentrification & bobo stronghold

SCHÖNEBERG, FRIEDENAU
Residential & literary

KREUZBERG
Alternative & arty

NEUKÖLLN
Multi-ethnic & shabby chic

FRIEDRICHSHAIN
Hip & bohemian

MOABIT, WEDDING
Administrative hub & social diversity

TEMPELHOF
Public park & regeneration

MITTE
City centre & major museums

Mitte is such a large borough that it encompasses thirteen *Stadtviertel* (smaller districts). The historic heart of the city, it became part of East Germany after the war and declined in importance. Following reunification, it has returned to the forefront again, becoming a bastion of *Neues Berlin* and a symbol of a resurgent Germany. It is home to the reunified capital's greatest monuments, museums and institutions. Among the embassies, grand hotels, ministries, TV studios and newspaper offices can be found the Brandenburg Gate, the Humboldt University, Museumsinsel, the Berliner Dom, the (disfigured) Alexanderplatz and the huge Stadtschloss, which is currently undergoing reconstruction. Between the Oranienburger Straße (where the Neue Synagogue is located) and the long, dreary Torstraße (home to cutting-edge fashion stores) is a vibrant neighbourhood of galleries, design showrooms and designer hotels and cafés. The edgy epicentre has shifted away from the now touristy Hackesche Höfe district and the Alte Schönhauser Straße towards Rosa-Luxemburg-Straße, the last bastion of resistance against the massive invasion of international stores. Rosenthaler Platz, on the other hand, has become the realm of low-cost hotels and an assortment of bars, cafés and restaurants. Brunnenstraße, running north from here, leads to the working-class Wedding neighbourhood.

TIERGARTEN
Peaceful parkland & new architecture

Now part of Mitte, this neighbourhood is named after the huge, wooded park that stretches from Zoo station to the Brandenburg Gate. This green lung is bisected by the interminable Straße des 17 Juni, a triumphant way punctuated halfway along by the Siegessäule (Victory Column), and is bounded to the north by the Spree. Nearby are the Haus der Kulturen der Welt (known as the "pregnant oyster"), the Reichstag building and the Bundestag, Schloss Bellevue, the Konrad Adenauer Foundation, the Bauhaus archives, the Gemäldegalerie, the Philharmonie and the new Potsdamer Platz, a large complex of shops, hotels and cinemas. Tiergarten is also, as it was before the war, the embassy neighbourhood. To the north-west is the Hansaviertel, with its architectural vestiges from the Interbau 57 international exhibition. To the south-east, is the Potsdamerstraße, an up-and-coming address since the arrival of numerous galleries and Andreas Murkudis's concept store. Finally, the formerly neglected areas around Zoo station and the Gedächtniskirche symbolize west Berlin's resurgence now that the possibilities of the east have been exhausted.

CHARLOTTENBURG
Smart residential & chic shopping

Since 2001, Charlottenburg and Wilmersdorf – formerly independent municipalities annexed by Greater Berlin – have formed a single borough. Nonetheless, in the eyes of Berliners and the local inhabitants, the two districts continue to exist as two distinct entities, physically separated by the Kurfürstendamm, or "Ku'damm". Paradoxically, this avenue 3 kilometres long could be a district in itself. It was Bismarck who, on his return from Paris in 1881, decided to transform a simple road into the German Champs-Elysées. The stamping ground of the liberal bourgeoisie, the Ku'damm became a centre of luxury, whereas today it offers a splendid diversity of stores. Charlottenburg lies to the north of the Ku'damm. It was nicknamed Charlottengrad when rich Russian families sought exile here following the 1919 Revolution, and the label has recently been revived now that Russians are moving in once again. Charlottenburg is peaceful, residential and well-heeled – the preferred residential district, in fact, of real Berliners, as well as newcomers, who plump for the area around the Schloss Charlottenburg, Savignyplatz and Lietzenseepark. Spared from the ravages of the Second World War, after which it was in the British zone, Charlottenburg, together with Schöneberg, is the district that best retells Berlin's past.

WILMERSDORF, GRUNEWALD
Affluent districts & woodland lakes
Wilmersdorf is south of the Ku'damm and takes full advantage of the bustling nearby retail and tourist activities. Formerly an independent district that was merged with Charlottenburg, it is a residential area – albeit a tad less affluent than the latter. It is broken up by broad highways, sometimes giving it the feel of a suburb. Wilmersdorf was mostly rebuilt after the Second World War and is a quiet, markedly unhip neighbourhood. It has a few pockets of well-preserved architecture, such as the streets running perpendicular to the Ku'damm and the area around the Ludwigkirchplatz. To the south-west, Grunewald is a district of forest and lakes, a residential enclave for the well-heeled, who live in lavish villas tucked away behind the trees. Dog-owners take their pets to the forest for exercise. You can also lunch or dine on the terrace of lakeside chalets, or bathe or go boating.

PRENZLAUER BERG
Gentrification & bobo stronghold
Now part of the borough of Pankow, Prenzlauer Berg (or Prenzl'berg, as it's known to locals) is located in the north-east of the city, beyond the Alexanderplatz. Less damaged by Allied bombing than the centre of Berlin, it was the first neighbourhood in the former East to emerge from the torpor brought about

by communism. It was situated in the soviet zone, but had a less industrial and working-class past. It was laid out at the beginning of the 20th century and has wider streets and pavements than most other parts of Berlin. This was the neighbourhood that Honecker chose to illustrate his propaganda speeches. It was used as a fake shop window for the communist good life. Some of its streets were restored – but only the facades. Now, after a period of being very fashionable, Prenzl'berg has lost a little of its edge due to its colonization by bobos, many of them foreigners, and the inevitable loss of its Ostalgie cachet. The latter gave it a subversive charm twenty years ago and led to many of its long-time residents being forced to move elsewhere. Those who remain now moan about the closure of the few remaining food shops, replaced by fashion boutiques and bars, cafés and restaurants, of which there are now almost one per inhabitant. On Saturdays, it is difficult to find room on the pavement amid all the buggies and prams. Indeed, the neighbourhood has acquired a new nickname, "Preganancy Hill", a reference to the high local birth rate.

SCHÖNEBERG, FRIEDENAU
Residential & literary
In the days of the Wall, the quiet working-class quarter of Schöneberg was in the American zone. It is in southern Berlin, adjoining Wilmersdorf to the west and Tiergarten to the north. Today it forms part of the Tempelhof-Schöneberg borough and is the new stronghold of moderate Berlin bohemians who are disdainful about almost everything that lies to the east, starting with Prenzlauer Berg. Schöneberg is a peaceful residential neighbourhood that's got more than its fair share of great places to go. It has a high percentage of vintage and organic shops, with chain stores almost non-existent. It is also a gay bastion, with a flourishing nightlife centred on Fuggerstraße and Motzstraße. There are

parks and wide, tree-lined streets, and the architecture is generally easy on the eye. Here one can live without fretting about what's going on elsewhere. The same is true in Friedenau, lying to the south-west of Schöneberg. This friendly residential district has traditionally been prized by writers, making it a well-known *Literatür-Bezirk* with its own dedicated hotel. Friedenau has a nice provincial feel about it and in its small cemetery you can find the graves of Bertolt Brecht, Marlene Dietrich and Helmut Newton, among other famous people.

KREUZBERG
Alternative & arty
Formerly known as Hallesches Tor, Kreuzberg, which was also in the American zone, was up until 1989 a dead end coming up against the Wall. During the Cold War, it was a border post where spies were exchanged. Bisected by the Kottbusser Damm and served by the Kottbusser Tor U-Bahn station, Kreuzberg continues to be referred to by its postcode, SO 36 (Süd-Ost, district 36). During the 1970s it housed Berlin's biggest, most militant community of squats. Kreuzberg remains etched into memories as the *Viertel* of violent clashes between anarchists and the police. A spirit of rebellion lingers on, with residents quick to protest against objectionable real estate projects. Kreuzberg is also a low-income, multiethnic area, with first-generation Turkish émigrés. It's a neighbourhood torn between its heritage of political radicalism and its present as a popular nightlife hotspot. It is Berlin's most densely populated neighbourhood, home, along with its neighbour Neukölln, to large ecumenical cemeteries. Berliners have recently taken to calling this frontier zone of streets straddling both neighbourhoods "Kreuzkölln", an epicentre of cool that is teeming with hip bars, cafés and shops.

NEUKÖLLN
Multi-ethnic & shabby chic
Neukölln, in south-eastern Berlin, is one of the city's largest districts, and also one of the most densely populated, with half of the inhabitants being immigrants – mostly and historically Turkish, to the point of earning it the moniker Little Istanbul. Once an independent town, enclosed by the Wall on the western side until 1989, Neukölln oscillates between multi-ethnicity perceived as a cultural asset – the 48 Stunden Neukölln (48 Hours) festival is one of the biggest cultural events in the city – and the endless inter-ethnic frictions in certain run-down areas. Neukölln has several architectural sites, including the Hufeisensiedlung (Horseshoe Estate) designed by Bruno Taut before the Second World War – a UNESCO listed site – and Gropiusstadt, designed by Walter Gropius in the early 1960s, a veritable town-within-a-town where the scandalous Christiane F. grew up. Around the Reuterstraße, to the north of this district, there are small signs of a burgeoning alternative lifestyle appearing, as a result of which Neukölln has been branded the hippest new quarter in Berlin.

FRIEDRICHSHAIN
Hip & bohemian
Administratively, Friedrichshain has been combined with Kreuzberg to form a single borough. On the ground, the two neighbourhoods are separated by the Spree and linked by three bridges that are a long way from each other. Formerly in the East, and still fairly desolate in the areas abutting the former trace of the Wall that bounded it, F'shain is dominated by a huge park, the Volkspark, and bisected by the Karl-Marx-Allee, the former proletarian Champs-Élysées, and its continuation, the Frankfurter Allee. The neighbourhood has gradually been absorbing the bobo overflow from its neighbour Prenzlauer Berg, and this partially residential neighbourhood has

been ironically nicknamed the "Prenz'l without kids". It is less built up and its liveliest areas can be found on the banks of the Spree, site of the East Side Gallery, an organized vestige of the Wall that prompts very strong reactions whenever the idea of moving it is mooted. Above all, there are the old quays of the Osthafen. The Mediaspree project proved very unpopular with local residents and has been scaled down as a result. The Universal Music building, Allianz tower and 02 World have already been built, together with the eye-catching Nhow Hotel. And disused port buildings are being colonized by start-ups.

MOABIT, WEDDING
Administrative hub & social diversity
Moabit, which shares its frontiers, naturally traced by the Spree, with Charlottenburg, Tiergarten and Mitte, and abuts Wedding, is an island formerly occupied by the French Huguenots. A former prison and sanitary quarter where thousands of workers used to be housed, Moabit was a centre for German communism before the war. After 1945, it was occupied by French forces, no doubt because the famous Paris-Moscow railway passed through it. The train of history: the historic Hamburger Bahnhof has been converted into one of the biggest museums of contemporary art in German. As for the gigantic new Hauptbahnhof (central station) which straddles the Berlin-Spandau canal on a site that was until not so long ago a wasteland, it will form the heart of what looks likely to be a rather soulless new neighbourhood. Moabit is also a neighbourhood of ministries and that of the tentacular Charité hospital complex. The western parts of Moabit are more working-class and ethnic, and can be interesting to explore. Multicultural Wedding, to the north of Moabit, is an up-and-coming neighbourhood with an emerging arts

scene. It is undistinguished architecturally, but has good transport links and, for the moment, relatively affordable rents.

TEMPELHOF
Public park & regeneration
Tempelhof, administratively joined to Schöneberg, is located in the south of Berlin and is bordered by Schöneberg, Kreuzberg and Neukölln. It is home to the former airport of the same name, the largest building in the world after the Pentagon and Ceaucescu's palace in Bucharest. Construction on it started in 1923, financed by Jewish investors subsequently expropriated by the Nazi regime, greatly expanded between 1934 and 1936 as part of Albert Speer's urban project. It was designed by Ernst Sagebiel in the rectilinear style popular during the Third Reich and was opened in 1941. Hitler disliked it, however, a fact that undermined the insinuations prompted by those opposed to its closure. But Tempelhof does not for all that embody rampant *Ostalgie*: situated in the West after 1945, the airport played a vital role during the blockade of Berlin in 1948 and 1949 decreed by Stalin to starve and punish the population. The airlift organized by the West, with cargo planes landing and taking off round the clock, saved the city from penury and famine. That is why the Tempelhof site has special poignancy for Berliners. After four years of struggle and a final contest opposing the left and the right, and Chancellor Angela Merkel and Klaus Wowereit, Berlin's former media-savvy social democrat mayor, the airport closed on 31 October 2008. Following opposition to an ambitious project to redevelop the Tempelhof site, a referendum was held in 2014, with locals voting to keep it unchanged. The Volksbühne has been using Hangar 5 as a temporary theatre for selected performances.

THE ESSENTIALS

Berlin is a city that is in a perpetual state of becoming. It's an ever-shifting work-in-progress that is pregnant with possibilities while being indelibly marked by its history.

Ever since the fall of the Wall that divided it, Berlin has been endlessly reinventing itself, responding to the changes imposed on it by a new modernity. As the permanent capital of a nation united at last, Berlin is now home to more than three and a half million inhabitants. The urban landscape is slowly healing: there are still gaps to fill and wounds to treat, colossal building sites and nostalgic restorations, but Berlin is coming to terms with its new status. Its symbolic structures have regained their lustre and their standing. What was once East Berlin has been revitalized, and it is now the turn of the former West, which has been stagnating since 1989, to undergo a vast programme of architectural and urban restoration. In setting out to reconquer the former West, Berliners are in danger of repeating the same mistakes made during the reconstruction of the 1950s. This time, however, the strong, vibrant counter-culture should exert a positive countervailing force.

The third most popular tourist destination in Europe after London and Paris, with visitor numbers rising every year, and permanent home to around half a million foreign residents from more than 185 countries, cosmopolitan Berlin has reclaimed its place as one of Europe's most dynamic and modern metropolises.

ARRIVING IN THE CITY

AIRPORT FORMALITIES

Of the four airports that served the city fifteen years ago, only two are still in service, Tegel (TXL) and Schönefeld (SXF). Eventually, they will be replaced by the new Berlin Brandenburg airport. Originally due to open in 2011, the project has experienced a series of embarrassing delays and cost overruns. Small airports unworthy of a major capital like Berlin, both Tegel (21 million passengers a year) and Schönefeld offer rapid passport control services for passengers from outside the Schengen zone. Non-EU passengers face waits of ten or fifteen minutes at most. The last flights of the evening are literally "fast-tracked". Of course, flights from countries deemed "sensitive" are subject to lengthier checks. Baggage collection is equally quick, as is exit from the airports.
Access to the passport control zone: 10 to 20 min
Checks: 10 to 15 min
www.berlin-airport.de

GETTING TO THE CITY
TRAIN

There is no rail line to the city centre from Tegel airport. However, Schönefeld, 20 kilometres from the centre, has a railway station where you can catch regional trains on the RE7 and RB14 lines (which act as an Airport Express), as well as S-Bahn lines S9 and S45 to the centre.
Airport Express RE7, RB14: 30 min, every 20 min, from 4:40am to 11:20pm, €3.20
S-Bahn S9 (city centre) or S45 (Südkreuz): 45 min, every 20 min, from 4am to 0:30am, €3.20
www.s-bahn-berlin.de, www.berlin.de, www.bvg.de

BUS

As Tegel airport has no train service to the city centre, it's best to take the TXL Express bus, which goes to Alexanderplatz

with a few stops en route. The X9 Express bus connects Tegel with the U- and S-Bahn station at Zoologischer Garten and the new Hauptbahnhof, the city's central station. There are plenty of buses from Schönefeld to the city centre. The X7 Express bus goes to the Rudow U-Bahn station.
TXL JetExpressBus (from Tegel to S-Bahn/U-Bahn Alexanderplatz): 40–45 min, departs every 7 to 20 min, 4:30am to midnight, €2.60
X9 JetExpressBus (from Tegel to S-Bahn/U-Bahn Zoologischer Garten): 20–30 min, departs every 10 to 20 min, 4:30am to 0:30pm, €2.60
X7 (from Schönefeld to U-Bahn Rudow): 7 min, departs every 20 to 30 min, 4:30am to 11:30pm, €3.20
www.berlin-airport.de
www.vbb.de

TAXI

Given the short distances between the two airports and the city centre and the fairly central location of the Hauptbahnhof, taking a taxi seems a sensible option, especially if there are two or three passengers. There are always taxis at the airport ranks, even during off-peak times and late in the evening. All taxis are obligated to take credit cards, so don't worry about keeping change on you. Tipping is not compulsory but is welcome. The driver will always get out of the vehicle and open the boot to get the luggage out.
From Tegel: 10 km, 20 to 30 min, €20 to €25
From Schönefeld: 22 km, 40 to 50 min, €35 to €40
Funk Taxi Berlin: tel 030 26 10 26,
www.funk-taxi-berlin.de
Taxi Berlin: tel 030 20 20 20,
www.taxi-berlin.de
TaxiFunk Berlin: tel 030 44 33 22,
www.taxifunkberlin.de
Würfelfunk: tel 030 21 01 01,
www.wuerfelfunk.de

892 km²
in surface area

3.5 million inhabitants

1,300 electric cars

16 metres
length of the shortest street,
Eiergasse, in Mitte

LIMOUSINE

Berliners hate drawing attention to
themselves, so hiring a stretch limousine
and driver is generally restricted to
international VIPs, rock stars on tour or
visiting celebrities. More restrained and
classy, the VW Phaeton and Class S
Mercedes-Benz are targeted at business
executives and art collectors on scouting
expeditions. Mercedes people carriers are
used by small groups or large families who
would find a taxi too small. Prices and
services are on demand and tailored to
the client. The Beverly Cars agency is one
of the most popular in the field.
Beverly Cars: tel 030 6331 3777,
www.beverlycars.de

FIRST IMPRESSIONS

Whether you arrive at Tegel (north-west)
or Schönefeld (south-east), which, despite
appearances to the contrary, are both
international airports, getting into the city
by road or by rail is very quick. Set right
on the edge of Berlin, Tegel's only real
attraction is its location. Once you're past
the vintage aircraft on show outside it,
the motorway into Berlin gets you to
Charlottenburg or Westend in a problem-
free 20 minutes, barely enough time
to notice you're entering the city.
No travelling through endless stretches
of suburbia, just some rivers and bridges
to cross. Schönefeld airport is even more
provincial, practically rural. Formerly
in the Soviet sector south-east of the city,
it has retained its almost rudimentary
appearance (it was built in 1946, and then
modernized). Passengers arriving here are
often surprised to see a number of people
in the crowd at the arrivals gate holding
bouquets of flowers or boxes of cakes as
a welcome gift for their visitors. As this
airport is beyond the border of the Berlin
Land (region), it obviously takes a lot
longer to get into the city, with a rather
featureless stretch of countryside to cross.
After dark, when public transport is less
reliable, a taxi is the best option. Watch the
street lighting become increasingly bright
the closer you get to the city.

GETTING AROUND THE CITY

TAXIS

Berlin's 7,000 taxis are operated by half-a-dozen companies and are all cream-coloured. The "For Hire" sign on the roof is easy to spot as it changes colour and can be seen from a good distance. The city has plenty of taxi ranks, but it is perfectly acceptable to hail a cab in traffic. When Berliners are travelling alone they generally sit up front with the driver, mainly as an expression of equality. Fares are best paid in small change or notes, rounding up the total, saying "Das stimmt so", which basically means "keep the change". If you need a receipt, say "Ich brauche ein Quittung, bitte" ("I need a receipt, please"). There is no additional charge for luggage.

Minimum fare: €4
Average fare: €8 to €15
Tip: round up the total or give an extra €1 to €5

Funk Taxi Berlin: tel 26 10 26,
www.funk-taxi-berlin.de
Taxi Berlin: tel 20 20 20, www.taxi-berlin.de
TaxiFunk Berlin: tel 44 33 22,
www.taxifunkberlin.de
Würfelfunk: tel 21 01 01, www.wuerfelfunk.de

ON FOOT

Berlin is very spread out, so no one really tries to cross the city on foot. However, Berliners are great walkers in their own neighbourhoods. The streets are very long and often served by two or even three U-Bahn stations, a great help when one has underestimated the distance between two points, the street numbering system being quite misleading. Berlin streets are numbered in sequence down one side of the street and when you reach the end the same system applies to the opposite side (so no. 1 can be opposite no. 225, for example).

U-BAHN AND S-BAHN

Berlin is comprehensively covered by a network known as the U-Bahn, operated by the city's transport authority (BVG). Its 10 lines serve 173 stations. The most

recent line, the U55, links the Hauptbahnhof to Brandenburg Gate, and it is being extended to join up with line U5.
The U-Bahn, indicated by a capital U, is supplemented by the S-Bahn operated by the Deutsche Bahn rail company, which shares a number of stations with it. An urban rail network, the S-Bahn has 166 stations served by 15 lines on a 328-km network, with an orbital line going right round Berlin city centre.

Daily from 4am to 1am, every 4 to 15 min
Single ticket (S-Bahn/U-Bahn)
Zone AB: €2.70, day ticket: €7
Berlin CityTourCard: €17.50 to €39.50 (from 48 hrs to 6 days)
Berlin WelcomeCard: €19.50 to €41.50 (from 48 hrs to 6 days)

www.visitberlin.de, www.bvg.de,
www.berlin-en-ligne.com

BUSES

Double-decker buses have been operating in Berlin since 1925. The 1,300 yellow BVG buses run on 17 lines, including the 100, nicknamed the Hop On/Hop Off, created after reunification to link east and west (Zoo-Alexanderplatz) and backed up by the 200. Note: don't confuse these bus services with the ones run by private companies offering the same services for much higher fares. When they want to get from one place to another quickly, Berliners avoid the bus, even though they travel quite fast along their special bus lanes. Night buses run throughout the night, although the routes differ from the daytime bus routes.
The same tickets are valid for all BVG services

www.visitberlin.de, www.bvg.de,
www.berlin-en-ligne.com

TRAMS

In old photos of Berlin, streets very often have tram tracks. The *Straßenbahn* was a practical and popular means of travel that was eliminated from West Berlin when the

city was divided in 1945, but was retained, modernized and even extended in the East. The tram, also operated by the BVG, still remains the best way to explore some of the outlying parts of the former East. There is a regular service and the trams run at the same speeds as before the Wall came down. **The same tickets are valid for all BVG services**
www.visitberlin.de, www.bvg.de, www.berlin-en-ligne.com

BIKES

Berliners love cycling, for environmental reasons as much as for convenience. The city has an extensive network of cycle paths – 700 km in all – going out as far as the lakes. A flat city, Berlin is great for cycling, except in winter. The Call-a-Bike service (www.callabike-interaktiv.de), set up by Deutsche Bahn, offers bikes for hire, with no deposit or minimum charge. To use one, you must first register a credit card. However, most tourists go to one of the innumerable small cycle hire businesses, often shops that sell and repair bikes as well. Berlin's main roads are generally wide, with a cycle path on the left-hand side of each pavement. Beware, as on these the cyclist is king. Bikes are welcome on public transport, on payment of an extra €1.50. A cycle-rickshaw service also available.
Call a Bike: €15 a day
Cycle-rickshaw: €15 basic fare
www.berlinerfahrradschau.de, www.veloberlin.com, www.bikedudes.de, www.bikesurf.org

ELECTRIC SCOOTER

Oddly, the scooter is not a popular means of locomotion in Berlin, probably because traffic still flows here. Launched in summer 2016, the Coup e-scooter rental system has a fleet of one thousand two-wheeled vehicles. There is no key, the helmet is under the seat, speed is limited to 45 kilometres per hour, and you can sign up on the app (iOS or Android). You must be over 21 years old and have a Category B driving licence. It costs €3 for 30 minutes. The Gogoro Smartscooter I series vehicles have a wonderful ovoid design.
www.joincoup.com

CAR HIRE

Thanks to congestion, the "green zone" (toll €5), the multitude of road signs in German, the difficulty of parking and the need to have a green sticker, it's not always easy to get around by car. Most Berliners use taxis in the evening for going out or when dining at a restaurant – very few offer valet parking. Most of the big rental agencies have offices in Berlin. Another option is car-sharing, which is flourishing in the city with companies like DriveNow, Car2go and Citeecar.
Avis: tel (0) 1805 21 77 02
Budget: tel (0) 1805 21 77 11
Europcar: tel (0) 1805 8000
Sixt: tel (0) 1805 25 25 25

BOATS

Most vessels navigating on the Spree are special tourist boats offering panoramic river cruises. A number of small companies offer excursions along the Landwehrkanal.

OFFBEAT TRANSPORT

A wide choice of alternative forms of transport are available, from cycle rickshaws and bikecabs to the nostalgic Trabants of Trabi Safari (in Mitte) and the vintage VW Beetles from Oldie Käfer Tour (Europa Center). Another cult VW vehicle is the "Bulli", or minibus, which can accommodate up to nineteen for tours of the city. There are also arty buses bursting at the seams with diurnal clubbers. And all kinds of other wheeled vehicles are authorized on Berlin's streets, including bicycle beer carts, which require you to pedal hard to pump the beer.
Trabi-Safari: www.trabi-safari.de
Oldie Käfer Tour:
www.oldie-kaefer-tour-berlin.de/en
Old Bulli Berlin: www.oldbulli.berlin
Rickshaw Tour: www.berlin-rikscha-tours.de

PRACTICAL MATTERS

COMMUNICATIONS
TELEPHONE
To call Berlin from abroad, dial the international access code, then the code for Germany (49), followed by 30 and the landline or mobile number of the person you are calling. To call abroad from Berlin, dial 00. To call a landline in Berlin from elsewhere in Germany, dial 030, then the number of the person you are calling. To make a local call in Berlin from a landline, dial the number direct without the 030; from a mobile dial 030 first; however, visitors using mobiles should dial 00 49 30 before the direct number to get a landline and 00 49 before the number when ringing a local mobile number.

E-MAIL/INTERNET
Although there are plenty of cybercafés in the city, restaurants and other cafés are not always generous when it comes to wifi. Hotels, which used to charge up to €25 per day and per appliance for in-room connection, have resigned themselves to general free access. In the city, the Public WiFi Berlin service has over 100 access terminals distributed across the four main neighbourhoods – Mitte, Charlottenburg, Prenzlauer Berg, Tiergarten – and also in Potsdam, offering 30 min free a day.
www.hotspot-locations.de
www.publicwifiberlin.de

POST
Public service provided by Deutsche Post: posting a letter in Germany costs €0.60, international letters and postcards €0.90, prices increase with weight.
Main post office: Georgenstraße 12, Mitte, S-Bahn and U-Bahn Friedrichstraße, tel 018 02 33 33, www.deutschepost.de Open 6am to 10pm, Saturdays and Sundays open from 8am

CURRENCY AND BANKS
EURO (€)
EXCHANGE RATE
€1 = $1.15 / €1 = £0.88
Unlike Paris or New York, there are few cashpoints (*Geldautomat*). Most are located inside bank branches or post offices through double-door entrances accessible outside branch opening hours. There is sometimes an extra charge of €3 to €8 depending on the bank, often indicated when it's too late to cancel the transaction. There is an increasing trend for bars and restaurants and even some small shops to refuse payment by credit card and accept cash only.
Banks: 8am to noon and 2pm to 4pm, closed Saturday and Sunday
Reporting stolen bank cards:
tel 0892 705 705 (7 days a week)
Reporting stolen cheque books:
tel 0892 683 208 (7 days a week)

AVERAGE PRICE INDEX
PRICE PER SQUARE METRE
€4,300
ANNUAL SALARY
€39,900
CINEMA TICKET
€10
BREAD ROLL
€1

CLIMATE/GEOGRAPHY
WEATHER
Berlin has a continental climate, with cold winters, temperatures sometimes descending as low as −15°C. In spring, the average temperature is around 10°C. A few days before Easter, the city sometimes experiences an early, short-lived spring with temperatures rising to 25°C. In summer, the thundery heat can send the thermometer up to 35°C. Autumn is more pleasant, but comes to a sudden end in late October.

SUNRISE AND SUNSET

MARCH 6:30am to 6:30pm
JUNE 5am to 9:30pm
SEPTEMBER 7am to 6:30pm
DECEMBER 8am to 4:25pm

TIME ZONE

GMT/UTC +1
GMT/UTC +2 (summer time)

ALTITUDE

Though the city is on a flat plain
35 metres above sea level, Teufelsberg,
an artificial hill in Grunewald, rises to
120 metres at its summit.

RIVER

The Spree is 400 kilometres long and
navigable along half its length. It winds
its way right through Berlin, joined by
a number of canals, and eventually runs
into the Havel, north-west of the city.
A number of artworks can be seen along
its route, such as the perforated metal
silhouette of Molecule Man, a rather
undistinguished sculpture. Several
floating swimming pools are anchored to
its banks. Of all the bridges that span it,
the Oberbaumbrücke, with its post-Neo-
Gothic brick turrets and battlements,
is the most spectacular. The bridge links
Kreuzberg and Friedrichshain.

PUBLIC HOLIDAYS

1 JANUARY New Year's Day
MARCH OR APRIL Easter
(Good Friday and Easter Monday)
1 MAY May Day
MAY Ascension Day
MAY-JUNE Whit Sunday and Monday
(Pentecost)
3 OCTOBER National Day
25 AND 26 DECEMBER Christmas

KEEP IN MIND

HOTEL TAXES

Tourist tax is charged at 5 %, but business
travellers are exempt.

ANIMALS

Under Schengen agreement rules, up to
five pets (dogs, cats, ferrets) are allowed,
provided they are tattooed or microchipped,
have been vaccinated against rabies
and their owner has their passport and
vaccination record. In the city, dogs are
very welcome in hotels and even
restaurants. Berliners like big dogs, which
they take for a morning run in the woods.

TOURIST OFFICE

Berlin Infostore Hauptbahnhof
Europaplatz 1, north entrance, level 0,
Tiergarten, S-Bahn Hauptbahnhof,
tel 030 25 00 25, open daily 8am to 10pm
Tourist Information Centre
Maschinenhaus in der Kulturbrauerei,
Schönhauser Allee 36, Prenzlauer Berg,
tel 030 4435 2170, 030 2500 2333
www.visitberlin.de
www.tic-in-prenzlauerberg.de
www.berlin.de
www.berlin-tourism.de

IMPORT/EXPORT

Non-EU residents may be able to claim
a tax exemption. Tax-free receipts
should be validated at airport customs.

EMERGENCY NUMBERS

Call **112** in a medical emergency,
110 for the police and **112** for the fire
and rescue service.
24-hour pharmacies:
Pharmacy at the Hauptbahnhof:
Europaplatz 1, Mitte, tel 030 20614190
Otherwise check local papers, pharmacy
shop windows or www.aponet.de/service/
notdienst/
Lost property:
Fundbüro, Potsdamer Straße 180–182,
Schöneberg, tel 030 19 449, 9am to 6pm,
Friday until 2pm, closed Saturday,
Sunday and public holidays

HISTORICAL AND MUST-SEE SITES

BERLINER DOM
Not to be confused with the German Cathedral (Deutscher Dom) on the Gendarmenmarkt, Berlin Cathedral was designed by Carl Julius Raschdorff and built between 1894 and 1905.
Am Lustgarten, Mitte

BRANDENBURGER TOR
The Brandenburg Gate is the city's most symbolic monument. It is crowned by the no less famous Quadriga, brought back from France in 1806 following the allied victory over Napoleon I. Contrary to popular myth, the Quadriga has always faced east, overlooking the main highway into old Berlin.
Pariser Platz, Mitte

DENKMAL FÜR DIE ERMORDETEN JUDEN EUROPAS (HOLOCAUST-MAHNMAL)
Designed by the American architect Peter Eisenman, the Holocaust Memorial is composed of 2,711 plinths of different heights and sizes, forming an open-air labyrinth. It is carefully monitored to ensure no one lies down on them for a rest.
Cora-Berliner-Straße 1, Tiergarten

EAST SIDE GALLERY
This is what remains of the Wall, an open-air gallery 1.3 kilometres long. It is a display space for 101 political and satirical murals painted by 118 artists from 21 countries, most of whom returned in 2009 for its partial restoration.
Mühlenstraße, Friedrichshain

FERNSEHTURM
A striking sight with its sphere and shaft, the television tower is an iconic Berlin landmark, comparable as an emblem to the Eiffel Tower in Paris. Soaring to a height of 368 metres, this is the tallest structure in the city – and in the country.
Panoramastraße 1a, Alexanderplatz, Mitte

GENDARMENMARKT
The most beautiful square in Berlin, its centrepiece is the theatre designed by Schinkel, now the Konzerthaus, flanked on either side by the German Cathedral and the French Cathedral.
Gendarmenmarkt, Mitte

GLIENICKER BRÜCKE
The suspension bridge over the Havel, west of Wannsee, used to be located at the south-westernmost tip of West Berlin. It was here, at the border crossing on the bridge, that high-value prisoners and spies were exchanged between East and West during the Cold War. Also worth visting nearby is Park Glienicke, with its summer houses, fountains and follies.
Berliner Straße 67, Potsdam

GRAVES OF THE BROTHERS GRIMM
The cemetery of the bucolic Sankt-Matthäus-Kirchhof in the heart of the "Red Island" is the final resting place of the illustrious Brothers Grimm. Wilhelm was buried here in 1859 and Jacob in 1863. Next to their gravestones are those of Wilhelm's sons.
Großgörschenstraße 12, Schöneberg

KAISER-WILHELM-GEDÄCHTNISKIRCHE
Purposely left since 1945 in its bombed-out state, earning it the nickname "the Hollow Tooth", the Memorial Church commemorating Kaiser Wilhelm I stands at the top of the Ku'damm. Dating from 1956, the glass memorial is the work of the architect Egon Eiermann. It is in the process of being restored and sausage sellers have temporarily colonized its protective fencing.
Breitscheidplatz, Tiergarten

KAPELLE DER VERSÖHNUNG
The (evangelical) Chapel of Reconciliation was built in 1999 on the old foundations of the Versöhnungskirche (Church of

Reconciliation), which was caught in the no man's land between West and East Berlin following construction of the Wall and was demolished by the GDR government in 1985. Located opposite the Gedenkstätte Berliner Mauer (Berlin Wall Memorial), the chapel was designed by Rudolf Reitermann and Peter Sassenroth and was consecrated in 2000. It consists of an outer wall made up of wooden columns and an inner structure made out of pressed clay. Simple and austere, it provides a moving experience for visitors.
Bernauer Straße, Mitte

KARL-MARX-ALLEE
Baptized "the Workers' Champs-Élysées", the widest boulevard in the former East Berlin is lined with post-Stalinist apartment buildings once occupied by the *nomenklatura*, and all clad in dull beige ceramic tiles, hand-made by the porcelain-makers of Meissen. The most impressive buildings are the ones built in the *Zückerbäckerstil* (wedding cake-style).
Karl-Marx-Allee, Friedrichshain

MUSEUMSINSEL
Classed as a World Heritage site by UNESCO, Museum Island is the site of the capital's principal museums, including the Altes Museum, Neues Museum, Alte Nationalgalerie, Bode-Museum and Pergamonmuseum. Of the various bridges linking the island, the most impressive is Schinkel's Schlossbrücke. Another, the Jungfernbrücke, is Berlin's oldest bridge, built in 1798. Spreeinsel, Mitte

NEUE SYNAGOGE
The Neue Synagoge was built in a mock-Moorish style in the 19th century. It was set on fire on Kristallnacht in 1938, but escaped complete destruction. Following restoration, the building was reopened in 1995 and is now closely guarded.
Oranienburger Straße 28–30, Mitte

180 km of navigable waterways
916 bridges

NIKOLAIKIRCHE
This is the oldest church in Berlin, built between 1220 and 1230. It was badly damaged by Allied bombing during the war and was eventually rebuilt in the 1980s. Inside, the bright colours of the ribs of the vaulted ceiling are based on a medieval pattern. Nikolaikirchplatz, Mitte

REICHSTAG
Home of the Bundestag, topped by a spectacular glass cupola designed by Lord Foster, the Reichstag is one of the most popular monuments in Berlin (entrance is free but by appointment), especially in the evening when it resembles a set from the film *Metropolis*.
Platz der Republik 1, Mitte

SIEGESSÄULE
Built between 1864 and 1873 by Johann Heinrich Strack to celebrate the victory of Prussia over Denmark, Austria and France, the "Victory Column" is topped with the famous bronze statue by Friedrich Drake of Viktoria (popularly known as Goldelse), which Wim Wenders used for the angel in *Wings of Desire*. The column was moved by Albert Speer in 1939 as part of the Germania project and ever since has stood at the centre of Großer Stern, on Straße des 17. Juni – regarded as a triumphal way at the time – halfway between Ernst-Reuter-Platz and the Brandenburg Gate.
Straße des 17. Juni, Tiergarten

EVENTS CALENDAR

JANUARY

1 JANUARY
Berliner Neujahrslauf,
the New Year race, starts
at the Brandenburg Gate.
www.berliner-neujahrslauf.de

FEBRUARY

EARLY FEBRUARY
Berlin Film Festival,
or Berlinale; Dieter
Kosslick is its charismatic
artistic director.
www.berlinale.de/en

MARCH

1ST WEEK
ITB, international travel
show. Every hotel is fully
booked.
www.itb-berlin.de/en
MaerzMusik, festival of
contemporary music.
www.berlinerfestspiele.de/
maerzmusik

MAY

EARLY MAY
Gallery Weekend.
www.gallery-weekend-
berlin.de
MID-MAY
Theatertreffen, international
theatre festival.
www.berlinerfestspiele.de/
theatertreffen
3RD SATURDAY
Lange Nacht der Museen,
museums and cultural
centres open at night.
www.lange-nacht-der-
museen.de
LATE MAY
Berlin Air Show (ILA):
the oldest airshow in
Europe at Schönefeld
airport. www.ila-berlin.de

JUNE

MID-JUNE
48 Hours Neukölln,
diverse arts festival around
the north of the district.
3RD WEEKEND
Christopher Street Day,
gay pride parade along
the Ku'damm.
www.csd-berlin.de
21 JUNE
Fête de la Musique.
www.fetedelamusique.de

JULY

EARLY JULY
Foreign Affairs,
international festival of
contemporary music,
dance and theatre.
www.berlinerfestspiele.de/
foreignaffairs

SEPTEMBER

1ST WEEK
Pop-Kultur: international
pop music festival at
changing locations. www.
berlin-music-week.de/en
3RD WEEK
Berlin Art Week,
comprising several art fairs
and plenty of openings.
www.berlinartweek.de/en
Berlin Marathon
The day before the main
marathon, there's a skater's
marathon, as well as
children's races.
www.bmw-berlin-marathon.
com

OCTOBER

END OCTOBER
Jazzfest Berlin.
www.berlinerfestspiele.de/
jazzfest

NOVEMBER

MID NOVEMBER
International Short
Film Festival Berlin
(over 500 films shown
in seven cinemas).
www.interfilm.de
**MID NOVEMBER–
LATE DECEMBER**
Christmas markets at
60 locations in the city.
www.visitberlin.com

DECEMBER

31 DECEMBER
New Year's Eve festivities
at the Brandenburg Gate
(fireworks, big public
party).
www.brandenburger-tor-
berlin.de

BERLIN LOUIS VUITTON

WHEN THE CITY SHUTS DOWN

The big increase in tourism has seen an extension to Saturday opening hours, especially in Mitte and Charlottenburg, often until 8pm. Elsewhere, the shutters still tend to come down early, between 2pm and 4pm. Good Friday and Easter Monday are undoubtedly the two quietest days of the year. Paradoxically, Sunday is a day when there is plenty going on.

BRUNCH IN A CAFÉ
Served until 4 pm, Sunday Frühstück is a religion in Berlin. Ranging from simple to highly sophisticated, it can be enjoyed at a corner café or in one of the big hotels. On some Sundays, it can even be the only activity you do that day.

BROWSE IN A FLEA MARKET
With no less than six markets and car boot sales every Sunday, Berlin is a goldmine for browsers. The best is probably in Fehrbelliner Platz, the most typically Berliner of them all.

VISIT MUSEUMS
They are all open (closed Mondays and Tuesdays), but close early, so it's best to go in the morning or straight after brunch, which you can have in the restaurant or café of the museum you are going to.

WANDER ROUND THE ZOO
A favourite with Berliners because the zoo is open every day. Go to ogle the orang-utans, pat a giraffe or contemplate the hippos.
www.zoo-berlin.de

GO TO THE CINEMA
Try the Zoo Palast, completely restored in amazing 1950s style. Its seats are more comfortable and luxurious than on a first-class flight (€13 a ticket, with drinks served at your seat).
www.zoopalast-berlin.de

GO OUT TO LUNCH
By the lakes, especially in fine weather, in one of the historic chalets or inns, where you can enjoy traditional comfort food at reasonable prices. It's a great way to relax and feel you're really experiencing the city, and in a lovely natural setting as well. The most charming is undoubtedly the Blockhaus Nikolskoe, open all year, on the shores of the Wannsee, looking out at Pfaueninsel (Peacock Island).
www.blockhaus-nikolskoe.de

GO TO A CONCERT
Classical music, singing, organ: Berlin has a vast array of choices for music fans. Check the culture pages of the daily papers to see what's on, at what time, where and with whom, or check out the websites
www.classictic.com, www.visitberlin.de

GO FOR A SWIM
Berlin has a large number of large, impressively designed municipal swimming pools, both indoor and outdoor. One of the most recent and spectacular is the one designed at the same time as the Velodrom by French architect Dominique Perrault as part of its Berlin's candidacy for the 2000 Olympics, which were given to Sydney. It is located in Prenzlauer Berg and is open 7 days a week.
www.berlinerbaeder.de

LIVING LIKE A LOCAL

Berliners are never in a hurry. They are rarely to be seen running – unless it's for exercise and then usually accompanied by big dogs. Depending on income group or professional status, schedules are carefully compartmentalized and leisure or personal life is not allowed to impinge on work time. And vice-versa.

UP AND RUNNING

Every morning from east to west by car or public transport: there are more Berliners who live in the east and work in the west than the other way round. This also applies to those who live even further east and work in Mitte. On average, Berliners spend 15 to 30 minutes travelling to work and many choose to live as close as possible to their workplaces even if they have to move house. The same process happens in reverse at the end of the day.

On Friday evenings, many dash off to catch a train to go back to their families or home to Frankfurt, Hamburg or Cologne: sent to the capital for short-term work, very few give up their family home. In addition to the million Berliners who use the U-Bahn and S-Bahn, many also travel by car, car pooling or car sharing.

THE WORKING DAY

Traffic queues, heavy but always moving, run from east to west in the morning between 7am and 9am and start in the afternoon at 4pm, going in the opposite direction.

Because breakfast or Frühstück, is the main meal of the day, Berliners spend plenty of time on it, starting at 6am, since they often start work early, from 7am.

Much too early for creative types, who start much later, about 9:30am, but everyone always has their *Frühstück*, whether at home or out – all the cafés, bars and restaurants display a breakfast menu served until noon.

Taken from about 11:30am, lunchtime is just a short break: Berliners lunch on the move, often standing, eating a sandwich or snack made in one of the city's 2,800 sandwich bars. Anyone taking the time to sit down restricts their meal to a bowl of soup, a salad or one light dish. All restaurants, and most open at lunchtime, offer a *Mittagsmenü* – a quick, hot, light lunch. White collar workers – managers, lawyers, etc. – take the same short lunch break and don't spend any more than everyone else – about €15.

Morning schedules end early and the same applies to the afternoons, as by 4pm workers and civil servants, among others, have finished for the day. Others finish later, often very late, especially those working in communications or entertainment.

THE EVENING

For many Berliners, the evening starts at 4pm, as soon as they leave work. They don't go home but rush straight to the gym. Having worked up a big appetite, they have supper early, at 6pm, alone, or

43 metres
height of the tallest tree, a larch that is 205 years old, in Tegel forest

10,000 clubbers
every evening at weekends

with one or two others. The high number of restaurants in the city – more than 6,500 – means that, with the exception of the most fashionable places, you don't necessarily have to make a reservation for dinner, though this is changing fast. Thirty-something Berliners who finish work later like to get together for a drink in a cocktail bar, where they often celebrate a birthday or a promotion. Their supper, eaten later, will be quicker and less elaborate. When the more middle-aged, middle-class Berliners go out for dinner, they take more time over it, but they'll still be going home by 10:30pm.

Whatever the case, on weeknights, unless it's during a special holiday period, Berliners go to bed early, except on Thursdays, when shops close later and the weekend is coming up. Anyone still partying after 10pm is either a German or foreign visitor staying in the city for a trade fair, conference or meeting.

THE WEEKEND

As we have seen, it starts on Friday at 4pm and finishes very early on Monday morning. During this short period, Berliners are capable of anything. From the worst to the best, from the healthiest to the most toxic. Nightlife and the electro music scene being what it is, everyone will find their niche, always reasonably priced, as low cost is practically a religion for Berliners.

Berliners do their shopping on Friday evenings – very few supermarkets offer home delivery – to keep Saturday free from this chore. The old market halls are back in fashion, now the province of "extreme" foodies and organic to the core, and provide another popular Saturday activity, until they close at noon, when it's almost impossible to get a seat for a lunch of *focaccia* or a salmon sandwich.

Saturday afternoons are spent visiting galleries in Mitte or alternative shopping in Prenzlauer Berg, where the stores keep outrageous hours for the city by staying open until 6pm – and are all closed in the morning. Elsewhere in the city, except on the *Ku'damm*, closing time is 4pm and not a minute later! At this point, many young Berliners go home for a nap, to regroup and build up their strength before spending the whole night out, right up to Sunday brunch, which ends at 2pm. More sedate forty-somethings go out at 6pm to the cinema, theatre or a concert.

Sunday mornings, depending on the weather, the dog is taken for a walk in the woods. Followed by brunch, a long one. Another religion. Afterwards, it's on to a museum to see an exhibition. Then home: on Sunday evenings the city is almost deserted, the restaurants often empty.

City habits are changing as well: wealthy Berliners are starting to get used to going away for the weekend, to the country or the Baltic shore, or even going as far as to visit another European capital. And their comings-and-goings have created a new soundtrack to Berlin weekends: the rumble of suitcase wheels on the pavement.

ETIQUETTE AND GOOD TASTE

For many years, Berliners were regarded by the rest of Germany, particularly Munichers, as rude, noisy people with a mocking sense of humour. Well, true Berliners undoubtedly have sarcasm in their DNA. It even has a name, Berliner Schnauze, and it hides the true character of Berliners, who are reserved and polite, but direct.

TIPPING

Service is included in the price displayed. Everyone pays their share and you should leave the waiter the change from the rounded-up bill, saying "Das stimmt so". However, don't tip if it's the owner. A person paying for the whole table, "zusammen" (all together), discreetly pays the tip him or herself: 10%.

DRESS CODE

These days, unless you're exploring one of the most distant districts of the former East Berlin, any differences in the clothing worn by west and east Berliners have disappeared, particularly in the generations born after the fall of the Wall. Though the west still offers examples of the over-sixties clad in a rather kitsch style, Berliners have eliminated their love of primary and fluorescent colours and gone over to the grey side. The same goes for their cars – bright colours are restricted to small French and Japanese makes.

After a rapid rise, soon over, Bavarian preppy style is right out of favour in the city. Clothes-conscious forty-somethings and ambitious thirty-somethings have turned to Italian fashion and international designers, following Paris, London and Milan in mixing low-cost and luxury. Suits for both sexes at the office

(plus tie for him); more elaborate outfits are reserved for special occasions (private views, first nights, museums). At the theatre or opera, older people opt for a very classic look; the youngest go out in whatever they were wearing during the day and no-one seems to mind.

THANK YOU

"Danke", "Bitte": two short but essential words, which you need to know how to qualify to get their meaning just right. "Danke" means "thank you". On its own, it is informal, used between colleagues and friends. With the addition of "Vielen" (very much), your thanks become more formal, as with "Danke sehr", as you leave a shop or restaurant. "Danke gern" (thank you most gladly), also often used, is the politest form possible. "Herzliche Danke" (thank you with all my heart) is generally used when writing a thank you note – as a letter or e-mail. Meaning "please", "Bitte" is given a more polite inflection when accompanied by "sehr" or "schön". It is also used in response to "Danke sehr" or "Danke schön", meaning "you're welcome", "it's a pleasure" or "don't mention it".

THE RIGHT ATTITUDE AT THE RIGHT TIME

Politeness. Punctuality. Simplicity. Berliners know their city is visited by people from all over the world and try to create a good impression to support its reputation. Having said that, rushing up to people without a "hello" or an "excuse me" in order to ask directions, and waving a map under their noses won't get you anywhere. Some will even have a little fun by giving you the wrong directions. Using a few words of German will be appreciated even though a good proportion of the population speaks English.

Though men will shake hands or give each other a brief hug, women are still quite reserved: a firm handshake and direct eye contact for a new acquaintance, perhaps a kiss on both cheeks once you know each other well. Say "Guten Morgen" (good morning) between 7am and 11am, then "Guten Tag" (good day) until 3pm, then "Guten Abend" (good evening) after 5pm. "Auf Wiedersehen" (goodbye) is used all day and all evening. "Gute Nacht" is restricted to family and close friends, as is the Italian "ciao" (also used by Berliners), popular and very informal, and used as a goodbye. "Tschüß!" means "See you!"

In shops, don't get impatient if you think the service is slow. Every customer is given time and served with respect.

WHAT NOT TO DO

Be late. Berliners are punctual and expect the same courtesy from others. However, phoning ahead if you are going to be late will be appreciated as a mark of respect. Berliners will then be surprisingly tolerant.

Be too critical. While they often make fun of themselves, Berliners avoid being negative about a restaurant, a film, etc. By the same token, they don't like visitors, whether from Germany or the other side of the world, criticizing their way of life, their food or their customs.

Spend money ostentatiously. Berliners are frugal and compare prices assiduously.

Be too shy – you must stand up for yourself. Because Berlin is still an urban jungle, shyness can be misinterpreted as fear. The fearful have no place in this city, where anything goes. By the same token, anyone apologising for a minor transgression will be considered weak. The Prussian heritage, toughness.

Click your fingers to call the waiter. There's nothing ruder. The same goes for summoning the waitress by shouting "Fraulein!" or a waiter with "Jung herr!" You should just say "Hallo!" and wave your hand: whatever happens, he or she will have seen you.

Cancel an appointment at the last moment. Berlin is not Los Angeles and Berliners are very organized people. Cancelling a business appointment at the last moment is an irreparable blunder. Doing the same if you're meeting a friend is less serious: the excuse generally used is that you can't come because you're ill, bedridden with a temperature.

Find fault with a Berliner. With their reputation for professional efficiency, a Berliner will be absolutely mortified to be found at fault by a foreigner. So refrain from any comments or ironic remarks to avoid making the situation worse: he will simply stop speaking to you. And since they never apologise . . .

Queue jump. Unthinkable, intolerable, sinful, uncivilized.

Smoke where it's not permitted and refrain from smoking where it is. Berliners are heavy smokers and have successfully got round the anti-smoking law by declaring a large number of places totally open to smokers.

ON TIME!
Berliners are punctual to a fault.
If you're invited to dinner you must arrive at the right time, though being a few minutes late is acceptable. Using heavy traffic or difficulty parking as an excuse is not. If it's at a restaurant, arrive when the table is booked; if there's a large group, sit down, order a drink and wait for the others.

HERE AND NOWHERE ELSE

Because of its own history, and that of its inhabitants, who are resolutely unconventional, Berlin remains an inexhaustible reservoir of everyday curiosities that Berliners nurture protectively and with great humour.

THE BEAR

The brown bear has been Berlin's mascot since the Middle Ages. Once a heraldic symbol it now appears on all the official flags of the reunified capital and is used in any number of ways in graphics, adverts and artistic projects. Even in the cinema, since the supreme prize of the Berlin Film Festival is a Golden Bear. As for the real sort, Knut, the zoo's star polar bear died in 2011, and the last brown bear, Schnute, to live in the strange enclosure in Köllnischen Park, was put to sleep in October 2015, after fierce campaigning from animal rights protesters. Given this patronage, it is perhaps not too surprising that Berlin produces its own honey.

www.kaiserhonig.de

THE SIXTIES TAXI

Beige, like all the other taxis in the city, this vehicle is an anachronistic Sixties Peugeot 404, registration number B ZR 404 H. It is driven by Matthias Zierau, who organizes tours and excursions. A change from the usual Mercedes or the spluttering Trabants of Trabi-Safari.

www.klassik-taxi-berlin.de

THE WATER PUMPS

These old-fashioned manual pumps are a curious sight, found on numerous streets, especially in the former West. Historic and popular, they still work and Berliners use them for washing their cars.

THE LOCAL CINEMAS FOR HIRE

Berlin is full of little local cinemas, often with just a few dozen seats. They are available for private hire for an evening to celebrate a birthday or other event, when you can show whatever film you choose. Prices depend on the number of seats in the cinema.

THE LESBIAN CEMETERY

Berlin is undoubtedly the European capital of the gay, lesbian and transgender communities. In spring 2014, to some media excitement, it opened the first lesbian-only cemetery in the grounds of the evangelical church of Georgen-Parochial-Friedhof, in Prenzlauer Berg.

BUYING A STORM

The Berlin Institut für Meteorologie in Grunewald, one of the oldest in the world, is known for the precision of its weather bulletins. What is unusual about the institute, however, is that it enables individuals to "purchase" the name of a European storm or an anticyclone. The practice began when the station was in the American sector and became all the rage when the Wall fell. Storms' names are cheaper because they are more frequent than anticyclones.

www.met.fu-berlin.de/de/wetter

THE CITY IN WORDS, FILM AND MUSIC

Berlin is home to Europe's most avid readers, although readership of newspapers and magazines still follows something of an east-west divide. The city, with its extraordinary history of division and reunification, has been an inspiration to numerous filmmakers, writers and musicians.

NEWSPAPERS AND MAGAZINES

B.Z. Not to be confused with the *Berliner Zeitung*, B.Z. was founded in 1877 and is published by Ullstein-Verlag, a subsidiary of Axel Springer AG. It is more benign than English tabloids and has an interesting cultural section.
www.bz-berlin.de

Berliner Morgenpost. This daily was launched in 1898 by Leopold Ullstein. Shut down by the Nazis, it reappeared in 1952. It is one of the capital's two biggest dailies.
www.morgenpost.de

Berliner Zeitung. From May 1945 to 1990, this was the Communist Party's local daily. Today it defines itself as a paper for the whole of the city, although it continues to be read more in the former East.
www.berliner-zeitung.de

Tagesspiegel. Co-founded in 1945 and mainly read in the former West, *Tagesspiegel* is a left-leaning daily close in outlook to the SDP. www.tagesspiegel.de

Die Welt. Founded in 1946 in Hamburg, today based in Berlin, *Die Welt* is one of the country's three main serious papers. It has a right-wing bias and a circulation of 200,000. Sunday supplement: *Welt am Sonntag*. www.welt.de

Exberliner. English-language weekly covering film, food, urban and social issues.
www.exberliner.com

TIP Berlin. Twice weekly magazine. Having fused with *Zitty*, *Tip* celebrated its 45th anniversary in March 2017. Magazine bihebdomadaire. *Zitty* is published every week and covers Berlin cultural life in full.
www.tip-berlin.de, www.zitty.de

BOOKS
What I Saw: Reports from Berlin, 1920–1933, Joseph Roth (translated by Michael Hofmann, 2003). Roth's writings dissect the decadent Berlin society that would soon be swept aside by the Nazis.

Berlin Alexanderplatz, Alfred Döblin (1929, English translation 1931). In his novel, Döblin describes the slums of Berlin, their poverty, crime and disease. Several attempts were made to adapt the novel to the screen, including Fassbinder's 15-hour version for TV (1980), with Hanna Schygulla and Günter Lamprecht.

Goodbye to Berlin, Christopher Isherwood (1939). Nostalgic, visionary novel set in pre-war Berlin. It has been adapted for the theatre and cinema, and then as the musical *Cabaret*. "Wilkommen, bienvenue, welcome . . ."

Berlin Diaries 1940–1945, Marie Vassiltchikov (1987). The diary of a young Russian aristocrat in Berlin during World War II up until the collapse of the Third Reich. It was published after the author's death in 1978.

Alone in Berlin, Hans Fallada (*Jeder stirbt für sich allein*, 1947). Inspired by the heroics of a real-life couple, Fallada's novel is regarded as the greatest literary work on German resistance to the Nazis.

Berlin Noir, Philip Kerr (*March Violets, The Pale Criminal* and *A German Requiem*). Pre-war Berlin seen through the prism of detective Bernie Gunther, a former policeman. Gritty, dark and sad.

Russian Disco, Wladimir Kaminer (2013). A slightly disjointed collection of tales of life in Berlin, where the author arrived as a Russian Jewish immigrant in the early 1990s. Funny and poignant.

Berlin Wonderland: *Wild Years Revisited 1990–1996* and *Berlin Heart Beats: Stories from the Wild Years 1990–Today* (2017): two volumes of black-and-white photos from the years following the fall of the Wall. Eloquent.

FILMS

Berlin Alexanderplatz, Phil Jutzi (1931). With Heinrich George and Maria Bard. Adaptation of Alfred Döblin's masterpiece. The hero, ex-convict Franz Biberkopf, becomes sucked into the Berlin underworld. Biberkopf is played by Heinrich George, a well-known leading man of his time.

Germany, Year Zero, Roberto Rossellini (*Germania, anno zero*, 1947). With Edmund Moeschke, Ingetraud Hinze, Franz-Otto Krüger. This masterpiece was shot in the ruins of West Berlin and follows the fortunes of a 13-year-old boy as he works the black market.

A Foreign Affair, Billy Wilder (1948). With Marlene Dietrich. West Berlin, 1948. A ruined city and the black market. American GI Captain Pringle has an affair with former Nazi turned nightclub singer Erika von Schlütow, who is hiding a Hitlerite dignitary thought to be dead. Typically sharp and wry.

Berlin, Ecke Schönhauser, Gerhard Klein (1957). With Ekkehard Schall, Ilse Pagé. Mostly shot on location in Prenzlauer Berg (East Berlin). The gang of delinquant

youths caused a scandal, because such people were not supposed to exist in the GDR. There was a sequel, *Berlin um die Ecke* (1965), which was banned until 1990.

One, Two, Three!, Billy Wilder (1961). With James Cagney, Horst Buchholz. An aggressive Coca-Cola exec (Cagney) tries to get ahead by selling the drink to Russia while trying to prevent his boss from finding out his ditzy daughter has married a rabid communist from East Berlin. A satire on American cultural imperialism.

Funeral in Berlin, Guy Hamilton (1966). With Michael Caine. Cold War thriller. Harry Palmer (Caine) is sent to Berlin to find out why a Russian intelligence colonel is keen to defect. Good location photography of Wedding.

Christiane F – Wir Kinder vom Bahnhof Zoo, Ulrich Edel (*Christiane F. – We Children from Bahnhof Zoo*, 1981). With Natja Brunckhorst. Adaptation of the non-fiction book based on tape recordings made by teenager Christiane Felscherinow (her real name), who turned to prostitution to support her heroin addiction. A box-office phenomenon.

The Wings of Desire, Wim Wenders (*Der Himmel über Berlin*, 1987). With Bruno Ganz, Solveig Dommartin, Otto Sander. Written by Wenders and Peter Handke. Two angels seeing everything in black and white want to become humans out of love for a trapeze artist. Followed in 1993 by *In weiter Ferne, so nah* with Otto Sander, Nastassja Kinski, Bruno Ganz. Lou Reed and Willem Dafoe play themselves.

Ostkreuz, Michael Klier (1991). With Laura Tonke and Suzanne von Borsody. An S-Bahn station at the easternmost point of the former East, Ostkreuz lent its name to the first post-Wall film, shot in a ghostly, run-down East Berlin, by a director from the West.

Run, Lola, Run, Tom Tykwer (*Lola rennt*, 1998). With Franka Potente. Red-haired Lola runs through Berlin in search of a bag filled with 100,000 Deutsche Marks forgotten on a train. Techno sounds and modern architecture of the new Berlin.

Good Bye Lenin!, Wolfgang Becker (2003). Daniel Brühl, Katrin Sass. The famous Ostalgie comedy was a global success. It's a gentle, thought-provoking satire on reunification. The films made by Dani Levy in its wake exploited the same comic vein. They include the funny *Alles auf Zucker!* (*Go for Zucker*, 2004), shot in apartments on the Karl-Marx-Allee.

The Lives of Others, Florian Henckel von Donnersmarck (*Das Leben der Anderen*, 2006). With Ulrich Mühe, Ulrich Tukur, Martina Gedeck. A critical and box office success. 1984, East Berlin (the film was shot in Friedrichshain, Karl-Marx-Allee, etc.), a Stasi officer is given the task of spying on a famous playwright and actress. Gripping, oppressive, magnificent.

Berlin Calling, Hannes Stöhr (2008). With Paul Kalkbrenner, Rita Lengyel, Corinna Harfouch. The trials and tribulations of a DJ in Berlin, with drugs and a techno soundtrack composed by Kalkbrenner, alias DJ Kalkito.

MUSIC
Das macht die Berliner Luft, by the famous librettist Paul Lincke for the operetta *Frau Luna* (1904). Berlin's unofficial hymn.

Berlin Berlin, Marlene Dietrich (1965). On the cult album *Marlene Dietrich singt Alt-Berliner Lieder*.

Das ist Berlin, Hildegard Knef (1966). The world-renowned German actress sang about Berlin. Her funeral was almost a national event.

Neuköln, David Bowie and Brian Eno (1977). Recorded at the Hansa Studios by Bowie during his Berlin period. Bowie's *Where Are We Now?* (2013) is also worth listening to out of pure nostalgia for this period.

Auf 'm Bahnhof Zoo, Nina Hagen (1978). From *Nina Hagen Band*, the album by ex-East Berlin punk diva. Listen to *Berlin (ist Dufte!)* as well.

Alexanderplatz, Milva (1982). The Italian singer, who is a popular personality in Italy, has also sung a lot of Brecht.

Summer in Berlin, Alphaville (1984). This cult German synthpop group borrowed their name from Godard.

Zoo Station, U2 (1991). The best-known song from the classic album *Achtung Baby*.

Born to Die in Berlin, The Ramones (1995). The American punk rock group is revered in Germany. A museum devoted to them has even been opened in Berlin, on Krausnickstraße.

Cabaret Berlin, Romy Haag (1999). Should be listened to alongside Liza Minnelli's *Cabaret* and Ute Lemper's *Berlin Cabaret Songs* in order to get the true measure of its trashy sophistication.

Dickes B, Peter Fox & Seeed (2001). The Basque Peter Fox, alias Pierre Baigorry, is a star in Berlin. *Dickes B*, Berlin's nickname, was a hit. Almost a classic.

106 days of rain

44% area occupied by green spaces, lakes and waterways

THE GREAT AND THE GOOD

WILHELM VON HUMBOLDT (1767–1835)
PHILOSOPHER

Wilhelm von Humboldt is best known for his theory of education, which focused on providing students with a well-rounded education, no matter what their future vocation, and became the standardised system of education implemented across Prussia. A keen linguist, he is credited as the first European to suggest that language is a rule-governed system. His brother, Alexander von Humboldt, was a well-known geographer and explorer.

KARL FRIEDRICH SCHINKEL (1781–1841)
ARCHITECT AND PAINTER

Schinkel's style has defined the centre of Berlin like none other. Named the state architect of King Frederick William III of Prussia 1815, he originally came back to Berlin from Paris to become a painter, but he turned to architecture instead, designing some of Berlin's greatest monuments: the Altes Museum, the Gendarmenmarkt and Konzerthaus, all in a Greek Revival style. A square alongside the Spree bears his name, with a statue of the Prussian architect.

ROSA LUXEMBURG (1871–1919)
ACTIVIST AND PHILOSOPHER

Though she was born in Poland, Rosa Luxemburg made an indelible mark on German politics, co-founding the Spartacus League that later developed into country's Communist Party. She wrote extensively on the power of working class people to mobilise effectively against war and imperialism. Her works were widely influential in Marxist circles, and she was despised by Stalin for her radical, hard-left views. She was murdered in the revolution following the First World War, along with her husband Karl Liebknecht (also a prominent revolutionary figure), and her body was thrown into the Landwehr Canal.

MIES VAN DER ROHE (1886–1969)
ARCHITECT

The modernist architect is often lauded for his work in America, but he also made significant contributions to the buildings in the capital of his homeland. The Aachen-born design pioneer was the architectural director of the Deutscher Werkbund, and subsequently the Bauhaus's final director, before the school finally closed under pressure from the Nazis. After his years of exile and a rich career in the US, Mies returned to Berlin, where he designed the Neue Nationalgalerie, which would be completed after his death.

BERTOLT BRECHT (1898–1956)
PLAYWRIGHT

Brecht came to Berlin in 1924 for a job as assistant dramaturge at the Deutsches Theater, and ended up setting up the Berliner Ensemble with his wife Helene Weigel. He is best known for his convention-defying, anti-bourgeois plays such as *The Threepenny Opera* and *Mother Courage and Her Children*, the latter of which was written in the playwright's exile from Nazi-era Germany. His work was forbidden and his books burnt. After losing his German nationality, Brecht was stateless; he ended up in Hollywood but was driven away. Forbidden to enter the FRG, he returned to East Berlin via Prague in 1947 and two years later founded the Berliner Ensemble there with Helene Weigel.

MARLENE DIETRICH (1901–1992)
ACTRESS AND SINGER

Marlene Dietrich was born at Leberstraβe 65 in the heart of "Red Island" (the left-wing workers' district in Schöneberg). Josef von Sternberg turned this chubby young actress into a star by casting her as Lola-Lola in *The Blue Angel* (1930). He also took her to Hollywood, where she became the goddess of cinema. Her immense fame enraged Hitler and Goebbels, who tried to get her to return to Berlin to embody the cinematographic ideal of the Third Reich. Fiercely opposed to the Nazis, she took US citizenship, created a fund to help Jews and political dissidents flee Germany and teamed up with US troops to fight Nazism. As her film career declined, she embarked on unforgettable concert tours, which took her to the FRG. The Blue Angel is buried in the Friedenau Cemetery in Berlin.

WILLY BRANDT (1913–1992)
STATESMAN
Born Herbert Ernst Karl Frahm, Willy Brandt changed his name on fleeing Nazi Germany for Scandinavia, where he worked as a journalist. Returning to his homeland at the end of the war, Brandt became the Governing Mayor of West Berlin, and continued to govern the city as relations with the Soviets worsened and the Berlin Wall was constructed. As part of the SPD, he became Chancellor of West Germany in 1969 and in 1971 received a Nobel Peace Prize for his efforts in maintaining European cohesion.

HILDEGARD KNEF (1925–2002)
ACTRESS, SINGER, WRITER
Hildegard Knef was Germany's first post-war star. Her first role was in the terrible 1946 film *The Murderers Are Among Us (Die Mörder Sind Unter Uns)*, the first East German production shot in a ruined Berlin. She created a scandal in 1950 by appearing in a brief nude scene in *The Sinner (Die Sinner)*. A big star in West Germany, the actress went to Hollywood, where she made a number of films. She acted on Broadway and made films in Paris. She was also a singer and recorded dozens of albums and singles. After many marriages and facelifts, this gay icon returned to Berlin after the fall of the Wall and has been resting in peace since 2002. Her songs live on, and the biopic *Hilde,* starring Heike Makasch, has brought her back into the public eye.

MARTIN KIPPENBERGER (1953–1997)
ARTIST
One the most influential German artists of his generation, Kippenberger moved to Berlin in 1978, where he created an incredible variety of works, including paintings made of latex, Richter paintings turned into coffee tables and a street lamp for drunks to congregate around. As the co-owner of SO36, Kippenberger was a Berlin personality, known for his hard drinking and jocular attitude.

NINA HAGEN (1955)
SINGER, PUNK DIVA
Nina Hagen was born in East Berlin, from which her mother, the great actress Eva Maria Hagen, was expelled. She was raised in West Berlin in an arty/radical environment and became a vociferous punk icon with remarkable vocal qualities. After forming several groups and making the rounds of provincial concert halls, she ended up in London. Her debut album, *Nina Hagen Band,* released in 1978, signalled the eruption of the phenomenon, amplified by the worldwide success of the song *African Reggae.* From Berlin to New York, the punk diva, who also made films, indulged in multiple provocations. She celebrated her 60th birthday on the stage of the Berliner Ensemble, where she sang – with great success – *The Threepenny Opera.*

PEACHES (1968–)
MUSICIAN
Merrill Nisker moved to Berlin from Toronto in 2000 and quickly made the city her home, signing with the Berlin label Kitty-Yo after just one concert. Six studio albums and a semi-autobiographical rock-musical later, she's still setting the scene alight with her outrageous self-representation, adorning her body with flesh-inspired stage costumes, and spitting her explicit, in-your-face lyrics, Peaches represents contemporary Berlin's eternal support for the attitude of punk.

24 HOURS IN THE CITY
TWELVE UNBEATABLE EXPERIENCES

7AM

Swim in a historic indoor pool, such as the spectacular Stadtbad Neukölln (page 196), with its two pools, one decorated like a basilica, the other like a Roman atrium, which have remained almost unchanged since they opened, in 1914. Early bathing hours run from Tuesday to Friday.

STADTBAD NEUKÖLLN
www.berlinerbaeder.de

9AM

Have breakfast at the Benedict (page 136), in the Max Brown hotel. Menu: New York eggs Benedict, mimosa cocktail, chachouka, bagels, pancakes.

BENEDICT
www.benedict-breakfast.de

10AM

Grab a quality coffee at the Kranzler (page 142), the famous red and white café on the Ku'damm now owned by well-known local roaster The Bar.

KRANZLER
www.thebarn.de

11AM

Have a massage, facial or body treatment at the Spa by Susanne Kaufmann (page 198), in the luxurious hotel Das Stue, designed by Patricia Urquiola (formerly the premises of the Danish embassy). An oasis of tranquillity on the edge of the Tiergarten.

SPA BY SUSANNE KAUFMANN
www.das-stue.com

1PM

Enjoy a great pastrami sandwich for lunch at Mogg (page 144), the delicatessen opened in the old refectory of the Jewish girls' school on Augustraße, in Mitte, before heading off to explore some of the contemporary art and photography galleries.

MOGG
www.moggmogg.com

3PM

Take in one of the exhibitions at the Martin-Gropius-Bau (page 261), which are always exciting and cleverly designed.

MARTIN-GROPIUS-BAU
www.gropiusbau.de

5 PM

Check out the graphic symbols from the typeface designed in the early 20th century by the great industrial designer Peter Behrens at the unclassifiable Type Hype concept store (page 220), near the Volksbühne theatre. The Berlin alphabet has been reinvented from A to Z, with a letter for each monument, printed on cards or posters. The most intelligent and unconventional souvenir shop in the capital.

TYPE HYPE
www.typehype.com

7 PM

Enjoy an early evening drink at the Bar am Steinplatz (page 135), in the hotel of the same name, where barman Christian Gentemann has banished gin from his bottles and created great new beers made in Berlin micro breweries.

BAR AM STEINPLATZ
www.hotelsteinplatz.com

8 PM

Attend one of the astonishing shows at the Komische Oper Berlin (page 237), directed by Barrie Kosky. One of the most creative theatres in the whole country.

KOMISCHE OPER BERLIN
www.komische-oper-berlin.de

10 PM

Have a Wiener Schnitzel for dinner, amid luminaries from the Berlin arts scene, at the Café Einstein (page 149), in the former villa of film star Henny Porten. Tarantino shot some scenes for his film *Inglourious Basterds* here.

CAFÉ EINSTEIN STAMMHAUS
www.cafeeinstein.com

12 AM

Begin the night at the Buck and Breck (page 156), a speakeasy in Mitte, before exploring some of the great bars nearby and hitting the clubs further on. Or else stay here until 4am, official closing time.

BUCK AND BRECK
www.buckandbreck.com

2 AM

Stave off late-night hunger pangs with a juicy burger at the Burgermeister (page 156), a former urinal converted into a top-notch burger joint, located under the elevated U-Bahn tracks in Kreuzberg.

BURGERMEISTER
Oberbaumstraße, under the railway arches, Kreuzberg, www.burger-meister.de

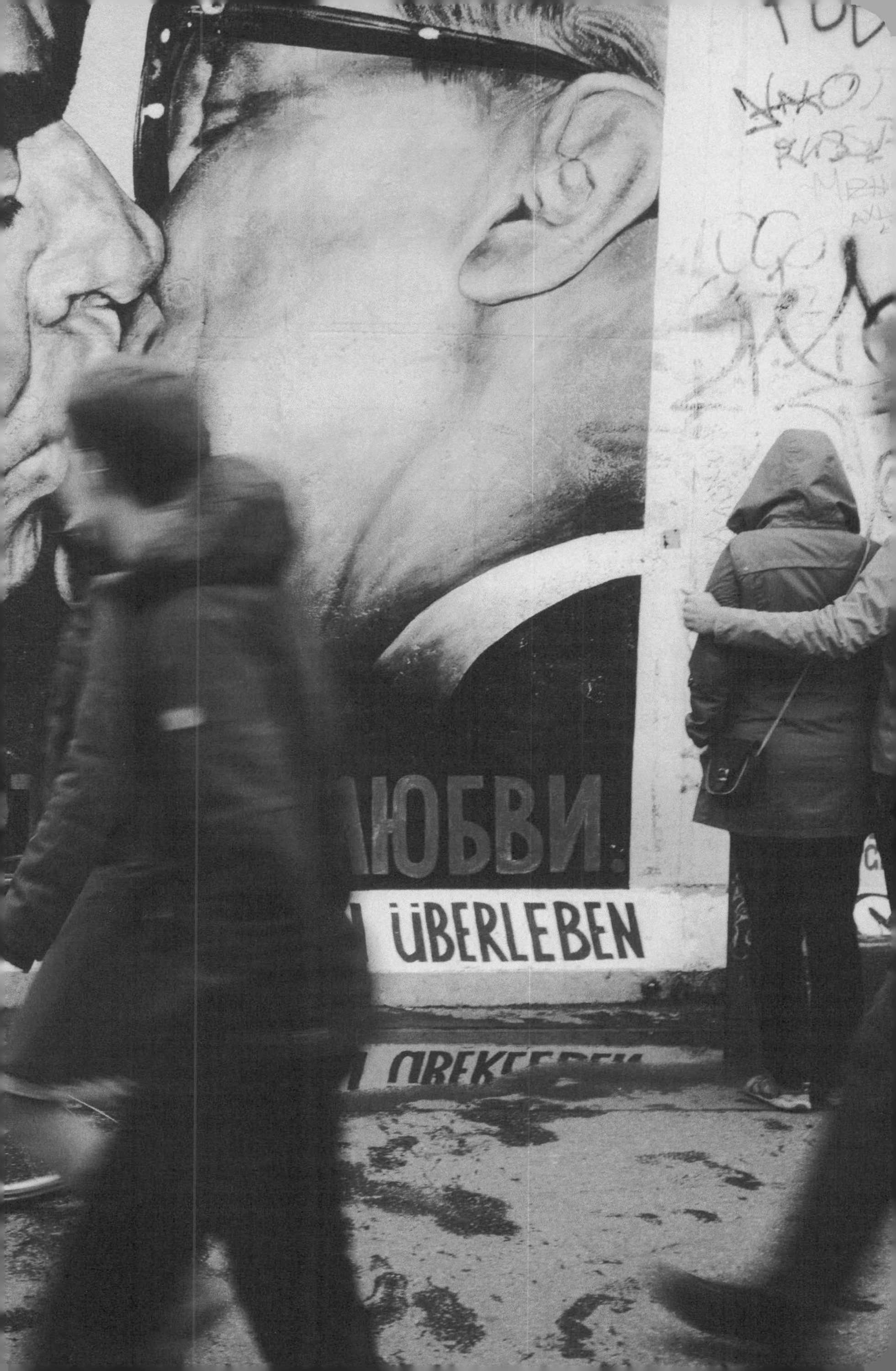
ЛЮБВИ.
ÜBERLEBEN

HOTELS

FIVE-STARS TO OFFBEAT HIDEOUTS: WHERE TO STAY IN THE CITY

Berlin is home to perhaps the most legendary hotel in the world, one that inspired first literature and later film. The Adlon is undoubtedly *the* great luxury hotel in the history of fiction, first recreated in Vicki Baum's novel *Grand Hotel* and later to leap from page to screen with the help of MGM, Greta Garbo and the Barrymore brothers. As for those run-down boarding houses you can still find in the west of the city, around the Ku'damm, they all summon up images of Sally Bowles in Christopher Isherwood's patron saint of a novel *Goodbye to Berlin*, later to be filmed as *Cabaret*.

Berlin is brimming with accommodation of all kinds, from the lowly student hostel to a cutting-edge five-star high in the sky. Often dubbed *Bettenburg* – Bed City – the German capital offers travellers the best value for money in Europe (room service included), whether you want international luxury, a fully equipped apartment, a serviced suite, a caravan, a lakeside cabin or something more hip or offbeat.

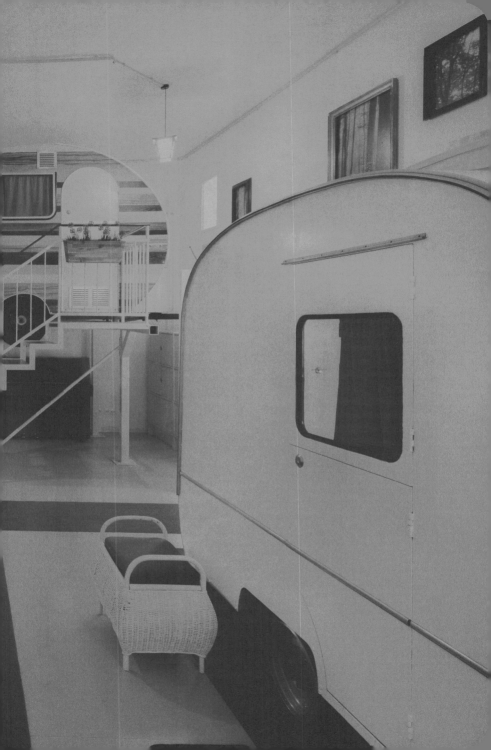

MITTE
City centre & major museums

CASA CAMPER BERLIN
Weinmeisterstraße 1,
corner of Rosenthaler Straße
U-Bahn Weinmeisterstraße
Tel 30 20 00 34 10
www.casacamper.com
48 rooms and 3 suites, €152 to €419
DESIGN HOTEL

Barcelona, 2005: Lorenzo Fluxà, founder of Camper shoes, a Majorca-based label, opened the first Casa Camper in Raval. The same team joined forces again to create a second establishment, in Berlin, which opened in 2009. The concept is much the same, although here the building is a modern one, and the number and size of rooms have increased (no room is smaller than 32 square metres and two of the suites are twice that). Bearing the same name as its Barcelona cousin, the **TENTEMPIÉ** buffet on the top floor is open 24/7 and has three separate areas, a wonderful view of the city, and drinks and snacks around the clock. The hotel's decor, liberally splashed with the Camper red, is highly successful. The beds are clouds of soft white percale, the lights are practical and there are electrical sockets galore within arm's reach. The Bakelite-style switches are user-friendly and there are pegs along the red walls on which you can hang your things. All the furniture is comfortable. The decor manages to be both practical and visually interesting – right down to the telephone, an old-fashioned one with very "last-century" buttons, and the grey-tiled shower, which is roomy enough for two and features a bizarre vertical bidet function. The bathrooms have huge windows, but an opaque panel prevents the toilet from becoming part of a peep show, while ensuring you still enjoy the view. The suites have fully equipped kitchens, including a Nespresso machine. Every room has the same wall decoration in the form of a handy map of the city. There is a basement fitness centre and sauna, and bicycles are available on request. The staff are never less than friendly and helpful. As for the fashionable restaurant on the ground floor, it has been replaced by pop-up stores devoted to labels from the Camper group, such as Medwinds. To set the seal on this four-star establishment, it is ideally located.

GORKI APARTMENTS
Weinbergsweg 25, Mitte
U-Bahn Rosenthaler Platz
Tel 30 4849 6480
www.gorkiapartments.com
35 apartments, €135 to €1,250
STYLISH APARTMENTS

Playwright Maxim Gorky was the official writer of the Soviet Communist regime, an early supporter of the Bolsheviks and one of Lenin's fellow fighters. Gorky was also famous for his full moustache, now used as the logo of the Gorki Apartments, a collection of thirty-six refined flats, including two extravagant penthouses, open-plan and loft-like. Gorki's portrait, complete with its impressive moustache, sits in front of the main entrance, beneath a neon sign bearing the playwright's name. The reception is on the first floor and each apartment is named after a fictional character under which you will be registered – Anselm Müller, Leo Sommer, Lorenz Winter, Caspar von Stein or Clara Ludwig – ensuring Garbo-like anonymity. The apartments, designed by Sandra Pauquet and Kim Wang, are divided into "Categorkis". Each has its own stylish, nostalgic, decorative flavour and radiates a homely yet very contemporary charm beneath the original mouldings. Tiled in white, black and green, the bathrooms hark back to the early 20th century, while the bedding, complete with soft duvet, is particularly comfortable. Choose one of the apartments with a large window overlooking the street for that typically

Berlin ambiance. You can eat a €13 Russian breakfast at the **GORKI PARK CAFÉ** down on the street, and you can buy vouchers to be redeemed there at the apartments' reception. Champagne and bicycles are also available.

HOTEL ADLON KEMPINSKI

Unter den Linden 77

S-Bahn Brandenburger Tor

Tel 30 22 610, www.hotel-adlon.de

307 rooms and 78 suites, €260 to €26,000

LUXURIOUS

The Adlon was founded by Lorenz Adlon, a wealthy hotelier and wine merchant, and opened in 1907 by Kaiser Wilhelm II, who made it his unofficial residence and loved to house his guests there. It overlooked Unter den Linden on one side and Pariser Platz on the other, and behind its massive four-storey Neoclassical facades was one of the most modern and luxurious of Berlin's hotels. Half the rooms were equipped with bathrooms boasting a bathtub and hot water. Frequented by the cream of the diplomatic corps and the aristocracy, it was the ultimate symbol of cosmopolitan Berlin in the 1920s and 1930s, when it was run by Lorenz's son, Louis. Its cellar was famous throughout Europe, as was its restaurant, whose chef was none other than the great Escoffier. Such was its fame, the Adlon inspired Austrian-born writer Vicki Baum's novel *Menschen im Hotel* (*Grand Hotel*), published in 1929. It was a huge bestseller, immediately translated into several languages, and was quickly made into a Hollywood film, with the Adlon's decor faithfully reproduced in the studio by MGM. In the mid-1950s, director Josef von Baky adapted the memoirs of the heiress Hedda Adlon for a West German film called *Hotel Adlon*, starring Nadja Tiller. Finally, as blood is thicker than water, the American director Percy Adlon, another heir to the name and famous for his *Bagdad Café*, directed a 1996 docudrama entitled *In der glanzvollen Welt of Hotel Adlon* (*The Glamorous World*

of the Adlon Hotel). During the war, it was partially converted into a military hospital, and in 1945 it was severely damaged by a fire, with only the cellar and one wing escaping unscathed. When the city was cut into two, the Adlon became part of the GDR. The surviving wing was reopened as a hotel, where the bellhops continued to wear the pre-war hotel uniform. It closed to guests in the 1970s, becoming a lodging house for apprentices. In 1984, the building was torn down. After the fall of the Wall, the Adlon family signed the name and site over to the Kempinski group, who eventually built an almost identical copy of the original. The central lobby with its skylight, the huge alabaster chandeliers and the famous elephant fountain, miraculously salvaged during excavations, have returned to their original locations. Since it reopened in 1997, the new Adlon has aimed for excellence in every area, and thanks to the presence of nearby embassies, it is almost always full. Since 2008, the hotel has been undergoing refurbishment, with new suites including three Presidential Suites, which are advertised as the safest in the country. For a perfect stay, take Albert Einstein's advice and ask for a room overlooking Pariser Platz with a view of the Brandenburg Gate – sublime at dawn and sunset – from your canopied bed. The ocean-liner-style mahogany bathrooms are supplied with JOOP! toiletries. The gigantic breakfast is delivered by a girl in a blue groom's uniform with a basket of warm pastries. Among the many bars and restaurants, keep an eye open for the **LORENZ ADLON ESSZIMMER**, a splendid dinner spot, and the glamorously fashionable **SRA BUA BY TIM RAUE**, which replaced Raue's earlier MA/Uma.

HOTEL AMANO

Auguststraße 43, corner of Rosenthaler Straße
U-Bahn Rosenthaler Platz
Tel 30 809 4150, www.amanogroup.de
163 rooms and apartments, €85 to €250
AFFORDABLE DESIGN HOTEL

While a few steps away, low-cost establishments compete for every corner of Rosenthaler Platz, the Amano wins votes as a well-appointed design hotel at prices that are decidedly downmarket. This is all down to the Süsskind family, who are based in Düsseldorf and for whom the Amano was their first hotel venture in Berlin. Their second, the **MANI** (Torstraße 136, Mitte, tel 030 5302 8080), opened in 2012 on the Torstraße. And the third – the 250-room **AMANO GRAND CENTRAL** (Heidestraße 62, Mitte, tel 400 3000) – opened in spring 2015, close to the wasteland of the former Tacheles squat. At their Auguststraße establishment, the fine exterior architecture is harmoniously echoed by the elegant interior design (both are by Ester Bruzkus from the Berlin-based Büro Gold agency), which ranges from shimmering glamour to velvety modern. The Amano has a fine terrace and a pleasant breakfast room with a decor that taps into the Thonet repertoire of orange, grey and white. The cocktail bar is excellent, if disconcertingly dark. Some of the rooms overlook the old Garnisonkirche cemetery dating back to 1722, which ensures that the neighbourhood is quiet. For extended stays, there is an apartment with a kitchenette. Excellent reception and service at (almost) Motel One prices.

HOTEL DE ROME

Behrenstraße 37
U-Bahn Französische Straße, Hausvogteiplatz
Tel 30 460 6090
www.roccofortehotels.com/fr/hotels-and-resorts/hotel-de-rome/
146 rooms and suites, €295 to €7,000
OPULENT

The Hotel de Rome occupies a stately edifice designed by Ludwig Heim in 1889. It is a prime example of the Wilhelminian architecture of "Greater Prussia" that characterized pre-war Berlin and provided the finishing touch to the remarkable Bebelplatz, where it rubs shoulders with the Staatsoper (under construction until autumn 2017), the former Royal Library, and Sankt-Hedwigs-Kathedrale. Miraculously spared during the bombing, it was the seat of the Dresdner Bank until 1945 and, until 1990, the home of the Central Bank of the German Democratic Republic, before lying vacant. It took the determination of Sir Rocco Forte to transform it into a luxury hotel. Its name evokes the Berlin legend of the almost forgotten Hotel de Rome, the first luxury hotel opened in the city at the end of the 19th century, ultimately outshone by the glittering, imperial Adlon Hotel. Following three years' work and the addition of two storeys, the old place has been brought back to life for the Rocco Forte Collection by Aukett + Heese, with input from interior designer Tommaso Ziffer and Olga Polizzi, the owner's sister. The four huge scarlet Medici vases and the floral compositions in the lobby bespeak a wittily revamped Schinkel-style classicism dotted with traces of the past, notably the impressive ballroom in the former cashiers' hall, and the spa and 20-metre swimming pool dug out of the old vault, where elegant Berlin ladies used to pick up their jewellery before heading for the Opera next door. The former offices on the second floor, with their traces of bullets and bombs in the woodwork, have now been transformed into executive suites. In the suites giving onto Bebelplatz, in particular, the ambience is intensely cosy, with hangings thick as eiderdowns, delectable linen bed sheets, satin-finish glass, velvet-upholstered furniture with scarlet highlights and an overall colour scheme of muted greys and blues. Set in the former entrance hall amid granite columns, the **OPERA COURT** is a high-tea must; and next door to the Bebel Bar is the **VELVET ROOM**, a small private lounge that is popular with Berliners. The

Roof Terrace is a lounge in the sky. The restaurant La Banca, recently renovated, is helmed by chef Jörg Behrend.

THE REGENT

Charlottenstraße 49
U-Bahn Französische Straße
Tel 30 20338
www.regenthotels.com/berlin
165 rooms and 35 suites, €250 to €3,700
CLASSIC, LUXURIOUS

A bit of history: the site used to be occupied by the residence of architect Carl Gotthard Langhans, who designed the Brandenburg Gate. It was damaged in 1945, then torn down. The current building was designed in the early 1990s by Berlin architect Josef Paul Kleihues, who was also in charge of redesigning the block known as Hofgarten (or Quartier 208). It is a vaguely postmodern design built out of marble, travertine and steel. The first hotel to occupy the building was opened in 1996 by the Four Seasons group and was considered to be the best hotel in Berlin at the time. It was sumptuously decorated by Bostonian designer Frank Nicholson, with lavish use of marble, gilt, a red and grey colour scheme, hangings, crystal, Biedermeier furniture and floral compositions for which the annual budget was around €50,000. A few years later, Four Seasons ceded the lease to Regent, but little has changed inside. The service remains impeccable, the bedding is wonderful and the decor is still immaculately classical in style. Every afternoon in winter, there's a warming fireplace in the tearoom and a tea master to share his expertise. The **FISCHERS FRITZ** gourmet restaurant is still overseen by the talented chef Christian Lohse, and each summer the Summer Lounge Orange sparkles thanks to the Veuve Clicquot Bar. Despite the lack of a pool, the Regent Health Club provides ample opportunities for physical exercise. And in a hotel where the sky's the limit, why not make the most of a deal with Air Berlin Service to take a helicopter tour of the city.

ALSO IN THIS NEIGHBOURHOOD

THE DUDE

Köpenicker Straße 92
U-Bahn Heinrich-Heine-Straße
Tel 30 411 988 177
www.thedudeberlin.com
30 rooms, €99 to €379
QUIRKY BOUTIQUE HOTEL

Located in the heart of Luisenstadt, on the eastern edge of Mitte, not far from Kreuzberg, this small, luxury boutique hotel was opened by advertising executive Alexander Schmidt-Vogel. It shares the same liquorice-coloured facade as **THE BROOKLYN**, which dates back to 1822. The interior, designed by Britta Bettendorf, looks as if it has escaped from the Berlin episode in *Casino Royale* with Peter Sellers and Joanna Pettet.

TIERGARTEN
*Peaceful parkland
& new architecture*

25HOURS HOTEL BIKINI BERLIN

Budapester Straße 40
S-Bahn and U-Bahn Zoologischer Garten
Tel 30 1202 210
www.25hours-hotels.com
149 rooms, €130 to €330
FASHIONABLE, DESIGN

25hours launched its first design hotel in Hamburg, at the entrance to the Otto von Bahren business park, following it with places in Frankfurt, Zürich and Vienna. The Berlin branch is a wonderful, slightly whacky wonderland occupying the ten floors of a former office building overlooking the Bikinihaus (now the Bikini Berlin, a shopping centre and office building). It has been a great success, due in part to the **NENI BERLIN** restaurant and the **MONKEY BAR**, both perched on the panoramic top floor, which is accessible via a separate lift. The ground-floor lobby features an old Austin Mini Countryman placed there like a relic, alongside suspended bicycles. Reception is located on the third floor, also reached by its own lift. Like the rest of the building, everything here has been stripped down, scraped away and exposed, brought up to standard and left as is. Designer Werner Aisslinger, whose handiwork is also on show at the **MICHELBERGER HOTEL**, has devised such ingenious decorative features as wooden pallet walls overgrown with ivy; emptied hi-fi speakers turned into bookshelves; hammocks; and curtained work booths. The reception desk is tiled in turquoise, and there's even a real bakery, open daily to hotel guests as well as outsiders, as well as the inevitable little café. The rooms upstairs are also smart, fun and practical, and have large windows to maximize views (ask for a room on the zoo side for a slightly surreal experience). The rooms abound in surprising, amusing, yet practical decorative details. For breakfast, try the **WOODFIRE BAKERY** or the **NENI**.

DAS STUE

Drakestraße 1
S-Bahn and U-Bahn Zoologischer Garten
Tel 30 311 7220
www.das-stue.com
79 rooms and suites, €230 to €2,700
LUXURIOUS DESIGN HOTEL

Built in 1939 by architect Johann Emil Schaudt near the zoo, the Royal Danish Embassy did not serve its country for long. Although it survived the bombing, it was unoccupied for many years and has now been given a new lease of life as a five-star hotel by a group of private investors. This is one of Berlin's most luxurious establishments, with a slight feel of a rural resort due to its location overlooking the Tiergarten. Unless you want to run in the woods or do some outdoor yoga, there is little compelling reason to step outside, even though the hotel claims to be just ten minutes from the Ku'damm – probably at the speed of an ostrich. Beginning with the alligator's head in the palatial lobby, wild animals play a major role in the decor, while rational animals like yourself with a liking for contemporary elegance will find everything they want without having to fight for it. Patricia Urquiola's decor is a fantasy of vivid colours and shapes in soft materials, including neon giraffes and leather turtles. The Stue Bar and the two restaurants, the gourmet **CINCO** and the **CASUAL**, masterminded by the Catalan chef Paco Pérez, have the same upbeat atmosphere. With beds floating on a bright island, and bathrooms scented with Molton Brown products, the rooms and suites have been artfully designed and are cosy and clean. On the wall, a white ceramic cockatoo on its blue perch reminds you, again, of the proximity of the zoo. From the large windows, the view of the zoo and the western horizon, with the Mercedes-Benz symbol crowning the Europa Center and the Kaiser-Wilhelm-Gedächtniskirche, is a striking sight when set against the backdrop of a dramatic sky. The wifi works well, the service is impeccable and the bedding above reproach. The gym is equipped with Technogym machines and the **SPA BY SUSANNE KAUFMANN** is highly recommended. On Saturdays, savvy Berliners come to lunch on an excellent breakfast club sandwich at the **CASUAL**, while evenings, showbiz people meet in the bar. A word of warning: there is another Drakestraße in the east of the city, so tell taxi drivers that you want to go to the Tiergarten.

GRAND HYATT BERLIN

Marlene-Dietrich-Platz 2
S-Bahn and U-Bahn Potsdamer Platz
Tel 30 2553 1234
www.berlin.grand.hyatt.com
342 rooms and suites, €190 to €3,500
LUXURIOUS

The Grand Hyatt, designed by José Rafael Moneos, stands next door to Renzo Piano's Daimler-Benz building on the new Potsdamer Platz. Opened in 1998, it is a superlative monument in itself, with a minimalist interior by architect Hannes Wettstein that has a peaceful, zen atmosphere, enhanced by the light flooding through the wide glass panels affording views of new Berlin. An impressive and annually enriched collection of artworks adorns the spacious lobby, the convention centre and the suites, including paintings commissioned from the Korean artist Jaehyo Lee. Upstairs, the American designer Tony Chi, responsible for the Andaz 5th Avenue in New York, has renovated the rooms with intelligence and taste, applying subtle, elegant,

contemporary touches to the strong Bauhaus heritage. The marble bathrooms with their steam-free mirrors and other refined accessories are a great success. The Grand Club on the seventh floor is a good place for business breakfasts and working one-on-ones. If you want a decent view, ask for a room or suite overlooking the Kulturforum and Hans Scharoun's Philharmonie. The **CLUB & SPA OLYMPUS** fitness centre on the top floor is open to non-residents for a monthly or annual subscription and has a vast mixed sauna, a large pool where you can swim looking out over the city, a brushed steel jacuzzi shaped like a panoramic Mediterranean washhouse and an outdoor solarium. Redesigned by the same Tony Chi, the **VOX RESTAURANT** serves a splendid buffet breakfast every weekday morning until 10:30am and on weekends until noon. The restaurant-bar Mesa has been replaced by a new concept called Jamboree.

THE RITZ-CARLTON BERLIN

Potsdamer Platz 3
S-Bahn and U-Bahn Potsdamer Platz
Tel 30 33 77 7
www.ritzcarlton.com
302 rooms and suites, 1 apartment,
€235 to €14,500
LUXURIOUS

This is the second establishment that was opened in 2004 in Germany under this name by the American group Marriott, following the one in Wolfsburg, designed by the late Andrée Putman. One of the striking features of this Ritz-Carlton is a superlative chandelier designed by Peter Silling, based in Cologne, who was inspired by the work of the famous Prussian architect Schinkel in trying to

"I love this sprawling town. I love the anarchy of stone and flesh visible only at night. The city is a web. The city is my mother. I love her ... I love how she can shine with splendour under the grime."
Paul Verhaeghen, Omega Minor, 2008

evoke old imperial grandeur, also evident in the grand central staircase and the profusion of lush flower arrangements. This comes as something of a surprise given the architectural style of the building itself, designed by Berlin agency Hilmer & Sattler und Albrecht, whose simple vertical lines call to mind the skyscrapers of Chicago and New York from the 1920s and 1930s. Set back from the Sony Center, the complex, called the Beisheim Center, houses lavishly appointed rooms and suites, including around forty club rooms on the tenth and eleventh floors specifically for business travellers, with easy check-in and various services. The **BRASSERIE DESBROSSES** is a little late 19th-century gem that was moved here piece by piece from Mâcon in France. The open kitchen, featuring an antique red enamel oven, creates a convivial atmosphere. There is also a tea lounge, the extraordinary cocktail bar **FRAGRANCES**, a well-equipped gym, pool and saunas, reserved for hotel guests.

CHARLOTTENBURG
Smart residential & chic shopping

HOTEL AM STEINPLATZ

Steinplatz 4
S-Bahn Savignyplatz
U-Bahn Ernst-Reuter-Platz
Tel 30 554 4440
www.hotelsteinplatz.com
84 rooms and 3 suites, €175 to €585
HISTORIC, LUXURIOUS

As the first hotel in the Autograph Collection to be opened in Germany by the American group Marriott, the Steinplatz has now regained its former ranking in the Berlin hotel industry. For a long time, the Hotel am Steinplatz was a pillar of hospitality, frequented in particular by artists, writers and actors. Its hundred years of history are described by Ilse Eliza Zellermayer in her book *Prinzessinnensuite*, in which she recalls her encounters and friendships with such luminaries as Vladimir Nabokov, Romy Schneider, Yehudi Menuhin and Heinrich Böll. Born in Berlin in 1920, the author, the German impresario for Luciano Pavarotti, is the daughter of Max Zellermayer, a prominent figure in the Berlin hotel world and the long-time owner of the hotel. The Steinplatz opened in 1913 in a Jugendstil apartment building built in 1907 by August Endell, designer of the famous Hackescher Höfe in Mitte. This historic building was damaged during the war, but after being restored and reopened it was converted into a retirement home when the hotel closed in 1976. A listed building, it remained empty for ten years until it underwent a three-year restoration, overseen by architect Claudia Dressler. The olive-green-and-cream facade was refurbished, as were the arched windows. Inside, the decor was designed by Tassilo Bost, who is based in Hamburg, where he was responsible for the interior design of the Westin Grand, part of the new

Elbphilharmonie complex designed by Herzog & de Meuron. No minimalist, Bost favours glamour and opulence, using an abundance of lacquer, mirrors and dark wood. The beautiful, bright bathrooms are impeccably equipped with Etro products. Each room has a minibar full of Berlin drinks – Our/Berlin vodka and Van Nahmen organic fruit juice – and an espresso machine and a kettle, plus an iron and board. Ask for one of the corner rooms (106, 206, 306 or 406) to enjoy the view over the Steinplatz. Opened in December 2013, rated five stars and managed by the charming Iris Baugatz, the Steinplatz is ideally located in Charlottenburg, close to Savignyplatz, as well as the C/O Forum, the Helmut Newton Foundation and the Max Hetzler gallery. The hotel has a wall of black-and-white photos featuring mythical names and places from pre-war Berlin. It also includes the **RESTAURANT AM STEINPLATZ**, overseen by Nicholas Hahn, the renowned **BAR AM STEINPLATZ**, a landscaped courtyard garden and the beautiful **SPA AM STEINPLATZ** on two levels (fifth and sixth floors), which is open to non-guests. And the golden sweets in the crystal candy dish at the reception are there to be gobbled up. Just like life itself.

HOTEL ZOO

Kurfürstendamm 25
U-Bahn Kurfürstendamm, Uhlandstraße
Tel 30 884 370
www.hotelzoo.de
131 rooms and 14 suites,
€130 to €1,500
DESIGNER HOTEL

There's no lack of hotels along the Ku'damm, but the Hotel Zoo is the one that best chimes with the Berlin legend. Opened in 1911 next to the Union-Palast, it miraculously remained intact in 1945 and became the stronghold for guest stars and the social whirl at the Berlinale, then held in West Berlin (the hotel's facade used to be adorned with a mass of national flags). Two glazed storeys were added in

the 1980s by architect Paul Baumgartner, reaching out over the pavement in a huge golden canopy, and the Hotel Zoo also underwent a sea change behind its listed Wilhelmine facade to remain in step with the transformation of the neighbourhood. It was bought by Manfred Weingärtner and Robert Hubner in 2005 and radically restructured and redecorated in a "New York meets Berlin" mode, mixing modern with vintage. The rooms on the top two floors were converted into penthouses in the sky, and the whole hotel was upgraded to a five-star, earning a Design Hotel label into the bargain. Maison Martin Margiela-branded bath towels and a limousine for airport arrivals and departures are a couple of the perks here, and the hotel is "connected" once again to the Berlinale. Shimmering, silky and velvety, the Zoo is a trendy enclave with lots of package deals and partnerships, including one with the Wheadon beauty institute. The rooms and suites offer optimal comfort and amenities aplenty.

SIR SAVIGNY HOTEL

Kantstraße, 144, Charlottenburg
U-Bahn Savignyplatz
Tel 30 3230 15671
www.sirsavignyhotel.com
44 rooms and suites, €105 to €275
URBAN ATMOSPHERE

Founded by Yossi Eliyahoo and Liran Wizman, the Entourage group manages all the Sir hotels in Europe: in Amsterdam there's the Sir Albert and Sir Adam, in Hamburg the Sir Nikolai and in Ibiza the Sir Joan. In Berlin, the Sir Savigny was opened on the site of a former rather nondescript design hotel. Of course, it's been totally redecorated, redesigned and launched into mega-cool orbit by the Baranowitz + Cronenbourg agency, who have restyled the lobby and the lounges. There's no reception as such: instead guests are welcomed by an informal reception service based around a large table loaded with vases and books. Friendly, stylish staff make sure you don't miss a thing: from the glass-roofed lounge with its central fireplace and **THE BUTCHER** restaurant (www.the-butcher.com) – another concept developed by the group and available in all Sir hotels – to the library, the art-filled interior garden, and the huge graffiti by Berlin graffiti artist Dome, aka Christian Krämer. Saar Zafrir has designed the rooms and suites, including the Sir Suite with a freestanding bathtub in the centre of the room, all immersed in an atmosphere of retro design. It's plush, amusing, cosy, comfortable, smart, chic, opulent and casual all at the same time: in fact the rich furnishings and colour palette work better in winter than in summer, not least the large collages by Berlin artist Katharina Musick hanging at the head of the bed. Nespresso machine, kettle, cosmetics and other little amenities are available in all categories of rooms. Conveniently located, truly welcoming, serving an impeccable breakfast, and filled with fun gimmicks such as the Call the Butchers bell for a room-service burger or the Dead Clean bath and shower products, the Sir richly deserves its aristocratic title, and has been endorsed by the Design Hotels brand.

WILMERSDORF, GRUNEWALD
Affluent districts & woodland lakes

ELLINGTON HOTEL

Nürnberger Straße 50–55, Wilmersdorf

U-Bahn Wittenbergplatz

Tel 30 683 150

www.ellington-hotel.com

285 rooms and suites, €118 to €460

CONTEMPORARY

Yes, the restaurant-bar is called **DUKE**. And yes, the whole place, right down to the Jazz 101.9 radio station broadcast here, is a homage to jazz. But there is nothing fake about this: in the early 1930s, before it was banned by the Nazis, this "new" music ruled the roost here. Built between 1928 and 1931 by Richard Bielenberg and Josef Moser, the Haus Nürnberg was better known to Berliners as the Tauentzienpalast, on the ground floor of which was the famous Femina dance hall. The building's long, sleek Bauhaus facades were designed by the great architect Erich Mendelsohn and were the modernist face of Neuer Westen. The building survived the war and since 2007 has housed a hotel, together with the "luxury" department of clothing retailer Peek & Cloppenburg. On the whole, the hotel's interior and amenities live up handsomely to the building's rationalist heritage. The staircases with their cream and celadon wall tiles and the light fixtures are original. Elsewhere, the decor designed by architect Luigi Lanzi is wholly contemporary. The minimalist, functional rooms, whose numbers are printed on the carpet in front of the door, have soothing white-beige-grey colour schemes. Only some of them have baths depending on the category. The overall effect is one of no-nonsense simplicity. The staff are young and enthusiastic. Not surprisingly, given the reasonable prices, the place is popular with groups. However, the hotel, which oscillates between three and four stars, is sufficiently large that you can escape from the crowds. The original shopping arcade on the ground floor includes a large florist, a hair salon and the Duke bar-restaurant (all have entrances on the street as well as from the hotel). The Sunday brunch is popular with Berliners, who generally know a thing or two when it comes to brunches.

HENRI HOTEL

Meinekestraße 9, Wilmersdorf
U-Bahn Kurfürstendamm
Tel 30 884 430, www.henri-berlin.com
77 rooms and apartments, €78 to €285
RETRO MODERN

First launched in Hamburg in 2013, the Henri hotel group took a leap forward in 2016 when it opened a sister establishment located halfway between the Ku'damm and the Berliner Festspiele. This was once Berlin's former Western sector and it's now a decidedly fashionable part of town. The Henri occupies the former Residenz hotel, a beautiful late 19th-century building, in which interior designer Marc-Ludolf von Schmarsow has created an elegant decor that's a cosy evocation of the Bismarck style. Rooms are available in three categories – Kabinett, Les Chambres and Salon – and the ten or so apartments are equipped in the manner of charming small hotels for long-stay visitors. Whether it's the landing, with its beautiful Jugendstil mouldings painted in floral tones, the Roter and Blauer salons, or the Damenzimmer, all the public areas are gleaming and comfortable. Food is served at the counter in the kitchen, which is decorated to look like an early 20th-century middle-class home. In a decor of wall tiles, dressers and gleaming brasswork, this is where the self-service breakfast happens – it's all "sehr gut" and extremely reassuring. The **MINE & WINE** restaurant (www.minerestaurant.de), located on the ground floor, is not part of the hotel, but it contributes to the address's success – and to the rebirth of this major thoroughfare, once considered a little dull.

HOTEL AUGUSTA

Fasanenstraße 22, Wilmersdorf
U-Bahn Uhlandstraße
Tel 30 883 5028
www.hotel-augusta.de
42 rooms and 4 suites, €65 to €265
INTIMATE, DISCREET

Before the war, Berlin was full of furnished accommodation and boarding houses, and after the war this remained the case in the former West. Today, some of these establishments have disappeared, such as the legendary Hotel Bogota in Schlüterstraße, while others have lost their lustre, such as the Askanischer Hof on the Ku'damm. Others still have risen to prominence, as is the case with the Augusta, located opposite the Pension Funk and near the Haus der Literatur. This small yet charming hostelry is ideally located and has been modernized. The hotel is reached via a grand marble staircase with red carpet, as in days gone past. Run by Danuta and Julia Lippoth, mother and daughter, the Augusta has no other aim than to provide travellers with a pleasant, untaxing place to stay. The decor is for the most part comfortably classical, but with occasional touches of kitsch – in short, it could be ideal as a place for your parents to stay. The four suites all have espresso machines. The largest one, under the eaves, extends for 70 square metres and boasts a huge bathroom with jacuzzi. Although you have to pay for the breakfast, there is free parking and wifi.

HOTEL PENSION FUNK

Fasanenstraße 69, Wilmersdorf
U-Bahn Kurfürstendamm, Uhlandstraße
Tel 30 882 7193
www.hotel-pensionfunk.de
14 rooms, €45 to €129
INTIMATE, BELLE ÉPOQUE

The Danish actress Asta Nielsen was the leading star of German silent cinema, arriving in Berlin in 1909 and acting in seventy films, all shot and produced by her own studios. As the cinema's first sex bomb, she twice played Mata Hari, as well as Miss Julie and Hedda Gabler, but above all she starred in *Joyless Street* (1925), a G.W. Pabst masterpiece in which Greta Garbo made her debut. The actress spent a small part of her Berlin glory years in this huge fourteen-room apartment in this elegant, and at the time new, Jugendstil building built in 1895. She lived here from 1931 to 1937, during which time she appeared in a single talkie (a flop), acted in the theatre and turned down Goebbels' offer to become a leading producer. She then upped sticks and returned to Copenhagen. In 1956, the Funk sisters transformed the apartment into a boarding house that's now run by Michael Pfundt. Some of the rooms are adorned with ceiling mouldings and wallpaper based on original designs, while the most spacious look onto the Fasanenstraße, Berlin's most elegant thoroughfare. Breakfast, which is included, is served in the former dining room and the atmosphere is steeped in nostalgia for the long-gone Berlin of old. A unique, charming place to stay, where time seems to have stood still.

MAX BROWN

Uhlandstraße, 49,
corner of Pariser Straße, Wilmersdorf
U-Bahn Uhlandstraße, Hohenzollernplatz
Tel 30 217 826 39
www.maxbrownhotels.com
70 rooms, from €358
FUNKY, FASHIONABLE

The Domus Hotel, a faded 1980s design mecca still appreciated by a fringe of nostalgic travellers with low standards, is no more. It has been replaced with fanfare by Max Brown, tagged "Your Urban Residence", with a concept invented in Amsterdam in 2011. It is run by the atypical hotel group Europe Hotels Private Collection, which includes the Sir Hotels. Already present in Amsterdam and Düsseldorf, Max Brown has just taken Berlin by storm. It's a success, right from the entrance, decorated by Israeli designer

Alona Eliassi with gold embossed ceilings, black floors dotted with white, a red billiards table and a reception desk loaded with sweets, toys and amusing gadgets worthy of a bazaar of yesteryear. The rooms were done by interior decorator Saar Zafrir, in a joyful spirit. By the door of each room is a cactus in a white ceramic pot. The rooms have wallpaper, basketball hoops, tubular or vintage 1960s Scandinavian furniture, old phones and Crosley turntables to listen to the vinyl records provided by the label Unique Records. It's comfortable, fun and unlike the usual hotel room. The white-tiled bathrooms have retro fixtures and Dead Clean toiletries with argan oil. Rooms are sized "small" (rather cramped) to "extra-large", and they all have the same funky-retro spirit straight out of an Elke Sommer film. Or, even better, Rainer Werner Fassbinder's *Lola*. The **BENEDICT** restaurant, which takes up the entire ground floor, serves as the breakfast room and is a hotspot that contributes to the hotel's success.

PATRICK HELLMANN SCHLOSSHOTEL

Brahmsstraße 10, Grunewald
S-Bahn Grunewald
Tel 30 895 840
www.schlosshotelberlin.com
53 rooms and suites, €299 to €3,700
ELEGANT, REFINED

Built in 1912 as a place of entertainment by Walter von Pannwitz, a Silesian aristocrat married to a wealthy Argentinian, this small townhouse has enjoyed a curious history. Its heyday was short-lived: in the aftermath of the First World War, the Pannwitzes followed Kaiser Wilhelm II into exile in the Netherlands and then emigrated to Switzerland. When the Nazis seized power, they blackmailed the couple, demanding they sell the house in return for identity papers. The art collections in the house dropped straight into Göring's hands. In 1941, the Pannwitzes' townhouse became the headquarters of the Croatian Legation.

A hygiene blight affecting all hotel categories up to five-stars, the undersheet is supposed to protect the mattress. In reality, however, it serves as an instrument of nocturnal torture, and hotels across Germany, with those in Berlin leading the pack, appear to have made it their speciality. The traveller, unaware, perhaps distracted, lies down on delightful pure linen or percale sheet, falls asleep and suddenly begins to dream that his mattress is stuffed with crisp dollar bills. Suddenly he awakens, drenched in perspiration, realizing that no, he has not succumbed to a fever fit following a recent bout of malaria but, horror of horrors, rather to an abominable rubber undersheet crinkling and scrunching more loudly than a pallet piled with thousands of empty crisp packets. An undersheet? And why not a bedpan, as well, while you're at it? Welcome to the Intercontinental Hotel! You tear the bedding apart, rip off the undersheet and toss it in a ball in the cupboard, and whip the sheets back on the bed in an effort to remake it hastily – but the night is ruined. And no traditional cosy German duvet is going to make up for that lost sleep. Talking of which, we note that many major hotels have traded in their feather quilts folded in two – placed on a spacious king-size bed they look a bit like two raviolis on an overly large plate – for one huge quilt for two, but you have to request it specially. Confessing that they pay fortunes for five-star undersheets, hotel groups try to find alternatives, but even when these are invisible, silent and impalpable, even when made of pure cotton or linen or silk, even when they warm the bed, undersheets (which some hotels stupidly insist on tying over the mattress cover now so in vogue – yes, yes, we've seen it!) will continue to be as annoying as that famous pea that bedevilled the princess. The moral of the story: off with the undersheet!

Four years later, having miraculously escaped the bombing, it became a club for English officers in what was now the British sector. Converted into a hotel in 1951 known as Schlosshotel Gerhus, the house was then bought by five Berlin families who wanted to turn it into a luxury establishment. The hotel closed in 1991. At the same time, a team of Polish craftsmen was hired to restore the original interiors, with their panelling and stained-glass windows. This renovation work included a huge suite designed by Karl Lagerfeld. Launched in 1994 as part of the German Vier Jahreszeiten chain, the Schlosshotel boasted rooms and suites in different styles, although the whole was a luxurious echo of a time when the lobby and lounges overflowed with antiques, old paintings, panelling, gilded coffered ceilings and brocades. Nestling in the upmarket residential Grunewald district, and bathed in the peaceful atmosphere of a park, the property has seen many owners and operators, from The Regent to the Catalan Alma Hotels group. It is now in the hands of Patrick Hellmann. A fashion designer in charge of a men's style empire, Hellmann is a Berlin celebrity who has dressed may celebrities. In renovating this hotel complex, Patrick Hellmann called upon star architect Sergei Tchoban, sparing no expense to cover the dizzying lounges with gold and silver, and demanding the use of historic techniques and designs handed down from French Art Deco. Plush and boasting superlative comfort, the rooms and suites all bear his trademarks. Imbued with his favourite colours of black lacquer, simple white and Aegean blue, the rooms boast many drawings, sculptures, plasters, porcelains, sketches and other fantasies. The bathrooms display the same exceptional qualities, being both palatial and straightforward, with a penchant for the 1930s. Located on the ground floor, the spa and wellness centre with a beautiful swimming pool offer a range of treatments in individual cubicles, as well as a dedicated catering service. European firsts, opened in collaboration with Condé Nast Germany, the glamorous **VOGUE CAFÉ** and the **GQ BAR**, all lacquerware and Lalique, tweed and chevron-design wallpaper, attract a gilded clientele. A champagne lounge is planned in the former mirror room, while the former Vivaldi restaurant is to be renamed, redesigned and relocated. The black Rolls-Royce Ghost, parked in front of the hotel, is at the disposal of VIPs.

PRENZLAUER BERG
Gentrification & bobo stronghold

ACKSELHAUS & BLUE HOME
Belforter Straße 21–25
U-Bahn Senefelderplatz
Tel 30 4433 7633
www.ackselhaus.de
35 rooms and 4 suites, €120 to €340
OFFBEAT, SMALL

Strange as it might seem in view of the large number of tourists who flock here, Prenzlauer Berg has few hotels (but numerous B & Bs), with nearby Mitte, which boasts more than its share, absorbing the majority of visitors. Essentially a residential area, bastion of the yuppie set, Prenzlauer Berg is not the best place to look for accommodation, and only a few small establishments stand out. For his little hotel, Ulf Acksel went for an "exotic colonial" theme that is somewhat at odds with the neighbourhood, but is nonetheless rather beguiling. The rooms, suites and apartments spread across two 19th-century buildings have a rustic, ethnic, Balinese feel, creating a general mood of relaxation, lightness, and simplicity. Flower-filled, green and cooled in summer by several fountains and basins, the complex forms a curious oasis in the neighbourhood. A buffet breakfast is served every morning in the Café del Mar.

LINNEN
Eberswalder Straße 35
U-Bahn Eberswalder Straße
Tel 30 4737 2440
www.linnenberlin.com
4 rooms, 1 suite, 5 apartments, €85 to €185
OFFBEAT

Are we still in Mitte or already in Prenzlauer Berg? Are we closer to the Mauerpark and its Sunday flea market or to the Prenzlauer Berg bars? Starting with this hotel's own bar on the ground floor, a marvellous example of up-recycling. With its four rooms, two apartment and single suite, plus three other apartments in Mitte (Große Hamburger Straße 17 and Rosa-Luxemburg-Straße 3), the Linnen apartment house is spreading its intrinsically Berlin message of "more home, less hotel". Primarily targeting the young Euro-arty-urban set, the place looks like a movie set taken over by smart bric-a-brac, with a spiral staircase leading to the bedrooms decorated in the same tone, and bathrooms and toilets from Dr Bronner. The place fluctuates between a curio cabinet and a countertop in a bazaar, with much for the eye to enjoy. Breakfast is served in the above-mentioned café by staff who know how to smile and be friendly. In short, this is a relaxed, comfortable, funky place to stay, in a good location, at very reasonable prices.

SCHÖNEBERG, FRIEDENAU
Residential & literary

HOTEL FRIEDENAU – DAS LITERATURHOTEL BERLIN

Fregestraße 68, Friedenau
S-Bahn Friedenau
U-Bahn Friedrich-Wilhelm-Platz
Tel 30 859 0960
www.literaturhotel-berlin.de
20 rooms, €95 to €120
INTIMATE, CULTURAL

Friedenau is a quiet residential suburb in south Berlin between Schöneberg and Steglitz. It is off the beaten track for sightseers and museum-goers, but well worth a detour for its excellent pastry shops, such as **FRAU BEHRENS TORTEN** (Rheinstraße 65, Friedenau, tel 889 112 864), and also because, for years, it has been home to a wonderful little hotel. The "literature hotel" sits on a tree-lined street overlooked by attractive buildings, and is known for having long been the Berlin refuge of many writers of note, beginning with Günter Grass. The Friedenau's cultivated owner, Christa Moog, offers you the precious gift of being in Berlin without actually being there, and of basking in an aura of literary greatness. The word HOTEL on a yellow neon sign on the ochre-and-white facade calls out to you like a title on a book cover. On entering, you arrive in a little hallway, which is deserted. Keys are hung neatly on the wall and a photo of each room reveals its style. Welcome to Auntie's home, filled with her inherited Biedermeier furniture, particularly in the Johnson salon, named after the author Uwe Johnson, once a frequent guest here. Today, Frau Moog uses this lounge for readings, book signings and discussions about the works of Berlin writers, often in the presence of the authors. French, English, Italian, Russian, Swedish and Polish are all spoken here.

GOING IT ALONE

In terms of the sheer number of accommodation options and their variety, Berlin has few rivals in Europe. Here are some of the more offbeat possibilities.

ON WATER

If you are a fresh-air enthusiast with a preference for water, you can stay in a houseboat (*Hausboot*) at Marina Lanke in Spandau on the Havel River. They can accommodate from three to sixteen people. Alternatively, you could sleep aboard the Eastern Comfort or Western Comfort barge hotels anchored along the Spree, a few oar strokes from Oberbaumbrücke (prohibited for children under six, animals and non-swimmers).

MARINA LANKE BERLIN Scharfe Lanke 109–131, Spandau, 3km west of Grunewald, tel 362 0090, www.marina-lanke.de

EASTERN COMFORT and **WESTERN COMFORT** Mühlenstraße 73–77, Friedrichshain, S-Bahn and U-Bahn Warschauer Straße, tel 6676 3806, www.eastern-comfort.com

IN A MATTRESS FACTORY

At Daniel Heer's apartment and studio, you can sleep in a room with white walls, a double bed, a duvet, two bedside tables and a wood-and-leather stool. That's it. Herr Heer's idea is to give his customers a chance to sleep on one of his fantastic handmade horsehair mattresses for one night. They can also watch them being made. Books by the Swiss publisher Diaphanes are available, and guests can come and go as they please. Booking by appointment, seven days a week. If you buy a mattress, one night's stay is free; if not, it will cost €140, breakfast included.

SCHÖNEBERGER ZIMMER Blumenthalstraße 7, Tiergarten, U-Bahn Kurfürstenstraße, Bülowstraße, tel 30 340 85 194, www.danielheer.com

IN A CARAVAN

The delightfully whimsical Hüttenpalast in Neukölln offers an opportunity to sleep in a vintage caravan. The brainchild of Silke Lorenzen and Sarah Vollmer, this *Karawane-Hotel* is located in a former factory that now houses wooden shacks and old caravans decorated and furnished by young artists, such as Marion Andrieu from France and the Venezuelan Yoraco González. There are shared bathrooms and toilets (one for men, another for women), as well as tea- and coffee-making facilities. The concept has been so successful that the duo annexed a neighbouring space to house five new caravans, including a two-tone cream and emerald one that looks like a Schuco toy from the1950s. There are also six private rooms on offer for those who prefer their bathrooms to themselves. These include tea- and coffee-making facilities. Breakfast is served from 8am to 11am at a nice café overlooking the street.

HÜTTENPALAST Hobrechtstraße 65–66, Neukölln, U-Bahn Hermannplatz, tel 3730 5806, www.huettenpalast.de

FRIEDRICHSHAIN
Hip & bohemian

MICHELBERGER HOTEL

Warschauer Straße 39–40
S-Bahn and U-Bahn Warschauer Straße
Tel 30 2977 8590
www.michelbergerhotel.com
111 rooms, €60 to €450

FASHIONABLE, INEXPENSIVE

If it were not for the late 19th-century Neo-Gothic Oberbaumbrücke and the East Side Gallery, the rather dull Warschauer Straße spanning the Ostbahnhof railway tracks would be almost completely devoid of interest. However, in 2009 this unusual little hotel opened, quickly becoming the talk of the town. Trying to decipher the sign from a distance, you might think it was a salute to the late French singer Michel Berger. And why not? An **ABBA** hotel opened recently in Charlottenburg (a brief investigation has shown that, while its restaurant is called Mamma Mia!, the establishment has little to do with the famous Swedish pop group, Abba being the name of a Spanish hotel chain) and the city is regularly papered with posters announcing the triumphant return of Mireille Mathieu, though no one has yet thought to name a hotel after her. We're clearly on the wrong track: above the entrance to the Michelberger, you can read ever-changing mottos in black gaffer tape on neon: "I don't wanna wake you up, but I really wanna show you something" or "Small is beautiful". Inside, no attempt has been made to conceal the former factory's industrial past. Guests are greeted by untreated concrete, grillwork cages filled with old books, a wood-shingle-covered reception desk: the tone is set. Haphazard, funky, reused and recycled, tongue-in-cheek, ingenious, droll. Four minds are behind it: the owner, Tom Michelberger, who was in film production; designer Werner Aisslinger, who created the rooms; Anja Knauer, who designed the lobby;

and graphic designer Azar Kasimir. Four associates, four imaginative creators for a completely crazy and wonderful place that respects no rules but, in its anarchy, reminds you a little of the concept of the Lloyd Hotel in Amsterdam. From the immense cloche lampshades à la Kapoor, which are actually made of old book jackets, to the overall graphics, from the black-tiled bar to the luggage strap towel racks in the bathrooms and the breakdown of the rooms into size categories (Cosy, Loft, Band, Luxus and Big One, for from one to eight guests), the general and quite conscious effect is one of a crazy collage, resulting in a whimsical environment, where nothing is taken too seriously. Soap is provided by the litre; the washbasins double as night tables; the bunk beds and bookshelves are packing boxes; the mezzanines are edged with goalpost nets and reached via swimming-pool ladders; the electric wires are not hidden in any way. Before it opened in September 2009, there were hair-raising parties in the courtyard, including one given by *Vice* magazine. These days, things are more peaceful, but because the hotel prides itself on being a forerunner of the media takeover of the district, they are already starting to heat up again. When you book your stay, be sure to ask for the "Clever" room, designed by Aisslinger; it is papered with bad books, so if you get bored you can always read an old spy novel, the 1987 *Guinness Book of Records*, or perhaps the *Karl-Marx Album*. And lest we forget, a fabulous breakfast is served in the independent café, and the entire staff are really exceptionally nice. It's rather like another planet.

NHOW BERLIN

Stralauer Allee 3
U-Bahn Warschauer Straße
Tel 30 290 2990
www.nhow-hotels.com
302 rooms and 1 suite,
€120 to €2,500

OFFBEAT, CONTEMPORARY

The former Osthafen port on the Spree is gradually being redeveloped as new businesses put down roots. After Universal City set up shop here, it's now time for the Nhow, a striking music hotel launched by the Spanish group NH in a huge edifice designed by Sergei Tchoban and consisting of brown-brick buildings topped by a sort of giant sparkling diving board projecting over the river and reflecting the water in a stunning visual effect. The interior is funky in the extreme. From the lobby to the 300-odd rooms and suites, it's *Mars Attacks* all the way! And the invader in question is Karim Rashid, who has let rip with the colours, shapes and volumes, so you get combinations of purple, candy pink, violet, organic and stellar. The result is mind-blowing on all floors. You're almost ready for the defibrillator by the time you've reach the lobby, breathless with design fever. The **ENVY** bar is completely over-the-top, with a circular counter and a huge gilt piston dominating the fluo pink and green room. Upstairs, more than two-thirds of the rooms overlook the River Spree, the monumental sculpture of *Molecule Man* and the Oberbaumbrücke, the Neo-Gothic bridge with its little towers. The junior suites all feature a pivoting central unit containing a TV and desk. Each bathroom is decorated in spring-like pink or lime green mosaic. While pinks dominates in the east tower and blue in the west tower, the main ten-storey building has been decorated in grey. On the eighth floor, there are two well-equipped recording studios and Gibson guitars for hire via room service, which also offers on-demand DJ sets. Finally, the 258-square-metre Nhow Suite offers a fabulous setting and an amazing view. In the basement, there is a spa and fitness centre in orange, purple and white. You can work out like a fiend, but there is no pool, even though there seems to be enough room for one. Finally, the **FABRICS** restaurant has wide, panoramic windows and a more muted white and anise decor. Breakfast is served right next to the bar. Babies are entitled to an egg-shaped high chair designed by Karim, who considers the whole decorative scheme to be "music for the eyes". Beethoven would have needed to be blind. To really get in tune with it, just fill your ears with symphonic disco hits by the Electric Light Orchestra.

"Berlin is all about volatility. Its identity is based not on stability but on change. No other city has repeatedly been so powerful, and fallen so low." **Rory MacLean, City-Lit Berlin, 2009**

MOABIT, WEDDING
*Administrative hub
& social diversity*

ABION VILLA
Kirchstraße 13, Moabit
S-Bahn Bellevue, U-Bahn Turmstraße
Tel 30 3992 0399
www.abion-villa.de
10 rooms and 9 suites, €130 to €395
SMALL RESIDENCE

In the early 19th century, a small porcelain factory stood here. In its place, Carl Bolle founded a dairy empire whose name, Meierei C. Bolle, was as familiar to Berliners as is Nestlé to the Swiss. Throughout the city, little Bolle vans delivered fresh milk and ice cream produced by the company's 2,000 employees. After 1945, though it was located on the banks of the Spree in the Allied zone, the site was abandoned. It was rehabilitated after reunification and a modern edifice was erected to house the Sorat Hotel in 1994. It has now changed hands to become part of the Ameron group, switching name and decor in the process. Renamed the Abion, the hotel has a separate annex, the Abion Villa, which opened in 2008. With its red-brick facade facing the river, it looks vaguely like an industrial fortified castle, and was home for a time to some diplomats at the Swiss embassy. From the hotel, you reach the Villa by way of a little footpath lined with busts of famous figures, including Mies van der Rohe, Thomas Mann and Walther Rathenau. Nine vast, extremely comfortable suites decorated in a nautical mood have been created in this annex, with telescopes, antique boat furnishings and lovely bathrooms featuring Molton Brown products. This surprising little urban outpost, almost literally floating on the Spree, has all the usual hotel services, as well as use of the fitness centre, restaurant and bar in the main building. The Villa enjoys an unrivalled panorama of the beautiful old houses on Holsteiner Ufer, the curving shore between the Lessingbrücke and the Moabiter Brücke, whose landscape evokes a Berlin of yesteryear, with Parisian accents. Another wonderful plus is the elegant *Aida*, moored at the foot of the Abion, a Swedish motor yacht of teak and ebony that was built in the 1930s. From the end of March to the end of October, the vessel offers a splendid opportunity to explore the Spree while sipping a cocktail (€350 per hour). The Abion Villa's trump card, though, is perhaps the fact that it enjoys such a tranquil setting at the water's edge, seemingly far from the hubbub of the city, yet is actually very centrally located, close to Charlottenburg and Mitte.

CHECKING IN WITH BARRIE KOSKY

Barrie Kosky admits that he loves to imagine living in a hotel, "even if the idea of working there has no appeal for me. I sometimes shut myself up for two days in a luxury hotel in Sydney. I did the same thing in London. I didn't speak to anyone, and nobody knew where I was. Two days living on room service, taking long baths, watching lots of DVDs of films, reading, relaxing, sipping vodka martinis, which I love, while enjoying that inevitable sense of melancholy given off by hotel rooms. It would be enjoyable to try it again, but this time with a piano, my books and my dog, especially if I booked a room at the Adlon, right next to the Komische Oper Berlin. That would be slightly decadent, wouldn't it? Otherwise, when I go on holiday in January, I go to Australia or sometimes to Switzerland, where I stay in a family hotel that no one knows about." Evidently, this voracious reader is drawn to the idea of a magic mountain sanatorium.

HOTEL ADLON KEMPINSKI
Unter den Linden 77, Mitte, tel 30 22 610, www.hotel-adlon.de

RESTAURANTS
CULINARY CLASSICS TO BISTRO FARE:
EATING OUT IN THE CITY

In Berlin, and throughout Germany, people mostly eat at restaurants in the evening. Meals involve hearty set menus consisting of between three and ten courses (*Gänge*). Berlin may claim to have 6,500 restaurants, but most of these are cafés, diners, bistros and snack bars. Real restaurants are fewer on the ground and usually open only in the evenings, in some cases from 5pm. The exceptions are hotel restaurants, a handful of restaurants run by star chefs such as Tim Raue, pan-Asian places and large brasseries such as Borchardt and Einstein.

Berlin is an exciting gastronomic melting pot. Established chefs have reinvented themselves, winning awards in the process. Whether specializing in traditional German, exotic fusion or experimental cuisine, Berlin's restaurants have in general opted for local, high-quality produce. Many remain loyal to regional recipes that reinterpret hearty traditional Prussian dishes in a dynamic way. Assimilated by these talented chefs, Berlin classics such as *Königsberger Klopse* (veal dumplings) have been given a new lease of life, as have textbook recipes from Vienna and the Alps, all typical of the comfort food adored by Berliners, who made *Wiener Schnitzel* (pan-fried veal cutlet) their national dish. Wherever you go, service is bilingual, menus less so; delicious bread and butter is served as a matter of course. As for smokers, they are often given a dedicated space. However, the new mania for refusing credit card payments in gourmet restaurants for bills of more than €50 is regrettable. This is the 21st century, after all.

MITTE
City centre & major museums

3 MINUTES SUR MER

Torstraße 167
U-Bahn Rosenthaler Platz
Tel 30 67 30 20 52
www.3minutessurmer.de
Closed for lunch Monday to Friday
SOUTHERN CUISINE

The South of France seems to have moved to the dreary Torstraße: in addition to Bandol sur Mer, we now have 3 Minutes sur Mer, a must-stop for gourmets. It opened in March 2016 with a flamboyant neon sign worthy of a disco in Saint-Tropez and is run by Michael Päsler and David Schoensee. It serves food from breakfast to dinnertime. The menu offers oysters, fish soup with *rouille*, beef tartare, foie gras in brioche, fish of the day and the house speciality, bouillabaisse (for two). It has an authentic brasserie spirit and serves a very decent croque-monsieur, but, alas, it has the same flaw as many Berlin restaurants: credit cards are not accepted.

BORCHARDT

Französische Straße 47
U-Bahn Französische Straße
Tel 30 8188 6262
www.borchardt-restaurant.de
À la carte €50
CLASSIC, FASHIONABLE

Named, we presume, after the Berlin Egyptologist Ludwig Borchardt, who directed the excavations at Amarna, where he discovered the famous bust of Nefertiti in 1912, today on display at the Neues Museum? Not at all. This particular Borchardt, by the name of August, was the official purveyor of foodstuffs to the kaisers and a well-known figure in the late 19th century. Immediately after reunification, the exclusive early 20th-century brasserie and deli was restored, with its great faux leather benches,

Corinthian columns and period mosaics regaining their lustre of before. On summer days, the patio is a delightful open-air dining room, the perfect place to enjoy the best *Wiener Schnitzel* in town, highly popular with politicians, journalists and artists, not to mention members of the Munich *Schickeria*, who have made themselves at home under the wary eye of the waiters, who don't stand for any nonsense. The menu offers fairly standard brasserie fare, with more than a few hints of the South of France. Borchardt's owner Roland Mary manages various other establishments elsewhere in Berlin, such as the Café am Neuen See, and the Grosz brasserie located in Haus Cumberland on the Ku'damm.

COOKIES CREAM

Behrenstraße 55
S-Bahn Brandenburger Tor
U-Bahn Französische Straße
Tel 30 2749 2940, www.cookiescream.com
Fixed-price menu €44
Closed for lunch and all day Sunday
and Monday
CREATIVE VEGETARIAN

If heading for this place – which, despite the name, is nothing like an industrial ice-cream outlet – you might be advised to get hold of a compass, a GPS device, some tranquilizers and a few energy bars, because the route is labyrinthine. Oh, and since it's only open in the evening, a head torch may also come in handy. But let's start with the directions: get a fix on the entrance at the corner of the Westin Grand Hotel's hairdressing salon. There, running alongside the Opera building, a cul-de-sac leads to the theatre's backstage doors, cluttered with crates, vans and hoists for the scenery. First clue: the huge tacky chandelier, bristling with twisted candles and suspended in mid-air from steel girders. Second clue: none. Directed by a compassionate soul, you push on – left – no, right – up a staircase to the right – no, left. Thus, in a state of total confusion and dishevelment,

À LA CARTE

À la carte indicates the average price of a three-course meal, excluding wine.

you at last enter Cookies Cream. And now you reel back: the room's all coarse, whitewashed concrete, a featureless block with only one plate-glass window looking out onto God knows what. Oh, a neon Aeroflot sign! Then, in the flickering light of white candles, your eyes accustom themselves to one of the most awesome surprises Berlin has to offer, a brilliant veggie UFO in a cosmos of uniform predictability. Since 2007, Stephan Hentschel has been slapping white tablecloths on a jumble of tables, all placed within earshot of neighbouring diners – a motley crew of good-natured folk, from radical hard rockers and vegetarians in Trippen pumps to dedicated fashionistas, from hardcore nighthawks to white-collar wimps. In other words, an absolutely delightful mix of good old *Homo sapiens*. Settling down on your bench seat or 1970s stool, you begin to get your composure back, aided and abetted by the discreet welcome and service. As open-plan as a station concourse, the kitchen produces bread, main meals and desserts that are all tasty, creative and hearty. Selections include quail's egg in brioche with shallots, potato foam and truffle jus; sheep's milk yoghurt with hibiscus, radish and Roquefort; Parmesan *Knödel* (dumplings) with artichokes; and cauliflower and rocket polenta with Swiss cheese and sesame. As for dessert, why not try the jackfruit salad and coconut dacquoise, among others. Any lingering sadness at the passing of Cookies, the long-running club that used to be located on the ground floor, is quickly dispelled by the addition of **CRACKERS** (Friedrichstraße 158, Mitte, tel 680 730 488), whose menu may not be entirely vegetarian but is equally creative.

EINSUNTERNULL

Hannoversche Straße 1
U-Bahn Oranienburger Tor
Tel 30 2757 7810
www.einsunternull.com
Fixed-price menus €29 to €117
Closed all day Sunday and Monday lunch
MINIMALIST, CREATIVE

"Eins unter Null" means one floor down. In this case, such modesty is belied by some unique talent, which has already been on the receiving end of many awards. Ivo Ebert, recently arrived from Reinstoff, and chef Andreas Rieger, previously at Horvath, took the plunge in 2015 and their brilliant cooking has kept them afloat ever since. Located in Mitte, in a street still untouched by the hordes of backpackers, their restaurant exudes calm hipness, with its beautiful contemporary decor of unvarnished wood, which is laid out over two levels – one devoted to lunch service, the other to dinner. Large glass preserving jars filled with vegetables grown in Dahlem's kitchen gardens provide amusing visual appetisers. Taking an almost mystical approach that regards nature as the source of surprising and outstanding food, the pair don't go in for showy names for their creations. At both lunch and dinner, their menus are understated and intriguing. German coffee. Black salsify. Braised onion. Kale. Mushroom bread. Desserts are summed up in one word: sweets. In other words, just let yourself go, be surprised, seduced and spoiled. Both the presentation and flavours are heightened and exquisite, with unique creative combinations. An outstanding experience.

LORENZ ADLON ESSZIMMER

Hotel Adlon Kempinski, 1st floor,
Unter den Linden 77
S-Bahn Brandenburger Tor
Tel 30 2261 1960
www.lorenzadlon-esszimmer.de
Fixed-price menus €145 to €205,
à la carte €140
Closed for lunch and all day Sunday
to Tuesday

CREATIVE CUISINE

The Hotel Adlon is home to numerous bars and restaurants, including the Quarré and the Sra Bua, a luxurious pan-Asian place masterminded by Tim Raue. With its high ceilings, the Lorenz Adlon's dining room is located on the first floor, boasting seven tables plus a beautiful panelled library, which can be booked for private parties. It's all – or almost all – exactly as it was at the start of the 20th century when this luxury hotel served what was considered the epitome of gastronomy in Berlin, and the great Escoffier himself even directed operations from time to time. With its wood panelling, fireplaces, haughty bust of Kaiser Bill, champagne-coloured table linen, silverware, KPM (Königliche Porzellan-Manufaktur) china and view of the Brandenburg Gate, the setting is exclusive, theatrical and sumptuous. Since spring 2010, the Esszimmer has been run by chef Hendrik Otto, who has worked at some of the greatest grand hotels in Hamburg, Cologne and Berlin. Overseen by Boris Häbel, the splendid dining room, a combination of tradition and modernity that manages to feel both exclusive and vibrant, is but a prelude to the short menu whose concise entries – goose liver, bouillabaisse, sturgeon caviar, pigeon – give little hint of the chef's fabled mastery. Presented like works of art, his dishes enrapture diners. It may say "goose liver", but it's undeniably foie gras with coffee, truffles, polenta, thyme and brioche. The bouillabaisse is deconstructed and disconcerting – but just right. The pigeon takes flight with juniper, vegetables and garden herbs. For dessert, the chocolate cream is a crunchy breath of fresh air, gliding between dill ice cream, yoghurt with carrot and apple jus. Dazzling. Reservations well in advance are a must.

PARIS-MOSKAU

Alt-Moabit 141
S-Bahn Hauptbahnhof
Tel 30 394 2081, www.paris-moskau.de
Fixed-price menus €66 and €83,
à la carte €65
Closed for lunch Saturday and Sunday

GASTRONOMIC BISTRO

Formerly a railway snack bar, this authentic remnant of a bygone Berlin, situated atop a bridge, has been operating for over a century. For a long time a catering business, it was bought in 1984 by Wolfram Ritschl, who initially called the place Josef, before changing his mind four years later and opting for the more evocative Paris Moskau. It was also more appropriate, since the building is located on the very line that linked the two capital cities via Berlin. Adored by locals, the establishment is valued as much for its anachronistic historical character and its continued existence, which always seems to be hanging by a thread, as for its no-nonsense, mouth-watering food, served in a timeless atmosphere after a glass of Alfred Gratien champagne beneath the opalescent ceiling globes. The steak tartare with char caviar, anchovies and beetroot is delicious, while the monkfish with fennel and saffron, enlivened with a fennel and celery salad, is well nigh perfect.

PAULY SAAL

Auguststraße 11–13
S-Bahn Oranienburger Straße
Tel 30 3300 6070, www.paulysaal.com
Fixed-price menu €76, à la carte €55
Closed Sunday and Monday

BERLIN CUISINE

Before the war, this austere, brown-brick, Rationalist-style building was home to a Jewish girls' school, which closed down decades ago. Redeveloped at the instigation of gallery owner Michael Fuchs, who installed exhibition spaces on the upper levels, the entire ground-floor complex comprises the delicatessen Mogg and Pauly Saal, a bar-restaurant opened by Stephan Landwehr and Boris Radczun, who also own the Grill Royal. Occupying the former school gymnasium with its impressively high ceiling, the restaurant is a design success. The walls are covered with champagne-coloured moire, huge amber Murano-glass lights twinkle overhead, the deep banquettes are upholstered in blue velvet, while stuffed foxes adorn the walls, their paws stuck in the plasterwork. Then there's the red-and-white rocket, which seems to be blasting through the back wall – in rather dubious taste given the building's history. With its perfect acoustics, comfortable ambience, starched white tablecloths, monogrammed tableware and speedy, friendly service, the Pauly produces modern interpretations of Prussian food, featuring homely Berlin dishes made with humble but good-quality ingredients. It's all been deliciously managed since 2015 by chef Arne Anker, who gained a Michelin star for the restaurant, and you'll clearly see why when you taste the entrecôte with risotto mushrooms and black pudding. In short, it's a treat. In the outer room, the chic **PAULY SAAL BAR** with its well-chosen background music offers a smoked-glass setting of tobacco-coloured cushioned leather and billiard-green walls.

REINSTOFF

Edison Höfe, Schlegelstraße 26c
S-Bahn Nordbahnhof
U-Bahn Naturkundemuseum
Tel 30 3088 1214, www.reinstoff.eu
Fixed-price menus €110 to €198
Closed for lunch and on Sunday and Monday
FUSION, FASHIONABLE

It was on this site that Thomas Edison and Emil Rathenau, the future founder of the mighty AEG, joined forces to create Deutsche Edison, the world's first factory for incandescent light bulbs. Completed in 1903, the Edison building was the operation's headquarters and production plant. Long abandoned, the site has now been refurbished. It is located within striking distance of several galleries and serves up pretty much the best fusion cuisine in Berlin today. The decor, designed by Christina Krüger of Bolwin Wulf architects, preserves some of the industrial heritage, with steel and exposed brick, combined with elegant contemporary touches. The lighting is a tribute to Edison's invention: the halos that fall onto the white tablecloths are pleasantly soft, and the guests, whether seated on black Eames chairs or nestling in alcoves, remain bathed in a flattering half-shadow. Meanwhile, in the kitchen chef Daniel Achilles produces dazzling food. From the starters to the main courses, from the nibbles to the desserts, everything is exciting and exquisitely prepared, with no trace of tricksy, fashionable "molecular" cuisine. The ingredients alone are enough, with Achilles fine-tuning the rest. There are two set menus: the *Ganznah* (quite near), which uses zero-food-miles ingredients; and the *Weiterdraussen* (faraway), which is more adventurous. The "quite near" selection features summer borscht with frozen sour cream and local vegetables or saddle of venison from Fürstenberg with red pepper and radish pods; while the "faraway" menu offers root plant curry with baby carrots and coconut or suckling goat's shoulder with salami, artichokes, poppy flower and broccoli. Both menus share one course as a palate-cleanser: the "long drink" of green juniper sorbet, Iris dry gin and tonic water. It's a triumph. To tantalize the taste buds even more, ask the excellent sommelier to recommend some of their German or Spanish wines. The whole venture is a thrilling combination of chic post-industrial setting, heaps of talent, attractive clientele and amazing cooking.

VOLTA

Im Pavillon, Brunnenstraße 73

U-Bahn Voltastraße

Tel 0176 77 55 64 22

www.dasvolta.com

À la carte €25

Closed Sunday and Monday

OFFBEAT GASTRO PUB

Are we still in Mitte, or over the border in Wedding? This gastro pub, taken over by Stephan Henschel, the chef at Cookies Cream, is located on the ground floor of a very unprepossessing block of flats. Is it possible to talk about gastronomy when the menu features just fourteen dishes, dessert included? Hard to say. Typical of the times, Volta's reservations system operates by text message, or WhatsApp, in other words, front-of-house is non-existent. The music is club-style, the other customers are hunched in front of their beers or lemonades and the food is served with barely more enthusiasm than in a fast-food joint. And yet the Volta Burger is juicy and delicious; the Wan-tan Pizza featuring black pudding, feta, red onions and fennel is finger-licking wonderful, while the Manchester Nuggets make you fall in love with chicken and mustard mayonnaise all over again. More Berlin than Berlin, Volta is an oddity that's worth a go, particularly as the prices are extremely reasonable. So which is it: Mitte or Wedding?

WEINBAR RUTZ

Chausseestraße 8

U-Bahn Oranienburger Tor

Tel 30 2462 8760

www.rutz-restaurant.de

Fixed-price menus €129 to €169,

à la carte €100

Closed for lunch and on Sunday and Monday

GASTRONOMIC WINE BAR

When it opened in 2001, this wine-bar-cum-restaurant was an instant success – and one that has lasted. After more than fifteen years, Rutz is today in the capable hands of chef Marco Müller, who left but came back, laden with awards. The interior

by Corrado Signoretti remains unchanged. The same can be said of the cooking, which has stayed ambitious and sophisticated. It is served on the first floor and comes in tasting menus of between six and ten courses, featuring duck, wagyu beef, king crab, king prawns cooked with herbs, spices, root and other vegetables. There are unexpected, Japanese-style experiences such as the exciting and surprising langoustines served with pigs' ears. It's a top-flight performance that has been deservedly recognized by international gourmets and critics. Another option is the ground-floor wine bar menu, which exploits the repertoire of German home cooking, resulting in Neukölln pork sausage, an excellent beef tartare, pork hock and roasted black pudding with mashed potatoes. The venue more than lives up to its reputation as a modern classic.

ALSO IN THIS NEIGHBOURHOOD

GRILL ROYAL

Friedrichstraße 105b

S-Bahn and U-Bahn Friedrichstraße

Tel 30 2887 9288, www.grillroyal.com

À la carte €90

Closed for lunch

BISTRO

Loved or loathed since it was opened in 2007 by Boris Radczun (of Pauly Saal), Stefan Landwehr and gallery owner Thilo Wermke, this home of Berlin bling looks like a Cannes casino and remains a classic venue for fashionable VIP frolics. Specialities include wagyu beef steaks, *la plancha* se a bass, grilled lobster and a gold-plated clientele. Located alongside the Riverside Hotel, in the shadow of a hideous tower block left behind in East Germany's death throes, the Royal enjoys views over the River Spree. In its offshoot in west Berlin, **LE PETIT ROYAL** (Grolmannstraße 56, Charlottenburg, tel 30 060 750), the kitchen is in the hands of the chef Sauli Kamppainen, who used to work in the Quadriga, the former restaurant in the Brandenburger Hof.

KATZ ORANGE

Bergstraße 22, at the end of the courtyard
U-Bahn Rosenthaler Platz
Tel 30 983 208 430
www.katzorange.com
À la carte €50
Closed for lunch

ORGANIC, WORLD

Occupying the same space as the old Maxwell restaurant in a wonderfully refurbished former brasserie, Katz Orange occupies two floors boasting a varied, exotic decor. Every evening sees freshly prepared dishes, including salads, gazpacho and fish, as well as a slow cuisine menu proposing meats roasted for twelve hours at low temperatures, known as "Candy on Bone". Added features are a cocktail bar, a terrace and a fun, casual atmosphere.

MANI

Hotel Amano, Torstraße 136
U-Bahn Rosenthaler Platz
Tel 30 530 280 8255
www.amanogroup.de
Fixed-price menus €12 and €15,
à la carte €40
Closed for lunch Saturday
and all day Sunday

MODERN ISRAELI CUISINE

The Argentinean chef Octavio Oses Bravo has travelled extensively, notably in Israel, from which he has brought back dozens of recipes containing cauliflower, a much-unloved vegetable in Europe. Hired to increase the appeal of the Amano hotel group, he has made a brilliant start, applying his creativity to both vegan and conventional recipes, such as aubergine with thyme and goat cheese; Roquefort, rhubarb and celery tart; lamb meatballs with tomato coulis and green beans; *shakshuka* with fried egg, tomatoes and chilli peppers; and sweet-potato, orange and cardamom granola. He is even capable of provocation with his *Kleine Schweinereien,* pancetta with crunchy vegetables and edible roots, and foie gras burger with truffles. The restaurant has a courtyard that is very popular as soon as the weather gets warm enough for lunch or dinner outside. Nice selection of gin at the bar.

"Almost every part of Berlin offers a pleasing picture. Its streets are a model of cleanliness."
Karl Baedeker, *Guide to Berlin,* 1912

TIERGARTEN
Peaceful parkland
& new architecture

5 – CINCO BY PACO PÉREZ

Das Stue Hotel, Drakestraße 1
Tel 30 311 7220, www.5-cinco.com
Fixed-price menu €165,
à la carte €120
Closed for lunch and all day Sunday and
Monday (closed 30 July to 30 August)
GASTRONOMIC, FUSION

Formerly the Danish embassy, Das Stue
Hotel on the edge of the zoological gardens
has managed to shake off its Nordic past
(with the exception of its name) and head
towards a Spanish future. Everyone and
everything is Spanish, from the investors
who are part of the hotel management, via
Patricia Urquiola the designer who created
the interiors, to the gourmet restaurant
5 – Cinco and its little brother, **CASUAL**,
run by award-winning Catalan chef Paco
Pérez. The name Cinco – the number
five – refers to the five senses, all of which
are set tingling here. The emphasis is
on visual as well as flavoursome effects,
in a contemporary decor that is more sober
and restrained than that of the hotel lobby.
A master of avant-garde haute cuisine,
Pérez seems in his element. Testing the
boundaries of his own culinary experience,
he performs alchemy in a menu of
twenty-six molecular concoctions where
bubbles and spheres (echoing the galaxy of
copper spheres that light the dining room's
ceiling) catapult around your palate like
dodgems. As for the daily breakfast at The
Casual, also part of Pérez's fiefdom, here
you'll find a totally different decor and
space where you can experience the chef's
talent for luxury snacks, reinvented with
cheeky élan: croquettes of *jamón ibérico*;
nachos with tuna and avocado; Caesar
salad; *spaghetti all'arrabbiata* with lobster;
and *crema catalana*. On Saturdays,
well-informed Berliners head over here
at around 1:30pm for the sole pleasure

LIQUID ASSETS

When water is ordered to accompany
your meal, you will usually be asked
"Mit Sprudel oder ohne Sprudel?"
(With or without bubbles?). The
best still mineral water is Vöslauer,
while the most common *mit Sprudel*
is Gerolsteiner. Both of these are
widely drunk in restaurants at
lunchtime. In snack bars, *Imbisse*
and cafés, Berliners tend to down
fizzy drinks and tea. Many people
eat a light lunch with a *Milchkaffee*
(coffee with milk) or a cappuccino.
In more formal restaurants,
lunchtime is a mineral-water-only
exercise. In the evening, though,
Berliners are happier to enjoy a glass
of wine. Indeed, gourmet menus
of four to twelve dishes, desserts
included, tend to come with
a sommelier's recommendation of
a sparkling, white or red, and sweet
wine or liqueur, all selected to match
the food. If you don't like mixing
your drinks, it is perfectly acceptable
to limit yourself to two or three
specific wines. But you'll have to get
the whole table to agree first! If you
eat à la carte, it's usual to drink
wine by the glass, especially as many
Berliners have become real wine
experts with discerning palates.
But during the week, for an informal
dinner in a brasserie or an exotic
restaurant, order a very bitter
draught beer – a classic that never
disappoints and allows Berliners to
show off their heritage, as Berlin has
many neo-breweries that produce
excellent, refreshing local beers:

IMPERIAL STOUT (SCHOPPEBRAÜ)
Berliner Weisse (Berliner Berg),
India Pale Ale (Bierfrabrik) and
Holzfassgereiftes (Lemke)

of tucking into a Das Stue club sandwich, which is a thing of wonder.

KIN DEE

Lützowstraße 81
U-Bahn Kurfürstenstraße
Tel 30 2155294, www.kindeeberlin.com
Fixed-price menu €45, à la carte €55
Closed for lunch and on Sunday and Monday

THAI TRENDY

An exotic satellite of the Royal Grill galaxy, this new gourmet Thai restaurant located near Potsdamer Straße is run by Thai chef Dalad Kambhu, an ex-model from Bangkok who was trained in the kitchen of the restaurant Dóttir. He is aided by the restaurateur Moritz Estermann, formerly of Pauly Saal. Open only in the evening, it has a refined decor and avoids the pitfalls of exoticism, concentrating on generous, authentic recipes. Aside from the traditional – and expected – green papaya salad, the charming Dalad's repertoire includes sea scallops marinated in an emulsion of lemongrass and coriander, accompanied by a salad of apples and peanuts; and octopus with chilli accompanied by a refreshing cucumber salad. Superior flavours can be found in the young cockerel legs in massamam curry and fish fried with spices and chilli.

MAULTASCHEN MANUFAKTUR

Lützowstraße 22
U-Bahn Kurfürstenstraße
Tel 30 6807 0943
www.maultaschen-manufaktur.de
À la carte €20
Closed Sunday

RAVIOLIS

Maultaschen, literally "bags with mouths", are big – really big – ravioli. This Swabian speciality is a favourite of the entire country. In Berlin, the best are handmade by Ulrich Morof, a Swabian who for more than fifteen years has been running his "factory" with all the seriousness of a regional ambassador. Prepared in homes and restaurants with myriad recipes and sauces, the *Maultaschen* are sold individually here to take away or eat on the spot, accompanied by a potato salad, the regional tradition. There is no decor here, but some of the photos on the walls are worthy of one of the neighbouring galleries.

NENI BERLIN

25Hours Hotel Bikini Berlin,
10th floor, Budapester Straße 40
S-Bahn and U-Bahn Zoologischer Garten
Tel 30 120 221 200
www.25hours-hotels.com
À la carte €30

MIDDLE EASTERN, HIP

In Berlin, it seems every day brings a new and different hotel. And the same goes for hotel restaurants. Quartered on the top floor of 25Hours alongside the new Bikini Berlin shopping centre, Neni is without doubt the most exciting and cosmopolitan establishment of its kind. Occupying the tenth floor along with the Monkey Bar, and sharing their toilets (don't miss the amazing views over the zoo from the gents), Neni boasts several imaginative gimmicks dreamed up by designer Werner Aisslinger, of which one of the simplest and most successful are the tables, whose wooden tops are fixed to bases made from old cast-iron drain covers. Flooded with daylight throughout the day, the restaurant welcomes an astonishing clientele, certainly the most varied in Berlin. Indeed, it's not unusual to see pensioners, artists, inquisitive tourists, locals, the young and the not-so-young mingling happily. This Neni-style inclusiveness, already tried and tested in Vienna and Zürich, is all down to the Molcho family, mother and son, whose Israeli, Romanian and Spanish roots have given them a taste for good, honest cooking. Try the Middle Eastern-style salmon, the Jerusalem plate, the *Tel Aviv sabich* (sandwich) with poached egg and chopped vegetables or the various kinds of hummus: it's all delicious, reasonably priced, exotic and surprising. Don't be deceived by the apparent informality here, you should book for Neni. You can't just turn up and expect to get in straightaway, as the queue on the ground floor testifies. Of course, the best seats are by the windows with a panoramic view, although those on the central podium or near the experimental kitchen garden aren't bad either. Yes, it's packed, but while you're waiting for a table in the evening you can always grab a drink at the lively Monkey Bar.

PANAMA

Potsdamer Straße 91
U-Bahn Kurfürstenstraße
Tel 30 983 208 435
www.oh-panama.com
À la carte €35
Closed for lunch and all day Sunday
and Monday

CREATIVE FUSION

Opened in 2016 and located at the back of a paved courtyard surrounded by yellow brick walls where several fashion showrooms are located, including that of Maisonnoée, Panama is linked to the Contemporary Food Lab, a food skills project started by Ludwig Cramer-Klett, who runs the restaurant Katz Orange. His focus is clear: humanism, nature, food and nutrition. The chef is a woman, Sophia Rudolph, formerly of Rutz, the crucible of a new generation of culinary talents who can now be found here and there around town. Among other dishes, Panama's menu includes a tempting venison tartare with red currants and shitake mushrooms; interesting shrimp with blueberries and vanilla; and a nice pikeperch with carrots, black beans and coriander. Enjoy this healthy meal in a postcolonial decor of blond wood, bare wooden tables, Thonet chairs in an immaculate basement enlivened by a few Pop touches like a neon sign on the wall and a potted cactus by the entrance. Just opposite, in a brick pavilion, the **TIGER BAR** offers before- or after-dinner drinks and has a terrace, open Tuesday to Saturday from 8pm.

VOX RESTAURANT

Grand Hyatt Berlin, Marlene-Dietrich-Platz 2
S-Bahn and U-Bahn Potsdamer Platz
Tel 30 2553 1772
www.vox-restaurant.de
Fixed-price menu €62, à la carte €65
Closed for lunch

GASTRONOMIC

Hannes Wettstein's original decor for the Grand Hyatt's gourmet restaurant has been subtly updated by New York interior designer Tony Chi. The place remains a great favourite with Berliners, who flock here for the breakfast buffet, one of the most lavish in town. In the evenings, Vox lowers its voice to an elegant murmur better suited to the intimacy of its booths, which are available if you prefer not to be "on show" to the boisterous Theater am Potsdamer Platz opposite. In the kitchen, on display to satisfy everyone's curiosity, chef Benjamin Haselbeck draws inspiration for his menu from southern Europe, with Japanese influences. Delicacies include rock octopus with miso and wild garlic; Iberico Presa with sauerkraut, apple and mustard, and back of venison with nori, chestnut and fig. The selection of largely French cheeses is almost a main course in itself, or as an alternative, the sushi menu created by the Japanese chef offers a welcome change for regulars. Vox has already established itself as a classic with its charming welcome, attentive service, flattering evening lighting, beautifully laid tables and atmosphere exuding international chic. Nearby, the **VOX BAR**, with its separate smoking lounge, provides similar charms with the bonus of music and cigarettes.

CHARLOTTENBURG
Smart residential & chic shopping

893 RYŌTEI
Kantstraße 135, Charlottenburg
S-Bahn Savignyplatz
Tel 30 9170 3121, www.893ryotei.de
À la carte €25
Closed Sunday and Monday
FASHIONABLE JAPANESE
No sooner had it opened than it closed
again – and then reopened, not without
some gnashing of teeth on the part of those
who had been lucky enough to eat here first
time around. The puppet-master of this
very West Berlin-style mini-Japanese gastro
restaurant is Duc Ngo, the same man who
created Kuchi, Madame Ngo and The Duc
Ngo, and who was in great demand at
the Provocateur Hotel. In short, he's a local
character. A million miles from the usual
Asian food, the cuisine at 893 is a cut above
the hackneyed dishes to be found elsewhere,
even though the names keep a low profile:
salmon marinated with sake and ponzu
sauce, filet mignon teriyaki and Japanese
mushrooms, *ika* (squid) tempura, and more.
When the food arrives and hits your taste
buds, by contrast, it's a whole other story.
Don't miss Daniel's Tartare, composed of
tenderloin, ginger, chilli, soy, crème fraîche
and char caviar. As for the sashimi and
ceviche, a sushi bar prepares and marinates
this cuisine with talent and expertise.
The restaurant is always packed, so expect
to make a reservation – for next month.

ALT LUXEMBURG
Windscheidstraße 31
U-Bahn Sophie-Charlotte-Platz
Tel 30 323 8730, www.altluxemburg.de
Fixed-price menus €52 to €79,
à la carte €60
Closed for lunch and on Sunday
FINE DINING
West Berlin, 1982. Hailing from the
Saarland, having worked in Switzerland

and France, chef Karl Wannemacher
and his wife Ingrid opened a successful
restaurant in the heart of Charlottenburg
serving French-influenced cuisine. More
than three decades later, the Wannemachers
are still here, smiling, friendly and
delighted to have created and established
a classic establishment, considered
one of the best restaurants in the city.
The elegant dining room is hung with oil
paintings and exudes serenity and comfort.
In the kitchen, the emphasis is more on
understated subtlety than culinary fireworks.
Several years ago, the tomato millefeuille
with lobster and the monkfish in saffron
sauce were the signature dishes. The
lobster cream soup, the soused herring
à sa façon, with apples, cucumber and
onions, and the breast of Barbary duck
with cherries, baby leeks and potato cake
demonstrate the expertise and care of
a chef who has lost none of his passion.
There's always a vegetarian option on the
menu, such as tabbouleh-stuffed peppers
with kohlrabi or courgette rolls filled
with small Mediterranean vegetables.
In summer, the selection of desserts is
deliberately weighted towards sorbets and
ice creams; while in winter they become
a touch richer, creamier and more
comforting, but always delicate. A classic
indeed, and one of the best.

DIENER TATTERSALL
Grolmanstraße 47
S-Bahn Savignyplatz, U-Bahn Uhlandstraße
Tel 30 881 5329, www.diener-berlin.de
À la carte €20
Closed for lunch
AUTHENTIC BERLIN
The walls? Brown. The floor? Brown. The
ceiling? Brown, with wood-grain Venilia
vinyl thrown in for free. The tables? Brown
wood, half of them with red-and-white
check tablecloths. The hunting scenes
on the walls? Brown daubs. The handsome
1930s overhead lamps? Dim. Result: the
countless black-and-white photos testifying
to the glorious past of the former owner

almost look like patches of colour. In his time, Franz Diener was a Lord of the Ring, a rival of the charismatic giant and world heavyweight champion Max Schmeling, and a passionate anti-Nazi. Here his fights, his friends, the stars who made this place their home are all brought together in a kind of wall album you work your way through once you've ordered. The menu is shot through with local slang, but the translation helps. So why not try *Hackepeter* (cold minced pork, raw egg, capers and anchovies) or the hearty *Königsberger Klopse*, the melt-in-the-mouth balls of minced veal that are a national dish here. A veritable Berlin institution, Diener Tattersall is a natural refuge for the locals from the worlds of theatre, literature and film. And after you've left, under the arches of the elevated railway on your right, you can relive Liza Minnelli's scream of liberation in *Cabaret*. It might not have been shot there, but it certainly looks as though it could have been.

LAMAZÈRE

Stuttgarter Platz 18
S-Bahn Charlottenburg
U-Bahn Wilmersdorfer Straße
Tel 30 3180 0712, www.lamazere.de
Fixed-price menus €38, à la carte €42
Closed for lunch and on Monday
FRENCH BRASSERIE

Régis Lamazère was to be found a few years ago working as maître d' at Hartmanns restaurant in Kreuzberg, which is now closed. So it's a surprise to find him in his own establishment, where since summer 2013 he's been running an authentic little brasserie of the kind that has become hard to find in Paris. Berliners love the place, some almost taking up permanent residence, encouraged by the modestly priced menu and the mastery of French cuisine displayed by chef de cuisine Liam Faggotter. Highlights include baked eggs with foie gras and duck confit with ratatouille. Designed by architect Torsten Elgt, the Montmartre-style interior of this restaurant joins in the French spirit, washed down with a fine glass of Morgon. The blackboard menu is a feast for the eyes and the stomach follows on rapidly behind. The rustic terrine is studded with pistachios, while the oxtail and mushroom *pithiviers* (savoury pies) are a minor miracle served in black cast-iron pots, and the blanquette of sea bass plays a wonderful variation on an old tune. The cheeses, supplied by Berlin company Maître Philippe & Filles and served with good Parisian bread, are a meal in themselves. For dessert, the strawberry millefeuille's pastry cream is flavoured with whisky. Lamazère is only open in the evenings, but its bar operates until 2am, although another option is available next door in the form of an after-dinner drink at the atmospheric and friendly Galander.

MARJELLCHEN

Mommsenstraße 9
S-Bahn Savignyplatz
Tel 30 883 2676
www.marjellchen-berlin.de
À la carte €40
Closed for lunch
TRADITIONAL PRUSSIAN

First, a bit of background. In the dialect of eastern Prussia (which stretched well beyond the city then known as Danzig, today Gdańsk), *Marjellchen* means a young girl. Although it no longer exists, of course, Prussia survives subliminally in terms of both language and tradition – and also through its cuisine. In Berlin, Marjellchen is an example of a dyed-in-the-wool Prussian institution. Despite her name, and having been born in Rome, owner Ramona Azzaro is one as well. Her distinctive, home-style cooking, using recipes inherited from her Prussian grandmother, is not recommended for anyone on a diet. Her hearty fare is served from 5pm in an intimate, cheerful, snug-as-a-bug setting, perfect for winter dining. The menu features herrings in cream sauce, smoked eel, potato soup

THE CITY SPECIAL
KÖNIGSBERG MEATBALLS

Traditional Berlin cuisine is varied, hearty and plentiful, and these days it is going through something of a revival. Home cooking, for example, is now being rediscovered and re-evaluated. Although the ubiquitous *Wiener Schnitzel* tends to head the list of Berliners' favourite restaurant dishes, it is in fact Austrian. Brandenburg provides its share of recipes that are thought to be rooted in the city's culinary culture, including *Eisbein mit Sauerkraut*, or pork knuckle in pickled cabbage, Havel pikeperch, Kaiser Wilhelm potato soup, *Rouladen* (minced meat rolls), *Leber mit Apfelringen* (Berlin-style veal liver with apples and onions) and the *Berliner omelett*, also called *Hoppel Poppel* (potatoes, onions, minced pork cutlet and three eggs per person). But there is one dish that wins all the votes and which young chefs strive to refine without betraying its uniqueness: *Königsberger Klopse*, or Königsberg meatballs (*Klopse* means "meatballs" in the dialect of East Prussia, of which Königsberg was the capital). Mixing together the surf 'n' turf ingredients from this Baltic province dates back to the 18th century. Some say it was invented by the king's chef, while others claim the chef worked for a rich noble. Whatever the truth, it was not until this dish was exported to Berlin that it came of age. Starting with stale bread soaked in hot water and then mixed with onions, ground meat – preferably veal – anchovies, eggs and spices, the KKs are boiled for twenty minutes in a seasoned broth and served topped with a thick lemon caper sauce, accompanied by steamed potatoes or rice. You can also add a big spoonful of candied beetroot. The anchovies (*Sardellen* in German) can be replaced by herring, which changes the dish's name to *Rostocker Klopse*. Or you can mix them both together, making *Soßklopse*. For the record, as Königsberg became Soviet after 1946 and was renamed Kaliningrad, East Berliners referred to KKs as *Koch Klopse*, or cooked meatballs. However that may be, *Königsberger Klopse* is a delectable dish that even in its most basic version is one of the ultimate comfort dishes. In Berlin, you can savour the best traditional KKs at **MARJELLCHEN** (www.marjellchen-berlin.de), the **DIENER TATTERSALL** (www.diener-berlin.de) and the **PRATER GARTEN** (www.facebook.com/pratergarten).

with shrimps and bacon, and venison and wild boar stew. The boiled beef with plums, for example, is a typically Mecklenburger recipe; and of course there's the indispensable *Königsberger Klopse* (veal dumplings) with capers and beetroot. At this rate, a dessert of apple fritters and Silesian poppy-seed dumplings is not going to make much difference. In short, it's all delicious, substantial, comforting and, for some people, almost a study in ethnology. The staff are conversant with several languages, as is the menu – which is just as well.

OTTENTHAL

Kantstraße 153
S-Bahn Savignyplatz
S-Bahn and U-Bahn Zoologischer Garten
Tel 30 313 3162, www.ottenthal.com
À la carte €40
Closed for lunch
AUSTRIAN

Situated a stone's throw from several cinemas, theatres and opera houses, Ottenthal benefits from the regular custom of a mixed clientele who dine with friends, either before or after performances, on the restaurant's impressive organic *Wiener Schnitzel* and Austrian wines. Located next door to the Paris Bar, Ottenthal is set in a kind of classically elegant white tunnel with a frieze around the top of the walls decorated, according to season or whim, with a herd of gilded Bambis or plaster busts of Mozart. The young, efficient waiting staff are always on hand with a smile. The traditional Viennese dishes are intelligently executed, and a menu of lighter options adds a creative touch, with marinated meat, game terrines, pasta and fish dishes delicately cooked and complemented with spices, herbs and top-quality vegetables. **Other location:** Knesebeckstraße 26, Charlottenburg, tel 30 8892 9226

PARIS BAR

Kantstraße 152
S-Bahn Savignyplatz,
S-Bahn and U-Bahn Zoologischer Garten
Tel 30 313 8052, www.parisbar.de
À la carte €50
TRADITIONAL

A book retraces the high points of this institution, which has been a magnet for Berlin's intelligentsia since the 1960s. This is a Paris brasserie-style venue, with a French-language menu (*boudin aux pommes, bœuf bourguignon*, homemade bouillabaisse and *tarte Tatin*) and prices to match. It continues to attract the *Film und Funk* – media folk, who sit on the left – and the *junge Wilde und alte Böcke* ("wild young things and old goats"), over to the right, with the *Arrivierten* ("newcomers" or "arrivistes") safely stowed at the back. All keeping a weather eye out for each other in a noisy, cheerful atmosphere presided over by owner Michel, beneath a decomposing mustard-yellow ceiling. The walls are decked with a host of horrors, including one or two gems, notably a wonderful chalk drawing on black paper. Unsigned it may be, but it's a Baselitz.

RESTAURANT AM STEINPLATZ

Hotel am Steinplatz, Steinplatz,
Charlottenburg
U-Bahn Ernst-Reuter-Platz
S-Bahn Savignyplatz
Tel 30 55 4444 7053
www.hotelsteinplatz.com
Fixed-price menus €59 to €69,
à la carte €50
Closed for lunch on Saturday and Sunday
CREATIVE GERMAN CUISINE

Restaurant am Steinplatz is part of a five-star hotel opened by the American Marriott group as part of its Autograph collection and, like the rest of the hotel, its interiors have been designed by Tassilo Bost. When chef Stefan Hartmann left for Vancouver to run the Bauhaus Restaurant, Marcus Zimmer, who became famous for having fed the film crews on George Clooney's *Monuments Men* (which was shot partly in Berlin), took over. Zimmer too went elsewhere, and insiders whispered that he might have gone to take over the kitchen at the five-star Hotel Palace, whose standards had fallen. Then Nicholas Hahn arrived, answering the call to pep up an elegant restaurant whose muffled mustard-beige decor is now promised a facelift to match Hahn's demanding and sophisticated cooking and presentation. Hahn is taking German cuisine to an astonishingly high level whose tone is set from the appetizers onwards. A chef who can transform the humble beetroot with such gastronomic and visual vitality surely deserves the highest praise. And the rest is a joy to behold – colourful and artistic food that excites the palate and thrills the taste buds. The only challenge comes when reading the menu, which offers, at most, the merest hint of the ingredients or list of courses: smoked eel/mustard seeds/red cabbage; zucchini/spinach/béarnaise; cod/leek/pear of the earth root (*yacon*); chocolate / wild rose / goat's milk. What Hahn makes of all this is pure genius. And the desserts look like miniature Frank Gehry buildings.

ALSO IN THIS NEIGHBOURHOOD

THE BUTCHER

Sir Savigny Hotel, Kantstraße 144
U-Bahn Savignyplatz
Tel 30 323 015 673, www.the-butcher.com
Closed Monday
JUICY BURGERS

The tone is set by a huge stuffed bull suspended from a hoof on the facade and in the window. The Butcher makes no concessions. Located in the Sir Savigny Hotel, the restaurant's concept is that of all Sir Hotels, in Amsterdam and elsewhere, and now Berlin. Based on Aberdeen Angus, the menu includes every possible preparation, right down to the room-service burger. Originating from the clinical butcher-shop restaurant space, service is provided throughout the hotel, in the lounges, around the big table in the lobby, around the central fireplace and on the courtyard terrace. This welcoming flexibility allows you to relax in the hotel's informal atmosphere while having a bite to eat. So, yes, the burgers are bloody generous, accompanied by chips, a poached egg or truffle sauce. The cocktails are like pharmaceutical concoctions. Choose your poison.

GLASS RESTAURANT

Uhlandstraße 195, S-Bahn Savignyplatz
Tel 30 5471 0861, www.glassberlin.de
Fixed-price menus €75 to €95
Closed for lunch and on Sunday and Monday
FUSION, FUTURISTIC DESIGN

Located near the Hotel am Steinplatz, this former office lobby, which can be spotted from the street thanks to its GLASS neon signage, has been converted into a fusion restaurant by its Israeli chef and owner Gal Ben Moshe. Its futuristic bistro interior, ever-changing, creative cooking and the mysterious sweet treat of the Candy Box dessert all combine to make Glass a truly astonishing experience.

WILMERSDORF, GRUNEWALD

Affluent districts & woodland lakes

CHÂLET SUISSE

Clayallee 99, Grunewald
U-Bahn Dahlemdorf
Tel 30 832 6362, www.chalet-suisse.de
À la carte €40

RUSTIC HIDEOUT

Like Hansel and Gretel's cottage lost in the Grunewald forest, but well known to all Berliners in the west of the city who walk their dogs here, the Châlet Suisse is a charming rustic oasis frequented by the political elite and the class of local celebrities known as *Promis*. Now refurbished and redecorated in a more contemporary style, the restaurant, which is open every day from noon, belongs to the Diekmann company, whose main restaurant on Meinekestraße has also been given a makeover. Alongside the dining rooms with roaring log fires (perfect for Saturday lunch, for example), the Châlet boasts a huge terrace and garden that echo to the happy chatter of trendy *Biergarten*-goers in summer. The menu offers equally elegant dishes – oysters, asparagus, celery soup, mixed salads or gazpacho with mascarpone. But star billing goes to the superb rösti, which come with salmon, mushrooms or meat stew. Afterwards, an excellent way to aid the digestion is a walk in the forest, a stroll round Grunewald lake or a peek inside the Jagdschloss Museum. The Brücke Museum is also within striking distance.

DUDU31

Bleibtreustraße 31, Wilmersdorf
U-Bahn Uhlandstraße
Tel 30 577 95 577, www.dudu31.de
À la carte €30

FASHIONABLE VIETNAMESE

Dudu means "papaya" in Vietnamese, but Dudu is one-hundred-per cent Berliner. Its founder, Nam Cao Hoai, works with his family. He opened the first Dudu in 2008 in a former soap factory on Torstraße in Mitte. It was a lasting success and counted many stars among its clientele. This recently opened Dudu replaces the Deli Bleibtreu in the Bleibtreu Hotel, a 1990s boutique hotel. Inside, there is (almost) nothing left of the original decoration by Herbert Jakob Weinand, a famous Berlin designer known for having created the sets for Robert van Ackeren's film *A Woman in Flames*. The New York-style bar, tiles and mosaics are gone, replaced by a new Asian-style decor of untreated wood, gilded metal and subdued lighting that is elegant, simple and comfortable. Seated at one of the large tables or on a stool at the counter, you can sample a papaya salad, shrimp tempura, tuna and avocado, beef ceviche or miso beef, a house speciality. Food is served from noon to midnight. And you may spot a few incognito stars.

HONÇA

Ludwigkirchplatz 12, Wilmersdorf
U-Bahn Spichernstraße
Tel 239 39 114, www.honca.de
À la carte €30
Closed for lunch Tuesday to Friday
and all day Monday

ANATOLIAN, GASTRONOMIC

The search for a decent Turkish restaurant in Berlin has been going on for years. During this time, the doner kebab ousted

"Berlin is a city of bold gestures and startling incongruities, of ferment and destruction." Brian Ladd, *The Ghosts of Berlin*, 1997

Currywurst from the top of the food hit parade, with almost 1,600 kebab shops in the city. Despite this, and the significant size of the Turkish community in Berlin, Turkish cooking – as rich as it is varied – played hard to get. Founded and run by the charming Volkan Kula, and attractively designed to look like an Italian hotel in Istanbul in the 1940s, lit by lots of tasselled lanterns (think Fortuny on the Bosphorus) and baroque Venetian mirrors, Honça promotes Anatolian cuisine, the mother of all forms of Turkish cooking. The dishes prepared by chef Nizar Alazi are so good you'll be unable to conceal your approval – much to the delight of the friendly staff and chefs, who work in full view of the customers. Particularly recommended are the *kuzu ciğer* (fried lamb's liver with caramelized onions), *zeytinyağlı enginar dolma* (rice-stuffed artichokes with pine nuts, raisins and dill) and *pastırmalı börek* with spinach and mushrooms – they're starters, but are rich enough to be main courses. The enchanting desserts include *incir hurma* (date and fig mousse with rosehip jam) and *sakızlı muhallebi*, a melt-in-the-mouth trifle with grapes and wild berry sauce.

MINE & WINE

Meinekestraße 10, Wilmersdorf
U-Bahn Kurfürstendamm
Tel 30 8892 6363
www.minerestaurant.de
À la carte €40
Closed for lunch and on Sunday and Monday
CHIC ITALIAN

Celebrity chefs know how to turn their media fame into commercial value, and indeed TV star Aram Mnatsakanov – nicknamed the Russian Jamie Oliver and already well established in Moscow – has done just that. Now in Berlin, on the ground floor of the building that houses the Henri Hotel, he runs this restaurant with his son Mikhail, a former student of the Ferrandi School in Paris. The black and gold decor hovers somewhere between urban glamour and trendy elegance. Whether it's the kitchen, the food or the menu, the language is Italian spoken with a French accent. Look out for caponata made with Sicilian aubergines; *casarecci* pasta with king crab; *maltagliati* pasta in Périgord duck stew; foie gras on toasted rye bread with grilled avocado and honey vinaigrette; grilled green asparagus with Parmesan sabayon; tortellini stuffed with burrata and ricotta and with shavings of white truffle; or lamb shoulder with roasted cauliflower and meat sauce. The combinations are imaginative and expertly handled. Berliners with long memories will remember that this location was the legendary home of Maître, the first restaurant in Berlin to be awarded two Michelin stars.

PRENZLAUER BERG
*Gentrification
& bobo stronghold*

LA BRICOLE

Senefelderstraße 30
S-Bahn Prenzlauer Allee
Tel 30 844 21 362, www.bricole.de
À la carte €30
Closed for lunch and on Sunday and Monday
HORS D'ŒUVRE BAR

Fabian Fischer is in tune with the times. After working at Borchardt and Grosz, he now has his own place with a *bar hors d'œuvre*, in French on the sign, differentiating his place from the Spanish-style tapas bars popping up in the area. He found a young chef, Steven Zeidler, immediately arousing interest and attracting success. In the kitchen, Zeidler draws on his imagination for a menu full of delicious little treasures that can be easily combined to make a full meal. This is neither a bar nor a restaurant, just an excellent gourmet address.

LA KÄSERIE

Lychenerstraße 6
U-Bahn Eberswalderstraße
Tel 30 3472 3400, www.lakaeserie.de
À la carte €20
Closed Sunday
CHEESE-CENTRED BISTRO

When it comes to cheese, the French are rarely far away. Behind this *Käserie*, a neologism based on *Käse* ("cheese" in German), there are two young, smiling Frenchmen – Roman Dumond and Bastien Slovinki – who began selling seasonal and refined French cheeses in 2012. As they grew successful, they eventually added a fine if humbly decorated bistro where you can sit down and play at being a taster. There is a large slate of cheeses that you can accompany with a glass of white wine, as well as a fondue, raclette or a warm Mont d'Or served with charcuterie and potatoes. For those who want to have a raclette at home, the Käserie rents out equipment. The restaurant also does breakfasts and takeaways.

PRATER GARTEN

Kastanienallee 7–9
U-Bahn Eberswalderstraße
Tel 30 448 56 88, www.pratergarten.de
À la carte €30
Closed for lunch except on Sunday
Biergarten open daily from noon
from April to September
POPULAR BIERGARTEN

The oldest Biergarten in Berlin, opened in 1837, is a multicultural institution where you can do more than just eat (rather well) and drink your fill. As soon as the Berlin Wall fell, young Berliners gathered here to take part in the intellectual ferment inspired by the reunification of Germany. While the wall still stood, Prater was one of the few cafés in East Berlin that was open on Sundays. The locals partied hard there, to the point that the Volkspolizei closed it down several times. Reopened in 1996, it now has a restaurant serving traditional German cuisine, open only in the evening and on Sunday from 10am for breakfast. Its famous summer Biergarten is open on fine days from noon and accommodates up to 600 people. In addition to these activities, the Prater pursues its eccentric-radical path, mixing people and genres to the point that even the most stuck-up customers forget themselves and let go, while sports fans are quick to vaunt the prowess of their teams. The large room has been refurbished, and the Königsberger Klopse are among the best in the city.

SCHÖNEBERG, FRIEDENAU
Residential & literary

BRASSERIE COLETTE

Passauer Straße 5–7, Schöneberg
U-Bahn and S-Bahn Augsburgerstraße,
Wittenbergplatz
Tel 30 219 92 174
www.brasseriecolette.de
À la carte €50

GASTRONOMIC BRASSERIE

Tim Raue's Parisian-style brasserie is located near KaDeWe on the ground floor of the Tertianum Residence, whose undulating facade houses luxury flats for the elderly. Branches have already opened in Munich and Konstanz. He serves all the classics of the genre – onion soup, duck confit, salade niçoise, black pudding, steak-frites and bouillabaisse – and even resurrects recipes from the past like tournedos Rossini and lobster Thermidor. For dessert, we appreciated the high-calorie crêpes Colette (with banana and salted-butter caramel). Seated on old wooden benches from the Paris metro and enjoying the bohemian bistro atmosphere, customers might imagine that they are in France. Credit cards not accepted.

RENGER-PATZSCH

Wartburgstraße 54, Schöneberg
U-Bahn Eisenacher Straße
Tel 30 784 2059
www.renger-patzsch.com
Fixed-price menus €28 and €33,
à la carte €20
Closed for lunch and on Sunday

ALSATIAN BISTRO

Exit Volker Hauptvogel and his popular Alsatian restaurant Storch ("Stork") in 2007. Following his departure, the nest was occupied by Oliver Schupp, who in turn left for pastures new (namely the Würgeengel, the Gorgonzola Club in Kreuzberg and the chic Bellmann cocktail bar). But Schupp has now returned with the aim of setting a flagging business back on its feet and saving a culinary heritage based largely on the *Flammekuchen*. In the kitchen, ex-Storch chef Hannes Behrmann (previously of the Cochon Bourgeois) presides over a fabulously good, classy menu, in tandem with Oliver Schupp. The duo run a tight ship, with simple, unpretentious bistro decor featuring walls with wood panelling and grey-blue paintwork. The place is invariably packed with a loyal clientele, chattering elbow-to-elbow at the communal tables in each of the three dining rooms. For a cut above, ask for the table-for-two perched high up on the right, next to the entrance, offering a bird's-eye view and a great spot for chatting with the waiters and barman – provided you don't mind passing for Statler and Waldorf from the *Muppet Show* in their theatrical box. On the menu, traditional authentic *Flammekuchen* – crispy, salty, sweet, delicious – and, inevitably, a Sauerkraut of the first water. As for the name, it refers to photographer Albert Renger-Patzsch, high priest of New Objectivity and a close friend of Schupp's paternal grandfather. The latter was himself a distinguished architect and owner of a photographic collection bequeathed by Renger-Patzsch, whose value on the collectors' market is on the rise.

SISSI

Motzstraße 34, Schöneberg
U-Bahn Nollendorfplatz
Tel 30 2101 8101, www.sissi-berlin.de
À la carte €13
Closed for lunch and on Monday

AUSTRO-GAY

A faded old sign on the front of the building bears ghostly witness to the past: *Paketversand nach Ost und West*, meaning "Parcels sent to East and West". Sissi, with its green-and-red decor, its loyal clientele and its afternoon cakes, sits squarely where it belongs, in the middle of the gay street in Schöneberg. You can drop in for lunch or dinner, but the place is primarily

TERRACES AND SECRET GARDENS

A green and peaceful city, Berlin is an ideal place for restaurant and café owners to extend their business *draußen* – outside. And there are certainly plenty of fresh-air opportunities out there: wide shady sidewalks, large panoramic terraces, courtyards, gardens along the Spree, canals and lakes. Most major cafés and *Biergarten* make the most of them, and almost all the small restaurants, *Imbisse* and bars spill over onto the pavement with a few tables and chairs or even plain wooden or plastic boxes with camping cushions. The best are naturally to be found in parks and along lakeshores, packed out when it's sunny. In the Grunewald woods, the CHÂLET SUISSE is a perfect spot with its beautiful rustic terrace under the trees. In Mitte, the gourmet restaurant FACIL, up on the fifth floor of the Mandala Hotel, opens when the weather's fine onto a mid-air terrace for twenty guests, who have to book in advance. Choose lunch rather than dinner to enjoy it to the full, far from the bustle of Potsdamer Platz.

The most secret garden in Berlin, however, forms part of the excellent FRÜHSAMMERS restaurant in Wilmersdorf, where Peter and Sonja Frühsammer, a couple of award-winning chefs, have set up shop inside a sumptuous orange villa surrounded by a beautiful garden, now owned by the Grunewald Tennisclub. The house was once owned by the Austrian singer and actress Fritzi Massary, an operetta star in the 1920s who participated in the creation of some of Oscar Straus's compositions. You can eat lunch and dinner outdoors on sunny days in this classically refined restaurant with its Art Deco bourgeois decor. A delight.

CHÂLET SUISSE Clayallee 99, Grunewald, U-Bahn Dahlemdorf, tel 832 6362, www.chalet-suisse.de

FACIL The Mandala Hotel, Potsdamer Straße 3, Tiergarten, S-Bahn and U-Bahn Potsdamer Platz, tel 590 051 234, www.facil.de

DIE QUADRIGA Dormero Hotel Brandenburger Hof Berlin, Eislebener Straße 14, Wilmersdorf, U-Bahn Augsburger Straße, tel 2140 5650, www.brandenburger-hof.com

FRÜHSAMMERS Flinsberger Platz 8, Wilmersdorf, S-Bahn Hohenzollerndamm, tel 8973 8628, www.fruehsammers-restaurant.de

a *Gaststube* (lounge), no larger than the sewing basket of the Austrian empress whose name it bears, although the space has been extended to the rear. With its wood-burning stove, this is a wonderfully cosy place in winter, where you feel a bit like a cat in front of a fire. The rather jokey serving staff declaim the very international menu and the daily specials, such as soup or goulash. After much hesitation, you ask for a *Schnitzel*. Pork or veal? *Ach,* another choice to make! Servings are so copious that they offer doggy-bags here. In short, Sissi is a little classic.

ZSA ZSA BURGER

Motzstraße 28, Schöneberg
U-Bahn Nollendorfplatz
Tel 30 2191 3470, www.zsazsaburger.de
À la carte €20
Closed for lunch
BURGER MANIA

The Zsa Zsa Burger is situated in the gay Motzstraße, just up the street from the Viennese café-bistro Sissi, and offers its own decorative daring in a kitsch chalet style of grey walls and black ceiling with a large "suction cup" crystal chandelier – a nod to the jewellery of the real Zsa Zsa (Gabor). Open only at night and very popular with locals, it is owned and run by Oliver Schneider, while Ernesto Kuoni prepares the dishes and comes up with the suggestive titles, such as The Silence of the Lambs, The Hangover Burger and The Bangkok Bang. As well as the delicious burgers – Argentinean beef, ground chicken, lamb, turkey and vegetarian – sauced up with mango chutney or curry mayonnaise and accompanied by excellent chips, there are salads, soups and desserts, including a fried vanilla ice cream topped with maple syrup. Expect a cheeky service and a merry mix of typical Berliners sporting leather trappings, hipster couples, grandpas on their own and chatty groups of friends.

KREUZBERG
Alternative & arty

ALTES ZOLLHAUS

Carl-Herz-Ufer 30, U-Bahn Prinzenstraße
Tel 30 692 3300
www.altes-zollhaus-berlin.de
À la carte €50
Closed for lunch and on Sunday and Monday
MODERN BERLIN CUISINE

The historic, bucolic Altes Zollhaus lies off the beaten track in a residential neighbourhood, on the banks of the Landwehrkanal. The building used to be a river customs post that was restored and converted into an inn in 1979. The restaurant belongs to Herbert Beltle, who also owns the Aigner brewery on Gendarmenmarkt and the Weingrün bistro in Mitte. It serves new modern German cuisine concocted by chef Günter Beyer, one of its finest exponents. There are two dining rooms, both with an understated, elegant, rustic-modern decor. A mixture of small and large tables cater for couples and larger groups. On sunny days, you can eat outdoors on the garden terrace. The food ranks the place among the best tables in Berlin, and it is worth having the full works of starter, main dish and dessert, starting, for example, with a cake of smoked trout and marinated beefsteak tomatoes, continuing with an oven-roasted breast of free-range Brandenburg duck accompanied by a pancake of cabbage and potatoes, and ending with a *Rote Grütze*, a contemporary version of a very traditional dessert. For the unenlightened, the *Rote Grütze* is to Berliners what blancmange is to Londoners – a gruel of red fruit, the sort of typical dessert that was the glory of the now-defunct Mohring café but which the post-war food industry turned into something grotesque. Here, however, you can taste the real thing. Another great house speciality is the KPM, which apart from the physical dish itself has very little to do with the Berlin porcelain factory of the same name. Here we are talking about the *Königliche Preußische Mahlzeit* – a Prussian royal meal that features a generous plate of chops and free-range lamb meatballs accompanied by courgette dumplings with cheese. With all these culinary delights, you hardly have time to notice the very Tamara de Lempicka pictures, the beautiful flower arrangements, the sumptuous and much-used meat slicer, and the fact that you are comfortably seated on benches covered with big linen cushions. The service by staff in large aprons is simple, playful and effortlessly bilingual. The menu features a wine of the week from the Horcher vineyard, also owned by Herbert Beltle. But you can also drink beer with such feasts; the bitter Progusta from the Braufactum is pure nectar. When it's all over, the bill comes in a music box, but shouldn't cause any surprises. Booking is recommended. Dogs are welcome.

E.T.A. HOFFMANN

Yorckstraße 83
U-Bahn Mehringdamm
Tel 30 780 98 809
www.etahoffmann-berlin.de
Fixed-price menus €38 to €76
Closed for lunch and on Tuesday
CLASSIC CUISINE

In the heart of Kreuzberg, two Baroque Atlases frame the porch of a late 19th-century housing estate surrounding a large courtyard garden. The apartments and studios are inhabited by young artists and intellectuals. The Riehmers Hofgarten hotel is located next door to the Yorck, an art-house cinema with many branches in the city. Independent from it, but located in the same place, is the restaurant e.t.a. hoffmann, named for the famous writer and composer Ernst Theodor Amadeus Hoffmann. This is where chef Tim Raue made his debut several years ago. Other chefs have also passed through the kitchen, and the restaurant has now become a classic, with a new gourmet life under

Thomas Kurt, whose savoury Italian cuisine is made with herbs and vegetables he picks himself in the adjoining kitchen garden. Dishes include lobster pot-au-feu with red curry, fillet of veal and deglazed asparagus, and duck foie gras coated with chocolate. The menu also offers two excellent fixed-price vegan meals (€38 and €45). And the assortment of cheeses, rare in Berlin, is superb. In fine weather, diners leave the warm dining room to enjoy the courtyard terrace.

HERZ & NIERE

Fichtestraße, 31, U-Bahn Südstern
Tel 30 690 01 522
www.herzundniere.berlin
Tasting menu €38, à la carte €35
Closed for lunch and on Monday
GERMAN CUISINE

Travelling gourmets will remember that Stephan Hartmann's restaurant used to be located here before he went to the Restaurant am Steinplatz and then moved to Canada. The space is now occupied by the young chef Christoph Hauser, first spotted at Rutz. Open only the evening, like most of Berlin's fine restaurants, it makes its direction clear with its name: Herz & Niere means "heart and kidneys", almost provocative considering all the vegans around. We approve with all our heart. So, meat and offal are the specialities, simply described on the menu, which changes every day. Dishes include beef brawn salad with gherkins and pink radishes, chicken stock with duck hearts, vegetables and *Knöpfle* (pasta), pork belly with hazelnut and apple crust, and beef tongue with chopped lamb. The most extravagant dish, with the same name as the restaurant, a kind of hunter's trophy, might defeat the weak of heart. Again, we approve. The decor is simple, and the service friendly and attentive. Credit cards are not accepted, an old local custom that we thought had changed but that has recently reappeared.

HORVÁTH

Paul-Lincke-Ufer 44a
U-Bahn Schönleinstraße
Tel 30 6128 9992
www.restaurant-horvath.de
Fixed-price menus €89 to €129
Closed for lunch and on Monday
and Tuesday

GOURMET

There are several restaurants and cafés
along the northern bank of the Landwehr
Canal, and they all have terraces that are
taken by storm when the weather permits.
But while these places seem to come and
go with depressing frequency, the Horváth,
together with the Volt further on, has
remained a fixture. Named after German
playwright Ödön von Horváth, it has
been here for years, unperturbed by the
succession of owners and chefs. Things
are changing now though, since the young
award-winning chef Sebastian Frank has
taken over with his partner Jeannine
Kessler. While the decor still sports wood
panelling and gleaming brass, and the
atmosphere remains quiet, the modern
Austrian cuisine is now reaching for the
skies. It must be said that Frank has had
a stellar career since his time at the
Steirereck in Vienna. His surprise menu
of ten starters, main dishes and desserts
is a veritable symphony of flavours and
textures. On paper, it all looks so simple,
with three words and three ingredients:
radish/mackerel/apple; suckling pig/
onion/acacia; carrot/almond/thyme.
Prepared with great talent, the food speeds
from plate to palate with an explosion
of favours. Before you get started, though,
try the house drink, a Horvatini (vermouth,
celery and lime), to stimulate your appetite.
Open evenings only, from Wednesday to
Sunday, this café-restaurant with a billiards
table used to be called Exile and was one
of David Bowie's favourite hangouts during
his long stay in Berlin.

KIMCHI PRINCESS

Skalitzer Straße 36,
entrance via Manteuffelstraße
U-Bahn Görlitzer Bahnhof
Tel 48812460
www.kimchiprincess.com
À la carte €25

KOREAN, ATMOSPHERIC

This Korean canteen, opened in 2009,
is quite simply one of the best of its kind
in Berlin. The "designer construction site"
decor by Felix Pahnke features scarlet
Algeco units, huge, long wooden tables,
assorted benches and occasional seating,
including Diamond chairs by Harry
Bertoia (also scarlet, like the lighting). The
atmosphere is relaxed, chatty and musical
(Claudja Barry, a brave choice indeed)
and the house speciality is Korean-style
fondue, served in large pans on tabletop
hotplates, around which clusters a striking
concentration of Julian Schnabel lookalikes
(of all ages). Steel chopsticks in hand,
diners pick their white rice from the iron
bowls, and wolf down their *bibimbap* or
their *bulgogi*. It's delightful, convivial and
unpretentious, and typical of Berlin's youth
scene. Just one catch: due to the kitchen
odours, you need to wear disposable
clothing or take out a subscription at the
cleaners. The Kimchi's owners, Young-mi
Park-Snowden, Andrea Volpato and Baris
Ergün, have opened an offshoot round
the corner, the **ANGRY CHICKEN** diner
(www.angry-chicken.com).

RESTAURANT RICHARD

Köpenicker Straße 174
U-Bahn Schlesisches Tor
Tel 30 492 07 242
www.restaurant-richard.de
Fixed-price menus €64 to €94
Closed for lunch and on Sunday and Monday

FRENCH CUISINE

The Swiss owner, Hans Richard, has his
two chefs, Tino Scodeller and John Richter,
to thank for earning him a star rating with
their four- to seven-course gourmet tasting
menus, with a light or more pronounced

French influence, depending on the recipe. Examples are the sumptuous foie gras accompanied by crunchy pepper biscuits; and sea bass with capers and lemony *beurre blanc*. The handsome decor intelligently combines the Brutalist style popular in Kreuzberg with rather exotic shimmering fabrics.

TIM RAUE

Rudi-Dutschke-Straße 26, U-Bahn Kochstraße
Tel 30 2593 7930, www.tim-raue.de
Fixed-price menus €38 to €168,
à la carte €120
Closed Sunday and Monday
WESTERN-ASIAN FUSION

Tim Raue, the poster boy of Berlin gastronomy, shot to fame in the city when he opened the 44, the Swissôtel's gourmet restaurant. Before that he was chef at Die Quadriga, a gourmet restaurant in the former Brandenburger Hof Hotel. Festooned with prizes and honours, Raue made a triumphant comeback to the Berlin scene in 2008 with MA, the wildly successful restaurant in the Adlon Hotel. Also the firebrand behind La Soupe Populaire in Prenzlauer Berg (which was short-lived), he opened a restaurant in his own name on the border between Mitte and Kreuzberg, close to Checkpoint Charlie, taking the hummingbird as his mascot and logo. His cooking, steeped in Asian wisdom, is rich in quality and invention. His choice of neighbourhood may seem odd – one side of the street is teeming with tourists heading to Checkpoint Charlie. The decor has the feel of a business lounge at a Danish airport, with office chairs a marble bar, banquettes and a cosy corner with panelling. The menu gives succinct descriptions to better stimulate fertile imaginations: imperial caviar/sprat/yuzu; cod/lemon/lettuce; Jerusalem artichoke/black truffle/ red grapes; veal/celery/jalapeno; vanilla/ passion fruit/caramel. In the end, it all comes together like a torpedo that hits its target.

TULUS LOTREK

Fichtestraße 24
U-Bahn Südstern
Tel 30 419 56 687
www.tuluslotrek.de
Tasting menu €69
Closed for lunch and on Monday
CREATIVE, FASHIONABLE

Ilona Scholl and Maximilian Strohe have given Toulouse Lautrec's name a Turkish spelling, a successful move for this neighbour of Herz & Niere, making this cobblestoned street a favourite destination for gourmets. The atmosphere is friendly and welcoming, and wine is served by the glass, offering an opportunity to discover exotic Serbian biodynamic wines from the Budmir vineyards. The restaurant fuses street food and gastronomic dishes, elevating chicken nuggets and cleverly combining duck foie gras with venison tartare. You'll also find scallops with celery purée, apricot and *poutargue*, and halibut with almonds, wild broccoli, carrots and red curry. Credit cards not accepted – no surprise there!

ALSO IN THIS NEIGHBOURHOOD

JOLESCH

Muskauer Straße 1
U-Bahn Görlitzer Bahnhof
Tel 30 612 3581, www.jolesch.de
Fixed-price menu €12, à la carte €30
Closed for lunch during the summer
VIENNESE, CONTEMPORARY

This outpost has been flying the Austrian flag here for more than twenty years. Despite the invitation waltz of different owners, Jolesch is still on course. The lunch menu is unbeatable, the cakes are Vienna-ishly good and the evening menu is Austro-contemporary. It is said that film director Tom Tykwer was a regular.

VOLT

Paul-Lincke-Ufer 21
U-Bahn Schönleinstraße
Tel 30 338 402 320
www.volt-restaurant.de
Fixed-price menus from €58
Closed for lunch and on Sunday and Monday

ATMOSPHERIC, NEO-GERMAN

Volt opened in 2010 in an old power plant built in 1928 beside the canal, and has kept the high brick arches of this industrial cathedral, now lit by beautiful copper globes. Chef Matthias Gleiss simmers up contemporary German dishes with commendable vegetarian variants. Top marks for both presentation and service.

NEUKÖLLN
Multi-ethnic & shabby chic

FILETSTÜCK PIGALLE

Sanderstraße 17
U-Bahn Schönleinstraße
Tel 30 239 39 663
www.filetstueck-berlin.de
À la carte €40
Closed Sunday

MEATY

The Filetstück on Ultstandstraße has closed, and Martin Hader's restaurant has moved to Neukölln to a former brothel, which explains the "Pigalle" in the name. Human flesh is no longer for sale, just grilled, seared, roasted and raw animal meat, a welcome change in this area full of vegan restaurants. Like most others, however, *nicht* credit card.

INDUSTRY STANDARD

Sonnenallee 83, Neukölln
U-Bahn Rathaus Neukölln
Tel 30 6272 7732
www.industry-standard.de
À la carte €35
Closed for lunch (except on Sunday)
and on Monday and Tuesday

NEW GENERATION GOURMET

This is the heart of the multicultural district of Neukölln, surrounded by shops selling "fast" everything, so the presence of a gourmet restaurant seems a tad incongruous. But we are in Berlin, after all, and we've already waded through worse in search of other gems. Ramses Manneck, who, despite his name is Mexican, and his Canadian associate, are at the helm. It's all a bit confusing, but we are in Berlin after all. On the menu you'll find French dishes with a twist, featuring tartare of beef with Parmesan and chanterelles, black pudding cake with fried egg and apple, pork tongue with tomatoes and wild garlic, braised endives with Stilton, walnuts and Granny Smith apples. Wash it all down with the help of an amazingly extensive wine list.

It's a great reason to head across town, but be warned, this is another place that doesn't accept credit cards.

LAVA

Flughafenstraße 46, U-Bahn Boddinstraße
Tel 30 2234 6908, www.lava-berlin.de
À la carte €30
Closed Monday and Tuesday
EXPERIMENTAL, ATMOSPHERIC

An offshoot of the amazing **LAVANDERIA VECCHIA**, Lava initially comes across as a beautifully appetizing butcher's shop specializing in quality hams, cooked up in various dishes to be taken away or eaten in. But when night falls it turns into something out of the *Dance of the Vampires*. Once through the kitchen, where various tattooed figures are busy, you spot a Marat-style bathtub full of red water oozing down a gutter somewhere. The dining room at the back has an Art Nouveau look with cracked green wallpaper. It might have been the scene for an attempted murder inspired by the Addams family: there's a copper chandelier on the black-and-white tiled floor that must have missed its target. Atmosphere, atmosphere! Sat at wooden tables brandishing antique, probably Russian silverware, you sample creative and experimental meals, such as pumpkin soufflé, skrei (young cod), swordfish with gnocchi; pappardelle with cocoa-mushrooms and radicchio, and atomic asparagus. Everything has an alchemical, deconstructed, pulverized feel, and it's delicious. That said, even a simple dish of the finest hams mentioned above is a bit of an adventure, as is the Caesar salad, in which the usual chicken is replaced with sardines. The dessert is decidedly normcore, featuring the comeback of the dreaded banana split. Alternatively, you can have a crazy pina colada with lashings of rum spray. The service, care of an adorable Cure fan, adds to the oddity. And note the old medicine cabinet hanging in the hallway, packed to bursting.

LAVANDERIA VECCHIA

Flughafenstraße 46
U-Bahn Boddinstraße
Tel 30 6272 2152
www.lavanderiavecchia.de
Fixed-price menus €11 to €60
Closed Saturday
ITALIAN, OFFBEAT

This "old laundry" is Lava's parent company. It is tucked away in a double courtyard with just a simple plaque by the gate to identify it. You enter via a corridor adorned with street-art frescoes. The trattoria occupies a former industrial laundry and uses its own laundry as decoration, with shelves loaded with boxes of sheets, full washing machines, tea towels drying from the ceiling and even an empty pram – a Berlin version of *A Special Day* with Sophia Loren, perhaps. You can get a lunch here almost for the price of a wash and spin dry in a laundromat: *penne alla ricotta* and aubergine, asparagus and chicken risotto, fish fillets of the day, soups and salads. There is a single set dinner every evening, with the dishes for that day listed on the chalkboard above the cash register and served on large oilcloth-covered tables under the fake laundry drying overhead. The place is located fairly far from the centre, so the clients are mostly Neukölln neighbourhood regulars.

FRIEDRICHSHAIN
Hip & bohemian

MUTZENBACHER

Libauer Straße 11
S-Bahn and U-Bahn Warschauer Straße
Tel 9561 6788,
www.mutzenbacher-berlin.de
À la carte €30
Closed for lunch Monday to Thursday
AUSTRIAN SPECIALITIES
Equidistant from the Michelberger Hotel
and Boxhagener Platz – you just have
to cross the railway tracks, which is a little
less dramatic than exchanging a spy
on the Glienicker Brücke in the middle
of the Cold War – the Mutzenbacher has
brought its Austrian doe eyes into the
heart of a neighbourhood that doesn't
warrant them. More than ten years
after Schneeweiss, the alpine hut niche
market continues to enchant the locals,
who make short work of the *Fleischkäse*,
Kasspatzen, *Zerletts Eier* and other typical
Kaiserschmarrn. The pink Schnitzel-
Puff sign (it can translate as "brothel
cutlets", and that's just the polite version)
sets the tone for this kitsch urban chalet,
which is both relaxing and charmingly
light-hearted. The place is oozing with
beer, white wine and good humour.
You're forcefully reminded, in case you
needed to be, that you're in Friedrichshain
and nowhere else. Behind their white-
and-red shutters, Marcel Schnabel and
Franz-Josef Steiner also run a delicatessen,
open from noon until late into the night,
that does takeaway snacks.

ELSEWHERE

BLOCKHAUS NIKOLSKOE

Nikolskoer Weg 15, Steglitz-Zehlendorf
S-Bahn Wannsee, then bus
Tel 30 805 2914
www.blockhaus-nikolskoe.de
À la carte €25
Closed for dinner
LAKESIDE CHALET
On the way to Potsdam over the Glienicker
Brücke stands a liturgical curiosity –
the evangelical church of St Peter and Paul,
built in 1837 at the request of Frederick
William III, where sacred music concerts
are held. Overlooking the waters of the
Havel, towards Peacock Island, there is
another, more secular curiosity –
a restaurant bound by force to the history
of the church. It also began with a black
wooden dacha built in 1819 by the same
king for his beloved daughter, Charlotte,
who had just married a Russian prince, the
future Tsar Nicholas I. Over a century ago,
one of the king's coachmen, a Russian
named Ivan, lived there and acted as the
church caretaker. In the end, he turned the
house into a sort of refreshment bar where
he served cold cuts and bread and butter.
Time passed and the River Havel flowed
softly past. The neat little cottage with its
geraniums was bought by the Bossier family,
who kept up the tradition of the little bar
and its sausages and pastries. Inside,
the large tiled stove still warms the place
in winter, but once the weather improves,
choose a *Biergarten*-style table with a view
of the lake, opposite Peacock Island, where
you can watch the boats plying the waters
of the Havel. Headlining asparagus in the
spring and mushrooms in the autumn, the
menu is inexhaustible. It includes good
greasy herring *matjes* with parsley potatoes,
filet of pikeperch, plump *Königsberger Klopse*
and trout (*Forelle*) meunière. It won't be
the meal of the century, but coming here for
a change of scenery near the city while
sipping a brown beer or an *Apfelschorle* is
one of Berlin's special pleasures.

DINING OUT WITH BARRIE KOSKY

I don't cook much, so I eat out a lot in restaurants. In the evening, I love going to Pauly Saal, which was opened by the owners of the Grill Royal inside a former Jewish girls' school. I love this place, although I find the "decorative" presence of the rocket slightly odd. I also go to the Italian restaurant Bocca di Bacco quite often, as it's my favourite pasta cantina. And then there is a Vietnamese restaurant I love, but I'll never give its address away to anyone! That said, I don't understand why Asian restaurants in Berlin are usually so dreary and bad. They're a disaster.

PAULY SAAL
Auguststraße 11–13, Mitte, tel 30 3300 6070, www.paulysaal.com

BOCCA DI BACCO
Friedrichstraße 167, Mitte, tel 30 2067 2828, www.boccadibacco.de

GOOD THINGS
GOURMET DELIS TO FARMERS MARKETS: THE TASTE OF THE CITY

Perhaps because Berlin is so profoundly marked by the memory of the Soviet blockade – an attempt, defeated by the Allied airlift, to starve out the population of West Berlin – Berliners have an ambivalent relationship with food. Their combination of thrift, passion and moralistic fatalism leads some to criticize others for their supposed extravagances. As soon as the Wall fell, East Berliners flocked to KaDeWe (Kaufhaus des Westens) to slaver over the piles of delicious and exotic foods, whose fame had travelled to Moscow.

Time has passed and Berliners have fully embraced the organic movement, supplying themselves from farms and market gardens in the Brandenburg countryside. Though *Imbiss*, the local snack stands, still exist, gourmet food counters and specialist stores are popping up, along with food halls and luxury supermarkets. Berliners are gourmets, connoisseurs with very high standards – and they know what they like. Choices have grown exponentially, diversifying along the way.

Updated, healthier versions of traditional food stores place the emphasis on excellence. There are more patisseries than ever before. Wine merchants and cheese shops are springing up everywhere. Coffee is now firmly in the hands of baristas, the new purist designer teas are all the rage and the city distils its own spirits and brews its own local beers. The covered markets are a paradise for foodies, with little snack bars, stalls, kiosks and food wagons particularly busy on Thursday evening and Saturday morning. These days, you have to try really hard if you want to eat badly in Berlin.

ABSINTH DEPOT BERLIN

Weinmeisterstraße 4, Mitte
U-Bahn Weinmeisterstraße
Tel 30 281 6789, www.absinth-berlin.de
Open 2pm to midnight, Saturday from 1pm,
closed Sunday

ABSINTHE

This alcoholic vestige from the Berlin of
East German days has lost nothing of its
unique charm. It has tightened up the
menu and got rid of the deadweight in the
liqueur and anisette selection, reintroducing
absinthe, the supposedly madness-inducing
liqueur that was banned for many years.
Absinthe is back in style, and this is one
of the best places to sample it. You can also
pick up a copy of the store's original poster,
featuring a striped russet cat on a green
(absinthe) background in an alcohol-
vapour-induced swoon. Quite conveniently,
the place is open until midnight.

ANDRASCHKO

Industriestraße 18, Tempelhof
U-Bahn Kaiserin-Augusta-Straße
Tel 30 69598687
www.andraschkokaffee.com

COFFEE ROASTER

Andraschko is an authentic Berlin-style
coffee house that roasts beans from
small-scale suppliers and cooperatives.
It doesn't have its own retail outlet, but
its beans are distributed by several
vendors in the city, starting with KaDeWe,
of course, but also by **GOLDHAHN UND
SAMPSON** (Dunckestraße 9, Prenzlauer
Berg and Wilmerdorfer Straße 102–103,
Charlottenburg), a retailer combining
a cooking school, culinary bookshop
and delicatessen under one roof.

APFELGALERIE

Goltzstraße 3, Schöneberg
U-Bahn Eisenacher Straße
Tel 30 4470 5630, www.apfelgalerie.de
Open 11am to 7pm, Saturday until 3pm,
closed Sunday

APPLES

Goltzstraße has a great range of vintage
shops and outdoor cafés, and Apfelgalerie
is a unique new addition to its repertoire,
a speciality store devoted exclusively to
apples. It offers apples of every shape and
colour, so there's no getting bored with
just one kind, and apples are healthy,
à la "An apple a day keeps the doctor away."
The shop is run by Caty Schernus, author
of the all-about-apples book *Das Apfelbuch
Berlin-Brandenburg*. She has filled her store
with old and new apple varieties, guaranteed
locavore (zero food miles) as they are all
grown and harvested in Brandenburg.
"Old" here refers to long-forgotten varieties
now being regrown, including Reinettes
de Champagne, Belle Fleur, Kronzprinz
Rudolf and the amazing Macoun, a deep
damson colour. For a change, but still a
healthy one, you'll also find seasonal plums,
cherries, pears, mirabelles, cucumbers
and courgettes, all locally grown.

BERLINER KAFFEERÖSTEREI

Uhlandstraße 173–174, Wilmersdorf
U-Bahn Uhlandstraße
Tel 30 8867 7920
www.berliner-kaffeeroesterei.de
Open 9am to 8pm, Sunday 10am to 7pm

COFFEE ROASTER, SWEETS, CHOCOLATE

Making its own freshly roasted coffee,
sweets, chocolates, pastries and cakes, this
typically Berliner food store also has a café,
a restaurant and a Parisian-style terrace.
The smiling, friendly counter assistants
and waiters are happy to let customers take
their time hanging around amid the freshly
ground arabicas, chocolate bonbons
and cups of hot chocolate, knowing they'll
eventually give in to temptation. Opened
in 2001, the place feels like it's always
existed. Maybe it has.

BREZEL COMPANY

Lenaustraße 10, Neukölln
U-Bahn Schönleinstraße
Tel 30 612 4181
www.brezel-company-berlin.de
Open daily 6am to 7pm
PRETZELS, BREAD

There are all kinds of food producers in
Berlin: Strudel Manufaktur, opened by the
Austrian baker Wolfgang Ruhnau, Werner
Gasser's Knödelwirtschaftswunder,
Senf Manufaktur (mustard) and Blutwurst
Manufaktur (black pudding), even a Tofu
Manufaktur. Nestled in a quiet street not
far from Hütten Palast, Jörg Pfeifer's Brezel
Company is a proper bakery, producing
all kinds of bread and all sizes of pretzels –
fresh, crisp on the outside, soft in the
middle and with just the right amount of
salt. Fortunately, it doubles as a café serving
these delights. You'll want to go back often.
Ignore the decor – just enjoy the fine,
1930s Bauhaus tubular chairs, decidedly
different, and the quiet space to sip a large
cappuccino with a fruit tart or Bundt cake.
In December 2015, this Neukölln favourite
also expanded their pretzel empire to the
quieter streets of Schöneberg
(Kalckreuthstraße 16, Schöneberg).

CONFISERIE MÉLANIE

Grolmanstraße 20, Charlottenburg
S-Bahn Savignyplatz
Tel 30 313 8330, www.bei-melanie.de
Open 10am to 7pm,
Saturday until 4pm, closed Sunday
CHOCOLATE MAKER

The interior mezzanines create a 1990s
feel, as do the coffee cups. The preparation
area is open to view in the shop below.
Confiserie Mélanie has been creating
delicious chocolates for seventy years now.
Its current manager is Sabine Dubenknopp,
and it's still famous for its *Kugeln*, dark or
milk-chocolate truffles, filled with praline
or ganache flavoured with cardamom,
grappa, passion fruit, thyme, coffee or
Grand Marnier. Carefully choose one to go
with your cappuccino, as all café customers

are given one free. To take away: Valrhona,
Blanxart and Lauenstein chocolate bars
with almonds, limoncello or Black Forest
cherries; shortbread; biscuits. There's even
an old-fashioned "pick and mix" of loose
sweets and toffees. A few tables are set out
on the pavement on fine days.

DAS SÜSSE LEBEN

Salzburger Straße 7, Schöneberg
U-Bahn Bayerischer Platz
Tel 30 7476 0500
www.das-suesse-leben.de
Open 9am to 6pm, Saturday until 2pm,
closed Sunday
CHOCOLATE AND SWEETS

Berliners have a sweet tooth. Along with
the profusion of pastry shops, there's a host
of confectionery stores and chocolate
shops, most with a nostalgia theme, adding
the sweet touch that makes life more fun.
Ingrid Lang's little shop ("the sweet life")
seems almost made of candy. Just a few
metres from Café Tomasa, not far from the
Schöneberg town hall, this corner shop
seems straight out of a fairy tale (don't tell
the dentist!). The shelves are laden with
glass jars filled with sweets and pralines, as
well as foil wrapped chocolate bears, crisp
chocolate rabbits, chocolate bars, and boxes
and tubes filled with tempting but naughty
delights. The shop also sells jam, honey,
biscuits and other treats like the *Schokokuss*
that make perfect little presents. Life in
Berlin really is chocolate-coated.

DU BONHEUR

Brunnenstraße 39, Mitte
U-Bahn Bernauerstraße
Tel 30 5659 1955, www.dubonheur.de
Open 8am to 7pm, Saturday and Sunday
from 9am, closed Monday and Tuesday
FRENCH PATISSERIE

Brunnenstraße, which leads to the
Wedding quarter from Rosenthaler Platz,
has become Mitte's alternative street, with
galleries, bars and showrooms featuring
vintage design, mostly still at its lower end.
The location of this new patisserie further

THE PICK OF THE MARKETS

Berlin's open-air markets have traditionally been held all year long, even in midwinter, twice a week, on the esplanade of every district's town hall or on the nearest squares. The most entertaining is the one held every Saturday morning on the vast Winterfeldtplatz, in Schöneberg. The most eco-friendly and organic is at Kollwitzplatz, in Prenzlauer Berg, every Saturday from 9am. The cheapest is at Boxhagener Platz in Friedrichshain, on Saturday. Nevertheless, the most popular are still the ones fortunate enough to benefit from an indoor market hall, ensuring customers will always come, whatever the weather. Before the war, in addition to the two big central indoor markets, there were twelve smaller ones, one for each quarter. Some have disappeared, others have been renovated and house permanent stalls and shops, snack bars, bistros, cafés and a few non-food stalls selling useful things – bookstores, shoe repair shops, locksmiths, etc.

ARMINIUS MARKTHALLE The Arminius Markthalle was built in 1891 of red brick in a Brandenburg Gothic style. Designed by Hermann Blankenstein, who was responsible for most of the city's market halls, it is a popular local market and has been renovated in an attractive retro style. Along with the usual food stalls – butcher, baker, delicatessen, greengrocer – you'll find Vietnamese and Peruvian delis, Rosa Lisbert's specialities from Alsace, the Café Thussi & Armin, the palm court is popular for Saturday brunch from 10am to 3pm, with seating at big round tables and a wide choice of fast food outlets. The little blue and white Greek house adds another nicely exotic touch and makes excellent *Schnitzeln*. Arminiusstraße 2 – 4, Moabit, U-Bahn Turmstraße, tel 1511 5307 908, www.arminiusmarkthalle.com

MARKTHALLE NEUN This 19th-century iron and glass market hall was renovated and is managed by a young trio – Bernd Maier, Florian Niedermeir and Nikolaus Driessen. It's a paradise for foodies and locavores, with its old tram cabin used as a kiosk for the toilet attendant; its 1970s Photomaton booth; its stallholders of a Rasputin-meets-Druid sort, offering long-forgotten root vegetables and Jurassic potatoes; its cabbages, onions and garlic hung from black-market-style sacking from the free-spirited and politically active Rüdnitz gardeners; its sheds made from corrugated iron and wooden crates; and, of course, its organics, bobo, zero-food-miles customers. Its weekly Street Food Thursdays attract big crowds from 5pm to 10pm, and on fine Saturdays everyone spills out onto the pavement. Inside, don't miss **BERLIN BEEF BALLS** (www.berlinbeefballs.de), the Italian *focacceria* **SIRONI**, the **KANTINE NEUN** and its one-plate main courses, **FRAU ZELLER**'s patisserie (www.frauzeller.de), where you'll find delicious biscuits and cakes, including a memorable poppyseed cheesecake, or the stand with salmon in all kinds of sauce. It also holds barter and swap days: my homemade preserves in exchange for courgettes fresh from your garden. Eisenbahnstraße 42 – 43, Kreuzberg, U-Bahn Schlesisches Tor, tel 30 577 094 661, www.markthalleneun.de

MARHEINEKE MARKTHALLE This old market hall has also been beautifully restored and focuses on international products in stores like **PELLONI VINI E SALUMI**, **LES ÉPICURIENS** by Frédéric Gachelin-Verneuil and Éric Marette, **LE BRETAGNE** (croissants, crêpes), **OLGAS** (Greek grocer) and **TEESTUBE WERLER** (tea and herbal tea) with a range of groceries, wine, cheese, fruit and sweets. Worth visiting also are **KNIPPENBERGS** cheese shop and **YALDA** dried fruits. Marheinekeplatz 15, Kreuzberg, U-Bahn Gneisenaustraße, tel 30 50 56 65 36, www.meine-markthalle.de

THE UNMISSABLES

Christmas stollen:
BEUMER & LUTUM Cuvrystraße 22,
Kreuzberg, U-Bahn Schlesisches Tor,
tel 30 6167 5570, www.beumer-lutum.de

Knödeln: KNÖDELWIRTSCHAFT
Fuldastraße 33, Neukölln, U-Bahn
Rathaus Neukölln, tel 30 9660 0459,
www.knoedelwirtschaft.de

French pastries: DU BONHEUR
Brunnenstraße 39, Mitte, U-Bahn
Bernauer Straße, tel 30 5659 1955,
www.dubonheur.de

Poppyseed cheesecake:
FRAU ZELLER Markthalle Neun,
Einsenbahnstraße 42–43, Kreuzberg,
U-Bahn Schlesisches Tor,
tel 0178 132 08 28, www.frauzeller.de

**Late-night burgers and good
drinks: WHITE TRASH FAST FOOD**
Am Flutgraben 2, Alt-Treptow, U-Bahn
Schlesisches Tor, tel 30 551 506 587,
www.whitetrashfastfood.com

Quince lemonade:
GETRÄNKEFEINKOST
Boxhagener Straße 24, Friedrichshain,
U-Bahn Frankfurter Tor, tel 30 2593 3800,
www.getraenkefeinkost.de

up is therefore quite surprising, though less so considering the concentration of architectural offices, graphic design studios and artists' workshops that supply a clientele thrilled to be able to enjoy the impressive and delicious French-style gateaux that Anna Plagens makes. Following five years working with Pierre Hermé in Paris, she has now joined forces with Berliner Stephan Zuber. The café is decorated with random photos of Paris and is a real treat for the taste buds with its tarts, *canelés,* bread pudding, Parisian brioches, croissants, pains au chocolat, etc., and of course the "Hermé-tique" macarons, all beautifully displayed on pieces of slate. Other delicious treats include little Dulcey or Chococo domes, pure and sophisticated

creations with fantastic texture and flavour. There are jars of their own jam, blood-orange juice and friendly service as well. In short, it's the best patisserie in town.

ERICH HAMANN

Brandenburgische Straße 17, Wilmersdorf
U-Bahn Konstanzer Straße
Tel 30 873 20 86
www.hamann-schokolade.de
Open 9am to 6pm, Saturday until 1pm,
closed Sunday
CHOCOLATE

With its clean decor in silver maple and aluminium, this store in a Rationalist building designed by Johannes Itten in 1928 is a testament to the modernity, in their time, of Erich and Anne Hamann. The business remains in the Hamann family nearly a century after it was established in 1912, continuing to make excellent sweets and chocolates, such as the Weinbeißer and the Neue Ernte, as well as the beautiful, simple bars of dark chocolate whose wrapper remains unchanged, giving them the status of cult object. As you ponder what to buy, you get the feeling that nothing has happened in the city during the last century. Peerless.

FRAU BEHRENS TORTEN

Rheinstraße 65, Friedenau
U-Bahn Friedrich-Wilhelm-Platz
Tel 30 470 12 467
www.gugelhupf-berlin.com
Open daily 10am to 7pm
CAKES AND CHOCOLATE

A peripheral district of south-west Berlin, Friedenau is the peaceful, green refuge of numerous writers and intellectuals. On Sundays, young affluent families and shy singles take this small store by storm. It is located in a building whose small tower and steeply pitched roof give it the vague air of a shrunken French manor house. Having extended into the little shop next door, Frau Behrens Torten now has a lovely miniature tearoom. It has white tile walls and is furnished in the style of an Ibsen play, with marble pedestal tables and upholstered armchairs. It's the perfect setting for enjoying a slice of wonderful cream and fruit layer gateau or poppy-seed cake as you decide what to take away with you: some marble cake, shortbread and a big bar of Schoko-Gruß dark chocolate *aus Friedenau,* wrapped in a print illustrating the quarter. It has a small terrace open on fine days. After the branch in Charlottenburg, Frau Behrens opened a third address in Kreuzberg, which is even bigger and has a kitsch decor.

Other locations: Wilmersdorfer Straße 96–97, Charlottenburg, tel 30 8891 2864; Bergmannstraße 3, Kreuzberg, tel 30 20678257

FRISCHEPARADIES

Hermann-Blankenstein-Straße 48, Friedrichshain
S-Bahn Storkower Straße
Tel 30 390 815131
www.frischeparadies.com
Open 8am to 8pm, Saturday until 6pm, closed Sunday
CHIC DELI

Present in all major German cities, as well as Vienna, the FrischeParadies deli chain arrived in Berlin with a bang, opening two shops. The one in Friedrichshain, a striking edifice, was designed by the Robertneun agency, which was also behind the Tausend bar-restaurant, as well as the other branches of the FrischeParadies chain. The design received a prestigious BDA-Preis in 2009 (other winners that year included David Chipperfield for the wonderful Neues Museum and Realarchitecture for the Boros Collection building). The shop is situated in a district currently in the throes of renovation and is quite a walk from the nearest U-Bahn station. The sleek design creates a stylish, attractive atmosphere. The shelves are all fabulously stocked with thousands of succulent delicacies from the best suppliers. The selection includes fruit and vegetables, meat, fish, cold cuts and cheese, as well as wine and other beverages.

The restaurant section centres on a beautiful copper bar, on which customers can rest their elbows while they watch food being prepared by the French chef. The dishes of the day are copious and delicious. In winter, it's so cold you'll eat and shop wearing three down jackets.
Other location: Morsestraße 2, Charlottenburg, tel 30 3908 1523

G. BUCHWALD

Bartningallee 29, Charlottenburg
S-Bahn Bellevue
Tel 30 391 5931
www.konditorei-buchwald.de
Open 8am to 6pm, Sunday from 9am
HISTORIC PATISSERIE

Opposite the Moabiter Brücke, the bridge with the big bronze bear sculptures that takes you over the Spree to Moabit, you'll find this historic *Konditorei-Café* beloved of Berliners. Founded by Gustav Buchwald in 1852 in Cottbus, it soon moved to Berlin, where it occupies a corner at the edge of Hansaviertel. It soon became famous for inventing *Baumkuchen,* an iced layer cake, ancestor of all the world's Bundt cakes, and first choice of royalty. It was a favourite treat of the future Kaiser Wilhelm II, who appointed Buchwald as his official supplier. A real slice of history cooked on a spit, *Baumkuchen* are still made according to the original recipe and can take several shapes, be covered in chocolate or left plain, and have any number of creamy or fruity fillings, making them ever more tempting. Andrea Tönges is the fifth generation of Buchwalds to run the shop and is careful to preserve the timeless atmosphere of the place with its comfortable, old-fashioned tearooms where nothing – from the patterned wallpaper to the foliage motifs on the tablecloths and the flowery chairs – goes together. Nobody minds, because it is redolent of the indefinable essence of old Berlin combined with the best features of a good café. If *Baumkuchen* doesn't appeal to you, enjoy a restorative and perfect strudel or an enormous choux pastry filled with whipped cream. Look up as you leave: *Baumkuchen seit 1852* is inscribed on the facade and is visible for a good distance. Work it all off with a good walk straight on to Schloß Bellevue, one of the rare surviving Hohenzollern palaces in the city, or by setting off on a tour of the functionalist buildings of Interbau 57. No credit cards.

HOKEY POKEY

Stargarder Straße 73, Prenzlauer Berg
S-Bahn Schönhauser Allee
Tel 0176 8010 3080, www.hokey-pokey.de
Open 1pm to 7pm, in summer noon to 10pm
ICE CREAM, CHOCOLATE

Here there is just a counter, no tables or chairs. Hokey Pokey is a proper Italian-style artisan ice-cream shop, describing itself as an *Eispatisserie*, and Berliners, who love ice cream in all its forms, are happy to queue as they speculate on the flavour combinations they haven't ever tried. HP takes great care over its packaging as well as the contents. Try the delicious Sicilian pistachio, and the salty toffee flavour – a huge hit in cones or little pots. With a couple of fun kitsch toys and three squares of Marou chocolate, everyone's happy.

JUBEL

Hufelandstraße 10, Friedrichshain
S-Bahn Greifswalder Straße
Tel 30 5521 6150, www.jubel-berlin.de
Open 11am to 7pm, Saturday and Sunday until 6pm, closed Monday
PATISSERIE, TEAROOM

Kai Michels opened her fine patisserie in spring 2017 on an elegant street of restored apartment buildings, some painted in discordantly bright colours. Former head pastry chef at Weinbar Rutz, she joined forces with Lucie Babinska to convert this former butcher's shop, keeping its coloured wall tiles. It's a combined tearoom and shop, with a few tables for enjoying the sophisticated cakes and desserts. Tiny French-style gateaux, just a sweet mouthful, choux buns filled with rhubarb and whipped cream, coconut cakes (made

with rice, mango and a touch of spice), *Schoko-Kuppel* (pineapple, rum, nougat and mint), Snickers cake made with caramel and nougat, to be enjoyed there and then with a cup of Samova tea, a fresh fruit juice or a cappuccino, or taken home in a simple cardboard box. Right opposite, you'll find one of the **ROSA CANINA** (www.rosacanina.eu) ice cream shops, for a different kind of sugary treat.

KNIPPENBERGS LUST AUF KÄSE

Gorkistraße I–10, Tegelcenter, Tegel
U-Bahn Alt-Tegel
Tel 30 4360 4850, www.knippenbergs.de
Open 8am to 7pm, Saturday until 4pm, closed Sunday
CHEESE

Along with Maître Philippe, Knippenbergs is one of the great Berlin cheese shops. Ivo Knippenberg supplies his own stalls in several Berlin markets, including Arkonaplatz in Mitte, Domäne Dahlem in Zehlendorf and Boxhagener Platz in Friedrichshain. This enterprising cheesemonger, of comparable status to Pascal Beillevaire in Paris, also runs permanent counters in the food halls at Marheineke in Kreuzberg and the Tegelcenter in Reinickendorf. Committed to organic farming, whole milk, farmhouse produce and mature cheese, he offers no fewer than 150 varieties of cheese, all carefully stored at 15 degrees. The right cheese for the right season, from France, Switzerland, Italy, Holland, England and Germany, of course. Fancy some cheese? You bet. See website for other locations

KOCHHAUS

Bergmann Straße 94, Kreuzberg
U-Bahn Mehringdamm
Tel 30 577 089 100, www.kochhaus.de
Open 10am to 9pm, closed Sunday
FOOD SHOP

Kochhaus is a small chain of chic mini-markets with convenient hours and a franchise concept carefully managed by Ramin Goo and Dorothée Karsch since 2010. There are already three locations in Berlin and more in other major German cities. They offer a daily selection of meal ideas, according to season, with all the ingredients ready to buy in the store, dry, fresh, tinned and/or frozen. It's clever, and you can purchase the recipe alone, or get it free if you buy all the ingredients. The aim is to launch a revival in home cooking, striking a chord in a city where it's so easy to eat out. The shop, cleverly and stylishly designed, also sells a range of utensils and accessories. A contemporary idea, and there's even a counter selling cakes, coffee and sandwiches to take away or enjoy on the terrace. See website for other locations

MAÎTRE PHILIPPE ET FILLES

Emser Straße 42, Wilmersdorf
U-Bahn Hohenzollernplatz
Tel 30 8868 3610, www.maitrephilippe.de
Open 10am to 7pm,
Thursday until 8pm, Saturday until 2pm,
closed Sunday to Tuesday
CHEESE

As the doyen of a food store highly regarded by connoisseurs and supplier to the city's best restaurants, Philippe Causse is naturally an expert in his field. His fresh, matured French cheese is displayed in a decor echoing his native country, with Quinquina Bourin posters, photos of the Château de Chambord and a great wine selection. A must – and the prices are lower than at the KaDeWe department store.

MR. MINSCH

Yorckstraße 15, Kreuzberg
U-Bahn Möckernbrücke, Gneisenaustraße,
S-Bahn Yorckstraße
Tel 30 5266 4903, http://mr-minsch-torten.de
Open daily 10am to 6:30pm
CAKES

A patissier to the core, Andreas Minsch knew what he wanted to do from an early age. His shop, with its grey frontage and matching interior, is a bit of an oddity, a "sugarland" under glass with displays of

tarts, snacks and cakes that seem straight out of a disco video. The funky-trash collages on the walls don't help. What you can eat and enjoy here, sliced into individual pieces, is out of this world. The almond and apple tart is scrumptious, and the dark chocolate version is an intense and unique experience. The white-tiled space next to it looks like it's waiting to be decorated. In the meantime, when the weather's fine, take a table on the green bamboo terrace. Another oddity, on the pavement this time.

NOR – NOT ONLY RIESLING

Marheinekeplatz,
Schleiermacherstraße 25, Kreuzberg
U-Bahn Gneisenaustraße
Tel 30 6953 8866, www.not-only-riesling.de
Open noon to 10pm, Friday and Saturday
10am to midnight, closed Sunday
WINE MERCHANT, BAR

Not Only Riesling states its intentions clearly. The Rieslings here include one from Josten & Klein, strongly recommended. There's Bordeaux, too, and Burgundy, as well as wine from other small French, Austrian and Italian growers, and even a Kreuzberg pinot noir. You are encouraged to discover and taste in an uncluttered setting, where each bottle nestles in its own black-painted compartment. And all watched over by the colourful statue of a saint, escaped from a church. At the counter, by the light of the 1950s lamps, you can also try the little dishes of homemade appetizers – black pudding with apple, liver pâté – and then depart with a bottle of Berliner Brandstifter, a real grown-up drink. Open on weekdays until 10pm, NOR has the good taste to extend its hours to midnight on Saturdays and to have two different locations: this NOR, **NOR AM MAR** – Mar for Marheinekeplatz, with its celebrated, restored covered market – and a **NOR AM KAP** on Karl-August-Platz in Charlottenburg (Pestalozzistraße 85, tel 30 3470 9090).

ÖLMÜHLE AN DER HAVEL

Bergmannstraße 104, Kreuzberg
U-Bahn Mehringdamm
Tel 30 505 67 115, www.oelgenuss.de
Open daily 10am to 7pm

OILS AND SPICES

Berliners love everything that comes from the world's southern climes, from olive oil to peppers, spices and condiments. Sabine Stempfhuber and Frank Besingner more than meet this zesty yen with this new emporium packed with liquid, solid, grain, powder, and stick products, mixed with other foods to hybridise their flavours. Using mustard, linseed, sunflower, and hemp varieties, German regional oils are based on seeds or add in lemongrass as seasoning. They also sell salt of all kinds in jars, chocolate bars and Chocolain cocoa powder, Teanova teas and infusions, all elegantly packaged.

PAPER & TEA

Bleibtreustraße 4, Charlottenburg
S-Bahn Savignyplatz
Tel 30 555 798 071
www.paperandtea.com
Open 11am to 8pm, closed Sunday

TEA

His uncle was a tea trader, supplying luxury hotels, and he himself is a great traveller, admitting to an insatiable thirst for a well-brewed cup. Jens De Gruyter, the founder and artistic director of Paper & Tea, opened this tea store in late 2013, with an unusual decor by Fabian von Ferrari. Its packaging and Zen graphics have won prizes for this young company, including a Red Dot Design Award. Referring back to two historic Chinese inventions – paper and tea – P & T is brewing its own tradition: seeking out and inhaling the fragrance of green, white or black tea, using your nose as you would when creating a perfume. This cosmetological approach adds a whole new dimension to the concept, especially since the tea sold here is of such high quality, all sourced directly from the plantations where they are grown.

You'll also find contemporary accessories for making and serving tea, designed by Chinese and German artists. Don't miss the tasting sessions, a chance to experience the thirst-quenching power of green tea infused in cold water. **Other location:** Alte Schönhauser Straße 50, Mitte, tel 30 555 798 072

PAZIANAS OLIVENÖL

Senefelderstraße 4, Prenzlauer Berg
U-Bahn Eberswalderstraße
Tel 30 4404 9449, www.pazianas.de
Open noon to 8pm, Saturday 11am to 4pm, closed Sunday

OLIVE OIL

Themistokles Pazianas is Greek and owns olive groves in his home country, in the Peloponnese. He cold presses the olives to extract the oil and happily sells it in his simple little Berlin shop. A graphic designer in his previous life, Pazianas is a committed olive oil evangelist and his office contains bottles of olive oil from Sardinia and Umbria, as well as bulk supplies from Crete. In the space of ten years, Pazianas Olivenöl has become an essential part of the Berlin food scene. The owner is circumspect, though – no expansion plans in sight.

ROGACKI

Wilmersdorfer Straße 145–146, Charlottenburg
U-Bahn Bismarckstraße
Tel 30 343 8250, www.rogacki.de
Open 9am to 6pm, Thursday until 7pm, Friday 8am to 7pm, Saturday 8am to 4pm, closed Sunday

SMOKED FISH

Pay no attention to the acid green canopy, worthy of a service station or a university cafeteria. Nor to the building that would not look out of place north of Columbia in New York City. Since 1928, when it was founded, and 1932, when it opened at this address in Charlottenburg, Rogacki has been rated one of the best food shops in Berlin, even better than the

A TASTE OF BERLIN

From 1959 to 1960, on commission from *The Sunday Times*, Ian Fleming, creator of James Bond, wrote a series of articles on the world's thirteen most thrilling cities, including Macau, Las Vegas, Naples and Berlin. He started by using his nose: "Every capital city has its own smell. London's is fried fish and Player's cigarettes, Paris coffee, onions and Caporals, Moscow cheap eau de Cologne and sweat. Berlin smells of cigars and boiled cabbage." It's nothing like that today, apart from the tenacious aromas of *Bratwurst* sizzling on street corners. As it leaves its drab past behind it, Berlin is turning to sweeter things. To combat the cold, the dull grey skies, the overlong winters and the lack of sunshine, Berliners are eating more and more sugar. Always fond of their food, they take a more gourmet approach these days, enjoying cakes, chocolate, ice cream, pastries, toffee and other sweets. The city has never had so many patisseries and sweet shops, and very sophisticated ones, at that. Though Berliners like to start their day on a savoury note, with cold meat, sausage, liver pâté, eggs and herring, things get more sugary as the day goes on. For many, afternoon tea is sacred, with two cakes and a *krema* coffee or a cup of tea. By "cake" they mean a proper one, not a simple fruit tart, but a Viennese multi-layer cake, a heavy crumb cake or an enormous choux bun filled with whipped cream. Though *Arme Ritter*, a sort of bread pudding known as "poor knight", has almost disappeared, *Pfannkuchen* is hanging on well: known as a *Berliner* all over Germany and a Berliner bun by people who have never been there, it's a large doughnut filled with plum compote or raspberry jam, and rolled in icing sugar, proper comfort food for eating on the street when the cold wind is blowing. A popular treat, sold in bakeries, *Pfannkuchen* is a good barometer of the cost of living – its current price is €1.45. In addition to the *Alt Berliner Apfelkuchen* – apple cake – and the *Baumkuchen* invented by Buchwald – his patisserie still exists – Berliners also have their own typical cake, the *Berliner Luft*, or "Berlin air". It's really a dessert, made with egg yolks, white wine and whipped egg whites, hence the reference to air. The other super-popular, old-fashioned dessert coming back into fashion is *Rote Grütze*, or red groats, which is to Berliners what rice pudding or semolina is to Parisians: the best nursery food. Made with raspberries, blackcurrants, redcurrants and cherries in a thick purée and covered with vanilla custard or whipped cream, *Rote Grütze* has made it back onto the menus of leading restaurants.

KaDeWe food hall, mainly because of its extraordinary selection of smoked fish. Nowadays it is managed by Dietmar Rogacki, the founders' heir, and has a bistro alongside its international delicatessen – a great idea, as you can sample almost all the products sold inside.

ROSA CANINA

Markthalle Neun,
Eisenbahnstraße 42, Kreuzberg
U-Bahn Görlitzer Bahnhof
www.rosacanina.eu
Open noon to 6pm, Thursday until 10pm,
Friday and Saturday until 9:30pm,
closed Sunday and Monday

ORGANIC ICE CREAM

Since 2008, this organic ice-cream parlour run by Reimar Philipps has been successfully holding out against increasing numbers of competitors each year. Faced

THE ART OF STREET FOOD

Long before the term became globally recognizable, "street food", or something very similar, had been sold in Berlin for centuries. *Berliner Bouletten*, meatballs for dipping in hot mustard, closely followed by *Frikadelle* (large flattened meatballs), were stuffed into a *Semmelbrot* (roll) with *Senf* (mustard) or mayonnaise. Though rivalled, even outdone, by the *Döner Kebab* (said to have been invented in Berlin in 1971 by a certain Mehmet Aygün), the *Currywurst* is putting up valiant resistance as a chic popular snack, depending on who is preparing and serving it, and a source of great pride for Berliners. It is eaten burning hot, with dramatic effects on the eyes and nose from the first bite. The queen of sausages, *Currywurst* is, when made properly, a sausage made with curry-spiced meat and when made badly, a sausage drowning in curry sauce. With or without casing, mild or strong, the sausage is always sliced into small pieces and surrounded by *pommes* (fries) – pronounced "pommess" – all served on a small, white, crimped paper tray, with a wooden or plastic fork. Some stands are even fully organic, down to the sausage and sauce. To order a *Currywurst*, you need to remember this phrase: " Mit oder ohne?" Or "With or without?" Meaning sauce. To top it all, there's even a Currywurstmuseum, where you'll discover it has its own mascot, called Qwoo, and that in Berlin you can make a museum for anything. Small consolation: if you don't like endless curry, you can buy a fake *Currywurst* made of marzipan, the perfect piece of kitsch. To find the real thing without needing to follow your nose, Berliners recommend the following places:

CURRY 36 The mindboggling queues stretching along the pavement are an accurate indication of the quality of the *Currywurst* sold here. Popular with local nightclubbers, the gay community and bus and taxi drivers. Fantastic organic option. Mehringdamm 36, Kreuzberg, U-Bahn Mehringdamm, tel 30 25800 88336, www.curry36.de; Hardenbergplatz 9, Tiergarten, tel 30 3199 2992

CURRY 195 This is the first sausage stall to sell champagne, Dom Perignon, as a sparkling addition to your *Wurst*. The evening sees it full of actors, the newly rich, nightclubbers and locals. Kurfürstendamm 195, Charlottenburg, U-Bahn Uhlandstraße, tel 30 881 8942, www.bier-s.com

CURRY & CHILI Lively Wursterie serving ten levels of hotness, bringing more than a bit of spice to life. Invest in a case of Gaviscon before you go. Osloer Straße, corner of Prinzenallee, Wedding, U-Bahn Pankstraße, www.curry-chili.de

DEUTSCHES CURRYWURST MUSEUM Berlin boasts museums of every kind, including one devoted to Currywurst, an important local speciality. After a fun visit to the museum, stop off in the shop to buy a kitsch mascot that you can hang from your rear view mirror. Schützenstraße 70, Mitte, U-Bahn Stadtmitte, tel 30 8871 8647, www.currywurstmuseum.de

with a selection of over forty flavours, connoisseurs will naturally opt for the chocolate-nutmeg-cardamom, the raspberry-basil, the alcohol-free *moscow-mule*, or the mango-lassi. Open all year round inside the Markthalle Neu, Rosa Canina works from March to October at its other locations, including a new one in the Hufelandstraße, opposite the Jubel pastry shop, and at the Günter Beltzig, signalled by its pavement terrace furnished in 1970s yellow plastic. **Other locations:** Pasteurstraße 32, Prenzlauer Berg; Hufelandstraße 7, Prenzlauer Berg

SALON SUCRÉ
Görlitzer Straße 32a, Kreuzberg
U-Bahn Görlitzer Bahnhof
Tel 30 612 2713, www.salonsucre.de
Open 10am to 6pm,
pastry shop closed Monday to Thursday,
hair salon closed Sunday to Tuesday
PATISSERIE, CAFÉ, HAIRDRESSER
When it comes to breaking down barriers, Salon Sucré, the brainchild of Frenchman Éric Muller, is leading the pack. It shares space with the hairdressing salon owned by his wife, Katia Barcellos, the reason for the many fine wall mirrors, ideal for inspecting your hairstyle from every angle. A shared arrangement that makes perfect sense once you make the hair/beauty/cakes connection. Of course, there's no chance of confusing a chignon with a meringue, and no one leaves here with a hairstyle like a millefeuille pastry, Muller's speciality, traditionally known in Berlin as a Napoleon. Originally from Strasbourg, Muller came to Berlin over fifteen years ago, and since then he has achieved hidden-treasure status in pastries, with fans crossing the city for his éclairs, croissants and lemon tarts, not to mention his truly delicious seasonal fruit tarts.

SAWADE
Hackeschen Höfe, Hof II,
Rosenthaler Straße 40–41, Mitte
U-Bahn Weinmeisterstraße
S-Bahn Hackescher Markt
Tel 30 9700 5363, www.sawade.berlin
Open 11am to 7pm, closed Sunday
CHOCOLATE MAKER
Those with long(ish) memories might remember the Sawade Feine Pralinen sweet shop in Grunewald, which was in business forty years. Located on Hohenzollerndamm, near Wiener Conditorei, it had to close when the lease expired. The original company's long history began in 1880 with Ladislaus Maximilianus Ziemkiewicz (ennobled in the late 19th century) when Sawade had its confectionery store on Unter den Linden. Defying all its setbacks, the business has bounced back with a new shop selling chocolates, truffles and marzipan in the Hackeschen Höfe, a tourist favourite. It has joined other venerable Berlin stores there, among them Askania watches and the Mühle barbershop. Designed by BFS Design (Stefan Flachsbarth and Michael Schultz), the decor has a real flavour of delicious past times and the beautiful chocolate boxes and tins are collector's items.

SÜSSKRAMDEALER
Varziner Straße 4, Friedenau
S-Bahn and U-Bahn Bundesplatz
Tel 30 8507 7797
www.suesskramdealer.de
Open 8am to 7pm, Saturday
and Sunday 10am to 6pm
CONFECTIONERY, COFFEE
Marlene Dietrich lived not far from here, in Bundesallee. Hildegard Knef grew up close by and mentions in her memoirs the tobacconists Loeser & Wolff, the original, historic, 1906 shop. The wood panelling and mahogany fittings are still here, with the original triangular layout, though the cigars, tobacco and snuff have been replaced by other addictions. Martin Hesse has opened a nostalgic sweetshop here,

with a small café alongside decorated in sugar almond white-pink-blue and pastel crepe-paper touches. You'll still find cigarettes here, but now they are chocolate ones, with chocolate bars and pralines sold loose or displayed in old cigar box cases, a link with the shop's history. The fan-shaped terrace on the little square outside catches the early morning sun.

WALD KÖNIGSBERGER MARZIPAN

Pestalozzistraße 54a, Charlottenburg
U-Bahn Sophie-Charlotte-Platz
Tel 30 323 8254
www.wald-koenigsberger-marzipan.com
Open10am to 6:30pm, Saturday until
3:30pm, closed Sunday
MARZIPAN

This historic store has a single speciality: marzipan. It was opened in 1947 by Paul and Irmgard Wald, and is now run by their granddaughter Gina Massey. *Königsberger Marzipan* is light and creamy, with a taste that is subtly bitter and not overly sweet. Gina's brother-in-law Ralf Bentlin makes them in the traditional form of braids (plain), hearts with fruit fillings or balls powdered with bitter cocoa. Fillings include pineapple, kiwi, raisin, apricot and hazelnut. There's even a sugar-free version, an unprecedented feat for this type of confection. You can order two days in advance, even by email, but your order should be eaten quickly – which is no problem at all. Among the house's loyal customers, count the sultan of Oman.

WEICHARDT BROT

Mehlitzstraße 7, Wilmersdorf
U-Bahn Blissestraße, Berliner Straße
Tel 30 873 8099, www.weichardt.de
Open 7:30am to 6:30pm,
Saturday until 2pm, closed Sunday
ORGANIC BREAD AND BISCUITS
Situated in the extreme south of Wilmersdorf, not far from the intersection of Berliner Straße and Uhlandstraße, this local bakery sells the best bread to be found for miles around. Customers include some of the biggest chefs and restaurants in Berlin. Biodynamic grain, certified by Demeter, is used, and the flour is milled in neighbouring premises visible from the street. In the shop, everything sells like hot cakes, even the large loaves with sesame seeds or nuts. Fresh and moist, the fruit pastries, cookies and doughnuts can't possibly leave you indifferent. In fact, the business has been so successful that other outlets have opened in Charlottenburg.
See website for other locations

ZEIT FÜR BROT

Konstanzer Straße 1, Charlottenburg
U-Bahn Adenauer Platz
Tel 30 8870 2424, www.zeitfuerbrot.com
Open 7am to 8pm, Saturday from 8am,
Sunday 8am to 6pm
BAKERY
Opened in Mitte just before Easter 2012, the first Zeit für Brot bakery was packed out right from the first day. And it's been full ever since. Encouraged by this, the bakery has opened a second store, moving further west to Charlottenburg. It's a huge place, with the same decor and specialities. More space, more tables and the same great organic quality. The men responsible for this runaway success are Dirk Steiger, who gave up a career in the film industry, and his associate Björn Schwind. Schwind is from Frankfurt where he ran a family bakery that used recipes handed down over several generations, including a traditional round wholemeal loaf weighing four kilos that keeps beautifully. As well as its excellent bread, certified organic and baked on the premises, Zeit für Brot offers some typical bakery fare with plum or apple cake, pretzels, brioches and rolls either plain or with tasty fillings. Its takeaway breakfast, served every morning, consists of a cappuccino and a choice of rolls packed for you in a paper carrier.

COOKING WITH BARRIE KOSKY

Barrie Kosky makes no secret of the fact that he can't cook.
In fact, he says he's a culinary disaster. He can't even cut a pepper
while downing a glass of white wine the way they do in films.

I can't even make the chicken soup I talk about in my book On Ecstasy.
*I just don't have the patience. And it doesn't relax me. But I love
to eat when someone else cooks for me. I'm a great guest when it comes
to sharing and friendship around a table. But I'm not at all fond of
German cooking, which I find too meat-heavy. As for Wurst becoming
a whole concept? I love everything in Germany except for its cuisine
and its humour, which doesn't have the irony or the sense of the surreal
of English, French or Russian humour. I'm a greedy guts, so I love cakes,
but I try to hold back. I have to watch my weight and my health.
So I just walk on as if I hadn't seen them.*

BARS, CAFÉS AND TEAROOMS

BREAKFAST TO DRINKS ON A TERRACE: TAKING A BREAK IN THE CITY

There's a bar for every Berliner, goes the old quip. And now it's almost true. There are ten thousand or so cafés, coffee shops, bars, pubs, taverns, brasseries and ice-cream parlours open for business in the city. You can find one on almost every street corner, as well as in museums, hotels, cinemas, concept stores, delis and *Imbissstuben*, as well as by lakes, rivers and canals. From *Stehcafe*, where you literally stand and gobble a quick snack, to the stylish new joints in the west of the city, cafés are a religion in Berlin. People spend lots of time in them with their laptop, or (more acceptably) their dog, or even a good book.

Most of Berlin's cafés serve breakfast all morning and provide a hot lunch *du jour* or even a full *Mittagsmenü*, followed in the afternoon by pastries, though the timetable is fairly elastic. The same goes for café-cake shops, where you can have breakfast, eat savoury dishes and snacks, and buy takeaways. People very rarely eat at the bar; the custom here is to be waited on at a table. And everyone pays their share. The quest for the best café for Berliners is rather like searching for the best gourmet restaurant.

1900 CAFÉ BISTRO

Knesebeckstraße 76, Charlottenburg
S-Bahn Savignyplatz
Tel 30 8871 5871
www.facebook.com/1900cafebistro/
CAFÉ

Stuffed to the gunwales with furniture, ornaments, lamps and mismatched place mats, the 1900 offers an unexpected interlude in the middle of the afternoon, when you get that uncontrollable urge for a spot of old-fashioned tart stuffed with rhubarb, plums, apples, red berries and brown sugar. They come homemade here, generous-sized, appetizing and delicious, and served by smiling young women who have replaced the moustachioed biker who was yesterday's waiter. They've kept everything as it was: grandma's dinner service is still (intentionally) mismatched and chipped as part of the scenery. In winter, eat your crumbles and strudels with an accompanying chamber-pot-sized bowl of ginger, mint and fresh fruit brew. The savoury odds and ends at lunch segue into an afternoon snack, and there's a flowery chalet-style mini-terrace for sun lovers.

ALPENSTUECKLE

Ludwigkirchstraße 3, Wilmersdorf
U-Bahn Uhlandstraße, Spichernstraße
Tel 30 8892 2255
www.alpenstueck.de
CAFÉ AND DELI

As well as taking over part of Schröderstraße in Mitte with her restaurant, café and bakery, Iris Schmied made her way to the west of the city to see whether the grass was greener, and opened this little piece of her Alpenstueck as an ideal café-deli-cum-refreshment-stand for breakfast and lunch on the go without asking (too) many questions. Everything is wholesome and tasty, from the elaborate sandwiches to the homemade soups.

BAR 203

Panoramastraße 1a, Mitte
S-Bahn and U-Bahn Alexanderplatz
Tel 30 247 575 875
www.tv-turm.de
PANORAMIC BAR

This famous bar is perched 203 metres above the city near the bottom of the "ball" on the Fernsehturm, or TV tower, which was erected in 1969 and has flashed interminably through Berlin's nights ever since. The tower was built as "a monument to the glory of socialist builders". The dismay of West Berliners at the construction of the tower turned to amusement when it transpired that sunshine reflecting off the globe formed a cross that was visible from their half of the city. The Bar 203 – formerly the Telecafé, where years ago party animals would absorb much-needed calories during a dizzying breakfast – shares the site with a panoramic restaurant on the floor above. To get there, you take a hair-raising lift, although you should be warned that the queues at the foot of the tower can be long (visitors to the restaurant would be advised to get a VIP ticket). At the circular bar, you order a recuperative Berlini made with white plum brandy, which you sip while you take in the 360° panoramic view. Intoxicating and sobering all in one.

BAR AM STEINPLATZ

Hotel am Steinplatz, Steinplatz 4, Charlottenburg
U-Bahn Ernst-Reuter-Platz
S-Bahn Savignyplatz
Tel 30 55 44 44 6054
www.hotelsteinplatz.com
CHIC BAR, CREATIVE DRINKS

Creative and something of a rebel, Christian Gentemann manages the bar in this five-star hotel in his own distinctive way. He's banned gin from its shelves, preferring to steer his customers towards (re)discovering the taste of German juniper schnapps. He's also worked with the Berlin brewery Schoppe Bräu to develop two new craft beers: August Pils and Endell Ale. Superb! It might seem a little cheeky in this ultra-bourgeois setting, but it's the perfect accompaniment to the reopening of the Am Steinplatz restaurant helmed by chef Nicholas Hahn, who has also developed the delectable menu served in the bar. To top it off, the Bar am Steinplatz won the Bar of the Year award.

BAR GRÀCIA

Göhrener Straße 5, Prenzlauer Berg
U-Bahn Eberswalderstraße
Tel 30 224 53 943
www.bargracia.de
TAPAS CATALANS
Barcelona-born Berlin actor Daniel Brühl (*Goodbye Lenin*, *The Lady in Gold*, *Alone in Berlin*, etc.) can claim a dash of *Hispanidad* as his mother is Spanish. Like Javier Bardem, he plays another role: that of restaurant owner. Partnering with Atilano González, he already has the Bar Raval, and he opened this Bar Gràcia in 2017. Tapas again, but this time more elaborate and creative so you can nibble them in good company. Not gourmet, but a great atmosphere. Book ahead via the annoying digital system.

BENEDICT

Max Brown Hotel,
Uhlandstraße 49, Wilmersdorf
U-Bahn Uhlandstraße, Hohenzollernplatz
Tel 30 9940 40997
www.benedict-breakfast.de
BREAKFAST
Four young men, Yair Kindler, Itay Pshigoda, Shay Kahana and Guy Osadon, all from Israel, launched this concept in Tel Aviv in 2006 with great success. They have now brought it to Berlin. Their eggs Benedict is now a must for any breakfast worthy of the name. Their establishment can be found in all the Max Brown hotels – here in Berlin and also in Amsterdam, with plans for more – and the hotel's guests can enjoy its breakfasts (included in the room price) at any time of day. With plenty

of space to welcome non-guests, who have made it an instant Instagram hot-spot, Benedict offers an all-day, all night "breakfast break". Table or counter, chairs or bar stools, on your own or in a group, there's good service at any time. On the menu: eggs in every form, cooked to order, with special emphasis on that New York classic, eggs Benedict, washed down with a mandatory mimosa cocktail or a coffee. Or opt for something different with a Texan breakfast or a toasted ham and cheese sandwich – with an egg – or perhaps some shakshuka, fresh bagels with avocado, pancakes and a wide choice of yoghurts, cereals, fresh fruits and more. Fresh from the ovens of the bakery counter, the bread is to die for. Packed, noisy, a mix of ages and style, this place is not to be missed.

BEUSTER BAR

Weserstraße 32, Neukölln
U-Bahn Rathaus Neukölln
Tel 30 4195 9780
www.beusterbar.com
BISTRO BAR
This section of Weserstraße has undergone a significant renovation in the past few years, with a third-wave coffee bar and snazzy concept store with exposed brick walls on every block. Opened in the summer of 2015 in a former physiotherapist's, Beuster Bar now sits in the middle of this neighbourhood, and represents something of a hub for the *Kiez*, where young professionals rub shoulders with out-of-towners hoping to enjoy some of the much-hyped Neukölln hipster lifestyle. And they won't be disappointed with what's on offer: the cocktails are the best in the neighbourhood and the small but refined food menu offers excellent French-German brasserie fare, such as *steak frites* and lightly grilled octopus with chickpea purée. With its green-tiled walls, wooden bar stools and cosy candles, this is a spot for intimate chats that go on for hours.

CAFE AM NEUEN SEE

Lichtensteinallee 2, Tiergarten
S-Bahn and U-Bahn Zoologischer Garten
Tel 30 2544 9300
www.cafe-am-neuen-see.de

BIERGARTEN

Berlin's largest beer garden (1,500 seats) is located in the heart of the Tiergarten by the very picturesque Neuer See. It combines outdoor friendliness with Bavarian-style wooden benches, stylish chic with white chairs and candle jars, and gourmet elegance with grilled specialities in a chalet decor, perfect for cold, gloomy days. Like a number of other establishments in town, including the sophisticated Borchardt brasserie and the Grosz on the Ku'damm, this tavern is run by the enterprising Roland Mary. The excellent Bavarian beer will quench your thirst when the heat of the day turns the city into a desert. The menu is rather limited, but the pizzas are good (indeed, beer and pizza seems to be the default combination for many). The staff can get a little overwhelmed on days when there are large numbers of visitors. After or before kicking back here, you can rent a rowing boat for a gentle outing on the waters of the lake. The Café am Neuen See is also within walking distance of the Das Stue design hotel.

CAFÉ FLEURY

Weinbergsweg 20, Mitte
U-Bahn Rosenthaler Platz
Tel 30 4403 4144
www.facebook.com/Café-
Fleury-108988229123298/

FRENCH CAFÉ AND DELI

This French café next door to the Gorki Park Café and the Gorky Apartments, has the charm of an old-fashioned grocery and offers eat-in or takeaway meals with a menu of soups, daily specials, homemade cakes, coffee, beer and breakfast. Consciously targeting women, it fits in with the provincial feel of the Weinbergsweg, which leads to the Weinbergsweg Park. The café is thus isolated from the din of the rowdy Rosenthaler Platz and its mega-cafés such as the St Oberholz, which should now be strenuously avoided.

CAFÉ IM LITERATURHAUS

Fasanenstraße 23, Wilmersdorf
U-Bahn Kurfürstendamm, Uhlandstraße
Tel 30 882 5414
www.literaturhaus-berlin.de

TRADITION

This magnificent neo-Renaissance villa, a stone's throw from the Ku'damm in the plushest street in Berlin, was built in 1889. It is part of the Haus Grisebach, which is also home to the **KÄTHE-KOLLWITZ-MUSEUM**. In the past, it has been a hostel for foreign students (where philosopher and essayist Emile Cioran once lodged), a soup kitchen, a brothel and a discotheque, before becoming the **LITERATURHAUS** in 1986. It is open to the public and houses a bookshop that sells old postcards of Berlin and books published by Kohlhaas & Co., whose offices are on the first floor. There is also a café and a restaurant beneath the large glass roof of the conservatory. In the summer, the restaurant moves into the garden, complete with its fountain. Reservations must be made in advance to lunch in this haven of peace. The café serves bistro-type fare and classic, comforting pastries. This is one of the most charming addresses in the west of the city.

CAFÉ KREDENZ

Kantstraße 81, Charlottenburg
U-Bahn Sophie-Charlotte-Platz
Tel 30 3270 4295
www.kredenz-cafe.de

TEAROOM

Located near the antiques shops on Suarezstraße, this café seems to have hoovered up all the available porcelain flowers and odds and ends of furnishings that remind one of Aunt Ursula's lounge. The mishmash of upholstered seats, charming old furniture, display cases full of silverware, framed napkins on the walls and fresh flowers make you think of doll's houses and tea parties in the nursery. Go for the excellent pastries and delicious cappuccino, served in delicately old-fashioned crockery. It all looks like (but isn't) something from an ancient dresser. Nicely done.

CAFÉ LINNEN

Eberswalder Straße 35, Prenzlauer Berg
U-Bahn Eberswalder Straße
Tel 30 4737 2440, www.linnenberlin.com
CAFÉ, HOTEL

Formerly called Liebling, as was the six-room boarding house upstairs, the Linnen has a number of owners, including Toni, a part-time DJ. It's located close to the Mauerpark and its Sunday flea market, and is decorated in an ingenious vintage-meets-contemporary style. It serves the best breakfast in the neighbourhood, and when the sun shines, the café spills out onto the pavement.

CAFÉ SAROTTI-HÖFE

Mehringdamm 57, Kreuzberg
U-Bahn Mehringdamm
Tel 30 6003 1680
www.hotel-sarottihoefe.de
CAFÉ, CONFECTIONERY

The story begins in 1852 when a high-class confectioner's shop named Felix & Sarotti opened on Friedrichstraße. A few years later, wealthy Berlin pastry cook Hugo Hoffmann bought the business. It shortened its name to Sarotti and went industrial, and by the early 20th century the Sarotti chocolate factory, established in 1882 on the edge of Belle-Alliance-Straße (renamed Mehringdamm in 1888), was the biggest in the world. Swiss group Nestlé bought the whole sprawling concern in 1929 and swallowed it lock, stock and barrel. Then, miraculously, the brand was resuscitated in 1998, when it was sold to German chocolate-maker Stollwerk, the inventor of the "dark chocolate bar for gentlemen". Like so many other relics of Berlin's industrial past, the warren of interlinked factory yards still had its old

name over the door, so a few years ago, when a small, respectable three-star hotel opened there with a café on the ground floor, it naturally named itself Sarotti. Dripping with moulded plasterwork, the decor looks as good to eat as the rich array of cakes on show, and the café's laid-back atmosphere makes it popular with the gay community. Hotel guests have the leisure of taking breakfast here until 11am.

CAFÉ STRAUSS

Bergmannstraße 42, Kreuzberg
U-Bahn Südstern
Tel 30 6956 4453
www.cafestraussberlin.de
CEMETERY CAFÉ

Using deconsecrated churches – and sometimes more ungodly buildings – as art galleries is now commonplace. But here is the only bar in the world to open in a former chapel of rest – that of the distinctly lively Friedrichswerdersche ecumenical cemetery. Last (unholy) orders, anyone? Under the red-brick arches and at the bucolic garden tables outside, the Café Strauss plays a different kind of waltz than "Wine, Women and Song". Yet queen of style Angelika Taschen did in fact celebrate one of her birthdays here, come to think of it.

CHOKOCAFÉ

Bleibtreustraße 15/16, Charlottenburg
S-Bahn Savignyplatz
Tel 30 6092 7872, www.chokocafe.de
COFFEE, ICE CREAM PARLOUR

Tiny and very red, just like the famous riding hood, the Chokocafé is located on the ground floor of a splendid neo-Renaissance residential building, with an entrance flanked by a toy-like bulb-topped sentry box. Outside on the granite pavement, there are three fair-weather tables sheltered by crimson parasols that add a dash of colour to this mini coffee and ice-cream parlour. At the rear, there's an equally minute club lounge with an artificial fireplace – a doll's waiting room perhaps. Fun.

COFFEE DRINK
YOUR MONKEY

Savignyplatz 11, Charlottenburg

S-Bahn Savignyplatz

COFFEE JOINT

Opened in spring 2017 near the S-Bahn
Bogen (arches), this new café comes from
the same team that cleaned up with the
vegan-healthy What Do You Fancy Love?
restaurant chain. Here they've successfully
rehabbed a former cafeteria with white
and pastel blue walls and Fermob furniture,
giving it a funky, dated decor to go with the
smiling welcome. Linked to the Schuhtick
shoes store CDYM, this new concept may
rapidly spread all over the city. Meanwhile,
the coffee is perfectly respectable. Terrace.

CONCIERGE COFFEE

Paul Lincke Ufer 39–40, Kreuzberg

U-Bahn Kottbusser Tor, Schönleinstraße

Tel 0176 84 19 59 15

www.facebook.com/ConciergeCoffee

COFFEE CULTURE

Coffee mania is sweeping Berlin, and you
don't need a vast space to make a quality
filter coffee. Namy and Benjamin are
seasoned baristas who worked at Bonanza
Coffee Heroes in Prenzlaeur Berg. Drinks
can be consumed inside or outside on the
small terrace on sunny days, taken away.
Each cup comes with comething to nibble.

DIE FISCHERHÜTTE
AM SCHLACHTENSEE

Fischerhüttenstraße 136, Steglitz-Zehlendorf,

10km south-west of the city centre

U-Bahn Alfred-Grenander-Platz

Tel 30 8049 8310

www.fischerhuette-berlin.de

LAKESIDE BIERGARTEN AND CAFÉ

The Schlachtensee in the Grunewald is
reputed to be the cleanest lake in Berlin.

In summer, Berliners are happy to swim
and cool off here, while in spring you can
see divers in coveralls, or stray sea lions.
This "Fisherman's Hut" has been a historic
monument here since the mid-18th
century. Following its restoration in 2005,
it provides customers with a combination
of café, Biergarten, wine bar, restaurant,
inn and Sunday brunch spot, opening every
day from 9am. Something for any hour,
mood or weather.

ELF

Paul-Robeson-Straße 11, Prenzlauer Berg

S-Bahn Schönhauser Allee,

Bornholmer Straße

Tel 30 23928 488, www.elfcafe.de

BREAKFAST

Here we are on the edge of the Arnimplatz,
a large flowery park north of Prenzlauer
Berg. Go any further north and you're
in Pankow. The street is named after the
famous black American singer and actor
Paul Robeson, the unforgettable performer
of the *Old Man River* number from the
musical *Show Boat*. A defender of human
rights, committed abolitionist, communist
sympathizer and victim of McCarthyism,
Robeson was a true hero in the Soviet
Union, where he was often an official guest.
This probably explains why this corner
of Prenzlauer Berg, untouched by the
trend for cool gentrification, still feels
as if the Wall has only just come down.
Note the old Wartburgs and Volvos parked
on the cobbled street. The Elf is the only
café around here, and its regulars are
on their guard against any foreign invasion.
The interior is large and cosy, and quickly
spreads outside when the weather
permits. The prices are so reasonable and
the service so friendly that checking out
the breakfast menu is a real pleasure. The

*"Anyone can feel at home in this city . . . The word normal
is extremely broadly defined in Berlin."* Jakob Hein,
Gebrauchsanweisung für Berlin, 2006

THE GRAND HISTORIC CAFÉ

CAFÉ EINSTEIN STAMMHAUS

In the middle of the 19th century, Berlin, like Vienna, became was one of the leading European capitals of cafés, those humble yet worldly hangouts for the intelligentsia, artists and politicians. The city's two focal points – Unter den Linden to the east and the Ku'damm to the west – teemed with taverns and *Kaffeehäuser* equipped with lounges, terraces and extensions of all kinds. They included the Romanisches Café, the Café des Westens, the Café Bauer and the Kranzler, originally located on the corner of Friedrichstraße and moved after the war to the Ku'damm in a rotating carousel-cum-pavilion that became a tourist trap and is now immobilized. A lot of the great cafés between Potsdamer Platz and Unter den Linden were destroyed by Allied bombing and rebuilt in the West after the city was split in two. But that was not the case for the Café Einstein, even though there was one on Unter den Linden in the 1920s. This famous and legendary café only dates back to 1978, opening on 21st May in a house that was steeped in history. The neo-Renaissance villa in which it is housed survived the air raids, and thus provides a glimpse of what the Kurfürstenstraße was like before the war, lined with elegant mansions where wealthy Berliners and film people used to live. Built in 1878 by architect Karl Schwatlo, the Villa Rossmann first bore the name of its owner, but was later bought by the banker Blumenfeld, who set up a private gambling den there before it was confiscated by the Nazi regime and "offered" by Goebbels to his mistress, the actress Henny Porten, the brightest star in the firmament of German silent and talking pictures, who lived there for two years from 1928 and 1930. People say that Porten returned to live and die there in 1960, but the jury is still out on that one. The myth of the Café Einstein, named after the opera *Einstein on the Beach* created by Bob Wilson and Philip Glass in 1976, lives on. Now a sanctuary of the spirit of Berlin, it featured the DAAD art gallery on the first floor, which was inaugurated by Ben and has hosted shows by Michelangelo Pistoletto, Daniel Spoerri and Damien Hirst. When it closed, it was replaced by the LEBENSSTERN. The scruffy mouldings, gilt and mirrors and decrepit panelling in the large dining room where there was once an illegal casino have seen the likes Rainer Werner Fassbinder, Jean Paul Gaultier, Vivienne Westwood, David Bowie and Quentin Tarantino, who turned some scenes of *Inglourious Basterds* here. You can sit on the Thonet chairs at a pink marble table, where a white-aproned waiter will serve you a delicious strudel. The place is busy throughout the day, a number of people reading the papers while waiting for an appointment. The best tables are perhaps those near the large windows overlooking the garden; the tables to the right as you go in, in the old library with its deep red moleskin banquettes, always seem to be reserved, even when there's nobody there. The Einstein is something of a tourist trap, but this isn't obvious. It is currently run by Philipp Hasse-Pratje. The Café Einstein's parent company has now opened several offshoots in the city (including one on Unter den Linden), as well as in other German cities. Kurfürstenstraße 58, Tiergarten, U-Bahn Nollendorfplatz, tel 263 91918, www.cafeeinstein.com

house also serves daily specials, toasted dishes, ciabatta, salads, sandwiches and soups, and litres of beer and coffee.

ESPRESSOBAR

Mommsenstraße 4, Charlottenburg
S-Bahn Savignyplatz
POCKET CAFÉ

As prices per square metre are rising in leaps and bounds in Berlin, midget eateries are starting to become fashionable in Charlottenburg, as this Espressobar successfully proves. The Espressobar testifies to its owners' passion for French pâtisserie. The lemon meringue pie, chocolate pecan or raspberry pies, and absolutely delicious orange *financiers* are among the best pastries in the city. The coffee is also excellent and can be savoured while perched on a stool, or outside if one of the three coloured tables is free.

GROSZ

Kurfürstendamm 193–194, Charlottenburg
U-Bahn Uhlandstraße
Tel 30 652 142 199
www.grosz-berlin.de
GRAND CAFÉ

Built in 1911 for Prince Ernest Augustus of Hanover, Duke of Cumberland, by the architect Robert Leibnitz, who had just completed the Hotel Adlon, the Haus Cumberland was converted into a 700-room luxury hotel after the First World War, before being converted into a government office building. After 1945, the walls remained intact and for a long time played host to Berlin's financial institutions. Used as a backdrop for many films, including *The Bourne Identity* with Matt Damon, the Cumberland has restored its own identity by remaining true to the original, with coffered panelling, chandeliers and balustrades. It now houses, among others, the Grosz café and restaurant, another outpost of the small gastro-empire built by Roland Mary, owner of the Borchardt. It operates throughout the day, especially at breakfast time, when

it serves the sort of French-style *Frühstück* they no longer serve in France. The pastries and bread come from the L'Oui bakery next door, which also supplies the café's puff pastry. All day long, the upholstered lounges with their chandeliers positioned at the entrance welcome drinkers and newspaper readers. Already a classic.

HAMMERS WEINKOSTBAR

Körtestraße 20, Kreuzberg
U-Bahn Südstern
Tel 30 6981 8677
www.hammers-wein.de
WINE BAR, DELI

Having cut his teeth at a number of well-known restaurants, including the Rutz, Jürgen Hammer has settled down in an old butcher's shop whose original neon "Fleischerei" sign still blinks away on the yellow-tiled storefront. Outside, a few garden tables under a red awning; inside, three pedestal tables and a counter piled high with cheese, charcuterie and other delicious treats to take out or enjoy on the spot, washed down with a glass of good wine. For Hammer is above all a sommelier who knows his field inside out. He also loves to shoot the breeze, so expect to find out all about the best new restaurants and food stores locally and across the city. The private apartment at the back of the shop is also used for wine tastings, by invitation.

JOSEPH ROTH DIELE

Potsdamer Straße 75, Tiergarten
U-Bahn Kurfürstenstraße
Tel 30 2636 9884
www.joseph-roth-diele.de
AUTHENTIC BERLIN

By running his quotes around the mouldings, this red-and-white bar-restaurant pays tribute to Joseph Roth, author of *The Radetzky March* and *The Legend of the Holy Drinker*, "who became a journalist out of despair", and who lived in the neighbourhood. Journalists from the nearby *Tagesspiegel* used to keep themselves going on the snacks and daily specials washed down with beer and spirits. Now that the editorial office has moved, they have been replaced by gallery owners and artists and the people working at Murkudis, which has taken over part of the huge building. But there are still old regulars, especially in the evening after the show at the Wintergarten Variété just opposite or from the Philharmonie further away, when they pack in under the huge Moroccan lantern. On the right as you go out, there's an Ave Maria religious trinkets shop: Roth would turn in his grave.

KRANZLER/THE BARN

Kurfürstendamm 18-19, corner of
Joachimsthaler Straße, Tiergarten
U-Bahn Kurfürstendamm
S-Bahn Zoologischer Garten
Tel 030 5527 8229
www.thebarn.de
PANORAMIC CAFÉ

First opened on Unter den Linden in 1825, the Viennese Kranzler café split in two in 1932 with a branch on Ku'damm. Post-1945, both were in ruins and the West Berlin café was the only one rebuilt. Overlooking the Ku'damm Eck, the vast, flashy junction with Times Square ambitions, now redefined by the city's new confidence, the Kranzler is a curiosity, a typical 1950s frivolity. Designed by the architect Hanns Dustmann, it opened in 1957, the year of the Interbau. Refurbished in 2000, it consists of a huge terrace and a red and white striped awning topping a circular building that looks as if it rotates, but doesn't. An optical illusion. Once popular with blue-rinsed ladies clutching handbags, the Kranzler had resisted all change to the point where it became irredeemably tacky. Now gutted and stripped, its fine woodwork has been exposed by Stefan Flachsbarth and Michael Schultz of interiors specialists BFS Design. It is run by Ralf Müller, who was the co-founder with Andreas Poulakidas of The Barn, coffee roasters

in Prenzlauer Berg, and one of the best in Berlin. Sheltered by the famous red and white striped awnings, the panoramic views extend to the outside with a circular terrace and gallery overlooking the Chicago-style architecture of the Swissotel and Sofitel. The huge letters of the neon KRANZLER sign are still in place on the roof. As well as coffee, it serves savoury snacks and Mast Brothers chocolates, and in the event of coffee overload, there's tea available at **PAPER & TEA** (www.paperandtea.de). Eat in or to go, seven days a week. Direct access by lift from street level (the courtyard) or up the stairs from the Superdry store below. See website for other locations

LE BON

Boppstraße 1, Kreuzberg
U-Bahn Schönleinstraße
Tel 30 6342 0794
www.lebon-berlin.com
À la carte €40
Closed for dinner on Sunday and
all day Monday
GERMAN NOUVELLE CUISINE

No, nothing to do with Simon and Yasmin Le Bon. Johanna Schellenbergian chose this name simply because she thought it sounded neat to use French for a new German restaurant. But all that has changed now the place has turned into a breakfast spot. And as Le Bon already worked in café-Frühstück mode during the day, it's all been a smooth transition. At the end of the street on the right on the Kottbusser Damm, you'll find the **MOVIEMENTO** (Kottbusser Damm 22, Kreuzberg, tel 30 6924785), the oldest cinema in the country, in operation since 1907. You're in the "Kreuzkölln" district here, at the frontier between Kreuzberg and Neukölln, where things are buzzing.

LUBITSCH

Bleibtreustraße 47, Charlottenburg
S-Bahn Savignyplatz
Tel 30 886 26 660
www.lubitsch-restaurant.de
BREAKFAST

The name obviously references the famous
Berlin film director Ernst Lubitsch, who
began his career at the Babelsberg studios
before emigrating to Hollywood in 1923.
But he probably didn't live around here.
This classic Charlottenburg café and
brasserie has made a powerful comeback.
From morning until 3pm, they serve
a splendid Berlin *Frühstück*, as well as
an attractive lunch menu based on hearty
German specialties. The clientele is
an elegant mix of regulars, politicians
and local shop-owners.

MANZINI

Ludwigkirchstraße 11, Wilmersdorf
U-Bahn Uhlandstraße, Spichernstraße
Tel 30 885 7820
www.manzini.de
MINI-BRASSERIE

An attractive, nostalgic bistro in the
heart of the Wilmersdorf artists' colony,
Manzini is a classic address frequented
by contemporary artists, actors and writers.
After a period of expansion, including
a new branch on the Winterfeldtplatz,
Manzini has now refocused its attention
on its original address, much to the delight
of regulars. Breakfast is a good time to go
there, but you can dine late into the evening
on a few well-cooked bits and bobs,
including a *Wiener Schnitzel* that is more
than acceptable.

MEIEREI

Kollwitzstraße 42, Prenzlauer Berg
U-Bahn Senefelderplatz
Tel 30 9212 9573
www.meierei.net
DELI, ALPINE BAR

When the new occupants of this old shop
in Prenzlauer Berg were refurbishing
the premises, they uncovered remains of
frescoes of mountains by Paul Wille dating
from 1905, a vestige of the creamery that
had occupied the premises for more than
a century. This was a boon and a blessing.
Meierei is a mountain outpost where you
can find canned goods, wool blankets,
jars, Ragusa chocolate bars and a counter
full of cold meats and cheeses cut to take
away or eat on the spot. You can also
sit down any time for a buttered pretzel,
a *speck* sandwich, a plate of goulash, or
a *Weißwurst* in its broth. It opens at 7:30am
for breakfast, or a bowl of Ovaltine.
Outside, the massive wooden table with
benches and smaller tables with orange
garden chairs offers a perfect vantage point
on sunny days.

MEIN HAUS AM SEE

Brunnenstraße 197–198, Mitte
U-Bahn Rosenthaler Platz
Tel 30 2388 3561 or 163 555 8033
www.mein-haus-am-see.club
POPULAR BAR

In the early afternoon, when the area's
residents are all still asleep, this fairly huge
space looks something like a giant
Czech furniture showroom after a nuclear
holocaust. The pictures pencilled on the
walls remind you of the mural drawings in
the subterranean city below Naples during
the Second World War. Come nightfall,
it all vanishes, swallowed up by the hordes

*"Everyone who came to Berlin . . . came to make or find themselves
in some way or other, their own creation changing the place
itself, making them a part of it, and it a part of them, becoming
Berliners."* **Rory MacLean,** *Imagine a City,* **2014**

of people clustered around the tables, and by all the music, noise, and comings and goings. The stage at the back of the room is also taken by storm, since it's a strategic vantage point. It's hard to tell who is serving and who is being served, and nobody much cares. What matters is to look and act like a regular, a permanent fixture. One question remains, however: does this endearingly beat-up bar take its name from "Haus am See", the song by Peter Fox, lead singer of the Berlin band Seeed, which features on his solo album *Stadtaffe*? Open 24/7.

MOGG

Auguststraße 11–13, Mitte
S-Bahn Oranienburger Straße
Tel 30 330 060 770
www.moggandmelzer.com
DELI

Refurbished under the supervision of gallery-owner Michael Fuchs, this former Jewish girls' school was closed for decades and now houses several galleries, the Pauly Saal restaurant and this café-deli owned by the caterer Mogg (formerly Mogg & Melzer) masterminded by Paul Mogg, whose entrance is to the right in the entrance – just follow your nose. This was apparently once part of the school canteen, so everything is a natural fit. The white tiled walls, opalescent globes, blue benches and a well-stocked counter give the stripped-down feel of a refectory, but the portions are more than generous so you don't need to ask for more. The pastrami sandwiches in two sizes served on wooden platters are a feast, yet lighter on the stomach than a portion of tofu. Good atmosphere + good food = good karma.

NOLA'S AM WEINBERG

Veteranenstraße 9, Mitte
U-Bahn Rosenthaler Platz
Tel 30 4404 0766, www.nola.de
HELVETIAN CAFÉ

Nola is Swiss, and appropriately located atop Volkspark am Weinberg, a rare piece of "downhill" Berlin greenery that adds to the panorama from the huge terrace overlooking Mitte and Prenzlauer Berg: the Zionskirche to the north, Rosenthaler Platz to the south and Nola in the neutral zone – a nicely contemporary topography. Indeed, people mostly come here for the view, and also, when the weather's fine, for a seat anywhere other than on a Berlin pavement. The menu features just about everything you can eat and drink throughout the day, with a Swiss accent.

OLIV

Münzstraße 8, Mitte
S-Bahn Hackescher markt
U-Bahn Weinmeisterstraße
Tel 30 8920 6540
www.oliv-cafe.de
BOBO HANGOUT

This modern corner café at the foot of the Müntz 8 building and its B&B apartments is the local social hub. With its charcoal, white and concrete walls and slab tables, it's an eye-catching place with a relaxed vibe. All the members of the fashion and design tribes operating in the area meet up here. Some spend a long while deep in a book or doing emails, while others come and go. It's a good place for a *latte macchiato* or a fresh ginger infusion, a house *Bircher Müsli* (in the morning), a piece of cake, and a mixed salad or a quiche. Oliv is not self-service or a *Stehcafe*; it goes in for *am Tisch* service. If you try to order at the counter, they will send you back to your seat.

OLIV EAT

Potsdamer Straße 91, Tiergarten
U-Bahn Kurfürstenstraße
Tel 30 5523 3823, www.oliv-cafe.de

COFFEE AND BITES

Act 2 for the olive tree planted in 2008 in Mitte by Oliver Mahne et Hans Thedieck. This branch is located on busy Potsdamer Straße, with people jostling inside and out. A former interior designer, Mahne, together with and his partner, has infused it with the same minimalist, modernist vibe, with lots of wood and charcoal-coloured walls. It serves the same excellent coffees, teas, and vegetable and fruit juices, as well as pastries, including outstanding apple crumble and carrot cake. The menu includes soup of the day, vegetable dishes, vegan concoctions and creamy quiches.

P103 MISCHKONZERN

Potsdamer Straße 103, Tiergarten
U-Bahn Kurfürstenstraße
Tel 30 5470 6000, www.p103.de

CONTEMPORARY GRAND CAFÉ

After setting up the taxi company Ans Netz Taxi, the trio of friends known only by their first names went even further. They got hold of a huge space being refurbished on Potsdamer Straße and opened this splendid bright 250-square-metre café, with its corners and comfortable rooms decorated in recycling mode and lit up by a collection of antique chandeliers. The walls and pillars have been scraped down to the brick to achieve a Berlin tone, the brown leather and almond-green velvet give it a post-neo-retro touch; there's fluid background music and some not uninteresting pictures (inevitably, the place is a gallery as well). The P103 is one of the best new cafés in the city, with a growing tribe of loyal regulars, such as the dapper gentleman who greets everyone courteously at the entrance, though he isn't the owner. The best tables and chairs are on the right behind the pillars. Order a cappuccino and cheesecake with whipped cream – wildly unreasonable but divine.

PARK CAFÉ

Fehrbelliner Platz 8, Wilmersdorf
U-Bahn Fehrbelliner Platz
Tel 30 8631 3838n www.parkcafe-berlin.de

SUNDAY CAFÉ

Berlin is full of cafés in pavilions bordering parks or large squares. This one, adjacent to Preussenpark, is ideally located for Saturdays and Sundays, when there is a flea market on Fehrbelliner Platz. You can have breakfast before heading off to hunt for antiques, and a good latte when you're done. This is a welcoming place, with a tastefully restrained retro 1950s setting and a friendly, family atmosphere. As soon as the weather permits, the large terrace allows a change of scenery, from 8:30am onwards.

RABIEN

Klingsorstraße 13, Steglitz
S-Bahn Rathaus Steglitz
Tel 30 7916 595, www.rabien-berlin.de

BREAKFAST

First opened in 1878 and once an official supplier to Kaiser Wilhelm when his court was transferred to Potsdam, this venerable family confectionery now in its fourth generation of cream whippers represents a sweet white stone in Berlin's gourmet memory. It offers several specialities, including *Baumkuchen*, blackcurrant mousse, cream cakes and petit-fours. But its the hearty, traditional breakfast that tempts people to trek out to Steglitz, located to the south-east, beyond Tempelhof, people. It's a good place for afternoon snacks, as well.

RASTSTÄTTE GNADENBROT

Martin Luther Straße 20a,
corner of Motzstraße, Schöneberg
U-Bahn Viktoria-Luise-Platz
Tel 30 2196 1786
www.raststaette-gnadenbrot.de

SELF-SERVICE

An old petrol pump topped with two cooking enamel pots recycled as flower planters acts as the shop sign, signal or beacon and sets the tone. Posted at the intersection of the gay district, this "service station" is a day and night spot where you can breakfast very late, inside or outdoors. The decor makes you think of the cover of a Boney M maxi single. Take time out to sip a Polish beer or have a quick self-service dinner. Help yourself to bread, cutlery, napkin, plastic cup, sausage and mustard, curried herring, and chocolate cake you dig into the fridge for. But there's a menu, too, printed on school exercise-book paper and telling you what you can sit down to eat at a table, if you can find one. On that elusive table is a lamp, and when it starts to flash it's time to go and collect your order from the counter. The music's chachacha, the clientele is mixed and the French fries are organic. And in fact, the food's pretty good and very reasonably priced.

SCHOENBRUNN

Am Schwanenteich, Volkspark, Friedrichshain
S-Bahn Landsberger Allee
Tel 30 453 056 525
www.schoenbrunn.net
BIERGARTEN

A combination of kiosk, bar, restaurant and *Biergarten* that can accommodate more than a thousand people, Schoenbrunn is a vast dining and refreshment complex located inside the Friedrichshain public park. Very popular for its Sunday breakfasts in fine weather and for relaxing out on the terrace, the restaurant has retained its East German design trappings, including balusters shaped like the ossicle that it uses for its logo. The *Frühstück* menu is so varied that you can spend a while deciding on what to have. After, you just keep sitting there in the sun, helped by a series of coffees. Around you are XL-sized families, young couples with double-strollers and accompanying children, or retirees who have probably been coming here for decades, despite the changes, long before the Wall came down. Closed from Monday to Friday in November and December.

SILO COFFEE

Gabriel-Max-Straße 4, Friedrichshain
U-Bahn Frankfurter Tor
www.facebook.com/silocoffee
NEIGHBOURHOOD CAFÉ

The coffees come from the best local roasters (The Barn), as well as from England and even Norway; and the bread comes from Sironi, the Milanese baker in the **MARKTHALLE NEUN,** so breakfast here is a European treat. Add in the toasts loaded with delicious, well-seasoned spreads such as hummus, crushed avocado and chorizo, the banana cake and a local *sehr gemütlich* (very comfortable) atmosphere, and this café is worth a (considerable) detour.

SOPHIENECK

Große Hamburger Straße 37, Mitte
S-Bahn Oranienburger Straße
Tel 30 283 4065
www.sophieneck-berlin.de
HISTORIC BISTRO

Duly listed in the directory of age-old Berlin *Kneipen*, like the Max und Moritz in Kreuzberg, the Sophieneck symbolizes a whole slice of raw Berlin life. It reopened in 1986, three years before the fall of the Berlin Wall, and resumed what it had been doing decades earlier before being hijacked into a bakery in 1926 by its then owners, thoroughbred Prussians Ernst and Gertrud Balzer. Acquired in 1994 by Henrik Nowack and Wolfgang Werba, the place has been updated, paradoxically, by emphasizing the Old Berlin aspect, with dark wood, shiny brass, green lampshades, old enamel advertising signs, bar stools and red moleskin seats. More a neighbourhood bistro than a fashion statement – and that's a good thing – frequented by real Berliners, Sophieneck offers Märkischer Landmann, Sion Kölsch, Berliner Pilsner and Irish stouts on tap, and no-frills family food such as pickled herring, meatballs and a daily special served until 1am.

SPLENDID DELIKATESSEN

Dorotheenstraße 37, Mitte
S-Bahn Friedrichstraße
Tel 171 5387 991
www.splendid-delikatessen.de
LUNCH ON THE GO

In 1904, on the foundations of an old shop, Gronau & Graul built the Hotel Splendid, which was rapidly bought out by the restaurant owner and caterer Julius Luthard Borchardt. A rare gem that was still standing after the war, following the fall of the Wall it was included in the expansion project undertaken by the Dussmann cultural megastore. In 2005, the latter opened the Splendid Dollmann, a food counter and confectioner decorated by the Berlin-based BFS Design agency with a red boar as its emblem. Now on its own, the Splendid is in the hands of Andreas Poulakidas (The Barn) who has recently reinvented himself by focusing exclusively on lunches of soups, quiches, sandwiches and cheeses, among other things. Welcome to an area ruined by junk food.

WIENER CONDITOREI CAFFEEHAUS

Hohenzollerndamm 92, Grunewald
S-Bahn Hohenzollerndamm
Tel 30 8959 6922
www.wiener-conditorei.de
CAFÉ, PASTRY SHOP

This café-tearoom-pastry shop is a good place to stop off for refreshments when visiting the Bauhaus housing project in Grunewald. Some Berliners routinely drive here on Sunday afternoons to buy cakes for teatime. The place only opened in 2003, but looks as though it has been in business for decades. The decor is vaguely imperial, as are the customers: silver-haired gentlemen in blazers and ladies in furs with eye-popping hairdos tinted in three colours that resemble the fruit tarts and layer cakes they gobble while chattering like birds. Run by the Otte family, cake-makers and confectioners since 1928 and owners of several other outlets in

Berlin, this place is hard to classify, since it also boasts a champagne and prosecco bar. The huge display case is crammed with desserts, sweet buns, fruitcakes, cream cakes and petit-fours "comme en France" (as in France), as a sign boldly proclaims. As in Orléans thirty years ago, maybe. It's easy to poke fun, but everything is freshly made and delicious, and served by friendly, smiling women. The kitchen, where the special orders (for wedding and birthday cakes) are confected, is worth a look. See website for other locations

WIRTSHAUS HEUBERGER

Gotenstraße 1, Schöneberg
S-Bahn Julius-Leber-Brücke
Tel 30 7895 7337
www.wirtshaus-heuberger.de
BIERGARTEN

To the south of Schöneberg, wedged between several S-Bahn bridges and lines, is the area known as the "Red Island", part of the city's political memory. It is so-named because between the wars it was home to many communist workers and their families. The Wirtshaus Heuberger is located at the point where Gotenstraße meets Cheruskerstraße. Outside, at the tip of the junction, there's a pleasant terrace where you can relax in the shade of the trees; inside, there are several rooms with red, white and brown walls and fine columns and mouldings. The atmosphere is relaxed and informal. You can have a beer and share a *flammeküche* appetizer served on a board, surrounded by families who are tucking into their dinners. This is a neighbourhood address that lies slightly off the beaten track, but if you're in this part of town it provides a good watering hole.

WOHNZIMMER

Lettestraße 6, corner of Schliemannstraße,
Prenzlauer Berg
U-Bahn Eberswalderstraße
Tel 30 445 5458
www.wohnzimmer-bar.de
CAFÉ

The "Living Room" is probably the most representative boozer in Prenzlauer Berg. It occupies the rustic floor of a very old storehouse, with a decor as eclectic as a rag-and-bone man's van. The furniture and seating suggest a taste for Spanish-inspired Jugendstil. The interior is divided into smoking and non-smoking areas and is more crammed with stuff than the living room of an ageing post-war coquette – think Marlene Dietrich in *A Foreign Affair*. In one corner, there's a small bar with three stools and a puppet decor resembling the backdrop in an old GDR TV show. Every Friday it hosts a barista or mixologist, come to concoct a cocktail for the house. The second room, arranged around a very "grand hotel" upholstered ottoman that must have been dredged up from the *Titanic*, is even more curious. People come here to drink, nibble, sip and munch organic fare ranging from muesli or Rita salad to croissants, lemonade and Czech beer. And please leave your dog outside, *danke*. Another plus: the Wohnzimmer is open every night until 4am.

A COFFEE WITH BARRIE KOSKY

I often go to the Café Einstein, where you bump into everyone who is anyone in Berlin arts and culture, but I don't have a regular table there.

CAFÉ EINSTEIN STAMMHAUS
Kurfürstenstraße 58, Tiergarten, tel 30 263 9190, www.cafeeinstein.com

NIGHTLIFE
JAZZ CLUBS TO TECHNO DANCE FLOORS: WINDING DOWN IN THE CITY

Though Berlin nightlife is still pretty much the same as ever, which is why partygoers flock here every weekend from all over Europe on low-cost flights, it is actually growing out of its binge-boozing kidult phase while still managing to attract the crowds. And Berliners themselves have matured, seeking new types of exhilaration.

The current trend is to move beyond the music – naturally still part and parcel of Berlin nights – and the legendary venues to explore new experiences. Mixology, for example, has attracted a more inquisitive, refined, cosmopolitan generation that wants to sit down, taste and enjoy things, rather than stupefying itself at any price. And the thirty-somethings are gradually gentrifying, while keeping one foot in the underground.

The world of speakeasies, cocktail bars and hotel bars is growing more intimate and opulent but is still informal enough to encourage all levels of society to mix and match. So VIPs (if they really exist) are now a dying breed. With their club or lounge mindset, people want sophisticated liquid menus and quality rather than quantity. They are (re)discovering forgotten drinks and unusual mixtures that are fun to sip rather than gulp down. In this *Cocktail-Kultur*, with a good-food focus against a background of jazzy funk, another style of Berlin nights is taking the high ground.

A-TRANE

Bleibtreustraße 1, Charlottenburg
S-Bahn Savignyplatz
Tel 30 313 32550
www.a-trane.de
Closed Sunday and Monday

JAZZ CLUB

Founded in 1992 by Sedal Sardan,
the A-Trane has been a signature hangout
for the world's jazz greats, from Herbie
Hancock, Wynton Marsalis and Ravi
Coltrane to Art Pepper, along with artists
such as Justo Gabriel Pérez, Eb Davis,
Roy Hargrove, Julia Kadel and the Susi
Hyldgaard Experience. The A-Trane is
still *the* great jazz club, with a live stage
where soloists, bands, trios, quartets and
groups that play anything from modern
and Latin jazz to blues and soul perform
and are filmed.

BAR SAINT JEAN

Steinstraße 21, Mitte
U-Bahn Weinmeisterstraße
Tel 30 24 08 84 64
www.barsaintjean.com
Closed Monday

COCKTAILS, GAY-FRIENDLY

Buried away on a mezzanine floor, the
Saint Jean is the white knight of the Berlin
cocktail circuit. Or black knight, rather,
as the place seems to have been burned out
before it opened. An iron ladder, twisted
by heat, hangs behind the bar and tends
to support this theory. Designed by Thilo
Reich, the decor is both raw and refined.
Behind the bar, the recently arrived
Frenchman Johann Courgibet is agreeably
taciturn, allowing his creative drinks to
speak for him. Every night, there's a good
choice of gin and tonic and bucks on the
slate, ranging from Moscow to Mexico City
mules and including a Jägermeister-based
Berlin mule. Try the fiery house cocktail,
naturally named Saint-Jean and made of
Aperol, rum, lime juice, sugar and a shot
of Laphroaig. Frankly, the best gay and
gay-friendly bar in Berlin.

BASSY COWBOY CLUB

Schönhauser Allee 176a, Prenzlauer Berg
U-Bahn Senefelderplatz
Tel 30 374 48 020
www.bassy-club.de

COSTUME CLUB

When it opened, Bassy revived long-
forgotten musical trends and is still strictly
committed to pre-1969 sounds – soul, R & B,
blues and more. It's something of a cross
between Perfectos and rock attitude, with
a rogue penchant for fringed-jacket country
music, Stetsons and cowboy boots. They
claim here quite bluntly to like the music
and outfits of Wanda Jackson, Etta James,
Andy Williams and Sky Saxon. Patrons also
dress the part, with a tendency for rig-outs
favoured by rockers, mods, cowboys, teddy
boys, modern fops and other circus freaks.
Buried deep inside a cellar, Bassy features
a gay-friendly programme of parties,
concerts and performances. A change from
techno-electro – a treat to the ears.

BERGHAIN

Am Wriezener Bahnhof, Friedrichshain
S-Bahn Ostbahnhof
Tel 30 29 36 02 10
www.berghain.de

TECHNODROME

Located in an immense vacant power plant,
the Berghain has been a haven since 1994
for clubbers disoriented by the closings and
frequent moves of other techno temples.
Run by Michael Teufele and Norbert
Thormann, it is above all a techno-electro-
gay club phenomenon, in the sense that
everyone wants in, at least once. As a result,
a packed crowd of "all sexes" waits more
or less patiently till five in the morning to get
in, with a doorman not easy to please and
happy to demonstrate physically that you're
not worth his time. With architectonics
on its side, it spares no decibels, although
some will appreciate the respite offered
by the Panorama Bar. The **LAB.ORATORY**
(www.lab-oratory.de) in the basement is for
hardcore gays, promising a few extra thrills
in a legendary back room often the subject

of dubiously salacious stories. Whatever the truth may be, the Berghain, where photos are strictly forbidden, warranted an entire chapter in the gay community's bible, Lost and Sound: Berlin, Techno und der Easyjetset by Tobias Rapp, a reporter and music editor for *Der Spiegel*, who describes it as the cathedral of techno and calls it "die Mitte der Welt" (the "centre of the world"). Now successfully put into orbit, the Berghain Kantine and its concert stage keep a low profile in the shadow of their monstrous elder sibling, while on the same site, the Biergarten plays it cool once the concerts are over. The Berghain starts early in the evening at 8pm, which is not to everybody's taste, and the club opens at midnight on Friday and Saturday. The site is also used during Berlin Alternative Fashion Week (www.bafw.de) for fashion shows and the Designers Market.

BRYK BAR

Rykestraße 18, Prenzlauer Berg
U-Bahn Eberswalderstraße
Tel 30 38 100 165
www.bryk-bar.com
Closed Sunday
COCKTAILS, CHIC

The Bryk opened in early April 2014 and mixes stylish cocktails you can sip while sitting in deep, blue-velvet, 1930s armchairs. Owned by the elegant Frank Besser from the five-star hotel world of Vancouver, Nice, Vienna and St. Moritz, and darkly and sophisticatedly decorated by Kathryn Bade of the Etage Vier architectural agency, the Bryk looks exactly like a private club, and in this area, it surprises people with its well-mannered style. The cloakroom is discreetly kept out of the limelight, the water coolers are of silver and crystal, the service is elegant and the whole venue is strictly non-smoking. Its two voluptuous lounges encourage intimate conversations over drinks priced in hundreds with simple yet zany names such as Kamasutra with a Hangover, Oily Bondage for Beginners and No More

Kinky Stuff Please, along with white chocolate mousse, Guinness syrup and horseradish as stimulants. The wiser choice of a Holy Shit, Is That Mary? takes the traditional Bloody M and whips it up with celery foam plus a shot of tomato schnapps. It's hard to catch the bartenders out by asking for a mixture not featuring on the menu. Bryk distils its own gin. It also serves refined snacks with a menu of charcuterie, roast beef sandwiches and elaborate desserts. One of the most dapper, debonair cocktail bars in Berlin.

BUCK AND BRECK

Brunnenstraße 177, Mitte
U-Bahn Rosenthaler Platz
Tel 176 3231 5507
www.buckandbreck.com
CONTEMPORARY SPEAKEASY

There's nothing on the street to show where it is or what it is. A speakeasy? Right on trend. Naming their bar after a forgotten American cocktail, Goncalo de Sousa Monteiro and Holger Groll deliberately decided to keep things small. No more than fifteen customers at a time. Seated around a single big black table designed by Zürich studio Bask. This convivial minimalism in no way reflects the expansive menu, featuring gin, vodka and whisky. The mixes and measures do the rest. With a sombre ambience pierced by pools of yellow light, the place exudes an air of mystery.

BURGERMEISTER

Oberbaumstraße,
under the railway arches, Kreuzberg
U-Bahn Schlesisches Tor
www.burger-meister.de
LATE-NIGHT BURGERS

True, this spot is neither a shop nor a mobile kitchen. Although located under the metal arches of the elevated S-Bahn at the curved Oberbaumstraße intersection, just at the exit of the amazing bridge with orange brick turrets and a few wild clubs, the Burgermeister stand is a former urinal (*ein Pissoir, ja*) which in 2006 was converted into a late-night burger joint popular with night owls, as it's a perfect stop-off between two club benders. It's not a cheapskate money-maker, either: it prepares and serves excellent, well-garnished burgers in several varieties, including a tofuburger and a "chilie" burger, together with "pommes" (fries) and a choice of sauces, including a must-have mango-curry. You eat standing, shamelessly, until 3am on weekdays and Sunday, and 4am on Friday and Saturday. The second location opened in 2015, with its indoor seating, is much more suitable for the freezing temperatures of Berlin's winter. **Other location:** Skalitzerstraße 136, Kreuzberg

CAFÉ M

Goltzstraße 33, Schöneberg
U-Bahn Eisenacherstraße
Tel 30 216 7092, www.cafe-m.de
1980S NOSTALGIA
Now a slightly forgotten classic still basking in its ageing reputation, the M was one of the bars that David Bowie and Iggy Pop used to frequent during their stays in Berlin, when they lived not far away on Hauptstraße. M for memory lane? Not really; the place runs all day and into the early hours, making it a must for a last nightcap when you don't really want to go back and sleep. Note that the happy hour here runs from 8pm to 10pm.

CLÄRCHENS BALLHAUS

Auguststraße 24, Mitte
U-Bahn Weinmeisterstraße, S-Bahn Oranienburger Straße
Tel 30 2829 2968, www.ballhaus.de
OLD-FASHIONED CHARM
Converted into a brothel in the 1920s – Alfred Döblin described the mirror room, the Spiegelsaal, in his novel *Berlin Alexanderplatz* – and then completely forgotten after 1945, the original Clärchens ballroom was exhumed by David Regehr, a painter and Christian Schulz, an actor. The old Clärchens (the little girl in

question was a certain Clara Habermann) has kept up its exceptional charm at the bottom of a wild garden impossible to discern from the outside. It reopened in 2004 with a breathtaking ballroom you enter by climbing a steep stairway. Every Sunday, in the lavish decrepitude of the decor, once used as a location for the film *Valkyrie* about Count von Stauffenberg's plot against Hitler, it puts on concerts of classical music and swing. During the week, in the other room on the ground floor with a more festive atmosphere, you can come and learn to dance the cha-cha-cha, tango, salsa, waltz or *schwoof* beneath a disco ball, while on Sunday afternoons, they hold a well-attended tea dance. The Ballhaus has also published a beautiful picture album recounting the entire history and destiny of this extraordinary venue that emerged from nothing to become a temple of twirls and two-step.

CODA DESSERT BAR

Friedelstraße 47, Neukölln
U-Bahn Herrmannplatz
Tel 030 91 49 63 96
www.coda-berlin.com
Closed Sunday and Monday
EXPERIMENTAL DESSERTS
What if a dessert could conjure the same alchemy of texture and taste as a cocktail? And what if, when it did, it was so good you had to have another? And what if you could get into some very bad habits here? The pair running Coda have the recipe just right: the avant-garde pastry chef René Frank and Oliver Bischoff, well-known for his restaurant interiors agency, ett la benn, have created the first dessert bar using fruit and vegetable juices and no added sugar. The result? Subtle and innovative concoctions for drinking and eating, selected from a menu featuring just two or three courses. An example chosen at random: aubergine, pecan nuts, cider vinegar and salty liquorice. It's often surprising, sometimes extraordinary and always wonderful.

DIE KLEINE PHILHARMONIE

Schaperstraße 14, Wilmersdorf
U-Bahn Spichernstraße
Tel 30 8872 7483
www.diekleinephilharmonie.eu
Closed Monday

GAY, AFTER HOURS

Together with the Neues Ufer (formerly Anderes Ufer), this is probably the oldest gay bar in Berlin, and the late Patrice Chéreau's favourite. It's an *Absacker* bar where you go for that last round at 5am, when they start doing social work at the bar. Die Kleine Philharmonie has been playing its own style of music since it opened in 1959, featuring the complete tunes of Mireille Mathieu in German, or a gang bawl of *The Winner Takes All* in French, or Udo Jürgens, or sometimes the Fortune Voices choir. For a long time it was run by Russian Wanda, who died a few years ago after fiercely reserving the bar for men only. It was then taken over by the blond and smiling Adrian Habel, who hardly so much as tweaked the original interior, which was cluttered with old chairs, padded, broken-down Regency sofas with lace-covered armrests, and macramé-topped tables that copied the Granny's neo-bars in Mitte and Prenzlauer Berg. But the dozens of open umbrellas hanging from the ceilings have gone, and regulars will point out that the most interesting of the atrocious daubs that once adorned the hummingbird wallpaper have begun a second life in the Schwules Museum. The young, very Jean Genet-style regulars, or those carbon-14-dated to 1976, still stand around jauntily cooing compliments to newcomers, who slouch to the end to down a beer and tuck into the homemade cakes – some of the best in town.

FRAGRANCES

Ritz-Carlton, Potsdamer Platz 3, Tiergarten
S-Bahn and U-Bahn Potsdamer Platz
Tel 30 3377 75403
Tel www.ritzcarlton.com
Closed Sunday to Tuesday

FRAGRANCE-THEMED BAR

Arnd Henning Heissen is a very unusual mixologist. His speciality: cocktails inspired by the flavours and aromas of perfumery. Since 2014, he has dedicated the bar of the luxurious Ritz-Carlton Hotel to this extraordinary alchemy, a global first. Heissen, a wizard Merlin of the cocktail universe, extends his innovative approach right through the glass, with drinks inspired by Guerlain, Armani, Bulgari and even Marie Le Febvre, French founder of Urban Scents, working with her to develop exclusive creations linked to her fragrances: Vetiver Réunion (mezcal, sake, vetiver, lemon juice, fresh grapefruit juice) or Lost Paradise (prosecco, hibiscus flower). An unusual experience.

GALANDER

Stuttgarter Platz 15, Charlottenburg
S-Bahn Charlottenburg
U-Bahn Wilmersdorfer Straße
Tel 30 3646 5363
www.galander-berlin.de

COCKTAILS, BERLINER SALON

Opened by Dominik Galander and Lars Junge, who also run other venues, including another Galander in Kreuzberg and a delicatessen next to the Lamazère restaurant, this stylish cocktail bar revives the spirit of the Berliner Zimmer with an interior of waxed woodwork, cordovan leather, moulded ceilings, a large crystal chandelier, ample armchairs, green marble tables and a dark wooden floor – though the floral arrangements might make you wonder where the funeral is. This is not a place for non-smokers, and cigars are welcome. Cooled by a large, slightly faded colonial-style fan, you order drinks from an iPad offered by a charming bartender in a waistcoat. The cocktails – Picon Punch,

Porto Flip, Pimms Cup – summon up evenings past and are really tempting.
See website for other locations

GRACE BAR

Kurfürstendamm 25, Charlottenburg
U-Bahn Kurfürstendamm
Tel 30 884 37 829, www.hotelzoo.de
HOTEL BAR

The Hotel Zoo reflects an important legacy in Berlin's luxury hotels. Its recent lavish renovation has naturally led to the introduction of a bouquet of fashionable lifestyle services. The Grace Bar was designed by Dayna Lee, with lots of purple velvet, exposed brickwork and glamorous touches. There's automatic access for hotel guests, but it's more selective if you're an outsider, as the hunk at the entrance will demonstrate.

GREEN DOOR

Winterfeldtstraße 50, Schöneberg
U-Bahn Nollendorfplatz
Tel 30 215 2515, www.greendoor.de
COCKTAILS

The green door really is. Green, that is. And it tends to stay closed if you don't ring or if, after doing so, you don't have the right style – that of being the person in the know, at ease in all situations. This cocktail bar, which occupies the space of the former Havana Bar, is run by Fritz Müller-Scherz, well known in cinema and publishing circles, and a trumpet player when the mood hits him. Known for having written several screenplays and worked with Wim Wenders and Werner Fassbinder, the good fellow willingly opens his bar for friends like Ulli Lommel, an actor and director of two films with Andy Warhol (including the famous *Cocaine Cowboys*), who had come here to exhibit his photos. Otherwise, the drinks menu proposes among other cocktails the Schönebergers Classics, including the famous Moscow Mule and vodka martini much loved by Barrie Kosky. A favourite of Berliners aged thirty and older who have not given up going out, the

Green Door is a chapel where people take communion standing up, so the rare seats here seem somewhat otiose.

JANSEN BAR

Gotenstraße 71, Schöneberg
S-Bahn Julius-Leber-Brücke
Tel 175 712 3173, www.jansenbar.de
Closed Monday
COCKTAILS, BERLIN CLASSICS

It's been two decades now that the Jansen Bar has ruled the roost of the working-class, communist enclave that was the Red Island of Schöneberg. It could have become a simple *Eckkneipe* – "local bar" – as found in every district of Berlin, but it did one better. Behind its metal door and British-style inn sign, the Jansen is a stylish cocktail bar whose owner, Oliver Mannal, has managed to build a Berlin classic. There's certainly a local clientele, but it's also very Schönebergian, with a mix of students and lawyers all enjoying the friendly, relaxed, almost family atmosphere. Although it is located in a former butcher's shop (note the old tiles), the Jansen is a quiet spot where the menu speaks louder than the regulars, as it lists more than forty whiskies and 180 cocktails. It's hard to stay silent about this amazing feat, especially after downing a couple of the drinks. Try the maitai, the Jay Beach (vodka and cranberry juice) or the Red Island Bug (gin, fresh ginger and ginger ale). A family place indeed.

JEDER VERNUNFT

Schaperstraße 24, Wilmersdorf
U-Bahn Spichernstraße
Tel 30 883 1582
www.bar-jeder-vernunft.de
CABARET

Created near the Berliner Festspiele in 1992 by Holger Klotzbach and directed by Lutz Deisinger, this miniature cabaret (200 seats) designed in the style of a circus tent, decorated with inlays and mirrors taken from a former Belgian carousel transformed into a chip shop, is a typically

Berlin theatrical speciality. It stages confirmed talents and rising stars ranging from Ute Lemper to Georgette Dee, who is regarded as a fortune teller in Germany, along with Max Raabe, Popette Betancor, Cora Frost, Otto Sander, Ulrich Michael Hessig enbodying Irmgard Knef, fake twin sister of the German star Hildegard Knef, a gay idol, and even the great Angela Winkler. All work the captivated audience members, seated either in the ring or in small boxes where they sip a beer and enjoy an assortment of charcuterie or cheese. One-(wo) man-shows, singing tours and witty operettas produced by Jeder Vernunft alternate with musicals such as *Cabaret* and *La Cage aux Folles*. In the Tiergarten, close to the Huître Enceinte but with a larger audience capacity, the **TIPI AM KANZLERAMT** (Große Querallee, Tiergarten, tel 030 3906 6550) puts on shows in its own tent, including the sassy review *Briefs* and concerts by the singer Gayle Tufts, a gay icon if anyone is.

KITKATCLUB

Köpenicker Straße 76, enter via
Brückenstraße, Mitte
U-Bahn Heinrich-Heine-Straße
Tel 30 787 1896, www.kitkatclub.org
Closed Sunday to Thursday
FETISH FANTASY

A nightclub that was frightfully fashionable one day and horribly cheesy the next, the Kit Kat Club has nothing to do with the venue shown in *Cabaret*. Even Sally Bowles would look like a nun here. For twenty years (so we can call it a classic), the Kit Kat has been feeding the fantasies of anyone who secretly gets a kick out of transgressive exhibitions but hasn't yet taken the plunge. Even after moving to its present address in 2007, the Kit Kat has always earned its keep due to its infamous reputation for exploring fetishist desires of all stripes with no holds barred, backed by heavy techno music. From latex wear to full nudity, the dress code here is cruelly strict, depending on the evening's theme. A word of warning: the Gegen gay nights are far from innocuous.

KLUB INTERNATIONAL

Karl-Marx-Allee 33, Mitte
U-Bahn Schillingstraße
Tel 30 24 75 60 11
www.klub-international.com
MONTHLY GAY NIGHTS

Housed in the Kino International, the prestige cinema of the East German regime built in 1960 by architects Josef Kaiser and Herbert Aust and still active through the sensible programming of Yorck Kinos, the KI makes a perfect excuse for hanging around the amusing Karl-Marx-Allee, because on the first Saturday of each month, they hold gay musical and theatrical celebrations here that would make the former heads of the Socialist nomenclature turn in their graves. Jurassica Parka and Äimi Weinhaus are the resident drag queens, while the electro combos Petting Psychos, Metanoize, La Schmock and Finkobot shake the walls.

LIMONADIER

Nostitzstraße 12, Kreuzberg
U-Bahn Gneisenaustraße
Tel 170 601 2020, www.limonadier.de
Closed Sunday
RETRO BEVERAGES

The wave of nostalgia for smart drinking has obviously reached Berlin, and with it, a tendency for French-style imbibing.

"Always in the background was Berlin. It was calling me every night, and its voice was the harsh sexy voice of the gramophone records. Berlin had affected me like a party at the end of which I didn't want to go home." **Christopher Isherwood,** *Down There on a Visit,* **1962**

Mon dieu, perhaps we will soon see waiters racing in long aprons down the Ku'damm. The Limonadier is taking a large-scale option on good old drinking habits. Instead of being a speakeasy, it offers a happy hour from 6pm to 8pm for aficionados of champagne, martini, whisky, rum and lemonade – as well it should, considering its name – with unusual versions featuring such ingredients as rhubarb, lemon balm, mint and even lime blossom. You can also find a dash of cocktail nostalgia in a Sazerac or a Colonies Françaises (white rum, vermouth and tonic), plus a robust commitment to Berlin at Night or a Kreuzberg Spritz. Trends being what they are, the Limonadier is also a gin-and-tonic bar with over ten versions on the menu. And there's a smoker's den.

MONKEY BAR

25Hours Hotel Bikini Berlin,
Budapester Straße 40, 10th floor, Tiergarten
S-Bahn and U-Bahn Zoologischer Garten
Tel 30 120 221 210
www.25hours-hotels.com
PANORAMIC VIEW, FASHIONABLE
First, you must get past the ground-floor bouncer who separates the hotel guests (lift on the left please) from the Neni restaurant diners (lift at the bottom right). In the middle there's an old, beatnik-looking Austin Mini Clubman. Up on the 10th floor, the Monkey Bar shares the whole floor with the restaurant and has a similar atmosphere. Designed by Werner Aisslinger, it is literally hanging in the air and offers the Zoo as a backdrop. You can sit down to a big snack burger on benches, cushions, armchairs, or on an open-sky terrace, and the place is packed with people of every age and style, drinking beer and cocktails. It has all been a very rapid, even feverish success story, and it's rare for an omni-clientele venue to be such a hit. The DJ booth with its turntables in a corner, under a Kapoor-style glass bell, features an ingenious rack for 33-rpm vinyl records, driven by pulleys and counterweights that keep it in motion, until it suddenly stops to deliver albums by Chaka Khan, Bryan Ferry, Al Green, Chic, Esther Phillips, En Vogue and so on. And the name? It comes from the primates you can spot in their enclosure in the zoo opposite.

NEUES UFER

Haupstraße 157, Schöneberg
U-Bahn Kleistpark
Tel 30 7895 7900, www.neuesufer.de
CULT, BOWIE
David Bowie lived just nearby at number 155 – same sidewalk, first floor. At the time (1977), the bar was called Anderes Ufer (The Other Shore) and boasted of being the first activist gay bar in Berlin. The inevitable noise and madness helped build its legend, whether or not Bowie played a role. But this famous bar celebrates Ziggy's birthday every year. Honed to the bone and threadbare, the decor is steeped in its own juices, between goose-poop paintings, tobacco-dyed walls and polished wooden tables. More than a classic, it's a legend. Open until 2am, which is reasonable.

PAULY SAAL BAR

Auguststraße 11–13, Mitte
S-Bahn Oranienburger Straße
Tel 30 3300 6070
www.paulysaal.com
Closed Sunday and Monday
CHIC COCKTAIL BAR
There is the Pauly Saal restaurant, which is located in the old gymnasium of the former Jewish girls' school, a functionalist building refurbished by gallery-owner Michael Fuchs. And there is the Pauly Saal Bar, which acts as a sort of antechamber to the restaurant with a decor of smoked glass, upholstered leather brown and billiards green that seems to have been there forever, serving as a setting for fashionable informal gatherings for a discerning clientele. There's an intoxicating list of champagnes, plus a plethora of gins, rums, tequilas and vodkas. Among the cocktails, the Dr Lakra

(mezcal, apple brandy, grapefruit, raspberry and lime) is a must, as are the disco long drinks and smart "borrowings" such as the GinGinMule, the Adonis or the Flannel Shirt, created at odd spots around the world by star mixologists. Adorable servers, who will bring terrific titbits such as fried cauliflower, charcuterie, and even a steak and mash!

PRINCE CHARLES

Prinzenstraße 85f, Kreuzberg
U-Bahn Moritzplatz
Tel 554 761 73
www.princecharlesberlin.com
NIGHTCLUB

The Moritzplatz is gradually changing. Opposite the homegrown vegetable idyll of the Prinzessinengarten stands the Aufbau Haus, whose owners have now developed the former factory into a utopia for modern gastronomy: relaxed European bistro Parker Bowles, Korean burger kitchen Pacifico and rooftop bar and event space Atelier have all moved in. Behind all these new ventures, tucked away in the courtyard, stands one of Berlin's hippest clubs, Prince Charles, in the former employee swimming pool of piano manufacturer Bechstein. It's hard to miss the aquatic connection, as the bar sits in the middle of where once there was water. In this party hub, there's a focus on nights that bring the music community together – from hip-hop crews to the finest electronic beat-makers. The low-key crowd dive right in and will still be swimming around the dance floor until the early hours, and beyond.

PROVOCATEUR BAR

Hôtel Provocateur,
Brandenburgische Straße 21, Wilmersdorf
U-Bahn Adenauer Platz, Fehrbelliner Platz
Tel 30 2205 6060
www.provocateur-hotel.com
HOTEL COCKTAIL BAR

Forget about the hotel opened with much razzmatazz by the Gekko company but frankly a laughable effort at being cool-chic-trendy-sexy-urban with its "burlesque hotel" concept and its Paris bordello decor borrowed from 1950s photos. And also forget about the place and the neighbourhood, which is as fun as a funeral procession on a rainy day in November. But do set your sights on the bar, since along with the restaurant, it was entrusted to Duc Ngo (398, Madame Ngo). Best to go there during the week, and avoid weekends, like most knowing Berliners. The provocation here sometimes borders on indecency and vulgarity, but it all adds to the local buzz.

RUM TRADER

Fasanenstraße 40, Wilmersdorf
U-Bahn Spichernstraße
Tel 30 881 1428
Closed Sunday
RUM

On a corner of Ludwigkirchstraße, Rum Trader shows few signs of life. With its blocked-off windows and black door implying that one simply drops in here for a quick gulp of grog, it's more like a well-sealed barrel. It's well worth going in, though, for the privilege of sipping a warming Shark's Tooth, a Fog Cutter or a Bucanero, and to enjoy a unique place, a favoured stop for the city's intellectuals. As it has never changed its ways, the Rum Trader has become another classic, caught up with the trend and now voted a place of worship by the cocktail society.

SCHWARZES CAFÉ

Kantstraße 148, Charlottenburg
S-Bahn Savignyplatz
Tel 30 313 80 38
www.schwarzescafe-berlin.de
Open 24/7
CLASSIC

Like the Paris Bar, which has been a long-time neighbour, this "Black" Café is a Berlin mother of all classics. Since 1978, its multi-coloured neon parrot has been illuminating the window, behind which an intense mix of clients, peaking around midnight, swarm over the two floors and the quiet backyard in fine, warm weather. There are bits and bobs to mop up the beer or more powerful kinds of liquid fuel. Especially as there's a plaque saying that Rudolf Diesel (yes, the inventor of the engine) once lived here.

SCHWUZ

Rollbergstraße 26, Neukölln
U-Bahn Rathaus Neukölln, Boddinstraße
Tel 30 5770 2270, www.schwuz.de
Closed Monday and Tuesday
GAY BURLESQUE

When the Schwules Museum moved to the Tiergarten, its former neighbour, SchwuZ, left the Mehringdamm in Kreuzberg to win the heart of Neukölln without losing any of its vitality or contagious, transgenerational – trans-anything – appeal. The nights are often hosted by a fabulous array of drag divas, with outlandish names such as Camelia Light, Hatice Osgur, Gloria Glamour and Kay P. Rinha, but no one comes anywhere near the resident star Gloria Viagra. SchwuZ was the venue of a song contest organized by Kriss Rudolph and chaired by a real jury including the singer Lisa Bassenge, the actress Maren Kroymann and Barrie Kosky, director of the Komische Oper Berlin, true to his broad tastes and mind.

TRESOR CLUB

Köpenicker Straße 70, Mitte
S-Bahn Ostbahnhof
U-Bahn Heinrich-Heine-Straße
Tel 30 6953 7713, www.tresorberlin.de
Closed Sunday and Tuesday
TECHNO, HOUSE

A temple of techno opened in 1991 in the old strongrooms of a department store, the Tresor Globus boasted the cream of international DJs, including Laurent Garnier and Dr Motte, fabled inventor of the Love Parade. It closed in April 2005, but only after a party that ran nonstop for

two weeks. Since 2007, after two years of Wednesday night fill-ins at the Club Maria am Ufer, it has occupied a disused power station right in the middle of Mitte. Blending *Blade Runner* with industrial nostalgia, this citadel of electronic culture has three dance floors that pack in 1,800 people spread between the Globus, dedicated to house music, the more experimental +4Bar, and the Vault, reverberating to its own obsessive sounds or digital concert performances. With a play list of nearly 200 works, the Tresor label, also founded in 1991, features such bands as Zenker Brothers, Peter Van Hoesen, Savvas Ysatis and Marcelus. You can download CDs and buy various bits of stuff via the online store. You pay to go in, and there are disabled facilities and smoking areas.

WÜRGEENGEL

Dresdener Straße 122, Kreuzberg
U-Bahn Kottbusser Tor
Tel 30 615 5560
www.wuergeengel.de
CHARMING, GAY

Depending on whether you mean Elfriede Jelinek or Luis Buñuel, the name of this diabolical angel of a club means either strangler or exterminator. It's run by Oliver Schupp, who also owns the Renger-Patzsch restaurant and the Gorgonzola Club, right next door. Which means that the angel has a faithful following of gay and gay-friendly folk with no age limit. In couples or in small talkative and cheerful groups, the customers sit around a table as if they were home with grandma and sip a Jewel or a Gimlet or a Bunueloni (Punt e Mes, vermouth and gin) that you would have liked Delphine Seyrig to drink, or more reasonably a Gingerengel (orange juice, ginger and ginger ale). If you're hungry, there are savoury odds and ends with an Italian accent. It's worth arriving before the end of the last screening at the Babylon art house cinema next door if you want to find a seat and replay *An Angel at My Table*.

A NIGHT OUT WITH BARRIE KOSKY

My favourite cocktail? A vodka martini. The best in town?
The ones served at the Green Door.

Located near Barrie Kosky's Berlin home, the Green Door cocktail
bar is both classic and offbeat, on account of its curious kitsch decor
with its undulating white lacquered wall, marble-cake pattern and
touches of gingham. Once past the emerald green door, you'll find
one of the best places in town – perhaps the best place. There are no
young partygoers or fashionistas here: the atmosphere and customers
are as sophisticated as the menu of cocktails mixed by Fritz Müller-
Scherz, patron saint, actor, writer, trumpet player and friend to
artists. Like the Moscow Mule, a Schöneberger classic, his vodka
martini is a drink to die for. Is it because it was once called a Kangaroo
that Barrie Kosky loves vodka martinis so much? The answer
lies in the olives. This cocktail, invented in the early 1960s and also
known as a Vodkatini, is derived from the dry martini. The latter,
which became a legend thanks to James Bond, who famously asked
for it to be "shaken, not stirred", is composed of four to six parts
vodka for two parts of dry (white) vermouth, with the addition
of stuffed green olives and cocktail onions, although opinions
on these vary. Vodka martinis faded out for a while but have once
again become a timeless global classic.

GREEN DOOR
Winterfeldtstraße 50, Schöneberg, tel 30 215 2515, www.greendoor.de

A SENSE OF STYLE
HIGH FASHION TO EMERGING DESIGNERS: SHOPPING IN THE CITY

With its free, liberal feel, Berlin is a city that encourages extravagance and resists regimented tastes. Years after the fall of the Wall, it has finally smoothed out its internal differences – it is now impossible to recognize whether someone walking down the street is from the west or the east of the city. The differences lie elsewhere.

Berlin is a capital of streetwear and even has a show for it, and it's the only city in Germany to produce whole generations of young fashion designers. Every new crop of them bursts with promise, and sometimes too much: the new darling of the day moves on, so you follow others who, in turn, form partnerships, split up and change directions. It's like a game of fashion snakes and ladders that only really dedicated fashion enthusiasts can hope to win. That said, some Berlin designers manage to take the high ground, with their shops, showrooms, global sales networks, parades and media coverage. Others who are equally talented prefer to keep out of the limelight, but they are happy to open up their studios to visitors by appointment.

In the street, anything goes – from neo-chic to the deliberately trashy, well-chosen vintage to international fashion, and Scandinavian streetwear to Japanese jeanswear. Freedom of choice is the name of the game, and there's no set dress code for evenings at the theatre or opera, although gallery openings and restaurant dinners provide good excuses to dress more elegantly.

FASHION AND ACCESSORIES

A.D.DEERTZ

Torstraße 106, Mitte
U-Bahn Rosenthaler Platz
Tel 30 9120 6630
www.addeertz.com
Open noon to 8pm, closed Sunday

DESIGNERS

Founded in 2000 by Wibke Deertz as
a unisex urban fashion label, ADD has
switched its gender target to men – urban
males who feel more comfortable in
the designer's trousers and Hirsch Natur
woollen socks. Offering a full wardrobe –
shirts, sweatshirts, T-shirts, jackets and
accessories designed by Deertz – this
simple boutique with a porch light in
Mondrianesque tints and two clothes
racks attracts arty-bobos from So-To
(South of Torstraße). Unique in Europe:
the indigo designs of the Vietnamese
label Kilomet109, handmade in Hanoi.

ADDDRESS

(Showroom) Weinmeisterstraße 12-14, Mitte
U-Bahn Weinmeisterstraße
Tel 30 2887 3434
www.adddress.de
Open noon to 8pm, closed Sunday

BERLIN LABEL

Andreea Vrajitoru founded her Adddress
women's label in 2003. Already a success
in Denmark and Japan, her designs are
very much of their time. Their balloon
shapes and girlie pleats have huge appeal
for thirty-somethings, and the neutral
colours are endlessly updated. The store
reflects the fluid understatement of the
collections. Very distinctive. Adddress
has opened a second store in the concept
mall Bikini Berlin.

ANDREAS MURKUDIS

Mercator Höfe, Potsdamer Straße 81e,
1st courtyard, Tiergarten
U-Bahn Kurfürstenstraße
Tel 30 680 798 306
www.andreasmurkudis.net
Open 10am to 8pm, closed Sunday

CONCEPT STORE

Since July 2011, Berlin fashion has had
a new home, in the former West, in
the huge interior courtyard of the former
headquarters of the *Tagesspiegel* newspaper.
The building and the site are nothing
special, but they have attracted a remarkable
concentration of art galleries. Andreas
Murkudis decided to come because he was
tired of the way Mitte was changing into
an open-air shopping centre. It also allowed
him to gather together into one large space
the AM1 and AM2 units scattered around
the "back backyards" of Münzstraße,
which Murkudis had pioneered. Brother
of the fashion designer Kostas Murkudis,
who presents his own collection here
(he lives and works in the courtyard across
the street), Andreas Murkudis called in
architects Pierre Jorge Gonzalez and Judith
Haase, who had already worked on the
Münzstraße shop, to remodel, all in white,
the 1,000 square metres of this former
print shop. The well-lit, shadow-free space
showcases more than 100 fashion brands
for men and women, including Jil Sander,
Ludwig Reiter, Lutz, Maison Martin
Margiela, Aspesi, Isaac Reina, Giorgio
Brato, Marsèll, Saskia Diez and Felisi,
as well as a growing number of exclusive
collaborations and cobranding partnerships.
In the home and design section, the
informed selection features iconic pieces
by Christophe Delcourt, e15, Lobmeyr
Glas and Nymphenburg porcelain. You can
also check out the entire Aesop range,
Susanne Kaufmann cosmetics and even
bottles of brandy from the venerable
Stählemühle distillery. Murkudis is a style/
lifestyle luminary and has been appointed
artistic director of the Bikini Berlin mall
concept (formerly Bikini Haus) tasked with

attracting Berlin's designers. He personally opened an AM + there in April 2014, using the same architects, but this time he chose a decor of yellow and orange, and supplied the store with a more affordable selection of brands.
See website for other locations

APRIL FIRST

Augustraße 77, Mitte
S-Bahn Oranienburger Straße
Tel 30 652 19 144, www.aprilfirst.de
Open noon to 7pm,
Saturday until 6pm, closed Sunday
DESIGNERS

After working for both Hugo Boss and Manon von Gerkan, Carolin Dunkel opened her multibrand store in April 2016. On the First, to be precise. Hence the name; it's also her birthday. A winning double: her silky-smooth boudoir displays tiers of highly desirable hand-picked fashions – See By Chloé, M.i.h Jeans, Mes Demoiselles, Hironaé, Ulla Johnson – as well as essential accessories, contemporary jewellery for daytime and that urban chic look that's starting to draw Berlin out of its streetwear phase. A great place.

BAERCK

Mulackstraße 12, Mitte
U-Bahn Weinmeisterstraße
Tel 30 2404 8994
www.baerck.net
Open noon to 8pm, closed Sunday
DESIGNERS

The former Fourstore has changed identity. It's still in the fashion business with a limited selection of sharp Berlin designers for men and women such as Études, Won Hundred, Vladimir Karaleev and Vibe Harsløf. But it's now into design, with French firms Petite Friture and L'Atelier d'Exercices and especially one of Baerck's three partners, Ilot Ilov, whose wooden furniture on rollers provides racks and display cases that can be easily moved around to match the mood of the occupant.

Don't miss the interior garden, and the basement where there are discount sales all the time.

BLESS

Oderberger Straße 60, 3rd floor,
Prenzlauer Berg
U-Bahn Eberswalder Straße
Tel 30 2759 6566
www.bless-service.de
Opening times vary
CONCEPTUAL, RECYCLED DESIGNS

Since 1977, Desiree Heiss and Ines Kaag have come up with about fifty conceptual exercises, under the Bless label, with each edition being something of a manifesto. They have constantly explored the edges of style, moving seamlessly between the fields of fashion and beauty, interior design, and art. They create unique products by recycling existing items in totally fresh and unexpected ways. Described by some as trash intellectuals and by others as cool provocateurs, they are actually faux radicals in the contemporary fashion world. To be able to express itself freely, Bless, which also exists in Paris, has left its storefront on Mulackstraße in Mitte and exiled itself to a third-floor apartment in a back courtyard in Prenzlauer Berg near Kastanienallee. You can't just happen upon the place by accident. But you can keep up with their parties, products and cult objects on their website.

BREE

Kurfürstendamm 36, Charlottenburg
U-Bahn Uhlandstraße
Tel 30 922 18 263, www.bree.com
Open 10am to 7pm, closed Sunday
BAGS

Wolf Peter and Renate Bree laid the foundations of their German leather bag empire in Hanover in 1970. Their first pieces were a satchel and a backpack. These days, their extensive collections are sold through a vast network of stores in Germany's major cities. In Berlin, in addition to its corner of the KaDeWe,

Bree has opened a shop in the gigantic Mall of Berlin, a recent addition to Leipziger Platz. It features everyday bags from the PB 0110 label founded by son Philipp Bree, for whom designers of the calibre of Ayzit Bostan and Christian Metzner have created some radical forms. Very popular with Berlin's urban nomads, who have had enough of Freitag bike bags.

BRILLEN SCHATZ

Postdamer Straße 79, Tiergarten
U-Bahn Kurfürstenstraße
Tel 30 6165 3702
www.brillenschatz.de/com
Open 11am to 7pm, Saturday until 5pm, closed Sunday

VINTAGE EYEWEAR

Unlike the shop of Swiss brand VIU, which has big windows giving onto the street, Brillen Schatz is hidden away in the entrance to the Mercator Höfe, and is only likely to be chanced upon as you head for the Andreas Murkudis concept store or one of the many galleries. The black, shiny decor has a hint of guitar hero mixed with Jules Verne submariner. There's a selection of sunglasses from the 1950s to the 1990s, including designs by top designers (Cartier, Dior, Jean-Paul Gaultier, Matsuda) and others by leading frame-makers like Alain Mikli and Robert La Roche. From the standard shapes and colours found everywhere – aviator, pantone – to the asymmetrical delights of the 1980s, it's a visual plunge into the recent past.

CAMPBELL

Kurfürstendamm 188, Wilmersdorf
U-Bahn Kurfürstendamm
Tel 30 8862 9809, www.campbell-optik.de
Open 10am to 7pm, Saturday until 6pm, closed Sunday

EYEWEAR

Campbell, self-proclaimed as the oldest eyewear shop in the world, was founded in Hamburg in 1816 by William Campbell and is still going strong on Neuer Wall,

with outposts in Stuttgart, New York, Palm Beach and here in Berlin. The firm designs and hand-makes unique collections for men and women. Its perfect, precise, assertive style has strong appeal for its customers – mainly architects, publishers and lawyers, who determinedly wear horn-rimmed glasses, the favourite material of this trusty brand. A second Berlin shop located at the foot of Gorki Apartments targets a younger clientele with tighter budgets: **CAMPBELL ZWEI** Weinbergsweg 21, Mitte, tel 030 8876 9040

CLAUDIA SKODA

Mulackstraße 8, Mitte
U-Bahn Weinmeisterstraße
Tel 30 4004 1884
www.claudiaskoda.com
Open 12:30pm to 6:30pm, closed Sunday

ICONIC DESIGNER

A pedigree Berliner, Claudia Skoda prides herself on being the oldest fashion designer still at work in the city, having started in 1973. Her first customers were men, and the most enthusiastic was the artist Martin Kippenberger, who just happened to share a squat with her in Kreuzberg. It was in this intensely arty, protest-driven neighbourhood that she opened her first shop, and David Bowie and Iggy Pop were customers during their Berlin days. Despite the times, Claudia was more Dominatrix than punk. She even made a record about it, and starred in three films, including one directed by Robert Van Ackeren. Her first husband decided that she should officially work in fashion. Good at drawing, she was also the first Berlin designer to open in New York in 1982, where Vivienne Westwood was a neighbour on Thompson Street in Soho. She spent five years going back and forth catering to an elite clientele led by Veruschka. Back in Berlin, Claudia Skoda opened a high-impact spot on the Ku'damm, designed by Marc Newson. It closed ten years later and the decor was auctioned by de Pury. The Wall came down, and Claudia escaped to Mitte.

Always close to young people, she gave up on avant-garde experiments and switched to what people wanted to wear. Her hallmark: colours and knits for women and men recognizable from afar. After Linienstraße and Alte Schönhauser Straße (which reminded her of Soho), she ended up in Mulackstraße. She has taken some of her bits and bobs, and Andreas Tesch has created an amazing ceramic wall. Easy to wear, and so comfortable (you'll never want to take off her tracksuits), her clothes come in vibrant colours and lines, fades and slightly acid geometries.

THE CORNER BERLIN

Französische Straße 40, Mitte
U-Bahn Französische Straße
Tel 30 2067 0940
www.thecornerberlin.de
Open 10am to 7pm, closed Sunday
DESIGNER COLLECTIONS

This is a must-see address in a neighbourhood better known for luxury hotels than shopping till you drop, even though the Q206 and Galeries Lafayette are just a flip of a credit card away. The Corner is a distillation of all the gimmicks of international concept stores. Founded in 2006 by Josef Voelk and Emmanuel Bayser, this cool shop has a twin that opened in the West, beautifully decorated in 1950s Milanese style where there is a sharp, glamorous, international and eclectic selection including Alaïa, Victoria Beckham, Rick Owens, Balenciaga, Maison Michel, Christian Louboutin, Céline and Isabel Marant. **Other location:** Wielandstraße 29, Charlottenburg, tel 30 206 13 764

DARKLANDS

Lindower Straße 22, Wedding
U-Bahn Leopoldplatz
S-Bahn Wedding
www.darklandsberlin.com
Open noon to 7pm, closed Sunday
CULT FASHION

Campbell McDougall is Canadian by birth. Following a few years in Canada spent developing retail fashion concepts like Komakino, he is now in Berlin, very busy clothing the city's underground ultra-techno scene in his futurist and extravagant outfits, available in one colour only: black. In store, the big guy is firming up exclusive brand partnerships with Alexander Fielden, Kuboraum, Boris Bidjan Saberi, MA+, Julius, Leon Emanuel Blanck, Sandrine Philippe, Carol Christian Poell, Cédric Jacqemyn and, counter-intuitively, the veteran Geoffrey B. Small. Esoteric, neo-Goth, avant-garde but not into trends, he seems to move to a new place every six months. The previous one, a perfect, Brutalist concrete cavern, was on Heidestraße, in Moabit. The new one – but for how long? – is up on the second floor of a huge former workers' hostel at the back of an abandoned courtyard in Wedding. Ideal for wrecking your look before you even get there. One to track.

DAS NEUE SCHWARZ

Mulackstraße 38, Mitte
U-Bahn Weinmeisterstraße
Tel 2787 4467
www.dasneueschwarz.de
Open noon to 8pm, closed Sunday
VINTAGE MEN'S AND WOMENSWEAR

The New Black is aptly named, because apart from rare exceptions, you'll only find black (or very dark grey) clothing and accessories. This shop specializes in young branded vintage and tries hard to stick to a clear stylistic line, despite the diversity. And as vintage is a second religion in Berlin, everyone is happy to take communion here. Meaning women *and* men.

DO THE DONT'S

Mommsenstraße 3, Charlottenburg
S-Bahn Savignyplatz
Tel 030 407 45 563
www.dothedonts.com
Open 2pm to 7pm, Saturday 11am to 5pm,
closed Sunday
REBEL LABEL

Or the contemporary Berlin version of the famous slogan "banning is banned". And it's creative. First off, the choice of location, very Westens-chic for a project that might have been better somewhere between Brunnenstraße and Prenzlauer Berg. Proof that following on from the Wall, Berlin's social partitions are falling too. A collective, bringing together all kinds of artists, designers and creatives, DtD occupies an unglamorous showroom/corridor. A nice bike, T-shirts on a rail arranged by colour, a few objects: the company is just starting out but already has a commitment to highlight sustainable design in all its forms. And at all prices. No falling back onto useless gadgets.

ÉCOLE BOUTIQUE

Torstraße 3, Mitte
U-Bahn Rosa-Luxemburg-Platz
Tel 30 2236 1206
www.ecole-boutique.com
Open noon to 8pm, closed Sunday
GLAMOROUS DESIGNER COLLECTIONS

Viola Jaeger is the proud founder and owner of Très Bonjour, a sexy-chic latex dressmaking salon, whose next-door neighbour was a driving school. When this closed down, she kicked into gear and took over the premises, retaining the name École. She placed a fine old trunk found in a Paris flea market right in the middle of the place, and architect Adrian Bleschke built a glass cage around it, in a creamy, white-lacquered decor studded with niches for light-filled mirrors. She also uses glass cages to exhibit the tribal jewellery by Tel Aviv brand Adi Lev and the Australian designer Mariposa, as well as Berlin-based Kjelf. Without reneging on her appetite for

sexy wear, Jaeger packs plenty of avant-garde into her selection of urban glam designs that perfectly match the London touch on the net-like designs of Sasha Louise Latex. Well-schooled, indeed.

EDSOR

Hotel Adlon Kempinski,
Unter den Linden 77, Mitte
U-Bahn Brandenburger Tor
Tel 30 40 054 666, www.edsor.de
Open daily 11am to 7pm,
Saturday and Sunday 10am to 6pm
NECKTIES

Despite the very English-sounding name standing for Edward Windsor, this silk tie and accessories factory, the oldest in Germany, is fundamentally Berliner. Founded in 1909 and capitalizing on the Windsor knot, it even supplied the Kaiser. Hence its name Edsor Kronen. Its fame continued into the Second World War. The company removed "crown" from its company name in 1954, but kept the symbol in its embroidered logo. Taken over in 2010 by Jan-Henrik Scheper-Stuke, heir to the founders and fifth-generation tie-maker, Edsor, with a factory still in Kreuzberg, opened its first shop in the touristy Hackesche Höfe, and now sells its high-quality, well-designed items from its shop in the stunning Hotel Adlon Kemplinski.

ESTHER PERBANDT

Almstadtstraße 3, Mitte
U-Bahn Rosa-Luxemburg-Platz
Tel 30 8853 6791
www.estherperbandt.com
Open 10am to 7pm, Saturday noon to 6pm,
closed Sunday
EMERGING DESIGNER

In 2009 Esther Perbandt was, together with Frida Weyer, the big discovery of Fashion Week thanks to a New Faces Award. She was also seen in Tokyo and Paris taking part in specialized shows. Based in this shop where she regularly presents her collections in the form of

shows, Esther Perbandt is popular
with women Berliners who like to strike
a balance between style and individuality.
With its white walls, round coat-pegs,
and stray pieces of furniture provided
by Marie-Pascale Charles of Deco Arts,
the decor is basic, like her fashion; black
and off-white, accessorized by a stylish
collection of leather bags. A personality,
most certainly.

FALKE

Kurfürstendamm 36, Charlottenburg
U-Bahn Uhlandstraße
Tel 30 8855 3565, www.falke.com
Open 10am to 7pm, closed Sunday
SOCKS
Located in Schmallenberg, Falke is
a Rhenish family firm with a glowing
reputation. Linked to Christian Dior from
1953 to 1999, it acquired the Burlington
brand in 2008 to swell its emblematic
graphic heritage. After the closure of
its small outlet in Friedrichstraße, a store
within a store at Quartier 206, Germany's
best-known brand of hosiery took its
time relocating. Opened in 2006 by the
Ku'damm, this new store was designed
with intelligence, style and some daring.
It displays the label's whole range of
women's tights and stockings, as well as
men's socks. The latter are available long
or short, in cashmere or cotton, merino or
Scottish wool, coloured or neutral, plain
or striped – and lasting, to boot. Using
an ingenious colour system, one chooses
the styles like one would a painting, a tile
or a set of writing paper. In the back,
you can find children's and sports items,
including incredible walking shoes with
extra comfortable pads. Otherwise,
Falke is constantly expanding its collections
with cashmere and merino knitwear and
ultra-thin sports sweaters.

FIONA BENNETT

Potsdamer Straße 81–83, Tiergarten
U-Bahn Kurfürstenstraße
Tel 30 2809 6330
www.fionabennett.com
Open 10am to 7pm, closed Sunday
THEATRICAL HATS
A very smart woman and a talented
Anglo-German milliner, Fiona Bennett
dropped off the radar after closing her salon
in Mitte and only emerged occasionally
to dress the hotel staff here or a celebrity
there. But now she's back, debonair as ever,
another migrant to the west of the city.
Her shop is near Andreas Murkudis, and
has large windows through which you can
see the stacks of wooden forms in her
workshop. She has reinvented her decor as
round pink niches in which her adorable
titfers made of feathers, velvet, plumes, fur
and jet summon up memories of George
Cukor's film *The Women*. So it's hardly
surprising that she supplies hats for film
and stage, especially the musicals at the
Theater des Westens. Her black-and-white-
striped hatboxes, recalling Buren's columns
in Paris, complete her aesthetic agenda,
while the yellow cover of her book
Vom Locken der Federn adds a dash of dazzle.

GARAGE

Ahornstraße 2, basement, Schöneberg
U-Bahn Nollendorfplatz
Tel 30 211 2760
www.kleidermarkt-vintage.de
Open 11am to 7pm,
Saturday until 6pm, closed Sunday
SECONDHAND CLOTHING
A Tatort-style impasse and a consulate,
opposite a grey block of social housing.
Down on the right, a yellow sign. Take
the stairs down to the basement. There
you find something between a garage and
a Berlin thrift shop much pawed-over
by fashion people who want more than
a choice of white teddy bears and green
military coats. There's an inevitable smell
of disinfectant, but also a more exciting
scent of unexpected treasures. Just keeping

searching and sorting. Wednesdays from 11am to 1pm, Garage has a happy hour with at least 30 percent off all items.

GOLETZ BOWTIES
Paul-Lincke-Ufer 30, Kreuzberg
U-Bahn Kottbusser Tor
Tel 176 7045 606
www.goletzbowties.com
By appointment only
BESPOKE BOWTIES

The ultimate in men's fashion, and with a delightful feminine twist, these bowties are the creation of just one young designer: Daniel Goletz. He ties them with the dexterity of an entomologist into fun and elegant accessories for day or evening. From the true classics to the most extravagant, his creations, the fruits of an exuberant imagination, suit every mood and material. Particularly special: his feathered ties, a real touch of fantasy. The address is for information only: Daniel Goletz comes to you, at home or at your hotel, and creates your dream bowtie in just six days.

HANNES ROETHER
Torstraße 109, Mitte
U-Bahn Rosenthaler Platz
Tel 30 4737 7375
www.hannesroetherinternational.de
Open daily 11am to 7pm, closed Sunday
MEN'S KNITWEAR

Based in Munich, where he also has his own shop, Hannes Roether is a proven name in knits that he designs, cuts, rolls and mixes in anything from thick twisted wool to the finest merino. His simple, creative, attractive and off-beat collections for men include curly felt, velvet and linen blended into sweaters, jackets, vests, T-shirts, trousers, and hoods, always in black, grey, brown, navy, khaki, steel blue and white, but incredibly comfortable; they can be worn anywhere and radiate a unique charm. Both of his Berlin stores are decorated with a studied sense of shabby chic and are well worth a visit, one

for men and one for women. You pop in for a hat and a belt and you come out with a bulging suitcase. **Other location** (women's store): Brunnenstraße 6–7, Mitte, tel 30 9606 1066

HAPPY SHOP
Torstraße 67, Mitte
U-Bahn Rosenthaler Platz,
Rosa-Luxemburg-Platz
Tel 30 2900 9501
www.happyshop-berlin.de
Open 11am to 7pm,
Saturday noon to 6pm, closed Sunday
COLOURFUL DESIGNERS

It's official, Torstraße is now divided into two distinct zones, NoTo and SoTo; North of Torstraße and South of Torstraße. This contagious New Yorkism was immediately adopted by the store **SOTO** for men (Torstraße 72, tel 030 2576 2070). Just opposite, Mischa Woeste opened the Happy Shop in January 2011. Although it looks like a pop-up store with its black-and-white-striped facade and its very 1980s LA green-neon sign, the shop is a permanent one. Mischa's selection is designed to attract hip thirty-somethings, with men's and womenswear by Kitsuné, Minä Perhonen, Yohji Yamamoto, Uslu Airlines, Cat's Tsumori Chisato and Toga Archives. Designed by Fingerle & Woeste, the decor, with wooden racks and hanging shelves, is perfect for this niche. The welcome here is warm and happy.

HEIMAT BERLIN
Kastanienallee 40, Prenzlauer Berg
U-Bahn Eberswalder Straße
Tel 30 889 48 059
www.heimat-berlin.eu
Open noon to 7pm, closed Sunday
HATS, ACCESSOIRIES

Not far from Prater, Heimat is making "a little go a long way" with two stores along this same street (nos. 13/14 and 40). This one is for men, with caps and hats – Stetson predominates – shoes, socks, artefacts, small fun trinkets, skincare

products and beard-care kits for the type sported by Captain Fawcett. Plus a few books on how to do the hipster thing properly and a bunch of gifts (or treats for yourself) to help you look good.
Other locations: Bergmannstraße 19, Kreutzberg; Kastanienallee 13/14, Prenzlauer Berg

HENNEMANN & BRAUN

Senefelderstraße 32, Prenzlauer Berg
U-Bahn Eberswalder Straße
S-Bahn Prenzlauer Allee
Tel 30 4004 2861
www.massschuhmacherei.de
Open 10pm to 6pm, Saturday 11am to 4pm, and by appointment, closed Sunday and Monday
CUSTOM-MADE SHOES
Shaping, sizing and assembling women's shoes, from classic lace-ups and extravagant slip-ons to red ankle boots with a Louis XV heel and hunting boots, Kirstin Hennemann remains the only well-established *Maßschuhmacherei* in the city. This young bootmaker has a devoted clientele of thirty-somethings who will stop at nothing to get their hands on a pair of her creations in cordovan leather, crocodile and ostrich. Boosted by her success, she has also expanded her range for men by making Budapesters, lace-ups, Oxfords, derbies and ankle boots. As part of her ready-to-wear collection, she also has hunting and rain boots in rubber and tweed, as well as the stout Bavarian Haferl shoes by Trabert with side laces.

HERR VON EDEN

Alte Schönhauser Straße 14, Mitte
U-Bahn Weinmeisterstraße
Tel 30 288 74 354
www.herrvoneden.de
Open 11am to 8pm, closed Sunday
NEO-VINTAGE FOR MEN
Originally Germany's main specialist in rare vintage menswear, Bent Angelo Jensen has moved on to design collections based on the classic tailored three-piece suit,

along with a myriad of accessories. Though he's based in Hamburg, HvE has another store in Cologne, and in Berlin, of course, where he supplies smart wear for anyone who's had enough of urban or goth. This showroom-store would put any neo-dandy at ease: its first section contains impeccable rows of suits, from the very sober to the very playful, and suitcases full of ties scattered here and there. Past the sales desk as frontier post and the cologne bars where you can try his own fragrances and look through the selection of Mühle shaving accessories, there's a second space, less formal but just as select, offering evening wear, double cuff shirts, hats and bowties. A retro style from the 1930s to the 1960s, between Joe Jackson and Bobby Darin in Las Vegas, gives way to a more funky contemporary look, moving between John Waters and David Bowie.

JGL JOHN GLET

Mehringdamm 27, Kreuzberg
U-Bahn Gneisenaustraße
Tel 30 695 860, www.john-glet.de
Open 9am to 6pm, Saturday until 2pm, closed Sunday
PRACTICAL CLOTHING
Just opposite the windowless fortress of a tax office, JGL is a store specializing in work clothing and accessories for building sites or repair jobs, including plumbing, carpentry and other trades that require robust, practical gear. All this is of little interest to most people, of course, but those who have a thing about thick, bright yellow and orange T-shirts, split leather belts, chain belt key-rings, work boots and driller's gloves – in other words, the trappings of a Village People highlander that sex shops sell for a fortune – then this place is a gold mine. Here, it all costs next to nothing, but you have to pay cash: credit cards are not accepted.

JIL SANDER

Kurfürstendamm 185, Charlottenburg

U-Bahn Adenauerplatz

Tel 30 886 7020, www.jilsander.com

Open 10am to 7pm, Saturday until 6pm,
closed Sunday

ICONIC DESIGNER

The story that began in a small clothing store in Hamburg in 1967 is well-known, as is Jil Sander's own saga. One day the designer sold her revered, minimalist, yet globally popular brand to Prada Group and then shut the door. What followed was a game of musical chairs among artistic directors until Raf Simons calmed things down. Jil Sander's own whereabouts kept fuelling fashion news about the sale and resale of the brand. A regular Swiss cuckoo clock of transactions. But the talent remained intact, and that became a global hit at Uniqlo as part of a capsule collection. Jil Sander herself returned as a consultant and then quit again, this time for good, promise. In 2014, by which time the company had been bought by the Onward group, she was replaced by the Italian Rodolfo Paglialunga, who arrived from Vionnetex having previously been at Prada. Opened in 1994, the immense flagship store on Ku'damm has moved on and been replaced by Louis Vuitton. It is now a little further down the street. Its strikingly simple interior, completed in 2016, was designed by the Milanese architect Andrea Trognon. It's the ideal setting for showing new developments in the collections, now under the artistic direction of Lucie & Mike Meier, reinjecting some pan-Germanic DNA into the brand.

JIYOUNG KIM

Postdamer Straße 91, Tiergarten

U-Bahn Kurfürstenstraße

Tel 30 2579 7004, www.theslowissue.com

Open noon to 8pm, closed Sunday

CREATIVE SHIRTS

Since studying fashion in Berlin, the Korean Jiyoung Kim has focused her attention on one major item of the female wardrobe: the shirt (or blouse as the nuns at her old convent school would have it). A shirt in extra-basic colours – black, white, grey – thinly striped, cotton, in sizes from S to XXL, aimed at a clientele who like the style twists she puts on the usual patterns for its shape. Sleeves, neck, buttons, length, width, volume: the repertoire is disrupted, perfectly in tune with an urban generation besotted with purist and minimalist textile designs, and always *made in Berlin*. On a mezzanine in the same courtyard as the Panama Restaurant and Maisonnoée, it's well worth going down the few stairs to her studio for an insight.

J.R. LEDERMANUFAKTUR

Gipsstraße 7, Mitte

U-Bahn Rosenthaler Platz

Tel 30 2838 7136

www.ledermanufaktur-berlin.de

Open noon to 6pm, Saturday until 5pm,
closed Sunday and Monday

LEATHER BAGS AND ACCESSORIES

Jörn Rischke has had a workshop-boutique in Mitte for many years and his brand is now almost a local classic. Always sporting his leather apron as he bends over his bench, he crafts bespoke bags, suitcases, briefcases, knapsacks and travel bags from very, very thick leather that he dyes himself and then polishes with olive oil. These manly, timeless and indestructible pieces come with a twenty-year guarantee.

JÜNEMANN'S PANTOFFELECK

Torstraße 39, Mitte

U-Bahn Rosa-Luxemburg-Platz

Tel 30 442 5337, www.pantoffeleck.de

Open 9am to 6pm,
closed Saturday and Sunday

SLIPPERS

Since 1908 the Jünemann family has been making every imaginable style of felt slippers. Their curious shop near Alexanderplatz, tucked away in Torstraße, has been extended and modernized. Günter and Reno (third and fourth generations) carry on the tradition by supplying Berliners with slippers, carpet slippers and clogs they can slip on as soon as they remove their Birkenstocks. The "Berliner" model, yellow and checked brown (up to size 52), also known as the Niedertreter, remains a best-seller, representing impeccable stylishness. However, choosing curtains or a bedspread to match would be an act of extreme bravery.

KADEWE BERLIN

Tauentzienstraße 21–24, Schöneberg
U-Bahn Wittenbergplatz
Tel 30 21 210
www.kadewe.de
Open 10am to 8pm, Friday until 9pm,
Saturday from 9:30am, closed Sunday
LUXURY DEPARTMENT STORE
The Kaufhaus des Westens was designed by Johann Emil Schaudt for its original owner, Adolf Jandorf, and opened in 1907. Its name was soon shortened to KaDeWe (pronounced "Kah-day-vay"). Hermann Tietz added it to his collection of Berlin department stores in 1927, but when the Nazis came to power, KaDeWe was confiscated from the Jewish owners. Totally destroyed in the Allied bombings of 1943, the store was rebuilt, remodelled and enlarged in the 1950s. It stood as a cheeky champion of capitalism throughout the Cold War, its shelves groaning with Western novelties and luxury goods from around the globe, full of fantastic items mocking East Berlin. In 1990, when the East Germans came in droves to see and touch this cathedral to consumer society, the store underwent another makeover, designed by architect Hans Soll. On the first day, over 180,000 people flocked to see the new KaDeWe with their own eyes. Three years later, it treated itself to an extra floor and a rooftop restaurant designed by Strömming Ernst & Partner. The sixth-floor food hall is one gigantic banquet, featuring an upscale food supermarket with prices to match, and various specialist

gourmet sections with food counters where you can sample oysters, lobster, bouillabaisse, champagne, shrimp sandwiches, cooked fish, pastries, and much, much more. But be warned, you'll need a few words of German to know exactly what you're getting. The staff won't speak a word of any other language, which is odd for a place whose client base is 70 percent foreign. The chocolates and confectionery department is a folly of sugar, and the Lenôtre stand is rightly regarded as the best cake shop in town. The breathtaking toy department and the lavishly stocked men's department on level 1 are both well worth a visit. The top luxury goods brands and beauty products are sumptuously spread out in their individual display areas on the ground floor. The recent renovation by Rem Koolhaas marks the beginning of a new era for Germany's most famous department store.

KAVIAR GAUCHE

Linienstraße 44, Mitte
U-Bahn Rosa-Luxemburg-Platz,
Rosenthaler Platz
Tel 30 2887 3562
www.kaviargauche.com
Open noon to 7pm and by appointment,
closed Sunday
ELEGANT WOMENSWEAR, BRIDAL WEAR
The name, of course, comes from "gauche caviar". Graduates of the Berlin branch of Esmod, Alexandra Fischer-Roehler and Johanna Kühl created their label in 2004, and were first noticed in London two years later. Their dresses and accessories have already caught the eye of the likes of Charlize Theron and Heike Makatsch. Their ready-to-wear collections, previously available only in their workshop, are now sold in a beautiful store with a black parquet floor and glowing with smoked glass. A line of wedding dresses and another of bags have been added to their existing collections of cocktail and evening dresses, displayed on curving racks in arabesque shapes. The **VINTAGE STORE**

(Brunnenstraße 6, Mitte, tel 30 95611044)
sells items from past collections together
with high-quality finds.

KONK

Kleine Hamburger Straße 15, Mitte
U-Bahn Rosenthaler Platz
Tel 30 2809 7939, www.konk-berlin.de
Open noon to 7pm, Saturday until 6pm,
closed Sunday
CONCEPT STORE

For years, Konk has been an address that
counts for established and emerging
designers where they get serious exposure
and reach customers in the know. Founded
by Ettina Berrios-Negrón, who handed it
over to trained tailor Edda Mann when she
left to focus on her brand Thone Negrón,
Konk ignores the trappings and gets
straight down to the labels, such as the
promising Berliner Isabell de Hillerin, Hui
Hui, Hanna Pordzik and Nico Sutor.

LABO.ART

Bikini Berlin,
Budapester Straße 38–50, Tiergarten
S-Bahn Zoologischer Garten
Tel 30 920 34 992, www.laboart.com
Open 9am to 8:30pm, Sunday noon to 6pm
RADICAL FASHION

Ludovica Diligu is Sardinian. Her label,
Labo.Art, founded in 2006, is based
in Milan, where she opened a shop
on via Maroncelli long before it became
fashionable. The Berlin store followed,
on Brunnenstraße in Mitte, and was a big
success, the decor and collections chiming
better with Berlin attitudes and habits.
Time has passed. Milan has moved on
to new trends, while Berlin has become
more conservative. So Labo.Art has moved
on to Bikini Berlin, which is undergoing
a commercial transformation three years
after it opened. The post-industrial raw
concrete structures sit well with Ludovica
Diligu's radical roots and cachet,
and her collections, season after season,
achieve near-classic status among her
committed and loyal clientele.

LALA BERLIN

Alte Schönhauser Straße 3, Mitte
U-Bahn Weinmeisterstraße
Tel 2009 5363
www.lalaberlin.com
Open 11am to 7pm, closed Sunday
FASHIONABLE DESIGNER

Lala Berlin, alias Leyla Piedayesh, is one
of the most prominent designers of the
moment, partly because she has clothed
Claudia Schiffer and some well-
photographed emerging stars. Following
a period when she met with her (female)
customers in the workshop where she
continues her dressmaking, she opened
a Lala store where her Lala style became
synonymous with contemporary, sexy
ready-to-wear that her customers love.

LIENERIE

Linienstraße 75, Mitte
U-Bahn Rosenthaler Platz
Tel 30 537 94 971
www.lienerie.de
Open 11am to 7pm,
Saturday until 6pm, closed Sunday
LINGERIE

Now Blush has pulled down the shutters
and Schiesser has completely obliterated
its "100% cotton" quality reputation,
this new store selling underwear for women
(and men) is the place to go for your pure
Baumwolle. It's amazing how many brands,
styles and patterns can be stocked in
such a small space, a lace-edge away from
Linienstraße, hence the play on words.
You'll find Asceno, 1979, November,
Sommerfeld, Zimmerli, Hanro, About
Underwear, esSeawear, Falke, and more.
Items are sourced in Switzerland,
Scandinavia and Belgium, the heartlands
of top-quality lingerie. The swimwear is
great, as well. Fantastic.

LOUIS VUITTON

Kurfürstendamm 185, Charlottenburg
U-Bahn Adenauerplatz
Tel 882 52 72, www.louisvuitton.com
Open 10am to 7pm,
Saturday until 6pm, closed Sunday
LUXURY HOUSE

Since 2000, Louis Vuitton can also be found in the large KaDeWe department store, where it has a sumptuous space on the ground floor showcasing luggage, leather goods, accessories, shoes and fragrance. Louis Vuitton was one of the first luxury houses to open on the Ku'damm following the fall of the Wall, helping to turn this section of one of Berlin's most emblematic streets into a bastion of international luxury. The house now occupies the huge spaces of the former Jil Sander store, which has moved a few metres further on. The store sells luggage, leather goods, accessories, shoes, fragrance and ready-to-wear, while its windows are scrutinized by all the students of the city's fashion schools.

LOUIS VUITTON

To contact the customer relations service covering all Louis Vuitton stores in Berlin: 0211 864700. For news on all Louis Vuitton activities go to: www.louisvuitton.com

KURFÜRSTENDAMM
Kurfürstendamm 185, Charlottenburg,
U-Bahn Adenauerplatz, open 10am
to 7pm, Saturday until 6pm,
closed Sunday

Luggage, leather goods, accessories, ready-to-wear, shoes and fragrance

KADEWE Tauentzienstraße 21-24,
Schöneberg, U-Bahn Wittenbergplatz,
open 10am to 8pm, Friday until 9pm,
Saturday from 9:30am, closed Sunday

Luggage, leather goods, accessories, shoes and fragrance

LUNETTES SELECTION

Torstraße 172, Mitte
U-Bahn Rosenthaler Platz
Tel 30 2021 5216
www.lunettes-selection.de
Open noon to 8pm, closed Sunday
EYEWEAR

Attention all eyes: run smoothly and seriously by Uta Geyer, the Lunettes Selection branch of the eyewear shop Lunettes is a small *Mad Men*-style design miracle, with contemporary wooden furniture, a big mirror, two flowers in a glass vase and neon lighting. On the displays and in the drawers there is nothing but certified, good-as-new vintage and hip brands such as James Long and Cooperative Design, in the form of limited-series co-branding models. To have a pair of glasses with prescription lenses made for you, allow one week.
Other location: Dunkerstraße 18, Prenzlauer Berg, tel 30 4471 8050

MAISONNOÉE

Potsdamer Straße 91, Tiergarten
U-Bahn Kurfürstenstraße
Tel 30 8010 5028
www.maisonnoee.com
Open 10am to 8pm, closed Sunday
WOMEN'S FASHION

Located in a quiet interior courtyard, also home to the Panama restaurant and the Tiger Bar, Maisonnoée sells its range of elegant and timeless fashion. Square concrete blocks on the floor, white walls, furniture by Eileen Gray: the designer Sophie Oemus, née Böhmert (she insists), who launched the company in 2013, displays her collections with sophisticated flair, exporting them with great success across the world – even to Los Angeles, with a pop-up store on Abbot Kinney in Venice. Muted, neutral colours, astute cutting, skilled leatherwork, short, long, knitted.

MICHALSKY GALLERY

Potsdamer Platz 4, Tiergarten
S-Bahn and U-Bahn Potsdamer Platz
Tel 30 2693 3280
www.michalsky.com
Open noon to 7pm and by appointment,
closed Sunday and Monday
DESIGNER
Dynamic designer Michael Michalsky was
artistic director for Adidas (the lines on
the Y–3 sneakers are thanks to him), Stella
McCartney and Missy Elliott, as well as less
iconic names like Munich brand MCM,
a kind of sub-Escada of handbags, and even
Tchibo, a popular brand, although you
never knew if it sold coffee or terry towels.
Now the slate is clean. In late August 2009,
he opened the Michalsky Gallery right
next to the Ritz-Carlton, where he sells
a selection from his collections for women
and men, sunglasses, luxury sneakers and
Urban Nomads fragrances, together with
work by others he is particularly fond of.
In the middle of this black and gold space
is an ancient Persian chest set with
precious stones and duly encased in glass,
an object that on its own justifies visiting
this address. Michalsky is also trying his
hand at decoration with a rug collection.
To be continued.

MIMI

Goltzstraße 5, Schöneberg
U-Bahn Eisenacher Straße
Tel 30 2 363 8438, www.mimi-berlin.de
Open noon to 7pm,
Saturday 11am to 4pm, closed Sunday
COLLECTIBLE CLOTHING
Despite growing competition from cheap
clothing and fake vintage items, and the
death of the manager of vintage outlet
Sterling Gold, who made *Dynasty* look like
Mother Courage (www.sterlinggold.de),
Mirjam Grese's wonderful vintage store
was saved by nearly fifteen years of the
unique work, culture and taste of Mirjam
herself. Collectors and wardrobe managers
flock here (the wardrobe manager for
Quentin Tarantino's *Inglourious Basterds*

came here to dress Diane Kruger, and
the wardrobe manager for the biopic
Hilde came to clad Heike Makatsch).
Mimi also does designs for many theatrical
productions and operas, and dressed
Daniel Brühl for a Western. Passing visitors
remain for hours in this pretty setting
where the (totally intentional) cutie style,
hatboxes and glass cabinets create the
atmosphere of a small museum. With
jewellery, accessories and menswear
straight out of Polanski's *The Pianist*, the
place is a real must and has the added
advantage of being on a pretty Schöneberg
street full of second-hand shops, fashion
boutiques, cafés and pastry shops. Just
opposite, for instance, is the delightful
MAMSELL (www.mamsellberlin.de) where
you can feast on cakes and chocolates to
console yourself for not fitting into those
marvellous 1954 Hermès gloves.

MYKITA SHOP

Rosa-Luxemburg-Straße 6, Mitte
U-Bahn Alexanderplatz
Tel 30 6730 8715, www.mykita.com
Open 11am to 8pm,
Saturday until 6pm, closed Sunday
EYEWEAR
A Berlin label, Mykita opened its first store
right here in 2007. It is intelligently laid
out with a white background, assorted
perforated back panels and furniture from
former Swissair planes. It's perfect for
presenting and storing all their eye- and
sunglass lines, including their capsule
collections designed with Romain Kremer
and Bernhard Willhelm. This highly
creative venture has expanded to include
Damir Doma and Maison Martin Margiela,
as well designer Kostas Murkudis and
singer Beth Ditto at times. Manufactured
and assembled by hand in a factory that
was moved from Brunnenstraße to the
Pelikan-Haus, a listed industrial hotel
located in Kreuzberg, Mykita frames are
sold worldwide in Mykita Shops with
the same interior design in Paris (in the
Marais), Tokyo, New York, Vienna and

Zurich. In Berlin, Mykita has also gone West with a second boutique inside the Bikini Berlin concept mall. Of the original quartet, only Moritz Krueger remains, now working with the charismatic Bernd Beetz, manager of the Coty group. **Other location:** Budapester Straße 38–50, Tiergarten, tel 30 2847 4114

NO 74

Torstraße 74, Mitte
U-Bahn Rosa-Luxemburg-Platz
Tel 30 5306 2513
www.no74-berlin.com
Open noon to 8pm, closed Sunday
SNEAKER CULTURE
It's No. 6 in London and No. 42 in Paris – the numbers on the street where Adidas opens special shops showcasing its partnerships with designers around the world. Since 2008, Berlin has been No 74 and sells Adidas sneakers by Stella McCartney, Adidas by Rick Owens, Adidas by Tom Dixon, the Y-3 collections, and the Adidas Originals and Performance models. There's an adrenalin rush of collaborations with designer brands Jeremy Scott, Opening Ceremony, Kazuki and Raf Simons for the legendary Stan Smith sneakers. The designers can show installations here and design performances that keep customers on their toes.

ODEEH SPACE

Potsdamer Straße 81a, Tiergarten
U-Bahn Kurfürstenstraße
Tel 30 2639 1159
www.odeeh.com
Open 11am to 5pm and by appointment, closed Sunday to Tuesday
CREATIVE WOMEN'S FASHION
Odeeh is living proof that one can live and create in the provinces – in this case not far from Nuremberg – and be a smash hit in Berlin and myriad other capitals around the world. Behind this women's fashion label, founded in 2008, is a male design duo, Otto Drögsler and Jörg Ehrlich, who both love geometric shapes, colours

and prints. Popular with the world's best boutiques, including the demanding Luisa in Florence, their collections are perfectly in tune with the zeitgeist of the modern city. Since March 2017, Odeeh has had its own space on Potsdamer Straße, on the ground floor of Anton von Werner Haus, just two sleeves – or perhaps a skirt – away from the Andreas Murkudis concept store, the first one in the city to believe in and sell the brand.

ORIMONO

Joachimstraße 5, Mitte
U-Bahn Rosenthaler Platz
Tel 30 5565 6694
www.orimono.eu
Open noon to 7:30pm,
Saturday until 6:30pm, closed Sunday
CONCEPT STORE DARK
Far from a novelty in the fashion forward landscape of Mitte, Orimono resists all the trends flying across the city. Proof that dark post-punk-neo-gothic-crypto-vampire lives forever. A tone specialist, its male/female wardrobe is worn by a hip and stylish crowd, with pieces selected from collections by Rick Owens, Army of Me, The Last Conspiracy, First Aid to the Injured, Thom/Krom, Versuchskind and even Odeur. With one colour instruction: wear nothing except noir-*black-nero-schwartz*. In fact you can, as Orimono does permit its black mass liturgy to include white, grey and red. Shoes, accessories, travel bags.

OUKAN

Ackerstraße 144, Mitte
U-Bahn Rosenthaler Platz
Tel 30 2062 6700
www.oukan.de/home.html
Open noon to 7pm, closed Sunday
AVANT-GARDE CONCEPT STORE
After housing the Aanant & Zoo contemporary art gallery and ArtBar 71, this amazing structure by architect Hans Käsbohrer has now been taken over on two levels by the enterprising Huy Thong

Tran Mai, founder and purchaser of this concept store that emerged out of a charity project in Tokyo in 2011. In just a few seasons, Oukan has established itself as the gateway for pioneering Japanese brands intent on targeting the Berlin fashion market. There is also a well-edited selection from Henrik Vibskov, Barbara I Gongini, Damir Doma, Thom Krom, Rad Hourani, and Leon Louis. Check out the NoNoYes leather wallets, Anrealage's punchy prints and Nutsa Modebadze's handmade leather goods to see how daring this place is, and take a break in the Japanese restaurant, **AVAN** (www.avanberlin.com), open for lunch and dinner every day. The whole place is perfectly isolated from the usual anachronistic retail outlets.

PAUL KNOPF

Zossener Straße 10, Kreuzberg

U-Bahn Gneisenaustraße

Tel 30 692 1212

www.paulknopf.de

Open 9am to 6pm, Wednesday and Thursday from 2pm, closed Saturday to Monday

ANTIQUE BUTTONS

Strange but true: in German, a button is a *Knopf*. And what does Paul "Button" sell? *Knöpfe*, of course. His shop has been here for years and contains an arsenal of buttons in their tens of thousands. And in almost as many different shapes, colours and materials. Customers come here ostensibly for a few buttons to facelift a faded trench coat or thrift-shop jacket and then spend hours combing through everything, especially as Herr Knopf is not the sort who buttons up when it comes to sharing information and stories. And, with a little luck, he will show collectors of old toys his riches, which occupy an adjoining shop. No credit cards.

RIMOWA

Kurfürstendamm 231, Charlottenburg

U-Bahn Kurfürstendamm

S-Bahn Zoologischer Garten

Tel 30 8800 30

Open 10am to 8pm, closed Sunday

LUGGAGE

Founded by Paul Morszeck back in 1898 in Cologne, still its main base, this celebrated brand of metal luggage waited until 2005 to open its first exclusive shop (in Munich, in the same location as the Porsche Design showroom), before opening in Berlin, though its products are also sold at KaDeWe. In 1930, Paul Morszeck became famous as the first manufacturer to use aluminium in suitcases and trunks for overseas travel. In 1950, he produced and marketed the Topas, Germany's first all-aluminium suitcase, which is still in the catalogue, along with a Gold version. As for the characteristic grooves found on all Rimowa luggage and the source of their enduring solidity, these were the work of the founder's son, Richard Morszeck, who based his design on the ribbed undercarriage of the Junkers Ju 52 aeroplane. Waterproof since 1976, fitted on two, or even four, wheels since 1996, Rimowa cases are available in several formats. The largest is a favourite with cameramen and film directors and has featured in some thirty films, including *Ocean's Twelve*, *Spider-Man, M. & Mrs. Smith* and *Taxi*. The aluminium version is still made in Cologne, with the newer coloured polycarbonate models produced in the Czech Republic. The historic collections have now been joined by some ultra-sophisticated travel accessories, such as a travel humidor and a special champagne case. In addition, following an agreement with Lufthansa, today's Rimowa cases are fitted with a Bluetooth tag to make check-in easy. Early in 2017, the third generation of Morszecks sold an 80% stake in Rimowa to LVMH.

SCHUH KONZEPT

Bleibtreustraße 24, Charlottenburg
S-Bahn Savignyplatz
Tel 30 3150 8067, www.schuhkonzept.de
Open 9am to 5pm, Saturday 10am to 6pm,
closed Sunday

SHOES

This shoe shop, which also houses
a high-quality repair service, sells every
accessory you need to keep your shoes
in good condition. The selection of shoes,
for men and women, spans the world's
leading manufacturers, from John Lobb
and Church to Borgioli and Cheaney,
and from Allen Edmonds to Heschung.

SONNENBERG

Lietzenburger Straße 62, Wilmersdorf
U-Bahn Uhlandstraße
Tel 30 887 09 640, www.sonnenberg.berlin
Open 10am to 7pm, Saturday 11am to 6pm,
closed Sunday

PET SHOP CHIC

Black walls decorated with white chalk
drawings, wooden cash registers, black and
white tiled floor, shelves that look more
like an apothecary than a pottery: this little
department store for dogs and cats sells
water and food bowls, baskets, brushes,
lotions and 100% natural food with a
whole pack of specialist brands: Wolfsblut,
Icepaw, Edelbeiss, Para Perro, Pfoody.
Plus a bespoke service available for pet
beds, mattresses and coats.

SPITZE

Suarezstraße 53, Charlottenburg
U-Bahn Sophie-Charlotte-Platz
Tel 30 313 1068
www.spitze-berlin.de
Open 2pm to 7pm, Saturday noon to 4pm,
closed Sunday to Tuesday

VINTAGE CHIC

Herbert Mayr and Axel Noltekuhlmann
moved to this address on Suarezstraße
a few years ago, after spending twenty-six
years on Weimarerstraße. They are
acknowledged experts in fashion history
and their assistance is regularly sought by
costume designers (in 2009 they supplied
the outfits for the Michael Haneke film
The White Ribbon). Then there are the
collectors and the merely curious, drawn
to the shop by chance. You'll find a whole
century of clothes here – accessories for
men and women, kaftans, hats, bags and
jewellery, a thousand wonderful examples
of trimmings, costume jewellery, and
much more. There are irresistible selections
of wing glasses, sleeve buttons, powder
compacts, purses and minaudières.

STARSTYLING

Mulackstraße 4, Mitte
U-Bahn Weinmeisterstraße
Tel 30 9700 5182
www.starstyling.net
Open noon to 7pm, closed Sunday

PARTY T-SHIRTS

The shop window stops you in your tracks.
Has Kristel Carrington returned and is she
about to do the Ferrero Rocher thing at
the ambassador's dinner party in a golden
dress, you wonder? Or better still, have The
Three Degrees got back together and are
they going to sing their disco music with
Boney M? The rather pretentious name
of this shop, which conjures up a celebrity
hairdresser, conceals an extraordinary duo,
Katja Schlegel and Kai Seifried, whose
imagination and creativity have nothing
to do with peroxide. Ever since Björk and
Brad Pitt were seen wearing them, people
have been fighting to get hold of their
T-shirts. It is impossible to categorize their
creations, however, as they are inspired
by thousands of influences and references,
including the very trashy. Illustrators and
photographers who work with them can't
stop singing their praises. Neither can we.

STUDIO 183

Brunnestraße 183, Mitte
U-Bahn Rosenthaler Platz
Tel 157 72547723
www.studio183.co

UP-AND-COMING LABELS

The endless Torstraße has seen plenty
of fashion concept stores come and go.
The one run by Mark Hunt and Katrina
Marie Ryback stands out from the rest.
The pair stock a sharp selection of labels
and collections that changes every
three months, making their store a sort
of seasonal shelter, including the inevitable
barista point, essential element of any
project these days. So it's purely by chance
that we discovered jewellery here by the
Danish designer Malene Glintborg,
merino and mohair knitwear by Frëtt, street
fashion from Buffet Clothing, urbanwear
by Bonboz, ranges from Louloublanche,
Temper, Chyarny, and even work by the
Russian designer Sonja Litichevskava,
plus work by a Berlin-based Korean, who
hides behind the label Assembled Half,
and by Studio Gampe, based in Berlin.
In other words, a fashion moment,
endlessly reworked and retouched. Studio
183 is also working in a space on the first
floor of Bikini Berlin.

TALBOT RUNHOF

Schlüterstraße 50, Charlottenburg
U-Bahn Uhlandstraße, S-Bahn Savignyplatz
Tel 30 233 63 170
www.talbotrunhof.com
Open 10am to 7pm, Saturday until 6pm

ELEGANT WOMENSWEAR

A dark and realistic satire about fame and
the theatre, *All About Eve* showed the fall
of a star, played by Bette Davis, pushed
out of the limelight by her young rival,
Eve Harrington, played by Anne Baxter
(grand-daughter of Frank Lloyd Wright).
The film was also a portrait of elegant
1950s New York society. When the
American-German duo of Johnny Talbot
and Adrian Runhof, then based in Munich,
got into fashion, they called their company

FOOT NOTES

Berliners walk a lot, and their main
concern is comfort. Especially the
need to protect themselves in winter,
when it freezes enough to split stones
apart, and the pavements are strewn
with salt so you can't go out in your
favourite sneakers. What you need
are big boots, hobnailed clodhoppers
fitted with soles thick as a snow tyre,
plus thick, woollen mountain socks
slipped over them, so you don't slip.
Once believed to be an urban legend,
this counter-style that thrilled the
Charlottenburg ladies is perfectly
real, though actually only applied in
extremis. But winters can be long and
harsh. So for women, it's boots in
winter, high heels in the spring and
early autumn, and flat sandals in
summer; men wear work shoes, biker
boots, or clodhoppers if they don't
work in an office. When they have to,
Berliners show an unfortunate
tendency to like either big, cheap,
ugly square shoes or tapered Italian
pumps. Needless to say, neither look
is recommended.

after the film. The fabric version of the
story of *All About Eve* followed a similar
plot: it was replaced by a ready-to-wear
label, Talbot Runhof, still sophisticated
but more commercial. Their showroom,
designed by Uli Tredup, opened in
2000 in Munich on Klenzestraße and
moved to the prestigious Palais Preysing
in Munich in 2015. A hit in Asia and
Australia, it took the company a few years
to travel west to Berlin, via KaDeWe,
of course. Now it is settled in the heart
of on-trend Charlottenburg in a glossy
interior, selling its collection of gowns
for evenings, weddings and the red carpet,
with all the requisite accessories.

THATCHERS

Kastanienallee 21, Prenzlauer Berg
U-Bahn Eberswalder Straße
Tel 30 246 27 751
www.thatchers.de
Open 11am to 7pm, closed Sunday

BERLIN FASHION

This fashion label, named as a cheeky reference to Margaret Thatcher and founded by Ralf Hensellek and Thomas Mrozek in 1994, was part of the Kastanienallee transformation in the post-Wall years. Hensellek and Mrozek belonged to a generation of designers who were self-taught and eclectic. Having recently celebrated its twenty-fifth anniversary, the brand now seems like a veteran pioneer. Sadly, the double act became a solo following the death of Hensellek in 2011. Since then, Mrozek has redefined its basic, classic and couture collections, and increased collaborations with visual artists through the Thatchers Salon, while remaining true to his heritage. Quite an achievement.

THONE NEGRÓN

Linienstraße 71, Mitte
U-Bahn Rosenthaler Platz
Tel 30 5316 1116
www.thonenegron.com
Open noon to 7pm, Saturday until 6pm,
closed Sunday

INNOVATIVE DESIGNER

If you want something done, do it yourself. Ettina Berrios-Negrón founded the Konk concept store and retailed her collections there under the Thone Negrón label until 2012, when she left to focus on her own label. Her space on Linienstraße is succinctly decorated, with a beautiful Dieter Rams sofa, a 1970s totem, as the reference point for the rest. The collection of short and long women's dresses, shirts, blouses and skirts offers a glossy Latin touch to brighten up life beneath the Berlin sky.

TO.MTO

Torstraße 22, Mitte
U-Bahn Rosa-Luxemburg-Platz
Tel 30 9700 4733, www.tomto.de
Open 10am to 6:30pm and by appointment,
closed Saturday and Sunday

CORSETS

Whether or not it's exactly fetishism, the corset is to Berlin what Scholl shoes are to nurses in a Black Forest clinic: a second skin, deep DNA, a source of pride. Once overshadowed by Revenge of the Woman or Hautnah, there is no question about Tonia Merz's skills at meshing together whale bones. Since she began in 2002, the lady has been corseting everyone, and delivering handmade corsets to operas, theatres and film sets, including *Carmen*, *Cabaret* and even the film *Speed Racer* by Andy and Lana Wachowski. The singer Barbara Schöneberger, Katy Perry and Nina Hagen for a Converse ad were corseted up by TO. Take another look at *The Girl Rosemarie*, a classic German post-war film with the gorgeous Nadja Tiller and see what a corset can do for you.

TRÈS BONJOUR

Torstraße 3, Mitte
U-Bahn Alexanderplatz, Rosa-Luxemburg-Platz
Tel 30 2280 3180
www.tresbonjour.de
Open noon to 8pm, closed Sunday

LATEX COUTURE

Viola Jaeger's latex couture salon is a little marvel of sensual teasing mixed with a healthy dose of suggestive humour. Opened in 2009, almost right opposite TO.mTO, Très Bonjour is both a workshop where all this latex lingerie is made by hand, and a shop which titillates, displaying latex jewellery by Denise Julia Reytan, latex charms by Anna Block and, above all, the panoplies and accessories of Viola herself, who has a soft spot for pasties (nipple bobbles). The style is closer to Dita von Teese than to Latexa Gummi, queen of the night. An address that is both pleasing and stimulating.

TRIPPEN GALLERY

Alte Schönhauser Straße 45, Mitte
U-Bahn Weinmeisterstraße
Tel 30 2463 2284, www.trippen.com
Open noon to 7pm, closed Sunday
ICONIC SHOES

In the Middle Ages, *Trippen* were "wooden soles". Developed in the mid-1990s by designers Angela Spieth and Michael Oehler, the Trippen brand took up the old idea again in a renewed craft workshop in the north of the city, turning Trippen into a successful, exportable Berlin product. It won an award from the Chicago Design Museum for its fashion shows for Claudia Skoda, Barbara Bui and Yohji Yamamoto and opened shops in London and Tokyo. It then melted back into the landscape for being too square, slightly overplaying its stylistic tourism number. Now it's made a comeback. In addition to its principal outlet in Hackescher Höfe and its new shops in Cologne and Munich, Trippen took a left turn with Trippen Gallery for its more radical, experimental lines. **Other location:** Hackesche Höfe, 4th courtyard, Rosenthaler Straße 40–41, Mitte, tel 30 2839 1337

TRÜFFELSCHWEIN

Rosa-Luxemburg-Straße 21, Mitte
U-Bahn Rosa-Luxemburg-Platz
Tel 30 7022 1225
www.trueffelschweinberlin.com
Open noon to 8pm,
Saturday until 7pm, closed Sunday
DESIGNER MENSWEAR

There is no lack of men's clothes shops in Mitte in general, all of them more or less interchangeable and carrying the same brands. This "truffle pig" stands out from the crowd by dint of its flair for bringing to light more specialized labels that deserve to be given a chance, such as Armor Lux, Hannes Roether, Hentsch Man and Dr. Bronner's toiletries, all presented in an amusing decor of wide-open antique wardrobes. The staff will even serve you a complimentary coffee.

ULF HAINES

Rosa-Luxemburg-Straße 24–26, Mitte
U-Bahn Rosa-Luxemburg-Platz
Tel 30 2887 3628
www.ulfhaines.com
Open noon to 8pm,
Saturday until 7pm, closed Sunday
INTERNATIONAL DESIGNERS

The Ulf Haines label, part of the Chambers group that also owns the Lux 11 and Weinmeister hotels, is the outlet in Berlin-Mitte of international labels like Ann Demeulemeester, Giuliano Fujiwara, Christian Wijnants, Stephan Schneider and Comme des Garçons. The collections for women are displayed in an angular interior designed by Frank Drews, with an atmosphere that is calm and relaxed. For menswear, head to nos. 24–26 on the same street.

VLADIMIR KARALEEV

Leipziger Straße 66, Mitte
U-Bahn Stadtmitte
Tel 30 9700 5218
www.vladimirkaraleev.com
Open by appointment
COUTURIER, WORKSHOP

Perfectly at ease with his Bulgarian origins, Vladimir Karaleev set up his promising Berlin fashion business in 2010. He joined in the Vogue Salon event intended to promote young German design, and has also been retailed at Baerck. His intensely monochromatic or mixed men's and women's clothes can also be custom-tailored in his workshop.

VOO STORE

Oranienstraße 24, Kreuzberg
U-Bahn Kottbusser Tor
Tel 695 797 2710
www.vooberlin.com
Open 10am to 8pm, closed Sunday
CONCEPT STORE

Mainstays of the Kreuzberg night scene, brothers Yasin and Kaan Müjdeci own the Luzia bar, and to keep the party going they opened the Voo Store in November 2010 on the same side of the street – in a decrepit locksmith's way back in a courtyard – the perfect setting for their idea of style. They were savvy enough to entrust the artistic direction and purchases to Herbert Hofmann, a young denizen of Kreuzberg associated with the Scandinavian designer Sigurd Larsen. Thanks to him, many designers and labels have managed to create an outlet in Berlin. Through his flair and sense of taste, he can blend the fashion of Kris Van Assche, Mad Len, The White Briefs, Issever Bahri, Hien Le, Stutterheim, Henrik Vibskov, Stine Goya, Uniforms for the Dedicated, and Silent by Damir Doma, with Six Scents perfumes, Uslu Airlines cosmetics, Field Notes notebooks, Astier de Villatte ceramics, sneakers by Adieu Paris or NikeLab x Marc Newson. Signalled by flashy green neon, this space features a brick facade with a cream-and-bottle-green glaze and 300 square metres of concrete that has more cracks than the walls around Chernobyl. A small café on a raised platform adds a peaceful touch. The wood and cement tables, together with the furniture, have been designed by Larsen. The old barrels and wooden crates help display a small selection of design and graphic objects. As soon as it opened, Voo Store became one of the most cutting-edge venues in Berlin, almost in spite of itself. In fact just as Luzia is more than a bar, Voo Store is more than a shop. It regularly holds meetings and puts on creative, graphic, and musical performances in this raw concrete setting.

WOLFEN

Auguststraße 41, Mitte
U-Bahn Weinmeisterstraße
Tel 30 4978 1966
www.wolfengermany.com
Open 11am to 7pm, Saturday until 6pm, closed Sunday

MINIMALIST MEN'S AND WOMENSWEAR

A former architect who successfully moved into fashion, Jacqueline Huste started out in a first-floor studio-showroom in a drab street in Mitte. Now she has a proper window display. Her pretty matt grey shop is fitted out in a minimalist, practical style. At the front of the store, you'll find womenswear, knitwear and scarves, which are austere, almost monastic in style. To the rear is her men's range: essential and understated. The architects, who have forgiven Jacqueline for deserting them – or are jealous of her – love it.

YVA BY KATHARINA SIGWART

Bleibtreustraße 20, Charlottenburg
U-Bahn Uhlandstraße
Tel 30 2838 4595
www.yva.de
Open 11am to 7pm,
Saturday 10am to 4pm, closed Sunday

STYLISH HATS

Else Ernestine Neuländer Simon, better known as Yva, was a great Berlin photographer who died after being deported. She was also the mentor of the young Helmut Newton before he left Berlin. So why the hats? No need for any head-scratching: Yva's mother was a milliner. Which is why Katharina Sigwart pays a jaunty homage to the lady by affording a stylish cover for men's and women's heads. In her corridor of "capital"

"Liberty is in the very air of Berlin now. It is good to be alive here, and to be young must be heaven. Everything is in flux, everything is changing, new horizons open, and nothing demands unqualified respect or allegiance." **Jan Morris, A Writer's World, 2003**

pleasures, the pretty hats for the dolls come with such suggestive names as Nadja, Filomena and Pia Stenja, while those for the guys are Anatol, Quentin and Max. In winter, go for the incredibly flattering caps and in summer a cream-blue Hugo panama. Big heads should choose bespoke.

ZEHA BERLIN

Prenzlauer Allee 213, Prenzlauer Berg
U-Bahn Senefelderplatz
Tel 30 4401 7214
www.zeha-berlin.de
Open noon to 8pm,
Saturday 10am to 6pm, closed Sunday

CULT SHOES

First stitched together by bootmaker Carl Hässner in Weida, Thuringia, in 1897, Zehas were immediately walking the high road to success, and by the 1920s the entire Berlin intelligentsia was sporting them. The factory was in the East, and after the war it went on to become official supplier for the GDR and Soviet Olympic teams. With the fall of the Wall, the once-revered Zehas were callously cast aside and by 1993 the brand was no more. And then, ten years later, stylish Berlin designers Alexander Barré and Torsten Heine brought them back, triply revamped: the Streetwear collection; the Urban Classics – and most famously of all – the Carl Hässner historic sneaker collection, inspired by 1950s football boots. Now run solely by Barré, the brand they opened this store in April 2014 as an outlet selling cheap pairs from previous collections. The iconic boots can also be found in Kreuzberg or at the Schöneberg branch, which is frequented by Barrie Kosky, director of the Komische Oper Berlin, who loves Zehas so much he owns dozens of pairs. **Other locations:** Belziger Straße 21, Schöneberg, tel 30 7895 0993; Friesenstraße 7, Kreuzberg, tel 695 38 855

WATCHES AND JEWELLERY

ASKANIA

Hackesche Höfe,
Rosenthaler Straße 40–41, Mitte
S-Bahn Hackescher Markt,
U-Bahn Weinmeisterstraße
Tel 30 2408 3169
www.askania-berlin.de
Open daily 10am to 8pm, Sunday to 5pm

HISTORIC COLLECTION

In the interwar years, Askania timepieces were found in the cockpits of Messerschmitts and the planes of the first German pilots to cross the Atlantic. The company was created in Berlin in 1871 by Carl Bamberg, himself the son of a watchmaker and adjuster of precision instruments for ships, observatories and geographic expeditions. In 2006, the brand returned to its roots thanks to the enthusiast Leonhard R. Müller. With a wide product range evoking the history and famous places of Berlin, Askania produces timepieces that refer to its own illustrious history, for example the Bremen and Heinkel watches, or that refer to the important people behind them, such as the aviator Elly Beinhorn and Carl Bamberg himself. Each model is available with a choice of four different straps. The whole collection is on display, alongside examples of the earliest models, in premises with a late Jugendstil decor at the Hackesche Höfe – a further link with Askania's heyday.

BREEDE

Fasanenstraße 69, Wilmersdorf
U-Bahn Uhlandstraße
Tel 30 8868 3123, www.breede.de
Open Monday by appointment only,
Tuesday to Saturday 10am to 6pm,
Saturday to 3pm, closed Sunday

ANTIQUE JEWELLERY, CLOCKS

Heir to a dynasty of gold- and silversmiths established in 1859, the elegant Ulf Breede cultivates discretion and distinction.

Behind the heavy door with its fake-rust effects, his store has a contemporary decor. In fact, it's a gallery of precious objects, where a fine selection of Art Deco silverware leads on to a splendid collection of jewellery from the 1860s to the 1960s, with a marked preference for the 1920s and 1930s. He also sells clocks and watches from the best Paris, London and Berlin designers. A true connoisseur, Ulf Breede attends all the leading trade fairs, such as the unmissable TEFAF in Maastricht.

DZIUBA JEWELS

Rosa-Luxemburg-Straße 25, Mitte
U-Bahn Rosa-Luxemburg-Platz
Tel 30 2462 5280
www.gabidziuba.de
Open 1pm to 6pm, Saturday until 3pm, closed Sunday to Tuesday or by appointment
CONTEMPORARY STYLES
A disciple of Reinhold Reining, inventor of contemporary art jewellery in Germany, Gabi Dziuba came from Munich, where she worked with a range of artists and painters, especially Martin Kippenberger, to create unique pieces of jewellery. With her turban, artist's smock and busy mien, this feisty and creative jewellery artist "came up" to Berlin a few years ago while exhibiting her work in design and fine arts museums across the country. Now that she's settled, you'll hear her talk about her career and her infatuation with other artists such as the South African Daniel Kruger, Christian Philipp Müller and her compatriot Karl Fritsch, if you're lucky.

RHEINFRANK – ANTIQUE & VINTAGE JEWELLERY

Linienstraße 44, Mitte
U-Bahn Rosenthaler Platz
Tel 30 2068 9155
www.antique-jewellery.de
Open 11am to 6pm, closed Sunday
ECLECTIC, INTERNATIONAL COLLECTION
Oliver Rheinfrank, a former designer for photo shoots, commercials and catalogues, opened this large showroom for vintage

jewellery in 2010. Displays are laid out by period – 19th and 20th centuries, Biedermeier, Victorian, Art Nouveau, Art Deco – and material – Italian cameos, Bohemian garnets, English jet and Wedgwood china. In the middle, there's a glass counter showcasing a varied selection of fantasy cufflinks from the 1920s to the 1950s from Germany, Slavic countries and even Russia, with dark green agates and at very affordable prices. A treasure trove.

SABRINA DEHOFF

Torstraße 175, Mitte
U-Bahn Rosenthaler Platz
Tel 30 9362 4680
www.sabrinadehoff.com
Open noon to 7pm, Saturday until 6pm, closed Sunday
GLITZY COLLECTION
A graduate in women's fashion at the London Royal College of Art, Sabrina Dehoff began working in Paris under Alber Elbaz at Lanvin. Moving to Berlin in 2000, she worked for several fashion brands before launching her own contemporary jewellery label in 2006. Three years later she opened her own shop. Her jewellery collections have made her the favourite designer for Berlin ladies and such stars as Martina Gedeck, Halle Berry, Heike Makatsch and Charlize Theron. Her exuberant, colourful, glitzy style has earned her enviable media coverage and plenty of work with Swarovski and Uslu Airlines, while her rings, necklaces, bracelets and earrings are carefully produced in her workshops in Berlin. Her most enthusiastic foreign retailers include Colette in Paris, Henrik Vibskov in Copenhagen, and the small Simons fashion and luxury department stores in Canada.

TREYKORN

Savignyplatz 13, Charlottenburg
S-Bahn Savignyplatz
Tel 30 3180 2354, www.treykorn.de
Open 11am to 7pm,
Saturday until 4pm, closed Sunday
GOLDSMITHS, CONTEMPORARY

More than twenty years ago, Sabine and
Andreas Treykorn, a pair of creative
goldsmiths, opened their studio/gallery
with other artists and goldsmiths including
Françoise and Claude Chavent, Michael
Becker, Jacqueline Ryan, Giovanni Corvaja
and Batho Gündra. Today, while retailing
their own contemporary, Berlin-style
work, they also showcase the creations of
Carl Dau, Daniela Gillardon, Andrea Hiebl
and a few other designers that have been
with them since they started, including
Sophia Epp. You'll find the place down
a narrow walkway lined with bookshops
and clothing stores.

UHREN BISCHOFF

Pestalozzistraße 54, Charlottenburg
U-Bahn Sophie-Charlotte-Platz
Tel 30 323 2163
www.uhren-bischoff.de
Open 1pm to 6pm, Saturday 10am to 1pm
ANTIQUE TIMEPIECES

Duly listed in the directory of antiques
dealers on nearby Suarezstraße, Friedrich
Bischoff's watchmaker's shop is perfect
for time travellers. Especially for those
whose timepieces have stopped or need
repairing, or those who have lost their
way and need to wind themselves up again.
Inside the shadowy store, time seems
to have stopped, while Herr Bischoff,
a heavy smoker, repairs and restores
age-old clocks, grandfather clocks, table
clocks, cuckoo clocks and watches in his
next-door workshop.

WAGNER PREZIOSEN

Mommsenstraße, 4, Charlottenburg
U-Bahn Uhlandstraße, S-Bahn Savignyplatz
Tel 30 8870 7773
www.wagner-preziosen.de
Open 10:30am to 6:30pm,
Saturday until 4pm, closed Sunday
DESIGNER JEWELLERY

Those with good memories will confirm
that the location of this new niche jeweller
was occupied a few years ago by the
excellent bespoke shoemaker Alexander
Breitenbach, who has now moved on to
pastures new. Clemens Ritter von Wagner
had a long career with Cartier and has now
launched his own venture, opening his own
shop here. The decor is soft and muted,
grey and silken ivory tones contrasting with
purple in an all-over couture chic. Friendly
and enthusiastic, Clemens loves explaining
the history of his treasures. Some pieces
are antiques from the major Paris
jewellers, others are designed by leading
contemporary designers such as Victoire
de Castellane and the Tom Muntsteiner
workshop. As for the signet rings, necklaces,
rings or cuff links, they are unique pieces
he has designed himself. And finally, the
highlight of his sparkling and fascinating
selection must be the collection he calls,
with a touch of iconoclasm, the Trash
Treasures. There are vintage pieces taken
apart, reassembled, cut and recut by him
and by jewellery designers such as Loukia
Richards, Christoph Ziegler and Tine
Steen. Jewellery Meets Recycling, or
the slightly irreverent art of embracing
a new and gorgeously dazzling modernity.
Unique pieces, naturally. Amazing and
expensive. Very, very expensive.

A SENSE OF STYLE WATCHES AND JEWELLERY

HEALTH AND BEAUTY

ADLON SPA BY RESENSE

Hotel Adlon Kempinski,
Behrenstraße 72, Mitte
S-Bahn Brandenburger Tor
Tel 30 2261 1220
www.kempinski.com/berlin
Open 10am to 9pm,
Sunday and Monday until 8pm
LUXURIOUS TREATMENTS, MASSAGES

There's a separate entrance, a hair salon on the ground floor, a cosy corner with fireplace, drinks that are warm or cool in keeping with the season, and booths upholstered with cream leather downstairs. The decor is sleek and luxurious, with subtle Oriental accents. The Adlon's day spa comprises several suites leading off a corridor of linen-lined walls. Each suite has its own speciality, ranging from facials or body treatments to manicures, massages, yoga and much more. Treatments are available for men and women separately or as a couple. All the suites are equipped with a shower, locker and toiletries kit with hairbrush. This cocoon of calm is open seven days a week, as is the health club and extravagant Versace-style pool. The spa is open to residents and non-residents alike, whether members or not. A car park and valet parking are also available.

BECYCLE

Brunnenstraße 24, Mitte
U-Bahn Rosenthaler Platz
Tel 30 280 35 570
www.becycle.de
Open 6:30am to 9pm, Saturday 7:30am to 2pm and 5:30pm to 7:30pm, Sunday 10am to 3pm and 5:30pm to 7:30pm
INDOOR CYCLING, CORE CLASSES

Opened in summer 2016, BeCycle sees itself as a chic riposte to the Soul Cycle concept, with a decor redolent of a nightclub by Lien Tran, the young designer of Vietnamese origin who is building a great reputation in Germany and Turkey. The glossy gold of the changing room lockers sets the tone, echoed in the display of sleek racing bikes and the New York products (Malin+Goetz) in the bathrooms. Spin, barre, HIIT and yoga classes: aimed at sedentary nomads and incorrigible slackers, the disciplines are quintessentially urban. The same glamorous vibe can be experienced in the various rooms, where 45-minute programmes such as Ride or Refine take place to beats from a DJ to boost your performance. Becycle provides towels and velcro spin shoes in every size, as well as shower facilities. The adjoining **MY GOODNESS** café (www.mygoodnessberlin.com) squeezes the right juice mixes to boost energy levels and reconnect with your inner clean.

BREATHE FRESH COSMETICS

Rosa-Luxemburg-Straße 28, Mitte
U-Bahn Rosa-Luxemburg-Platz
Tel 30 2434 2577
www.breathe-cosmetics.com
Open noon to 8pm, Saturday until 7pm, closed Sunday
NICHE PERFUMES, COSMETICS

This is the third address for niche perfumer Gregor Vidzer. Since 2007, his store has been located next door to the men's and women's underwear salon Blush Dessous. This latest Breathe has opted for essential purity – in other words, a clinically bare decor with a wooden counter and the use of immaculate white gravel – and offers an extremely wide selection of products: Wode by Boudicca, Dr. Alkaitis, Liebling, Mark Buxton Perfumes Collection, Ormonde Jayne, Escentric Molecules and indeed "local" fragrances by Humiecki & Graef, Biehl.

HARRY LEHMANN

Kantstraße 106, Charlottenburg
U-Bahn Wilmersdorfer Straße
Tel 30 324 3582
www.parfum-individual.de
Open 9am to 6:30pm,
Saturday until 2pm, closed Sunday

ICONIC PERFUME

During the period between the late
19th century and the interwar years,
Berlin's many perfume makers enjoyed
their heyday, but today hardly any survive.
The J.F. Schwarzlose brand, for example,
once perfumer to the royal court and
whose golden age was the 1920s, has now
been relaunched in "well-kept secret"
style (www.schwarzloseberlin.com). Harry
Lehmann is also celebrated as a historic
brand. Established near Potsdamer Brücke
in 1926, the company relocated six times
thereafter, arriving in West Berlin in 1958,
and hasn't moved since. The shop's facade
and interior attest to this, its neon lights
and lino floors embodying the essence of
the German economic miracle. Large glass
carboys with spigots are filled with
the house's signature perfumes, as once
worn – one might imagine – by Marlene,
Hildegard, Nadja or Elke. Habanera, Sucre,
Surabaya, Singapore Patchouly, Fougère
and Cochabamba – what evocative names.
There's also Russische Eau de Cologne,
Titano Man aftershave and a wide range
of extracts such as rose, neroli, vetiver,
frangipane and lily-of-the-valley, all
fragrances used to create custom-made,
personalized perfumes. Don't leave without
a bottle of Eau de Berlin, a light cologne
invented in 1986 for the city's jubilee.
Unfortunately, Lehmann's has discontinued
its Eau de Portugal hair tonic – a wonderful
summer fragrance. The artificial flowers
on sale are another throwback to years
gone by, as are the prices of the perfumes,
which astonishingly start at €3 for 100 ml.

LA MAISON VALMONT

Fasanenstraße 72, Wilmersdorf
U-Bahn Uhlandstraße
Tel 30 3464 9471
www.boutiquevalmont.com
Open daily by appointment

BEAUTY TREATMENTS

The former Dermalogica facial spa is
the new home of Valmont, the famous
Swiss cosmetics company, a familiar sight
in luxury hotels and now branching out.
Discreet and elegant, bathed in simple
whites, welcoming and responsive, the
salon offers its ultra-exclusive treatments
using its own high-performance Valmont
products. Anti-ageing facials can be booked
for three different time periods, from
45 to 90 minutes. For the body firming or
body energy treatments, allow at least an
hour. All are delivered by the expert hands
of its highly trained staff. The ultimate
is the facial and body treatment using the
Elixir des Glaciers range, restoring inner
glow and vitality. You'll leave its relaxing
treatment rooms and return to everyday life
radiant and at ease.

MDC COSMETIC

Knaackstraße 26, Prenzlauer Berg
U-Bahn Senefelderplatz
Tel 30 4005 6339, www.mdc-cosmetic.com
Open 10am to 8pm, closed Sunday

SKINCARE, NICHE PRODUCTS

A close associate of Andreas Murkudis,
Melanie Dal Canton has recently
opened her own beauty store that includes
a small treatment room for facials, body
treatments and manicures using completely
natural product ranges such as Susanne
Kaufmann, Julisis and Skin Regimen.
Upstairs the same products are on sale in
a pure white concept store, where Melanie
mingles perfumes, lotions, creams and
other potions with jewellery, design objects
and small fashion accessories. As the
exclusive Berlin outlet for the skincare and
fragrances of the famous Florentine brand
Santa Maria Novella, MDC puts its faith
in tried and tested niche brands as well,

WHERE TO SWIM IN THE CITY

For Berliners, swimming is one of life's essentials. Apart from the lakes, where they love to go as soon as the mercury hits 20°C, Berliners enjoy access to around forty municipal pools (*Stadtbäder*) almost all of which are enormous, measuring 25 or 50 metres in length and heated to between 25 and 30°C. Some are indoor pools (*Hallenbäder*), others are open-air (*Sommerbäder*). And then there are the *Kombibäder*, facilities that offer both types of pool. Finally, *Strandbäder*, or artificial beaches, refer to the lakeside resorts on the Wannsee, Müggelsee or Weissensee, among others. In the city, three pools are worth visiting for their design alone.

STADTBAD NEUKÖLLN

Built in 1914 by architect Reinhold Kiehl, it has been magnificently renovated, boasting two pools of 19 and 25 metres. The women's pool is designed in the style of a basilica, and the men's resembles a Roman atrium with colonnades, arcades, sauna and steam room. Ganghoferstraße 3, Neukölln, U-Bahn Rathaus Neukölln, tel 30 221 190 011, www.berlinerbaeder.de

STADTBAD CHARLOTTENBURG

With its fitness-themed tiles, frescos and huge, light-filled glass roof, the "old pool" at offers a Belle Époque atmosphere and a pretty 19-metre pool, while the "new pool" boasts a decidedly modern design, coming in at 25 metres. City regulations that limit bathing hours to take account of school users can be rather dispiriting, but there are also private swimming options offering more tranquillity, though in less impressive surroundings. Krumme Straße 10, Charlottenburg, U-Bahn Bismarckstraße, tel 3438 3860, www.berlinerbaeder.de

CLUB & SPA OLYMPUS

Perched on the top floor of the Grand Hyatt, this pool is available to hotel guests or with monthly or annual membership: it's the best hotel pool in town, offers a panoramic view, and you can plough your lengths from 6am to 11pm. Grand Hyatt Berlin Hotel, Marlene-Dietrich-Platz 2, Tiergarten, S-Bahn and U-Bahn Potsdamer Platz, tel 2553 1890, www.clubolympus.berlin.hyatt.com

such as Perricone MD and Malin & Goetz of New York, the Australian range Aesop, the Viennese company Saint Charles, and French products from Astier de Villatte. But Dal Canton doesn't ignore exclusive Berlin names such as Biehl Parfumkunstwerke, or the long-established perfume maker Stählemühle and its nutritive Wadenbeisser body rub with thyme and rosemary. Finally, look out for Frank Leder, the leather goods manufacturer, who has made the leap to another part of the retail forest with a modern apothecary range of creams, lotions and liquid soaps made from plant and flower extracts and packaged in vintage-style bottles with Bakelite caps.

MÜHLE

Rosenthaler Straße 40–41,
Hackesche Höfe, Hof IV, Mitte
S-Bahn Hackescher Markt
U-Bahn Weinmeisterstraße
Tel 30 6026 9429
www.muehle-shaving.com
Open 11am to 7pm, closed Sunday
BARBER

Long-standing manufacturer of shaving equipment and accessories, Mühle has come a long way. Founded in 1945 by Otto Johannes Müller in a country in ruins, his small factory making *Rasierpinseln* (shaving brushes) was an instant success, at home and abroad. Named Mühle – the "mill" – the factory, located in the GDR, was nationalized. After the Wall came down, it was re-privatised by Hans-Jürgen Müller, the founder's son, starting again from almost nothing. It is now one of the flagship brands of European shaving culture, and part of the HJM group. The company recently opened this barbershop selling the full range of Mühle accessories and shaving accoutrements and, of course, offering shaving services, haircuts, beard and moustache trimming, and more. As well as Mühle, you will also find shaving products from Proraso, Baxter of California and, naturally, HJM. A quick

beard trim with clippers: €15; standard shave: €35; beard spa: €60. In short, their shaves come at a price. But they're a great treat.

SHAN RAHIMKHAN

Kurfürstendamm 196–196, Wilmersdorf
U-Bahn Uhlandstraße
Tel 30 88 717 900, www.shanrahimkhan.de
Open Monday 9am to 6pm,
Tuesday and Wednesday until 7pm,
Thursday and Friday until 8pm,
Saturday 10am to 7pm, closed Sunday
HAIRDRESSER, BEAUTY, FASHION

A native of Tehran, Shan Rahimkhan lived in Vienna before arriving in Berlin in 1996 where his first job as hairstylist was with star hairdresser Udo Walz, the city's premier salon. Shan went on to open three salons of his own, including a salon plus lifestyle store and café on the Gendarmenmarkt, before turning up here on the Ku'damm. Covering several floors, all designed by Davide Rizzo, the place also has an excellent café called **SHAN'S KITCHEN**. Upstairs you'll find the beauty salon featuring Shan's haircare programme True, developed in partnership with Elemental Herbology. Allow forty-five to ninety minutes, depending on the treatment. The salon also provides express makeovers and manicures for women and men. **Other location:**
Markgrafenstraße 36, Gendarmenmarkt,
Mitte, tel 30 206 7890

SPA AM STEINPLATZ

Hotel am Steinplatz,
Steinplatz 4, Charlottenburg
S-Bahn Savignyplatz
U-Bahn Ernst-Reuter-Platz
Tel 554 4446 080, www.hotelsteinplatz.com
Open daily until 10pm, by appointment
LUXURIOUS BERLIN-STYLE TREATMENTS

The 200-square-metre Steinplatz spa is located on the fifth and sixth floors of an almond-green building dating back to 1907. Designed by architect August Endell in a Jugendstil spirit, the building is once again home to a luxury five-star hotel, whose guests and non-residents alike may enjoy the spa. Unfortunately, there's no pool, but the spa does offer two saunas, a steam room, a Technogym fitness suite, four treatment rooms, a terrace and a glorious panoramic view of the city. The treatments feature Thalgo products: choose the energizing, revitalizing Romy Schneider Express. It takes 25 minutes, after which you are offered a glass of sparkling wine to lift the spirits. Another exclusive treatment, the Berliner Adel, is a facial that includes champagne and fresh fruit dipped in melted chocolate to ward off the harsh Berlin winter. Reading matter is provided by the Do You Read Me?! bookstore, in partnership with the hotel. Valet parking also available.

SPA BY SUSANNE KAUFMANN

Hotel Das Stue, Drakestraße 1, Tiergarten
S-Bahn and U-Bahn Zoologischer Garten
Tel 30 311 722 160
www.das-stue.com
Open daily 6am to 10pm
ALPINE AUSTRIAN TREATMENTS
Austrian Susanne Kaufmann opened her first, crowd-pleasing salon in Munich, then set up another popular beauty institute at the Post Hotel in Bezau, in the middle of the Bregenz Forest. Other locations followed, all in Austria, while at the same time concept stores and exclusive, contemporary perfume shops from Augsburg to Berlin began selling her product ranges. Her arrival in Berlin caused a stir, and locals adored her face and body treatments for men and women, all created uniquely from herbs, flowers and other plants picked fresh from the fields. Kaufmann's first boutique spa opened near Monbijouplatz in Mitte – frankly, not the best place for appreciating the benefits of her alpine Austrian products. She has now graduated to the far more suitable climes of the Das Stue hotel. The spa is designed around a bracingly cold

swimming pool with sauna upstairs, plus three treatment rooms, including one double, all bathed in a perfect, soothing light. With soft music, a friendly welcome, and excellent long-lasting massages administered on wide, extremely comfortable couches, the atmosphere is ideal. Depending on skin type the therapists choose organic products from the T, F or A ranges for women, and M for men. Both men and women can choose from treatments including sugar waxing, alkaline pedicures, body scrubs with *echinacea purpurea*, or a Hawaiian *lomi-lomi-nui* massage ritual – all of which contribute to a restorative result. As well as these treatments, the spa sells the excellent Susanne Kaufmann products.

SPA DE ROME

Hotel de Rome, Behrenstraße 37, Mitte
U-Bahn Französische Straße
Tel 460 6091160
www.roccofortecollection.com
Open daily 6:30am to 10pm
LUXURIOUS BODYCARE, POOL
Buried in the basement of the Hotel de Rome and open to non-guests at daily, monthly or yearly rates, this splendid spa has an understated interior by Tommaso Ziffer (who also designed the hotel), with plenty of Bisazza mosaic. It includes a handsome 20-metre pool you can really swim in (you can even check the quality of your backstroke in the judiciously placed mirrors), a sauna, a hammam, a fitness centre and treatment booths where Organic Pharmacy products are used. Ironically, the manicure booth is in the former "Treasury" – the strong room. Who would have thought nails and cuticles were so precious? A fifty-minute anti-jet-lag massage is available, as are day-long sessions. There is also a pre-wedding package (massage and facial for groom; make-up, manicure and massage for bride and bridesmaids). Valet parking.

TECHNIK & DESIGN

Rankestraße 8,
corner of Augsburger Straße, Wilmersdorf
U-Bahn Kurfürstendamm
Tel 30 885 4565
www.braun-spezialist.de
Open 10am to 6:30pm, Saturday until 4pm,
closed Sunday

CUTTING-EDGE ELECTRIC RAZORS

Braun is considered *the* German brand bar none, and the name that revived German design during the reconstruction period of the 1950s. Thanks to Dieter Rams and Hans Gugelot, Braun based its reputation on radios, record players, TVs, small electrical goods and also – perhaps above all – on electric razors. A symbol of modern masculinity in tandem with Mennen toiletries, Braun razors, both mains and battery, have become essential accessories, always at the cutting edge of technology. Alongside multi-blade wet razors, the brand competes for the privilege of shaving half the planet. Like all towns in Germany, Berlin boasts an official Braun outlet, which both sells and repairs razors and clippers (both hair and nose), as well as electric toothbrushes and Braun hairdryers. This store, managed by Thomas Ebendorf, is also the official supplier of Swiss knife manufacturer Victorinox.

TODI'S BARBER SHOP

Konstanzer Straße 8, Wilmersdorf
U-Bahn Adenauer Platz
Tel 30 914 77 771
www.todis-barbershop-berlin.de
Open 10am to 8pm, Saturday until 6pm,
closed Sunday

BARBER

Strictly men only, too bad for the women – though there's no shortage of *Friseure* in the city. The barber shop owned by Aleksandar "Todi" Todorovic, doesn't split hairs. From Belgrade, he's a big strapping chap, bearded, of course, perfect poster boy for a new production of the musical *Sweeney Todd*, the demon barber of Fleet Street. It's got everything, even the decor,

clearly inspired by traditional British barbershops. Hair, moustache, beard, scalp: armed with his tools, Todi trims, cuts, shaves and designs precisely and carefully. Virile, tattooed, loyal, his clients are the sort you don't mess with. Todi is the polar opposite of those wannabe barbers springing up all over the city and best avoided. He offers a friendly welcome and a good, efficient service. Down to the last hair.

URBAN SCENTS

Eisenacher Straße 57, Schöneberg
U-Bahn Eisenacher Straße
S-Bahn Julius Leber Brücke
Tel 159 0104 9818
www.urbanscents.de
Open 11am to 6pm, closed Sunday

NICHE PERFUMES

Marie Le Febvre has a passion for flying and admits to an earlier life working for a major fragrance company. She is married to Alexander Urban – who has lent his name to her exclusive fragrance brand, produced in Grasse by the great Roudnitska. In 2015, she founded her laboratory of unique, exclusive fragrances in Berlin. She sells them in an art gallery – CavuSpace – where she blends special fragrances to go with the artist's work on show, responding to the visual invitations and interpretations. Like Michel Granger and his India inks for Au Nom de la Terre and Pauline Bazignan for Vulcano. Future projects involve the Colombian artist Daniela Elorza and the illustrator François Cadière. Packed in a special box, each perfume bottle, inscribed by the artist, is available in a limited edition only. The main Urban Scents range comprises Gunpowder Cologne, Desert Rose, Singular Oud and Sensual Blend. Marie Le Febvre has also worked with the mixologist at the Ritz-Carlton, Arnd Henning Heissen, to create two cocktails inspired by her perfumes: Vetiver Reunion and Lost Paradise. Try them in the **FRAGRANCES** bar.

WHEADON

Steinstraße 17,
corner of Gormannstraße, Mitte
U-Bahn Weinmeisterstraße
Tel 30 5266 0621
www.wheadon.de
Open noon to 7pm, closed Sunday

BARBER, FACIALS, FRAGRANCES

Delightfully effusive Nicole Wheadon is the life and soul of her salon, with its boutique on the ground floor, plus treatment room and barbershop in the basement. It's all decorated in upcycle style by Davide Rizzo, who seems to have had great fun on a limited budget by blending white-painted palettes, metal chain curtains, huge swivelling mirrors and black walls. More like the dark room in a gay bar than the usual image of a beauty salon or barbershop, the lower floor is totally disconcerting. Here Nicole administers her express facials including the pressurized oxygen jet treatment that's more effective than a Dyson, or serious procedures such as the Mount Everest Treat. The barbers provide traditional shaves, and trims beards and moustaches with rare dexterity and a keen eye. You'll emerge completely transformed. The shop stocks treatment products from Dr. Bronner, and fragrances and colognes from Humiecki & Graef, Parfumerie Générale, Pierre Guillaume, hair & skin care products by Susanne Kaufmann, plus Montale, Skin Design London, Ortigia Sicilia, Matriskin, Pai and the incredible and very expensive range from the Hungarian Omorovicza. Extending her beauty domain next door, Nicole has opened a women's salon, Frauenzimmer, also designed by Davide Rizzo. It offers cosmetics, nail and hairdressing services, with treatment rooms on the first floor (separate entrance) reserved for face and body treatments. And when the Berlin Film Festival is on, Nicole provides beauty treatments for the stars staying at the Hotel Zoo, on the Ku'damm.

WARDROBE TALK WITH BARRIE KOSKY

Although he has taken out his eyebrow piercing and cut back
on the heavy biker rings on his knuckles (a legacy from grandma?),
Barrie Kosky has not completely abandoned his urban rebel
paraphernalia. He wears khaki cargo trousers, a long-sleeved T-shirt
bearing a slogan or sign of some sort, and Zeha Berlin trainers.
*"I have ten pairs of them and as there is a shop in the street where I live
I'm often tempted."* He likes a casual, relaxed look: *"When I wear
a formal outfit for a premiere, everyone laughs."* He tries a bit of
everything. He has a weakness for Jil Sander and Agnès b., which
he buys when on the road, and Paul Smith socks.

JIL SANDER
Kurfürstendamm 185, Charlottenburg, tel 30 886 7020, www.jilsander.com

ZEHA BERLIN
Prenzlauer Allee 213, Prenzlauer Berg, tel 30 4401 7214, www.zeha-berlin.de

AGNÈS B.
Galeries Lafayette, Friedrichstraße 76–78, Mitte, tel 30 2094 8000, www.agnesb.com

PAUL SMITH
Mientus, Kurfürstendamm 52, Wilmersdorf, tel 30 323 9077, www.mientus.com

INTERIOR CACHET
QUIRKY ANTIQUES SHOPS TO CONTEMPORARY DESIGN GALLERIES: LIVING IN THE CITY

Together with Great Britain, Germany was the most industrialized country in Europe in the 19th century. In 1910, the powerful Berlin company AEG was the first to commission an architect (Peter Behrens) to design its corporate identity, embracing advertising, packaging and the look of its products. Nine years later, architect Walter Gropius opened the Bauhaus in Weimar, a school that aimed to unite art and industry by reflecting the newly inclusive avant-garde movements. The school comprised studios that were run by László Moholy-Nagy, Marcel Breuer, Paul Klee, Wassily Kandinsky, Marianne Brandt, Wilhelm Wagenfeld and Mies van der Rohe. The Bauhaus closed in 1933.

After the Second World War, despite being divided, Germany remained highly industrialized, although nothing was made in West Berlin any more. The major companies all moved to West Germany and opened design departments. In 1953, the German Design Council was created. The stated aim was "to design the best industrial and craft products possible in Germany in order to give the greatest satisfaction to the consumer". Germany remains synonymous with high-quality products to this day. In Berlin, if you're looking for antiques, vintage, contemporary, functional, the extraordinary or just one-of-a-kind, you'll find it in the city's shops, galleries, workshops and flea markets. And the "made in Berlin" hallmark confers added value.

ANDREAS MURKUDIS

Potsdamer Straße 77, Tiergarten
U-Bahn Kurfürstenstraße
Tel 30 7554 3879
www.andreasmurkudis.com
Open 10am to 8pm, closed Sunday
ULTRA-DESIGN

Right from his early days in Mitte, Andreas Murkudis showed excellent taste in design. Now occupying a vast Brutalist space in Potsdamer Straße, he has been able to give his passion free rein, with the results on display in this immense street-level showroom. Clean shapes, marble floors and grey walls form the perfect space for expanding his ambitions. Around a huge black monolith are arranged well-designed pieces of the finest quality that have a simple purity or display a radical, contemporary expressionism. They include designs by Christophe Delcourt, Michael Anastassiades, the Muller Van Severen duo, Bodo Sperlein and the German label e15, as well as products from ClassiCon, mattresses from his friend Daniel Heer, Venini glassware, textiles from Italian Society and strange terrazzo chairs by Max Lamb from Dzek. Another school of thought.
Other location: Potsdamer Straße 81, Tiergarten, tel 30 6807 98306

ART + INDUSTRY

Bleibtreustraße 40, entrance on
Mommsenstraße, Charlottenburg
S-Bahn Savignyplatz
Tel 30 883 4946, www.aiberlin.de
Open 2pm to 6:30pm, Saturday 11am to
4pm and by appointment, closed Sunday
DESIGN OBJECTS

Uwe Kniess sells everything, from Wagenfeld glassware and Bakelite radios to Murano glass and antique watches. All eras and styles are represented in his store, which is a real magnet for collectors, set designers and photo stylists. A classic design mecca, albeit now a little cramped, Art + Industry also has a warehouse space in the former office buildings of the old Tempelhof Airport.

Other location: Ringbahn Straße
16–20, entrance 3, 1st floor, Tempelhof,
tel 30 3270 6373

ATELIER OBLIQUE

Mulackstraße 20, Mitte
U-Bahn Rosenthaler Platz
Tel 42 80 36 19
www.atelier-oblique.com
SCENTED CANDLES

Over the past ten years, through his creative work for legendary music magazine *SPEX and art glossy Sleek*, Mario Lombardo has helped to reshape the contemporary face of the German graphic design industry. Throughout his design career, though, he has had a secret passion: fragrance. In 2015 the dream became a reality with the opening of his first boutique: a scented candle store on Mulackstraße. The scents are inspired by his native Argentina, which he left with his family when he was six, and have been crafted in collaboration with the French perfumery Robertet. The first collection of candles is twenty-seven strong: one for each letter of the alphabet, plus the ampersand. The French origin of the perfumes is reflected in the evocative name as well as the store design, which feels like a minimalist Parisian boutique, all eclectic bell jars and black lacquer. And, of course, the candles' graphic design is superb.

BLICKLE RÄDER UND ROLLEN

Potsdamer Straße 181–183, Schöneberg
U-Bahn Kleistpark
Tel 30 215 2900, www.blickle.de
Open 7:45am to 5pm, Friday until 2:45pm,
closed Saturday and Sunday
WHEELS

The shop window is fluorescent yellow. Inside, everything is perfectly sorted in orange boxes lined up immaculately on green shelves. What is in the window and in all these boxes? The answer is: wheels. All sorts of wheels and things that roll: small ones, big ones, enormous ones, tiny ones, streamlined ones, industrial ones, self-stopping ones, in wood, in steel, from the most rudimentary to the most sophisticated. A true fanatic's venture of the type you only come across in Germany. The company's factory, based in Rosenfeld, supplies the majority of firms in the country.

C. ADOLPH

Savignyplatz 3, Charlottenburg
S-Bahn Savignyplatz
Tel 30 313 804 445
Open 9am to 7pm,
Saturday until 2pm, closed Sundays

HISTORIC IRONMONGER'S
Founded in 1898, this shop still operates in its original location. The storefront and shop windows were modernized in the 1950s, of course, and since then it's had a minor facelift, but inside everything seems unchanged. Walls of drawers filled with door knobs, hooks, rivets, nails, label holders; shelves packed with traditional maintenance products, or stacked with pots and pans; and most importantly, Berlin's most wonderful selection of letterboxes and barbecues in brushed aluminium and steel.

CLASSIC REMISE

Wiebestraße 36–37, Moabit
S-Bahn Beusselstraße
Tel 30 364 0780, www.remise.de
Open 8am to 8pm, Sunday from 10am

VINTAGE CARS
This shrine to collectible vehicles is housed in a former tram depot built in 1901 and extended in 1924 by Jean Krämer, former assistant to the great architect Peter Behrens. The buildings were converted in 2003 by Martin Halder into Meilenwerk, a space dedicated to old cars, motorcycles and vintage boats. Meilenwerk has now changed its name to Classic Remise, but still offers sales, rentals, repairs and servicing, as well as renting out lock-up glazed garages. It's a veritable paradise for well-heeled collectors and petrol heads in general. And as the showroom is open on Sundays as well, you can spend the whole day here admiring these wonders after enjoying brunch at the onsite Trofeo restaurant.

DANIEL HEER

Blumenthalstraße 7, Mitte
U-Bahn Kurfürstenstraße, Bülowstraße
Tel 30 3408 5194
www.danielheer.com
Open by appointment, closed Sunday

LUXURIOUS MATTRESSES
Daniel Heer's family company was founded in Lucerne, Switzerland in 1907 and originally made saddles. It soon diversified and began making mattresses as well. Their horsehair stuffing places them at the luxury end of the market. So far, so logical. Having moved to Berlin, initially working in the obscurity of a workshop on the city outskirts, the young Heer, a trained saddler and upholsterer, built up an exclusive clientele from Los Angeles to Dubai, successfully soothed to sleep on his fabulous mattresses. Mattresses liberated from their usual night-time role to live a full life on the decks of Malibu's yachts and private pools, and all handmade in his factory. Still made of horsehair and with some highly unusual coverings, like deerskin, for example, the same used to make *Lederhosen* and Austrian riding breeches. Fantastic. Until recently he worked from a shop-workshop on Rosa-Luxemburg-Straße, but Daniel Heer decided to close the shop and return to work from home. He now has his showroom/workshop in his apartment, where he has cleverly installed a test bedroom to try out his mattresses. He is also running a charity project (www.projektmatrah.de), Matrah, that invites Syrian and Afghan refugees to share their textile skills and create unique cushions. All profits from sales go directly to assisting migrants.

DECO ARTS INTERIORS

Motzstraße 6, Schöneberg
U-Bahn Nollendorfplatz, Viktoria-Luise-Platz
Tel 30 215 8672, www.decoarts.eu
Open 3pm to 7pm, Saturday noon to 5pm
and by appointment,
closed Sunday to Tuesday

1950S AND 1960S

The store of Frenchwoman Marie-Pascale Charles, which she opened with Jo van Norden, who has now set up her own business elsewhere in the city, is in a street mostly given over to gay bars and sex shops. She is particularly interested in furniture and objects from the 1950s and 1960s, and the three rooms overflow with German items from the period of the reconstruction, a typical example being a rattan guitar-mirror. It's the kind of place where you might go in hoping to buy a Danish table and come out instead with an Italian lampstand.

DESIGN 54

Suarezstraße 54, Charlottenburg
U-Bahn Sophie-Charlotte-Platz
Tel 30 311 0209, www.design54.berlin
Open 11am to 7pm,
Saturday 10am to 5pm, closed Sunday

VINTAGE CURIOS

Suarezstraße, a quiet Charlottenburg street near Lietzensee, is famous throughout Berlin for its high concentration of antiques shops, specialist second-hand dealers and vintage clothes stores. Here you'll bump into ladies in hats straight out of a 1950s film, hordes of theatre and cinema designers and costumiers, and ordinary collectors looking for vintage lace or an unusual but pristine find. It's a good place to pick up reasonably priced pieces of furniture, paintings, watches and vintage design. Don't miss Magnus Ettlich, whose two-room store is packed from floor to ceiling with light fittings and unique items of furniture, as well as intriguing advertisements from 1970s Germany, including oddities such as a grey plastic dustpan inscribed with the legend *Let the*

Wall Fall. Candyass Visits Berlin. 1977. If you end up buying anything bulky, such as a 1960s German credenza with a swing lid, delivery can be arranged.

DIM 26

Oranienstraße 26, Kreuzberg
U-Bahn Moritzplatz, Kottbusser Tor
Tel 30 285 030 121
www.dim-berlin.de
Open 10am to 7pm, Saturday from noon,
closed Sunday

BRUSHES

The concept originated more than fifteen years ago with designers Oliver Vogt and Hermann Weizenegger: DIM (aka Die Imaginäre Manufaktur) was an initiative thought up for the Berlin Blindenanstalt (Institute for the Blind) to offer the visually impaired and disabled the opportunity to take part in a creative venture alongside German and international designers. Located in a 120-year-old former brush factory, it produces handmade brushes and brooms in classic, everyday designs, as well as brushes created by designers such as Matali Crasset, Volker Albus, Konstantin Grcic, Arik Lévy, Martí Guixé, Berit Burmester and Jana Gara. The selection includes ashtray brushes, coat-hanger brushes, ruler brushes, crucifix brushes, dumb-bell brushes and even an amazing nailbrush shaped like a set of false teeth. The range is still on sale in the glass cases behind the counter, now managed by the Union Sozialer Einrichtungen (USE), which keeps the original torch burning with a café and a new, more touristy range of brushes, items of jewellery and craft objects, a great way of showing one's solidarity with the cause as well as providing a great alternative souvenir of the city.

EINRICHTUNGSMEISTEREI

Oldenburgerstraße 3a, Moabit
U-Bahn Turmstraße, Birkenstraße
Tel 0174 748 7823
Open noon to 7pm, Saturday 11am to 4pm,
closed Sunday and Monday
VINTAGE HOMEWARE

Originally from Hamburg, the energetic
Katja Homann is the queen of everyday
vintage design from the 1950s to the 1970s.
A regular at flea markets, she has decided
to close her two shops, including the one
in Kreuzberg, to focus her operations here,
close to the Arminius covered market and
next door to the record shops. She stocks
glassware, Formica kitchen units, couches
and reupholstered armchairs, lamps
and various other objects. She even has
some cleaning-lady outfits that make a very
Berlin-style souvenir that's easy on the
pocket. Another address in the vicinity
worth visiting is Roland Hanne's store
MODERNES (Waldenserstraße 7, Moabit,
tel 0179 5124597), full of German
ceramics from the 1950s to 1970s and
other curios.

FIRMA LONDON

Bleibtreustraße 50, Charlottenburg
S-Bahn Savignyplatz
Tel 30 8321 0893
www.firmalondon.com
Open noon to 7pm, Saturday until 5pm,
closed Sunday and Monday
20TH-CENTURY DESIGN

As the name suggests, Florian von
Holstein arrived from London where
he ran Decoratum Gallery. The voluble
proprietor has no regrets about choosing
Berlin as the location for his new gallery,
which celebrates the history of design.
In its two rooms with their grey ceilings
and white walls decorated with paintings,
von Holstein exhibits furniture and lighting
by Marco Zanuso and Eero Saarinen,
with impressive lighting by Venini and
Arteluce. Since opening his doors in 2008,
he had already built up a loyal clientele
of artists and architects drawn by his eye

for good design, which is also in evidence
in the items on display in his 400-square-
metre warehouse near the Schloss in
Charlottenburg (Lise-Meitner-Straße 7).

HABIBI INTERIORS

Eisenacher Straße 56, Schöneberg
U-Bahn Eisenacher Straße
S-Bahn Julius Leber Brücke
Tel 30 239 15 605
www.habibi-interiors.de
Open 11am to 6pm,
closed Sunday and Monday
MOSAICS

Two showrooms in London but only
one in Berlin. That's because Habibi
founder Alexander "Sacha" Urban decided
to settle here, next-door to the **URBAN
SCENTS** laboratory-gallery opened by
his wife Marie Le Febvre, far from Berlin's
major decoration and design hotspots.
It is a resounding success, as Berliners
love his tiles and craft mosaics, which
are made in Morocco and sport a myriad
of motifs, colours and enamels. Urban
cleverly demonstrates this versatility
by showing visitors several in-situ settings.
The decorated, equipped and functioning
kitchens, bathrooms and hammams
can be rented by the night or for an event.
A unique mix of restrained exoticism
and expertise. Luxury.

HAUPTSAECHLICH LEINEN

Gutzkowstraße 4, Schöneberg
S-Bahn Schöneberg
U-Bahn Innsbrucker Platz
Tel 30 611 6208 or 0160 9683 9318
www.hauptsaechlich-leinen.de
Open Monday 3pm to 7pm,
the other days by appointment
HOUSEHOLD LINEN

Constanze von Papen is precisely the kind
of woman who washes her linen in public.
And since 2003 she has been doing just
that, sourcing all kinds of treated and
untreated linens, always top notch, from
France, Belgium, Italy, the Czech Republic,
Ireland and Lithuania. She creates sets of

bed linen and hand linen, table linen and bath linen, as well as napkins and tea towels. The quality and craftsmanship can best be appreciated by making an advance appointment, which also ensures enough time to choose carefully.

HOTEL ULTRA

Torstraße 155, Mitte
U-Bahn Rosenthaler Platz
Tel 30 275 811 00, www.hotelultra.de
Open 11:30am to 7:30pm, closed Sunday
CONCEPT STORE

Named after a fictional lodging in an Anton Corbijn-directed Depeche Mode video, the Hotel has 36 "rooms", or boxed showcase areas, each of which plays host to products from a single designer. The conceit continues to the cash register, or "reception", behind which a board of keys hangs, one for every room. The selection of items by international designers is intelligently curated, ranging from Jonathan Johnson's tongue-in-cheek jewellery made in Hamburg to contemporary Bosnian furniture from Zanat. Mo's taste tends towards surreal, cheeky designs, such as the clambering Seletti monkey lamps that fill the window, or Karsten Wegener's photographs of "Wurstkunst", which reimagine classic artworks from Van Gogh or Koons in meat form. Naturally, the selection obviously changes with the finds, acquisitions and exclusives. The café at the end of the shop is not unpleasant.

JAN KATH

Brunnenstraße 3, Mitte
U-Bahn Rosenthaler Platz
Tel 30 484 96 090, www.jan-kath.de
Open 11am to 7pm, closed Sunday
CONTEMPORARY CARPETS

Based in Bochum, Jan Kath is a German artist and designer who has invented a collection of hand-tufted carpets called Erased Heritage – the art of using the unusable, of consuming drawings and patterns as if they had been trodden underfoot for centuries. Each design

offers a visual subterfuge, referring to the ancestral art of knotting remixed using contemporary motifs. The visual effect is subtle, and you need to look closely and lose yourself in contemplation of these surfaces. And these carpets really do fly: Kath is distributed by a select network of galleries and showrooms in Miami, Vancouver, Munich and New York. This vast Berlin gallery has ended up in a neighbourhood somewhat unsuited to such purchases. More warp than weft?

JOCHUM RODGERS

Mommsenstraße 3, Charlottenburg
U-Bahn Uhlandstraße
S-Bahn Savignyplatz
Tel 30 882 1612, www.hpjochum.de
Open 2pm to 6:30pm,
Saturday 11am to 4pm, closed Sunday
20TH-CENTURY DESIGN

Hans-Peter Jochum and his associate Jett Sun Rodgers have an unrivalled selection of Bauhaus items. They also organize excellent monographic or thematic exhibitions devoted to post-war Italian and German design, featuring the likes of Egon Eiermann, Carlo Mollino, Franco Albini, Angelo Mangiarotti, Giancarlo Frattini, Osvaldo Borsani, Sergio Asti and Guglielmo Ulrich.

JUKELAND

Crellestraße 14, Schöneberg
S-Bahn Julius-Leber-Brücke, U-Bahn Kleistpark
Tel 30 782 3335, www.jukeland.de
Open 2pm to 6pm, Saturday 11am to 2pm,
closed Sunday and Monday
AMERICAN CULTURE

The cafés and terraces on the cobbled Crellestraße exude a rather provincial vibe. The street does, however, harbour a little treasure in Gerhard Mizera's Jukeland. The shop window boasts dolls of Elvis marrying Priscilla Beaulieu, while inside you can inhale the fumes of Route 66 with Texaco gas pumps, neon signage, No Parking signs, Wurlitzer jukeboxes and other retro machines. It's all evidence

A DAY AT THE FLEA MARKET

A day visiting the Berlin flea markets involves methodically criss-crossing the city on Saturday and/or Sunday, trying to pick up a bargain at a reasonable hour – between 10am and 11:30am and around 2pm – without getting caught up in the crowds that turn out on sunny days. Indeed, the real pros pray for grey and cold weather – but not rain. There are, depending on the time of year, no fewer than fifty flea markets and second-hand fairs (Flohmarkt and Trödelmarkt) dotted all over the city, in addition to car-boot-style operations that appear on Berlin's streets. The most famous fair is without doubt the one that takes place on **STRASSE DES 17 JUNI** (www.berlinertroedelmarkt.com) in Tiergarten, which has been infiltrated by quite a few stalls selling hideous paintings. It's reasonable in size, but much more touristy than the market on **FEHRBELLINER PLATZ** in Wilmersdorf, which is typical of Berlin (www.fehrbi.info) and adjoins the attractive **PARK CAFÉ** (www.parkcafe-berlin.de) – a great stop-off from 8:30am for breakfast on the terrace when it's sunny. On Saturdays and Sundays, there are plenty of bargains and really low prices (because it's a different set of vendors). Even more informal, the **FLEA MARKET AT SCHÖNEBERG TOWN HALL** (www.berlin-flohmaerkte.de) repays several thorough visits as the range changes from one week to the next. Coming across a Memphis-designed coffee set or a Roy Black LP will delight collectors, who can celebrate with a club sandwich at nearby **TOMASA** (www.tomasa.de). When it's not raining, the fair at **MAUERPARK** (www.mauerparkmarkt.de) on Bernauerstraße on the border between Mitte and Prenzlauer Berg attracts the city's hipsters, supplemented by back-packers visiting Berlin for the club scene (you can spot them from the club stamps on their hands). When it's raining, the free-for-all organized in tents may unearth a few treasures for anyone prepared to delve deeply into the boxes guarded by the dodgy-looking characters who perch on stools and invent their prices. The park's stone amphitheatre also plays host to a raucous post-club karaoke. Snack bars, *Currywurst* stalls and Turkish fast food pop up all over the place, so you can grab a bite standing in the mud before heading off to the **ARKONAPLATZ FLEA MARKET** (www.troedelmarkt-arkonaplatz.de) on the other side of Bernauerstraße and beyond – but only weather permitting. It's a hip, friendly market, frequented by those with a nose for up-and-coming trends: boys' toys, 1970s jewellery, really cool furniture and light fittings, for example. The prices themselves are not so cool, however, and some really uncool vendors just refuse to haggle. So you'll have to play it smart, or just walk away. There's no point venturing across to the flea market on Boxhagener Platz, which, for some strange reason, features high on the top ten list of Berlin flea markets. Here all the goods are rusty, broken or damaged, and almost as expensive as the flea markets in Paris. In another part of the forest, in Treptow near the Arena (also open on Saturdays) and at Friedrichshain, you have to be a real fan of junk to beard the groups of rag-and-bone merchants, who look like they've stepped out of a drawing by the great German caricaturist Heinrich Zille. Nevertheless, there remain a lot of small antiques and second-hand shops clinging on in Charlottenburg – and not only around Suarezstraße. Their prices are still reasonable by comparison with Paris and London, they're open all week, and they're happy for you to browse and even turn up some surprises.

of the American culture left behind by the former US occupation. Mizera also hires out his treasures to film sets, and his shop is the official German distributor of the cult classic Rock-Ola jukeboxes.

KAHLA PORZELLAN
Friedrichstraße 122, Mitte
S-Bahn Oranienburger Straße
Tel 30 278 74 590
www.kahlaporzellan.com
Open 11am to 7pm, closed Sunday
GERMAN PORCELAIN

In the aftermath of the Second World War, when Germany was split in two, much of its industry and many of the factories spared by Allied bombs ended up in Soviet hands. Taken over in 1949 by the Democratic Republic, Meissen, Kahla, Arzberg and many other porcelain manufacturers were grouped by speciality into *Combinats* (or VEB) and ordered to produce mass-market china for distribution in the GDR and all other Communist bloc nations and people's republics. So Kahla, founded in Thuringia by Christian Eckardt in 1844, became the Combinat of Fine Ceramics with seventeen factories to its name. This didn't mean that what was produced was devoid of creativity. In fact, most of the artists and designers who remained in the East worked towards modernising the designs and decorations, and these pieces in series are now much sought after by collectors. After the fall of the Wall, Reunification quickly led to the dissolution of the *Combinats*; Kahla was privatized in 1993, acquired by Günther Raithel, who used to work at Rosenthal, and quickly morphed into the most modern factory in Europe, winning dozens of prizes and awards. It has remained a family firm, now run by Holger Raithel Jr, and flourishing once again. Unlike Rosenthal, which has set up lots of its own stores, Kahla has maintained a very local footprint. So this Berlin flagship shop is the first of its kind, doubling up quite naturally as a café as Kahla produces cups, mugs

and bowls. The contemporary range of white and multi-coloured ware for kitchen and dining room is the work of some twenty designers and ceramists, including Lisa Keller, Barbara Schmidt and Speziell.

KPM
Königliche Porzellan-Manufaktur,
Wegelystraße 1, Tiergarten
S-Bahn Tiergarten
Tel 30 3900 9215, www.kpm-berlin.com
Open 10am to 6pm, closed Sunday
ROYAL PORCELAIN

Bought by the king of Prussia, Frederick the Great, in 1763 – the date when it assumed its current name – the Königliche Porzellan-Manufaktur (KPM) was set up close to the Charlottenburg bridge and operated there until 1918, mainly catering to the needs of the Hohenzollern family. During the interwar period, influenced by the Bauhaus, the factory flourished thanks to the dinner services designed by Trude Petri. Partly destroyed by the bombing, the Schloss Charlottenburg, situated in West Berlin, was meticulously rebuilt from 1948. Semi-dormant, the factory also benefited from this reconstruction and resumed manufacture of a number of its porcelain dinner services. In 1990, KPM appointed the Italian designer Enzo Mari as artistic director – his "Berlin" service was a bestseller – and manufactured the royal and noble collections in their entirety, including the great classic "Kurland", ordered in 1790 by Peter von Biron, duke of Courland. More recently, after coming close to bankruptcy, the venerable company closed its shop in Unter den Linden. The KPM Welt, however, continues to showcase the history and production of the company's most emblematic pieces. Situated between a loop in the Spree and the Ernst-Reuter-Haus, KPM Welt also has a café – where the china is made by KPM, of course. Another store is located on the ground floor of the Bristol Kempinski Hotel on the Ku'damm. The outlet in the concrete-and-glass box within the Hackesche Höfe, once home to the Leo Coppi gallery, looks like a pop-up store but was designed by Enzo Mari in a wooden-crate-and-straw vein.

KÜHN KERAMIK

Yorckstraße 18, Kreuzberg
S-Bahn and U-Bahn Mehringdamm
Tel 30 2838 4695, www.kuehn-keramik.com
Open noon to 7pm, Saturday 11am to 4pm,
closed Sunday and Tuesday

PUNK CERAMICS

Since 1993, ceramicists Bernhard and Claudia Kühn have been creating a world of random forms, printed with strange retro designs, meaningful words and aphorisms. The Kühns have set up their factory in the basement of a former pharmacy, the Anhalter Apotheke. At the back of the store, the countless drawers are still full of pharmacological boxes and accessories that Claudia Kühn enjoys unveiling for visitors. In this evocative, historic setting of sculpted wooden interiors, their collections of small and large bowls, egg cups, mugs, cups, saucers and other trinkets have usurped the pills, potions and other remedies. Some items are still given appropriate labels such as Poison and Toxic, and sit alongside the famous Alter Ego, Berlin, Vamp, Bitch and Sex. Kühn also produces some rather hideous, gilded items – but it's all part of the ultra-kitsch style.

MANUFACTUM

Hardenbergstraße 4–5, Charlottenburg
U-Bahn Savignyplatz
Tel 30 2403 3844, www.manufactum.de
Open 10am to 8pm,
Saturday until 6pm, closed Sunday

TRADITIONAL PRODUCTS

Manufactum was founded in 1988 by Thomas Hoof, a director of the Green Party, although it is now owned by a subsidiary of mail-order giant Otto. It continues to sell a wide range of products that all embody a commitment to quality manufacturing, classic designs and use of sustainable materials. In the beginning, Manufactum only sold its carefully selected products through its catalogue. The popularity of its goods with architects, designers and other trendsetters gave Thomas Hoof credibility in the eyes of manufacturers, whom he was able to persuade to revive forgotten products from the past. The reunification of Germany worked in his favour, as the former East Germany turned out to be an astonishing repository of pristine products. Updated to include French, Italian and English pieces, Manufactum's annual catalogue is a collector's bible, supplemented by thematic catalogues for clothing, gardens and summer goods. Manufactum opened its first physical store in Munich in 2001, soon followed by shops in Hamburg, Frankfurt, Cologne, Düsseldorf and elsewhere. The Berlin outlet, located opposite the Institute of Technology, incorporates a café-cum-deli called Brot & Butter. The prices are not cheap, but the market value of the goods is in this case outstripped by their traceability and provenance – something that gives their dustbins and roofing shoes alike a unique advantage.

MEISSEN

Unter den Linden 39b, Mitte
U-Bahn Branderburger Tor, Französische
Straße, S-Bahn Unter den Linden
Tel 30 2267 9028, www.meissen.com
Open 10am to 7pm,
Saturday until 6pm, closed Sunday

PORCELAIN

It was in Meissen, Saxony, that the manufacturing process of Chinese hard-paste porcelain was discovered in 1709 by the alchemist Johann Friedrich Böttger. Set up the following year by Augustus II the Strong, Prince Elector of Saxony and king of Poland, the Meissen porcelain factory was the first in Europe and today is the oldest in production. Eager to break the Chinese monopoly, the prince, who had asked the scientist E.W. von Tschirnhaus to study Saxon mineral and mining resources, kept Böttger prisoner in the Albrechtsberg fortress, ordering him to find the secret to the production of porcelain. The local soil abounded in kaolin, the pure, white clay that was central to the processes used by the Chinese. The sovereign set up his factory within the walls of the fortress and within the space of a few years, Meissen's porcelain dinner services began to appear on royal tables across the continent. Its famous decorative flowers and insects were widely copied. Meissen also became famous for the animal models created by Johann Joachim Kändler, who was appointed court sculptor in 1730, becoming porcelain modeller for Meissen the following year. The factory flourished for much of the 18th century, but when Louis XV founded the Manufacture de Sèvres (ex-Vincennes) in France in 1756, it marked the beginning of Meissen's decline. Brain drain was at its height, in a healthy atmosphere of artistic and chemical espionage; Paris, Munich and Berlin, Capodimonte in Naples, among others, entered into a fierce industrial war. The king of Prussia, Frederick the Great, founded the Königliche Porzellan-Manufaktur (KPM) in 1763 in Berlin, enticing away several of Meissen's talented craftsmen. Brought under GDR state control in 1949, Meissen, Kahla, Arzberg and many other factories were incorporated into industrial complexes (or VEB) for large-scale, low-quality porcelain production, which was then distributed throughout the communist bloc. Meissen manufactured the thousands of porcelain tiles that were used to cover the walls of the grand Stalinist buildings constructed in 1952 along Karl-Marx-Allee. Reunification led to the disbanding of the industrial complexes. Privatized in 1990, Meissen became the Staatliche Porzellan-Manufaktur Meissen, henceforth a registered trademark. The factory now turns out tableware, objets d'art, figurines, architectural ceramics and limited editions. To celebrate their 400th anniversary,

the factory produced several one-off pieces and limited editions, and completely refurbished its shop.

MÖVE

Stilwerk, Kantstraße 17, Charlottenburg
S-Bahn Savignyplatz
Tel 30 31 01 27 49, www.moeve.de
Open 10am to 7pm, closed Sunday
BATH LINEN

Almost as durable and renowned as Ruhr steel, Möve Frottana's terry products have been supplying the bathrooms of Germany's top hotels since 1927. After a difficult period, the "Seagull" (*Möve*) is once again flying high, thanks to its upscale collections for bathrooms and bedrooms, offering a texture borrowed ecologically from bamboo. The Stilwerk shop opened in Berlin in late 2008 is contributing to the development of the brand, now present in Hamburg and Düsseldorf and retailed in all department stores throughout the country. New: a Bath & Beauty line, developed with Biotherm, adds vitamin E to its terry products.

RADIO ART

Zossener Straße 2, Kreuzberg
U-Bahn Gneisenaustraße
Tel 30 693 9435, www.radio-art.de
Open noon to 6pm, Saturday 10am to 1pm, closed Sunday to Wednesday
OLD RADIOS

Experts in the history of the airwaves, Herr and Frau Schmahl repair, overhaul and generally maintain hundreds of radios, phonographs, transistors, record players and turntables dating from the 1930s to the 1970s. Siemens, Philips, Minerva, Grundig, Blaupunkt, Telefunken and Normende are some of the classic names; chrome, wood, Bakelite and plastic are some of the materials. As you leave, don't miss the former Besetzhaus, located opposite on the left. This was a notorious artists' squat, once home to talents such as Claudia Skoda, before she became a fashion designer, and Martin Kippenberger, at the time a star of contemporary West German art, who covered the wooden boards with plastic flooring. Before Kippenberger died in 1997 these floors were removed – after the last squatters still in residence were paid to decamp – and sold to a German museum for a million euros.

RASSELFISCH

Bergmannstraße 71–72, Kreuzberg
U-Bahn Gneisenaustraße
Tel 30 6120 1235
www.rasselfisch.de/berlin
Open 11am to 7pm,
Saturday until 5pm, closed Sunday
TOYS AND CHILDREN'S FURNITURE
Occupying a huge white space near the Passionskirche and the Marheineke covered market, alongside wine merchants Not Only Riesling (which adds a certain amount of interest), Rasselfisch swims cheekily along in the enchanted ocean of baby buggies. Its products look more like dragsters for infant boy or girl racers than Silver Cross perambulators, containing angelic baby accessories such as bassinets and educational playthings. The toys will also appeal to adults with only the slightest tendency to second childhood: for example, the large wooden fish that looks like a giant cheesy biscuit, or the Berlin-themed trinkets that make charming, reasonably priced souvenirs. The store also has a location in Prenzlauer Berg and, in late 2015, opened a third in the rapidly gentrifying Neukölln neighbourhood.

REISEANTIQUITÄTEN/ PRITI SHAMBHU

Suarezstraße 48–49, Charlottenburg
U-Bahn Sophie-Charlotte-Platz
Tel 30 208 2681
www.kunsthandel-antiquitaeten.com
Open noon to 7pm,
Saturday 11am to 3pm, closed Sunday
VINTAGE LUGGAGE
Located within the Antik-Center, which houses several specialist antiques stalls, Priti Shambhu's shop is a veritable mine of vintage travel and leisure accessories, such as suitcases, trunks, jewel boxes, toilet sets, hatboxes, glove boxes, map boxes, postcard albums, vintage travel guides, briefcases, parasols, shoes and handbags. Everything is either in perfect condition or else bears a patina that evokes a bygone world of high-class, elegant travel. Look out for the porcelain cups from Café Adlon scattered among the items of travel equipment.

RIANNA + NINA

Torstraße 62, Mitte
U-Bahn Rosa-Luxemburg-Platz
Tel 30 550 75 607
www.riannaandnina.com
Open noon to 7pm, closed Sunday
PSYCHEDELIC VINTAGE UPHOLSTERY
Nina Kuhn opened this shop in 2014 with Rianna Nektaria Kourou, whom she met at a vintage furniture show. Together they use unique fabrics from all over the world to festoon hand-made lamps with vintage stands, spatter silk cushions with ikat motifs or decorate them with delicate illustrations, hand-sew kimonos and scarves, and stitch together quilted bags from these same polychrome textiles. Other fabulous motifs await enthusiasts at the vintage store **RIANNA IN BERLIN** (Große Hamburger Straße 25, Mitte, tel 30 640 76 120).

ROSY'S PUPPEN & TEDDYKLINIK

Westfälische Straße 56, Wilmersdorf
S-Bahn Halensee
Tel 30 873 60 04
www.rosys-puppen-teddyklinik.de
Open Tuesday and Thursday 11am to 6pm
SOFT TOYS AND DOLLS
Since 1987 Rosy Blanke has been considered a kind of Florence Nightingale by collectors of vintage teddy bears and dolls, a title she treasures with pride. She has moved her shop-cum-clinic from Uhlandstraße to be closer to the Grunewald forest area of the city – doubtless a better environment for her patients both furry and porcelain, about whom she keeps

highly detailed medical notes. On entering the shop, with its dolls' clothes, miniature embroidered linen, vintage toys and doll's-house furniture, some collectors may start to feel faint with delight. Rosy herself, who boasts of not having lost a patient yet, keeps a close eye on things. All the reconstructive surgery takes place in a little outbuilding at the back of the courtyard.

SCHEE

Bleibtreustraße 48, Charlottenburg
S-Bahn Savignyplatz
Tel 30 889 20 134, www.schee.net
Open 11am to 8pm,
Saturday from 10am, closed Sunday
STYLISH DECORATIVE ITEMS
At first glance, you might be in Ibiza or Rome. The cold-climate Schee concept suggests something more southerly here with its washed-out floors and sun-baked furniture. The two-tone table, kitchen and cooking ceramics call out for tians, ratatouilles and shakshukas. Back to the north with the plaids, blankets and wooden toys. But what catches the eye is a whole wall occupied by framed graphic works. They are just numbered multiples, the number referring to a set of tokens whose number indicates that the drawing catching you eye is either available or out-of-stock. A sort of reverse lottery. They're very affordable, so go for that gift and/or impulse buy. And all the artists have a name: Flavio Morais, Elroyink, Sanna Maslander, Sanna Wieslander and Cat Coquillette. **Other location:** Rosenthaler Straße 15, Mitte, tel 030 526 46 987

SIBEL HUHN

Bleibtreustraße 19, Charlottenburg
U-Bahn Uhlandstraße
S-Bahn Savignyplatz
Tel 30 887 13 530, www.sibel-huhn.de
Open 10am to 7pm,
Saturday 11am to 6pm, closed Sunday
FURNITURE AND INTERIOR DESIGN
Sibel Huhn's showroom is immersed in an evocative darkness glinting with precious woods and rare objects. It feels like a UFO amid the efficient, Brutalist architectural rigor of Berlin-style interior design. A sumptuous showcase for an interior design agency that since 2009 has been specializing upmarket design in Berlin, Warsaw, Riga, Ibiza and Palma de Mallorca. Sibel Huhn, nicknamed "the VIP's architect", is the exclusive representative in the city for several high-flying firms, including Promemoria, belonging to the Italian cabinet-maker Romeo Sozzi.

SORGENFREI

Goltzstraße 18, Schöneberg
U-Bahn Eisenacher Straße
Tel 30 3010 4071
www.sorgenfrei-in-berlin.de
Open noon to 7pm, Saturday 10am to 6pm,
Sunday 1pm to 6pm, closed Monday
ANTIQUES, CAFÉ
Typical of the eccentrically charming attitude of inclusiveness that characterizes Schöneberg in general and Goltzstraße in particular, Sorgenfrei (literally, "no worries") is a haven of inexpensive amusing curios where you can nose around among occasional tables on which the owners serve drinks and cakes as you admire the vintage East and West German pieces with their aura of absurd nostalgia. There's a Sputnik-shaped standard lamp, a furnished 1950s doll's house, a shampoo bottle in the shape of a VW Cox, a Duracell bunny in a cosmonaut costume, an advert for John Player's tobacco, an illustrated book of 1950s West German film stars, extraordinary LPs, an electric hair dryer in the shape of a Vespa, and even a *Zu Gast in Berlin* guide dated 12 December 1970 – a real retro tourist barometer of West Berlin during the Cold War. The prices are as competitive as an East German athlete and they don't accept credit cards.

STEIFF GALERIE

Kurfürstendamm 38–39, Charlottenburg
U-Bahn Uhlandstraße, Kurfurstendamm
Tel 30 8862 5006, www.steiff.com
Open 10am to 8pm,
Saturday until 7pm, closed Sunday

TEDDY BEARS

The most famous of teddy bears, recognizable by its short velvety mohair fur and the metal "Knopf im Ohr" ("button in the [left] ear"), was invented in 1886 in Giengen an der Brenz by Margarete Steiff, a polio-afflicted dressmaker who made little stuffed animals to which her brother, Richard, added articulated limbs. The Steiff bear officially came of age in the US in 1902, when it was renamed Teddy as a tribute to President Roosevelt, who had once refused to shoot a bear. Ever since then there's scarcely a single German babe who has not been given a Steiff teddy as a christening or Christmas gift. The bears are the focus of a unique cult following and give collectors all over the world the vapours. The Steiff company is aware that they are custodians of a very special heritage and the source of an incredible teddymania, so every year they organize secret meetings in major cities to unveil their latest models and revivals of historic teddies. Still located in its original premises, the factory faithfully produces its collection of original toys. The bear family of Teddy, Moritz, Urs, Jona, Fynn, etc., now share their den with other animals, including the rabbit Lulac, launched in 1951, and the German Shepherd puppy Hasso, surely the cutest of them all. Owing to Steiff's proximity to the zoo, you can also buy life-size cuddly toys such as lions, giraffes and brown bears. There's also a range of pocket-sized mascots called Floppies. The little suitcase with a travelling teddy inside makes a perfect gift.

STUE

Torstraße 70, Mitte
U-Bahn Rosa-Luxemburg-Platz
Tel 30 2472 7650, www.stueberlin.de
Open noon to 7pm,
closed Sunday and Tuesday

SCANDINAVIAN DESIGN AND FASHION

Danish by birth, Heike Marie Rädeke left the Alte Schönhauserstraße some years ago when the rents went sky high, becoming one of the first to set up shop on Torstraße. She specializes in high-end Scandinavian design that she has selected intelligently and often restored herself, but also sells a small selection of contemporary art. This is the place to come if you're looking for a stylish vintage occasional table, a glass vase, a lamp, a sewing basket or a stoneware piece that would be an asset to any living room (in Danish, *stue* means living room). Heike Marie has a new associate, who restores vintage hi-fi.

TOBIAS GRAU

Stilwerk, Kantstraße 17, Charlottenburg
S-Bahn Savignyplatz
Tel 30 310 12 614
www.tobias-grau.com
Open 10am to 7pm, closed Sunday

LIGHTS

Tobias Grau is an interior designer who first made his name with the Luja low-voltage lighting system, invented in 1984. Further success came with his first collection, shown at the Cologne Fair in 1987. In 1999 he opened two showrooms simultaneously, one in Stilwerk in Hamburg and this one in Berlin. Winner of many prizes, Grau's work falls into four categories of lighting: suspension lights, floor lamps, wall and ceiling lights, and multi-directional systems featuring models that are available in four versions. Grau's bestsellers include Project X's UFO-style adjustable suspension lighting and George spotlights that look like the headlights of an old Citroën Traction Avant.

FIVE OBJECTS TO TAKE HOME

A MAP OF BERLIN drawn by the best cartographer in the world – Pharus. Available in specialist bookstores or direct from the publisher – a bit out of town, near Friedenau. Otherwise, for anecdotal interest or geo-historical comparisons, buy a 1952 Berlin map by Schaffmann, which has been reissued by Verlag Bien & Giersch (www.panorama-berlin.de) and is available in all good bookstores. **PHARUS** Rubensstraße 107, tel 3988 8883, www.pharus.eu, www.berliner-stadtplan.com

A WOOLLEN CAP that doesn't seem like one, but is! Very flattering, and made by Katharina Sigwart, the milliner whose company Yva provides hats for the coolest heads in town. Available in ready-to-wear or bespoke – but choose the camel rather than the black. **YVA** Bleibtreustraße 20, Charlottenburg, tel 28384595, www.yva.de

A BERLIN ALPHABET illustrating all the monuments and sights of the capital on cards, posters, etc. It's the most attractive of souvenirs – light in your luggage, and really creative. **TYPE HYPE** Rosa-Luxemburg-Straße 9 – 13, Mitte, tel 2759 1404, www.typehype.com

AN AMPELMANN: ONE RED, ONE GREEN – in the form of a keyring. Designed in 1961 by Karl Peglau, who was tasked with reducing accidents in city traffic, this little illuminated man appeared on East German, and thus East Berlin, traffic lights. The figure was designed so that anyone who was colour-blind could also see when to cross the street: if the little man is walking, you walk too; if he's standing with outstretched arms, you wait. The Ampelmann was still in use up to the start of the 1990s. When Berlin decided to change its signage, the population protested and the Ampelmann became a street cult, even in the West. Now a staple of the Ostalgia industry and reproduced on almost everything – and we mean almost everything – down to ice-cube trays, the Ampelmann has become a classic of Berlin design. **AMPELMANN** Hackesche Höfe, Hof IV, Mitte, tel 4404 8809, www.ampelmann.de

A PRODUCTION SUITCASE in cardboard with metal corners and bright colours, hand-made on historic machines dating from 1913 in full view of visitors to the workshops of the Deutsches Technikmusuem with the support of Rimowa, Samsonite and Bree. Three models, three sizes, in several colours and designs, sold in the museum shop: **DEUTSCHES MUSEUM** Trebbiner Straße 9, Kreuzberg, tel 030 902540, www.dtmn.de

TURBERG

Lietzenburger Straße 51, Schöneberg
U-Bahn Augsburger Straße
Tel 30 219 9900, www.turberg.de
Open 10am to 8pm,
Saturday until 6pm, closed Sunday
MODEL CARS AND TRAINS

No other Berlin store, not even KaDeWe's toy department, can compete with Turberg. In just a few years, the company has enjoyed astonishing success. The small original shop has been cast into oblivion, and today Turberg occupies two enormous adjoining stores, one for model cars, the other for electric trains. These are two typically German passions, represented here by both historic and trendsetting manufacturers. A temple for collectors, Turberg claims to be the biggest store of its kind in Europe, and its shop windows are magnets for collectors, who gaze transfixed for hours on end. In the train department, it's madness to even think about the lowest-price Märklin engines. In the model car department, prices are more modest, and you'll find all the classic brands: Schuco, Gama, Minichamps, Wikking, Herpa and Premium ClassiXXs from Germany; Motorart from Sweden; Abrex from the Czech Republic; Neo from Holland; and Brooklin from England, among many others. There's even the odd rerelease of the old 1:43-scale Märklin models, still packed in their little yellow 1970s-style cardboard boxes.

TYPE HYPE

Hotel Lux,
Rosa-Luxemburg-Straße 9–13, Mitte
U-Bahn Rosa-Luxemburg-Platz,
Weinmeisterstraße
Tel 2759 1404, www.typehype.com
Open 8am to 8pm, closed Sunday

CONCEPT STORE

Launched in December 2013 on the ground floor of the Lux 11 hotel, Type Hype is the brainchild of Kirsten Dietz and Jochen Rädeker, who founded the graphic design company Strichpunkt-Design, based in Stuttgart. They've set up a typographic business equipped with old print-shop furniture from Mainz, including a wonderful printing table with retractable stool and hundreds of narrow drawers. They sell a range of papers, textiles, porcelain, vegetable-tanned leather and enamelled kitchen wares, all printed from A to Z using various fonts they have invented themselves or based on Din Berlin, a typeface designed by Peter Behrens for Siemens in the early 20th century. Another addition to this elegant script is their collection of letters, graphically symbolizing, again from A to Z, Berlin's monuments and famous places, reproduced in formats from postcard to poster size: A for Alexanderplatz, D for Dom (the cathedral), O for Olympic Stadium, R for Reichstag, F for Funkturm, C for Checkpoint Charlie, P for Philharmonie, all the way to Z for Zoo, of course. From mugs to notebooks, it's all designed in Berlin and manufactured

in Germany, in particular by the venerable stationers Gmund, located on Lake Tegernsee in Bavaria, and porcelain manufacturer Reichenbach, based in Thuringia. One exception to the rule is the enamel kitchenware and cookware, such as the lunchboxes, saucepans and measuring jugs, which are produced by the Austrian company Riess. There's also a grocery department selling Type Hype branded coffee, jam, vinegar, biscuits, drinks, teas, spices, peppers and olive oils, all selected by the German branch of Slow Food. The Milk Bar in the middle of the shop refers to the beverage imbibed by printers in the olden days to counteract the supposed noxious effects of the ink and lead they worked with their bare hands. It serves fancy sandwiches, open sandwiches, cakes, fruit juices, cappuccinos and milkshakes. It's a great idea.

AT HOME WITH BARRIE KOSKY

For convenience sake, he could have chosen an apartment near the Komische Oper Berlin, but the Unter den Linden area wasn't what he was really after. So Barrie Kosky has chosen to live in Schöneberg – Belziger Straße, to be precise, a beautiful, wide retail and residential street, lined with elegant buildings that conjure up the Berlin of the interwar years. It's a broad street with a village feel. When you do the maths, Barrie Kosky only lives here half the year, but he's made this city his home port. Naturally, there's a piano, and, like his Komische Oper Berlin office lounge overlooking the Unter den Linden, there are columns and stalagmites of books.

There are even books in the bathroom. Berlin is a great city for bookshops. I mainly go to the Bücherbogen on Savignyplatz. That's the most dangerous one – I could buy the whole shop! I also go to the Eisenherz gay bookshop near my house, and often to Dussmann, a huge store on several floors, not far from the Komische Oper Berlin.

BÜCHERBOGEN
Stadtbahnbogen 593, Charlottenburg, tel 30 3186 9511, www.buecherbogen.com

DUSSMANN – DAS KULTURKAUFHAUS
Friedrichstraße 90, Mitte, tel 30 2025 1111, www.kulturkaufhaus.de

EISENHERZ
Motzstraße 23, Schöneberg, tel 30 313 9936, www.prinz-eisenherz.com

ARTS AND CULTURE

MAJOR MUSEUMS TO RADICAL THEATRES: EXPLORING THE CITY'S CULTURAL RICHES

Europe's third most popular tourist destination after London and Paris, Berlin has a rich cultural life, with a constant stream of commemorative events, crowd-pulling blockbuster exhibitions, biennales and festivals. Culture is everywhere in the city, from the frivolous and light-hearted to the challenging and serious.

Culture in Berlin is genuinely accessible to all, with literature and cinema being viewed with the same esteem as theatre, opera and concerts. Celebrated directors and conductors such as Thomas Ostermeier, Sasha Waltz, Barrie Kosky and Daniel Barenboim set the bar high on the Berlin arts scene. And with an increasing number of exhibition spaces in the west of the city, like the new C/O gallery and the Helmut Newton Foundation, photography is also making its mark.

Museum Island is still in the throes of redevelopment, but visitors continue to flock there. Part of the Dahlem museum complex will be transferring to the new Hohenzollern Palace, rebuilt to match the original. Grouped into a foundation, the other (real) Prussian royal palaces and parks welcome visitors on the lake shores and deep in the countryside. As for the contemporary art galleries, having made the former East Berlin their own, they are now eyeing up the former West, declaring it the new Eldorado, and moving into former post offices, redundant schools and deconsecrated churches. Culture for everyone. And controversies, of course. You are in Berlin, after all.

WORDS, FILM AND MUSIC

ANTIQUARIAT DÜWAL

Schlüterstraße 17, Charlottenburg
S-Bahn Savignyplatz
Tel 30 313 3030, www.duewal.de
Open 3pm to 6pm, Saturday 11am to 2pm
and by appointment, closed Sunday
SECOND-HAND GUIDEBOOKS

Antiquariat. The perfect word to describe old books and papers, it is more generally used by "antique" shops selling motley objects, unclassifiable curiosities, old toys, unusual items of furniture and knickknacks, although most of the shops specializing in old books continue to use the term. In the west of the city, the most interesting, specialized and diverse are in Charlottenburg, all around Savignyplatz and along Schlüterstraße. Well off the usual tourist trail, these old shops are a chance to experience a different, old-fashioned and erudite Berlin. That's certainly the case with this fine bookshop, where you'll find a friendly welcome and good advice, a great selection of vintage Baedeker guides, old books on architecture and geography and rare editions in both French and English.

AUTORENBUCHHANDLUNG BERLIN

Else-Ury-Bogen 599–600, Charlottenburg
S-Bahn Savignyplatz
Tel 30 313 0151
www.autorenbuchhandlung-berlin.de
Open 10am to 8pm, Saturday until 7pm,
closed Sunday
WRITERS' BOOKSHOP

This "writers' bookshop", located right next to the celebrated Bucherbogen bookshop, focuses on novels and other prose works. It moved from Cramerstraße in 2012, crossing Savignyplatz to nestle under the S-Bahn arches. It has that extra vital ingredient: a fine literary café, very popular with readers when it's not busy

with a reading or a stimulating discussion. Mad about books, Joachim Fürst and Marc Iven are really at home here, and so are their customers. Large selection of books in English.

BABYLON

Rosa-Luxemburg-Straße 30, Mitte
U-Bahn Rosa-Luxemburg-Platz
Tel 242 5969
www.babylonberlin.de
ARTHOUSE CINEMA

The Babylon, located opposite the Volksbühne, in Mitte, has an ochre and yellow façade designed by Hans Poelzig (1928) that conceals a cinema with the fullest programme in the city. A nostalgia treat, it still has its original cinema organ, a 1929 Philips with 66 notes and 913 pipes, and what's more, it has a resident organist (unique in Germany), Anna Vavilkina, who plays almost every evening before the main 8pm show.

BIBLIOTHECA CULINARIA

Zehdenicker Straße 16, Mitte
U-Bahn Rosenthaler Platz
Tel 30 4737 7570
www.bibliotheca-culinaria.de
Open 11am to 7pm, Saturday until 4pm,
closed Sunday and Monday
OLD COOKERY BOOKS

A former plants and fertiliser businessman, Swen Kernemann-Mohr nursed an unquenchable passion for old cookery books. He found and collected hundreds of them and associated items, never letting any go. When he retired, he found a new career: running a second-hand cookery bookshop. His bookshop is on the lower ground floor, the stock carefully arranged on Ikea bookshelves: by country, by discipline, by period. A glass-fronted cupboard holds a collection of cookbooks from the time of the GDR. He occasionally digs out a rarity like *Operation Vittles*, a little recipe book produced after the war by the wife of a US army officer living here during the Soviet blockade, when all supplies had to be brought in by airplane. Foraging about, one finds a bread slicer, a mincer, a coffee grinder and a cocktail set, all at reasonable prices. A treasure trove.

BORIS SCHOENHERR

Sophienstraße 20a, Mitte
U-Bahn Weinmeisterstraße
Tel 30 281 7064
www.holzblasinstrumente-schoenherr.de
Open 9am to noon and 1pm to 6pm, and
by appointment, closed Saturday and Sunday

WIND INSTRUMENTS

For more than twenty-five years Boris Schoenherr, celebrated master craftsman, has been making clarinets, flutes, saxophones and oboes of the finest quality, much sought after by leading musicians. Rather than trying to see something through the barred windows, it's better to go inside and start a conversation, even if the last time you touched a flute it had champagne in it. You'll see some amazing instruments, bringing back memories of childhood encounters with Peter and the Wolf, and leave refreshed by great sounds and stories.

BÜCHERBOGEN

Stadtbahnbogen 593, Charlottenburg
S-Bahn Savignyplatz
Tel 30 3186 9511, www.buecherbogen.com
Open 10am to 8pm, Saturday until 7pm,
closed Sunday

SPECIALIST BOOKSHOP

Ruthild Spangenberg's bookshop specializing in art, design, architecture, fashion, photography, theatre and new and second-hand rare books is flourishing under the S-Bahn arches near Savignyplatz. It opened in 1980 and annexed five extra arches in 2006, with interior design by architect Gerhard Spangenberg. The one devoted to Berlin – history, architecture, guides – offers the best selection in the city, while the section given over to journals, magazines and "mooks" (half-magazines, half-books) on fashion and fashion photography should not be missed.

CARAN D'ACHE

Uhlandstraße 29, Wilmersdorf
U-Bahn Uhlandstraße
Tel 30 885 51 655
www.carandache-deutschland.de
Open 10am to 7pm, Saturday 9:30am
to 6pm, closed Sunday

PENCILS AND STATIONERY

As Swiss as its graphite core, Caran d'Ache takes its name from the famous pseudonym used by the French illustrator Emmanuel Poiré. Born in Moscow, he simply Frenchified and ennobled the Russian word *karandash* (pencil) in order to promote his brilliant career as illustrator and caricaturist. He also used his made-up name for a collection of wooden toys, highly sought after by collectors. Caran d'Ache disappeared at the beginning of the 20th century but is still a legendary name in the field. When in 1924, the Swiss Carl Schweitzer bought the Ecridor Swiss pencil factory, founded in 1915, he renamed it Caran d'Ache. It has now been a century since the illustrious myth became a world-famous brand. Meanwhile, we've had the Fixpencil pencil clamp, and then the Prismalo, followed by a slew of cult pencils and pens. Picasso and Miro both consumed large numbers of these coloured pencils with cedar-wood bodies, and Karl Lagerfeld still uses them today. Paul Smith and Peter Marino have created capsule collections in limited editions. Still a Swiss family business, it has become synonymous with luxury pencils, with shops in Geneva, Zürich, Tokyo and also Berlin. You can find the entire collection of ranges, colours, graphites and pens produced by the firm, as well as paper and notebooks. Makes a change from Koh-i-Nor or Faber-Castell.

DO YOU READ ME?!

Auguststraße 28, Mitte
S-Bahn Oranienburger Straße
Tel 695 49 695
www.doyoureadme.de
Open 10am to 7:30pm, closed Sunday

FASHIONABLE BOOKSHOP

This stylish address, complete with
an esoterically punctuated name, is
a magazine-lover's paradise. Its black
shelves stock everything from the hippest
fashion bibles to self-published zines
on anything from gastronomy, bicycles,
photography, fashion, graphic design and
architecture. After a short-lived branch
in Potsdamer Straße, DYRM has opened
another store in **C/O BERLIN**.

DUSSMANN – DAS KULTURKAUFHAUS

Friedrichstraße 90, Mitte
S-Bahn and U-Bahn Friedrichstraße
Tel 30 2025 1111
www.kulturkaufhaus.de
Open 9am to midnight, Saturday until
11:30pm, closed Sunday

CULTURAL MEGASTORE

Opened by Peter Dussmann in 1997
in a new building designed by architects
Miroslav Volf, Mario Campi and Franco
Pessina, this "cultural department store"
caused a scandal by opening late into the
evening and also, to begin with, on Sunday.
In a town in which Sunday as a day of rest
is sacrosanct, this was deemed shocking.
Since then, the three floors, which are
flooded with light, have swarmed at all
hours. On the shelves: all the latest books
in the fields of the arts, politics, history and
crime fiction. In the basement: classical
music and opera on DVD and CD; on the
ground floor: a stationery shop and large
displays devoted to Berlin, Berlin writers,
and pop and rock, with a dedicated space
for independent labels. On the first floor:
children's books and jazz; on the
second floor, cinema (books and DVDs),
architecture, design, religion, sociology.
On the third floor: travel, learning and

foreign languages. Each floor is accessible
for the disabled and has toilets, a reading
lounge and even a baby-change room.

EINAR & BERT

Weinstraße 72, Friedrichshain
U-Bahn Senefelderplatz
Tel 30 4435 28511
www.einar-und-bert.de
Open 11am to 6pm, Saturday from noon,
closed Sunday

THEATRE BOOKSHOP

Located opposite Leise Park, this
specialist bookseller – with outlets in
several theatres such as the Berliner
Festspiele, the Schaubühne am Lehniner
Platz and the Thalia Theater in Hamburg
– has surprisingly chosen an area without
any theatre of note to set up its store
selling books, texts, essays, biographies,
CDs, works of criticism and history, all
focused on the theatre, which has such
a rich heritage in Germany. There's a small
café by the entrance with a few tables
outside, a smiling welcome and a guarantee
of finding titles that you won't find
anywhere else. A real theatre people's place.
They come here too, to sign autographs,
give lectures and enjoy its events.

EISENHERZ

Motzstraße 23, Schöneberg
U-Bahn Nollendorfplatz
Tel 30 313 9936
www.prinz-eisenherz.com
Open 10am to 8pm, closed Sunday

GAY AND LESBIAN BOOKSHOP

Prinz Eisenherz pioneered gay
bookshops in Germany, opening the first
one thirty-five years ago. It then crossed the
Ku'damm to a shop on Lietzenburgerstraße,
in Wilmersdorf, close to the gay bars,
cafés, clubs and hotels on Fuggerstraße.
With itchy feet again, the store has moved
to Motzstraße, in Schöneberg, in the heart
of the gay quarter. All literature on the
subject can be found in this bookshop,
from the most puerile to the most militant,
with comic books (naturally dominated by

the hilarious creations of Ralf König, a sort of gay Cologne version of Beryl Cook); DVDs of films that can no longer be found elsewhere (or are extremely difficult and complicated to find); and photography books. A suite of rooms at the rear of the store forms a gallery showing the work of visual artists – photos, collages, illustrations – from the LGBT community.

FILMTHEATER AM FRIEDRICHSHAIN

Bötzowstraße 1–5, Prenzlauer Berg
Tel 4284 5188, www.yorck.de
ARTHOUSE CINEMA
Considered Berlin's best art-house cinema, with five auditoriums, the Filmtheater am Friedrichshain, which has a very pleasant *Biergarten* as well, moves outdoors from June to August to show films in the park amphitheatre opposite. The Filmtheater belongs to the Yorck Kinogruppe, together with the Delphi Filmpalast, the Odeon, the Kant Kino, the Passage and the Arthouse, among others.

GRAMMOPHON-SALON-SCHUMACHER

Eisenacher Straße 11, Schöneberg
U-Bahn Nollendorfplatz
Tel 30 2147 4640
www.grammophon-salon.de
Open 2pm to 7pm, Saturday 11am to 2pm, closed Sunday and Monday
GRAMOPHONES, VINYL RECORDS
A few grooves from the apartment building at number 17 Nollendorfstraße where Christopher Isherwood lived in the 1930s, this gramophone and record shop harks back to the same period, when Sally Bowles sang her heart out on the *Cabaret* stage. More prosaically, but just as passionately, Kirsten Schumacher buys, repairs and resells these old ancestors of modern hi-fi, including old phonographs with their external horns, as well as accessories and LPs. Total nostalgia.

GROBER UNFUG

Zossener Straße 33, Kreuzberg
U-Bahn Gneisenaustraße
Tel 30 6940 1490
www.groberunfug.de
Open 11am to 7pm, Saturday until 6pm, closed Sunday
COMICS, MANGAS
This amazing comic bookshop has another branch in Mitte, on Torstraße. At both addresses, the sales staff are simply amazing. Novices determined to winkle out a first edition of the *Adventures of Tintin* might feel a tad out of their depth, but they'll soon learn from the friendly advice and encouragement they get here. Plus, since Grober is the leading store of its kind in the city, you'll find all the writers, illustrators, story boarders, collectors and publishers on hand whenever there's an evening book signing **Other location:** Torstraße 75, Mitte, tel 30 281 7331

HAMMETT

Friesenstraße 27, Kreuzberg
U-Bahn Gneisenaustraße
Tel 30 691 5834
www.hammett-krimis.de
Open 10am to 8pm, Saturday 9am to 6pm, closed Sunday
CRIME FICTION AND THRILLERS
A reference to the sombre Dashiell Hammett, inventor of the noir novel, this Berliner Hammett has specialized in crime fiction, noir and thrillers since 1995. And who profits from all this crime? It's Christian Bloch, an enthusiast who organizes book signings with many of the greats of the genre, such as Dennis Lehane. On the shelf, the Berlin of crime is one cruel city. From Grunewald to Köpenick, not to mention Unter den Linden, you'll find action, shooting, thrills. One title stands out: *Das tote Zimmermädchen vom Bahnhof Zoo*, a Berlin travel guide of crime, part of a series of novels featuring fifty tough-to-crack crimes, U-Bahn station by U-Bahn station, written by Rainer Stenzenberger and Ulrich Sackenreuter.

GREAT LIBRARIES

The mother of all the many libraries in Berlin is the former royal library, now part of Humboldt University. It stands on Bebelplatz and has a historic facade designed by Boumann (1775), a simple copy of another design, never built, by Fischer von Erlach for the Hofburg in Vienna. The **STAATSBIBLIOTHEK ZU BERLIN – PREUSSISCHER KULTURBESITZ**, or State Library, is divided between two sites that together form the largest research library in Germany, which has no national library. Haus Unter den Linden, Stabi-Ost, the east library, holds one of the world's largest collections of scores by Bach and Mozart. This enormous palace, built between 1903 and 1914 to a design by Ernst von Ihne in late Wilhelmine style, is currently undergoing large-scale reorganization. When completed it will house a book museum, with public access to the immense central reading room with its uplifting orange tones, designed by HG Merz. The history of the Western branch, Stabi-West or Haus Potsdamer Straße, is very different. After 1945, it transpired that most of the books not burned by the Nazis had been preserved in the Allied sectors and the architect Hans Scharoun was commissioned in 1964 to design a general library alongside the Philharmonie he had already designed. It was opened in 1978 with a large, luminous reading room with big windows looking out on the countryside. The powerful Humboldt University has built its own central library in Mitte, named **JACOB-UND-WILHELM-GRIMM-ZENTRUM** after the Brothers Grimm. Designed by Max Dudler, the rectangular building has an impressive layout that can feel claustrophobic, but its generous opening hours (until midnight) make up for this. Architecture enthusiasts will want to see the libraries at the **FREIE UNIVERSITÄT** in Dahlem, also home to the philology library designed in the shape of a brain by Lord Foster in 2011. If you want to learn more about Berlin's history and current affairs you should take out life membership of the **BERLINER STADTBIBLIOTHEK**, stakeholder in the union of Berlin's twelve excellent local libraries whose main project (**ZENTRAL- UND LANDESBIBLIOTHEK BERLIN**) seems endless: originally planned for the rebuilt Stadtschloss, the City decided instead to make it larger and more impressive and build it at Tempelhof airport, accompanied by a design competition. However, in a referendum in 2014 the public voted against turning the green space into a library. The saga continues.

STAATSBIBLIOTHEK ZU BERLIN Haus Unter den Linden, entrance on Dorotheenstraße 27, Mitte, S-Bahn and U-Bahn Friedrichstraße, tel 2664 33888; Haus Potsdamer Straße, Potsdamer Straße 33, Tiergarten, S-Bahn and U-Bahn Potsdamer Platz, tel 266 432 333, www.staatsbibliothek-berlin.de

JACOB-UND-WILHELM-GRIMM-ZENTRUM Geschwister-Scholl-Straße 1, Mitte, S-Bahn and U-Bahn Friedrichstraße, tel 30 209 399 370, www.grimm-zentrum.hu-berlin.de

FREIE UNIVERSITÄT BERLIN Habelschwerdter Allee 45, Dahlem, U-Bahn Dahlem-Dorf, tel 30 8385 8822, www.fu-berlin.de/sites/philbib

ZENTRAL- UND LANDESBIBLIOTHEK BERLIN / BERLINER STADTBIBLIOTHEK Breite Straße 30–36, Mitte, S-Bahn and U-Bahn Alexanderplatz, tel 30 9022 6401, www.zlb.de

The little room next door is devoted
to second-hand paperbacks in German
and English.

HORENSTEIN KLASSIKSCHALPLATTEN & CAFÉ

Fechner Straße 3, Wilmersdorf
U-Bahn Blissestraße
Tel 30 8639 6897
www.horenstein.de
Open 1pm to 7pm, Saturday 11am to 6pm,
closed Sunday to Tuesday
CDS, CONCERTS, CAFÉ

This extraordinary classical music store and
café was opened by the uncompromising
Wolf Zuber, a stickler for the finest sound
quality. The place has a strong air of vinyl
revenge, which has led to a stampede
from enthusiasts and collectors, flocking
here from Italy, Finland and even as far
afield as Japan. Zuber never takes the
easy option: not happy with offering an
extensive collection of LPs of classical
music from the post-war period to the last
recordings of the pre-CD era, he also has
top-quality equipment to play them on.
The store simply oozes 1950s and 1960s
nostalgia, with plenty of original items of
furniture. Pure bliss.

IMAGE MOVEMENT

Oranienburger Straße 18, Mitte
S-Bahn Oranienburger Straße
Tel 30 308 819 780
www.facebook.com/Image-
Movement-60553446463/
Open 11am to 7pm, closed Sunday
ARTHOUSE CINEMA

Image Movement portrays itself as a shop,
gallery and film library, with premises in
the city and an online store as well. It also
sees itself as a standard-bearer for the idea
of the moving image as art, working closely
with artists. To this end, they also host
an event series, held every two weeks, where
young filmmakers are invited to present
their work. With an enormous choice of
experimental and short films, this

mezzanine shop is a real gold mine, and
the book collection is growing by the day.

KLICK KINO

Windscheidstraße 19, Charlottenburg
S-Bahn Berlin-Charlottenburg
Tel 30 283 65 30
www.klickkino.de
ARTHOUSE CINEMA

Founded in 1911 as a neighbourhood
cinema, the Klick eventually clocked out,
turning into the DaWandsa Snuggery
concept store and café. Now it is back
giving public screenings ever since it was
taken over by Chritos Acrivulis, who
founded Missing Films, and Claudia
Rische, the former cinema PR. In March
2017, it opened with the premiere of the
documentary *Gaza Surf Club* directed
by Philip Gandat and Mickey Yamine,
promising a very bold art-house
programme. As it's in Berlin, the Klick
also has a café, ideal for gabbing about
movies after the show.

LUIBAN PAPETERIE

Rosa-Luxemburg-Straße 28, Mitte
U-Bahn Rosa-Luxemburg-Platz
Tel 30 8894 1192, www.luiban.de
Open noon to 8pm, closed Sunday
NOSTALGIC STATIONERY SHOP

Luiban opened its first shop in Nuremberg
in 2009. It opened an outpost in Berlin
in 2011, in the Kreuzberg neighbourhood.
It moved to this address in 2013, where
it rubs shoulders with fashion, perfumery,
hat and graphic design stores. Luiban is like
an enormous school pencil case, full
of all the things we used to use for writing,
underlining, sticking, pinning, clipping,
attaching, stapling, cutting out, correcting,
erasing and labelling. In this nostalgic, retro
shop you can rediscover the pleasures
of bottles of white glue, fountain pens and
small notebooks. It's impossible not to
buy something here: school supplies have
the same effect as Proust's madeleines.
Except they don't leave crumbs.

MODULOR

Aufbauhaus, Prinzenstraße 85, Kreuzberg
U-Bahn Moritzplatz
Tel 30 690 360, www.modulor.de
Open 9am to 8pm, Saturday 10am to 6pm,
closed Sunday

STATIONERY AND ARTISTS' SUPPLIES

Designers and artists in Berlin claim that
you only have to look at an installation,
a collage or a model here to know that the
person who made it got their supplies
from Modulor. Indeed, one begins to
wonder whether many creative people go
there with no specific objective in mind,
but simply to seek inspiration. In 2011,
Modulor moved from Gneisenaustraße
to Kreuzberg and is now housed in the
enormous Aufbau Haus, home of the
Aufbau publishing house, owner of Planet
Modulor. This massive, five-storey building
contains over eighty units, with studios,
workshops and design agencies, as well as
a theatre, the TAK, a bookshop, several
cafés and a number of graphic design
and art galleries, all linked to art and design
and all accessible from Modulor.

MOVIEMENTO

Kottbusser Damm 22, Kreuzberg
U-Bahn Hermannplatz
Tel 692 4785
www.moviemento.de

ARTHOUSE CINEMA

The Moviemento in Kreuzberg is proud
of its status as the oldest working cinema
in Berlin. Opened in 1907, it was here than
the cult *Rocky Horror Picture Show* was
screened continuously for ten years to the
accompaniment of fabulous over-the-top
audience participation and where the
director Tom Tykwer, now on Hollywood's
most bankable list, began his working life
as a projectionist in the 1980s. Films
shown all day, from morning till night, with
special programmes for children and even
a festival of arty porn films.

OCELOT – NOT JUST ANOTHER BOOKSTORE

Brunnenstraße 181, Mitte
U-Bahn Rosenthaler Platz
Tel 30 9789 4592, www.ocelot.de
Open 10am to 8pm, closed Sunday

BOOKS, NEWSPAPERS AND MAGAZINES

The delightful and pleasant-sounding
name of this bookshop might seem a trifle
enigmatic at first sight. In fact, these
qualities are the very reason for its choice:
for Frithjof Klepp, the young owner-
founder-director of this large general
bookshop, the word Ocelot has nothing to
do with a wild animal in a cage. Or free, for
that matter. It's just a symbol. The interior
is by Martina Zeyen, a Berlin designer
known for the Berlinomat concept store,
and its 260 square metres have been laid
out to provide a range of reading and
browsing areas. So you can take your time
here, sitting on a stool or sofa, choosing
books for children, or novels, essays,
art books, mostly in German. There's
a welcoming café and a newsstand on
your right as soon as you enter.

PRO QM

Almstadtstraße 48–50, Mitte
U-Bahn Rosa-Luxemburg-Platz
Tel 30 2472 8520
www.pro-qm.de
Open 11am to 8pm, closed Sunday

ARCHITECTURAL BOOKSHOP

In business since 1999, this unusual
bookshop focuses on the arts, design,
architecture, graphic design, politics and
urbanism. Its move from Alte Schönhauser
Straße, where it occupied the premises
of an old butcher's shop, resulted in the loss
of a charming setting, but the radical ethos
remains intact. Its newsletter is a gold mine
of information and literary discoveries.

THE RECORD STORE BERLIN

Invalidenstraße 148, Mitte
U-Bahn Rosenthaler Platz
Tel 30 2844 4680
www.facebook.com/TheRecordStoreBerlin/
Open noon to 8pm, closed Sunday
VINTAGE VINYL

Berlin is a mecca for music fans in general, and for vinyl enthusiasts in particular. You'll find plenty in every second-hand bookshop, packed in cardboard boxes, at a couple of euros each. The same goes for the flea markets, especially the ones near Schöneberg town hall, where you can unearth some amazing treasures. The Record Store is another good source, with a wide-ranging selection focusing on jazz, blues, early soul and classic rock. Having moved from its previous location just a needle's skip away on Brunnen Straße in 2015, its new, slightly smaller shop has retained the great display of 1950s and 1960s LP and singles sleeves on the walls, including Brigitte Bardot, Julie London, Billy Eckstine, MC5, Jan & Dean, Nancy Wilson, Gainsbourg, Adamo and Dalhia Lavi, who died recently.

ROBERT HARTWIG –
BERLINER BUCH- UND
MUSIKANTIQUARIAT

Pestalozzistraße 23, Charlottenburg
U-Bahn Wilmersdorfer Straße
Tel 30 312 9124
www.antiquariat-hartwig.de
Open by appointment
MUSICAL ANTIQUES

This dealer is unquestionably top dog in Berlin for musical antiques, something his competitors are happy to acknowledge. The price to pay for this reputation is that the opening hours are rather unpredictable. However, it's for a good cause: indeed, even if the shop is officially open at Friday and Saturday lunchtime, it is not uncommon to find yourself in front of a locked door, facing a sign saying "Closed to buy a book collection". Hardly surprising given that the shop specializes in the acquisition of prestigious private book collections. You are therefore strongly advised to phone ahead to make an appointment.

R.S.V.P. PAPIER IN MITTE

Mulackstraße 14 and 26, Mitte
S-Bahn Hackescher Markt
Tel 30 280 946 44
www.rsvp-berlin.de
Open 11am to 7pm, closed Sunday
STYLISH STATIONERY

After much smoking and drinking, Lisa von Treskow had an urgent need to write. Originally the founder of the Whiskey and Cigars cellar on the Sophienstraße, she switched to paper and writing accessories in 2001, a Berlin pioneer in nostalgically low-tech, high-powered new-wave stationery. Moleskine notebooks, G. Lalo writing paper, Delta pens and most importantly packaging papers and envelopes direct from old GDR stocks. *Tempus fugit*: a few years ago Meike Wander took over the business and in 2014 set up a second shop of this now historic enterprise.

SCHROPP LAND & KARTE

Hardenbergstraße 9a, Charlottenburg
S-Bahn and U-Bahn Zoologischer Garten
Tel 30 2355 7320
www.landkartenschropp.de
Open 10am to 8pm, Saturday until 6pm,
closed Sunday
MAPS AND GLOBES

With a number of universities as neighbours, this learned bookshop is full of maps and globes of all sizes. There are even maps of countries and regions you've probably never heard of. Regine and Robert Kiepert, a geographer and a living legend in the bookshop trade respectively, run this geographical oasis with erudition and good sense. Another world – ours.

SCHWESTERHERZ

Gärtnerstraße 28, Friedrichshain
U-Bahn Samariterstraße
Tel 30 7790 1183
www.schwesterherz-berlin.de
Open 11am to 8pm, Saturday 10:30am
to 7pm, closed Sunday
STATIONERY

This little stationery shop run by two
kindred spirits has been such a success
that they have opened a second branch
in Kreuzberg, near the Markthalle, next
door to the excellent wine merchant **NOT
ONLY RIESLING** (Schleiermacherstraße 25,
Kreuzberg, tel 030 6953 8866). There's
a juice bar and the whole venture has
a slightly girly vintage charm. You'll find
a huge choice of accessories and stylish
Berlin souvenirs and gifts. Have your
purchases wrapped in a sheet of
their pretty gift wrap. **Other location:**
KÜCHENLIEBE Gärtnerstraße 28,
Friedrichshain, tel 30 5449 0686

SODA BOOKS

Weinbergsweg 1, Mitte
U-Bahn Rosenthaler Platz
Tel 30 437 33 700, www.sodabooks.com
Open 11am to 7pm, Saturday from noon,
closed Sunday
BOOKAZINES

Soda came from Munich to compete with
the countless Berlin bookstores specialising
in bookazines, albums and reviews of art,
architecture, design, fashion, graphics
and even erotic books popular among the
creative urban tribes largely uninterested
in reading print. Along with a mass of
publishers and periodicals on the shelves
in glossy, recycled or crafted paper, there is
unsurprisingly a plethora of works on
graphics and tattooing. Curious publications
for curious people, goes the tagline. On a
practical note, Soda is located opposite the
Gorki Apartments. A captive, indeed
captivated, clientele.

UNTERWEGS ANTIQUARIAT & GALERIE

Torstraße 93, Mitte
U-Bahn Rosa-Luxemburg-Platz
Tel 30 4405 6015
www.berlinbook.com
Open 3pm to 7pm,
Saturday noon to 3pm and by appointment,
closed Sunday and Monday
TRAVEL BOOKS, PHOTO GALLERY

Marie-Luise Surek-Becker is a bona fide
archivist who has long collected,
catalogued and referenced the history
of travel writing and guides. This studious
address is a gold mine for people looking
for the 1923 Grieben guide to Baden-
Baden, the Baedeker to India and Russia,
Woerl publications for travel bookworms
and bibliophiles, or an intriguing guide
to hotels, boarding houses and restaurants
in East Germany, published in 1950.
In addition, there is a huge bookcase
filled with books on architecture and
photography in several languages, which
are listed in an impressive catalogue.
A photo gallery, focusing on Berlin
photographers such as André Kirchner
and Karl-Ludwig Lange, has also infiltrated
the bookshelves.

ZADIG

Linienstraße 141, Mitte
U-Bahn Oranienburger Tor
Tel 30 2809 9905
www.zadigbuchhandlung.de
Open 11am to 7pm, Monday from 2pm,
Saturday until 6pm, closed Sunday
FRENCH BOOKSHOP

This bookshop opened in 2003 by
Patrick Suel is the city's only bookshop
specializing in books in French. Zadig
stocks the latest hot fiction and non-fiction
works. Suel is the author of an amusing
blog where he promotes his current literary
favourites. He even published an anthology
of entries to celebrate his bookshop's
tenth anniversary. He also organizes plenty
of events in the shop in the form of
readings, meetings and book signings.

THEATRES AND CONCERT HALLS

BERLINER ENSEMBLE

Bertolt-Brecht-Platz 1, Mitte
S-Bahn and U-Bahn Friedrichstraße
Tel 30 2840 8155
www.berliner-ensemble.de
BRECHTIAN THEATRE
At the beginning, in 1892, there was
the Neues Theater where the great
Max Reinhardt staged his unforgettable
production of *A Midsummer Night's Dream*.
During the 1920s it became the National
Theater am Schiffbauerdamm, with
a marked political, left-wing bias.
The theatre finally took its permanent
name in 1949, when Helene Weigel and
Bertolt Brecht took over its management
under the watchful eye of the Soviet
authorities. It was in this theatre that
The Caucasian Chalk Circle and *Mother
Courage* were staged. And it is still here
that, season after season, the Brecht
catalogue is reinvented, from *The
Threepenny Opera* to *The Resistible Rise
of Arturo Ui*. Claus Peymann has been
its artistic director for over fifteen years
and the BE invites guest directors such as
Leander Haußmann, Robert Wilson,
Manfred Karge and Achim Freyer. It stages
plays from the classical repertoire –
Molière, Shakespeare, Goldoni, Schiller
– and more modern pieces by the likes
of Frank Wedekind, Samuel Beckett, Max
Frisch, Elfriede Jelinek, Botho Strauss
and Yasmina Reza. There are also fine
performances by German singers, including
Georgette Dee and the punk diva Nina
Hagen. Although the seats in the stalls are
old and a trifle narrow, choose one closest
to the stage, but avoid the second row,
as strangely the acoustics are bad there.
Brechtian right to the last.

BKA-THEATER

Mehringdamm 34, Kreuzberg
U-Bahn Mehringdamm
Tel 30 202 2007
www.bka-theater.de
CABARET
Founded by Jürgen Müller and Rainer
Rubbert and perched on the fifth floor,
the Berliner Kabarett Anstalt (BKA) has,
since 1988, been the typical Berlin-style
cabaret, with subdued lighting, café
atmosphere and refreshments. Onstage
are various brazen talents such as Sissi
Perlinger, Popette Betancor, Erkan und
Stefan, and Ades Zabel. Every Tuesday,
the "unconventional music" evenings
introduce listeners to new sounds.

DEUTSCHE OPER BERLIN

Bismarckstraße 35, Charlottenburg
U-Bahn Deutsche Oper, Bismarckstraße
Tel 30 343 8401
www.deutscheoperberlin.de
OPERA
In 1961 the biggest opera house in
Berlin was opened, replacing the former
Opernhaus of 1912, which was destroyed
during the war. It was designed by Fritz
Bornemann in a modernist style and has
nearly two thousand seats, all boasting
a perfect view. The repertoire includes
works in French, Italian and German, and
music directors have included Christian
Thielemann and the Scot Donald
Runnicles. The former West Berlin opera
house has expanded its programme to
include a broader spectrum of music (jazz,
for example). Productions have included
The Damnation of Faust and *Romeo and
Juliet* by Berlioz, *Samson and Delilah*
by Saint-Saëns, *Lady Macbeth of Mtsensk*
by Shostakovich and six operas by Puccini.
Naturally, the best seats are in the front
stalls and, more unusually, the small boxes
just to the side, but visibility and acoustics
are perfect everywhere.

HAU – HEBBEL AM UFER

Stresemannstraße 29, Kreuzberg
U-Bahn Hallesches Tor
Tel 30 2590 0427, www.hebbel-am-ufer.de
MULTIDISCIPLINARY THEATRE

A genuine Art Nouveau treasure built in 1908, the venerable Hebbel theatre is, with the **RENAISSANCE-THEATER** (Knesebeckstraße 100, Charlottenburg, tel 030 315 9730), one of the few Berlin theatres to have survived the vagaries of time and war. This 800-seat theatre, laid out for classical opera, is currently managed as part of the Theater am Halleschen Ufer, an institution lacking in charm but very effective. The merger led to the creation of HAU, or Hebbel am Ufer, a centre for international arts and performance. Its work is varied, ranging from local educational projects to interventions by foreign artists. You might see street art, Brazilian dance, a lecture on Cambodian pop music under the Khmer Rouge, indie music performances or discussions with performers.
Other locations: Hallesches Ufer 32, Kreuzberg; Tempelhofer Ufer 10, Kreuzberg

HAUS DES RUNDFUNKS

Großer Sendesaal des SFB – Haus des Rundfunks (Broadcasting House), Masurenallee 8–14, Charlottenburg
U-Bahn Theodor-Heuss-Platz
Tel 30 202 98710, www.roc-berlin.de
www.haus-des-rundfunks.de
RADIO CONCERTS

Designed by the architect Hans Poelzig in 1929–1930, Berlin's Broadcasting House (Haus des Rundfunks) has a striking expressionist brick facade 150 metres long. It stands opposite the Berlin Trade Fair ground and the Funkturm, the radio tower with Eiffel tendencies. Prior to the Second World War, it was the largest and most modern broadcasting complex in Europe; its three recording studios had perfect acoustics. In 1935, the world's first television programme was broadcast from here. During the war, concerts for the troops were held in the largest studio, with performances by Zarah Leander and other UFA singing stars. In 1956, West Berlin public radio successfully regained its right to broadcast from here, after many years managing with poor facilities in a tiny site in the British sector. Nowadays, Berliners come in large numbers to hear concerts by the radio orchestra and choir. Its lobby is still spectacular, as is the chain of continuous compartments on the rare paternoster lift, still in use.

KOMISCHE OPER BERLIN

Behrenstraße 55–57, Mitte
U-Bahn Französische Straße
Tel 30 4799 7400
www.komische-oper-berlin.de
COMIC OPERA

Before the war, the Metropol was one of the largest theatres in the city for variety and music hall. Rebuilt in 1947, it became the home of operetta, and pre-1990 it was a theatrical institution, not just in East Berlin, but the whole of Germany. Its directors and singers were regularly invited to perform in the West and even at Bayreuth, and it developed a tradition of staging light opera translated into German. This practice was dramatically reversed with the arrival of its new artistic director, the ebullient Barrie Kosky. In just a few seasons he has made it the liveliest venue in Berlin, winning it plaudits as the world's best opera house, with its dazzling sell-out productions. Encased in its socialist bunker overcoat, the Komische Oper's wonderful auditorium escaped the wartime bombings and its late 19th-century gilt and velvet are original elements designed by the Viennese architects Fellner and Helmer. The best seats? The boxes and the centre stalls, rows seven to fifteen, though the second row of the centre balcony provides a perfect view and better acoustics than the stalls. Wherever you sit though, every seat boasts an individual screen displaying simultaneous translations into English, French, Spanish and Turkish.

KONZERTHAUS BERLIN

Gendarmenmarkt, Mitte
U-Bahn Französische Straße,
Hausvogteiplatz
Tel 30 203 092 101
www.konzerthaus.de

CLASSICAL MUSIC

Poised elegantly on the city's most
beautiful square, between the French and
German cathedrals that were completely
rebuilt and restored by the GDR, this
classical building designed by Schinkel was
also rebuilt in the same style. It has four
auditoriums seating 1,500, 390, 230 and 80.
Reopened to the public in 1984 as the
Philharmonie for the GDR capital, it was
home to the Konzerthausorchester
Berlin, a formidable ensemble founded
in 1952 as the Berliner Sinfonie-
Orchester. The orchestra's fame increased
exponentially during the 1960s under
its longest-serving chief conductor,
the legendary Kurt Sanderling. A close
friend of Shostakovich, he had emigrated
to Leningrad, but returned for the sole
purpose of conducting this ensemble.
Sanderling conducted numerous superb
concerts, as well as legendary recordings
of the works of Shostakovich. The current
conductor is the Hungarian Iván Fischer,
and the Konzerthaus orchestra retains its
unique grasp of this repertoire. The venue
also hosts performances by a number
of high-quality ensembles, including
the Akademie für Alte Musik, and holds
concerts of contemporary music in its
ultra-modern modular performance space,
built with the aid of a donation by the
magnate Hans-Werner Otto, founder
of VPC Otto-Versand. The acoustics
in the four auditoriums have been greatly
improved. As in the cinema, the front
rows are not always the best.

MAXIM GORKI THEATER

Am Festungsgraben 2, Mitte
S-Bahn and U-Bahn Friedrichstraße
Tel 30 2022 1115
www.gorki.de

CONTEMPORARY THEATRE

The edifice was built in 1827 as the official
home of the Sing-Akademie zu Berlin,
a function it served for many years, and
was designed by the architect Friedrich
Schinkel. Its acoustics were so good
that the Electrola record company had its
studios here in the 1920s: the Staatskapelle
and the Berlin Philharmonic recorded
hundred of performances and Marlene
Dietrich came here to record *Ich bin von
Kopf bis Fuß auf Liebe eingestellt*. Damaged
in 1943, the building was requisitioned
in 1947 by the Soviet authorities. It became
the Soviet Union Cultural Centre and the
theatre was renamed in honour of the
writer Maxim Gorki. Now managed by the
City of Berlin, the Gorki theatre showcases
critical and dissident drama. Successors
to the energetic and controversial Volker
Hesse and Armin Petras, the intrepid
duo of Jens Hillje and Shermin Langhoff
has been managing the Gorki since the
2013–14 season. Born in Bursa, Turkey,
and deeply committed to radical theatre,
Shermin Langhoff was previously
artistic director of a celebrated fringe
venue in Kreuzberg.

PHILHARMONIE

Herbert-von-Karajan Straße 1, Tiergarten
S-Bahn and U-Bahn Potsdamer Platz
Tel 30 254 88 999
www.berliner-philharmoniker.de

CLASSICAL MUSIC

Designed by Hans Scharoun as the
cultural core of West Berlin, built very
close to the Wall in the midst of an urban
no-man's-land, the Philharmonie
opened in 1963 to praise from the writer
Max Frisch. Its 2,200 seats are arranged
in a revolutionary design, laid out in
a series of arcs, a layout since copied in
dozens of concert halls across the world.

Supplemented in 1987 with the addition of a smaller 1,200-seat auditorium, the Philharmonie is a source of great pride for Berliners. Its current chief conductor is Sir Simon Rattle. Another feature of the Philharmonie is its vast foyer, which features regular performances by leading musicians, as well as other Berlin ensembles such as the Berlin Radio Symphony Orchestra, the Stuttgart Radio Symphony Orchestra and Daniel Barenboim and his Staatskapelle Berlin. The best seats? All of them, of course.

PIERRE BOULEZ SAAL

Französiche Straße 33d, Mitte
U-Bahn Hausvogteilplatz
Tel 30 479 97411, www.boulezsaal.de
CONCERT HALL

Designed after the Second World War by Richard Paulick, a renegade from the Bauhaus and famous for designing the streetlights on Karl-Marx-Allee, the building was used for many years to store sets from the Staatsoper. It was then chosen as the permanent home for a new concert hall intended as a homage to the French composer and conductor Pierre Boulez, who died before the work was completed. At the helm of this centre for discussion, communication and intercultural openness is the star conductor Daniel Barenboim, who has worked tirelessly on the project to build the wood-panelled oval hall designed by Frank Gehry. It holds a mere 700 people, but every seat has a 360° view of the centre, creating an incredible sense of intimacy. Hence the reason for limiting performances to chamber music and recitals. The Boulez Ensemble has its home here, naturally, as well as the Barenboim-Said Academy, which trains musicians from the Middle East. They will have the opportunity to play in the West-Eastern Divan Orchestra created in 1999 by Daniel Barenboim and the Palestinian-American academic Edward W. Said, which aims to promote understanding between different communities through music. European

classical music, jazz, Arab music: the hall has already seen concerts by Lang Lang, John McLaughlin, Magdalena Kožená, with Simon Rattle, Denis Kozhukhin, Gidon Kremer and Pierre-Laurent Aimard. Already a major centre for music.

RADIALSYSTEM

Holzmarktstraße 33, Friedrichshain
S-Bahn Ostbahnhof
Tel 30 288 788 588
www.radialsystem.de
EXPERIMENTAL MUSIC

A centre for experimental art and music, housed in a former pumping station on the banks of the Spree which was restored by the architect Gerhard Spangenberg, Radialsystem is a radiant source of new ideas, whose non-hierarchical organization has been copied in Beijing, Buenos Aires and New York. It is here that the celebrated choreographer Sasha Waltz created all her dances, including *Dialogue 09,* produced for the opening ceremony of the Neues Museum in March 2009, and *Romeo and Juliet.* The centre's main focus is on music, both classical and contemporary, and the RS is host to concerts by the Mahler Chamber Orchestra, as well as all kinds of experimental ventures.

RENAISSANCE-THEATER

Knesebeckstraße 100, Charlottenburg
S-Bahn Savignyplatz
U-Bahn Ernst-Reuter-Platz
Tel 30 312 4202
www.renaissance-theater.de
CLASSICAL AND CONTEMPORARY THEATRE

Built in 1922, the Renaissance is the most beautiful theatre in Berlin. Situated in the West until the fall of the Wall, for a long time it was dedicated to staging comic plays and shows, as well as ambitious literary adaptations. Since reunification, it has opened up to contemporary drama, featuring modern writers such as Eugene O'Neill, Alan Ayckbourn, Erik Gedeon and Stella Müller.

SCHAUBÜHNE AM LEHNINER PLATZ

Kurfürstendamm 153, Wilmersdorf
S-Bahn Charlottenburg
U-Bahn Adenauerplatz
Tel 30 890 023
www.schaubuehne.de

CONTEMPORARY THEATRE

The Schaubühne company was formed in 1962 in Kreuzberg as a private theatre, though run on collective lines. It was aimed at students and staged contemporary works with social and political themes. In 1981 the company moved to a former cinema, the UFA, part of the old Woga-Komplex, a group of buildings designed by Erich Mendelsohn in 1926–28. Before the war, the complex included a modern shopping centre and the Kabarett der Komiker, a theatre equipped with a sophisticated staging system which cost a fortune at the time. The Schaubühne is a bastion of radical theatre, a place where directors and actors have artistic freedom. Thomas Ostermeier has been its artistic director since 2005. The repertoire includes works by Arthur Miller, Rainer Werner Fassbinder, Falk Richter, Sarah Kane and Franz Xaver Kroetz, as well as Alfred Döblin in the form of an interpretation of his *Berlin Alexanderplatz* by Volker Lösch. Each year, in April, it hosts a festival of new international drama.

STAATSOPER UNTER DEN LINDEN

Unter den Linden 7, Mitte
U-Bahn Friedrichstraße
Tel 30 2035 4555
www.staatsoper-berlin.de

OPERA

The Staatsoper returned to its historic home in autumn 2017, after an extended exile at the Schiller Theater, which was less than ideal for music. Renovation of its magnificent home, built for Frederick the Great in 1742 to a design by Knobelsdorff, took far longer than anticipated, turning into something of a long-running saga.

The state opera has a rich history dating back to the 18th century and its illustrious conductors have included Richard Strauss and Erich Kleiber.

VOLKSBÜHNE AM ROSA-LUXEMBURG-PLATZ

Rosa-Luxemburg-Platz, Mitte
U-Bahn Rosa-Luxemburg-Platz
Tel 24 06 55
www.volksbuehne-berlin.de

ICONOCLASTIC THEATRE

Erwin Piscator during the interwar years and Benno Besson in the 1960s jointly forged the legend of this theatre that had existed since 1914, remained in the East in 1945, and was housed within the walls of a building that was hideous enough (Soviet-Berlin rationalist designed by Hans Richter in 1954) to make you want to destroy it. From 1992 until recently, under the very active director Frank Castorf, the programme featured a cultural crossover of people and genres. His successor, Chris Dercon, from the Tate Gallery in London, was hired to propel the place into the video-cum-multimedia 21st century. Since September 2017, the Volksbühne has been expanding by taking over part of the disused site of the Tempelhof airport for its dance performances. In Hangar 5, they opened with *Dance-Ganz Berlin Tanzt auf Tempelhof*, a ten-hour long show choreographed by Frenchman Boris Charmatz. We are now waiting for a new cohort of Volksbühne directors – Suzanne Kennedy, Jérôme Bel and Tino Sehgal – to raise the curtain in this historic theatre.

ART GALLERIES

AANANT & ZOO

Bülowstraße 90, Schöneberg
U-Bahn Bülowstraße
Tel 30 8180 1873, www.aanantzoo.com
Open 11am to 6pm and by appointment,
closed Sunday to Tuesday

CONTEMPORARY ART

A year after moving into an amazing site designed by the architect Hans Käsbohrer, gallerist Alexander Hahn transferred his activities and artists to Schöneberg, playing the pioneer before more of his peers followed him to Bülowstraße. Some, such as **KUNSTSAELE** (www.kunstsaele.de) and **SALON POPULAIRE** (www.salon populaire.de), have even elected to share this same location. On the inevitable white walls, Hahn has shown work by Channa Horwitz and Dan Bayles (from the US), Kasper Pincis (UK) and Benjamin Yavuzsoy (Germany). The Croat poet and artist Vlado Martek and painter Merlin James have also exhibited here. As has Athanasios Argianas, with his sequential objects, and the photographer Lynn Hershman Leeson, who held her first Berlin show here. Why call it Aanant & Zoo? So that they're always first on the list.

BLAIN|SOUTHERN

Mercator Höfe,
Potsdamer Straße 77–87, Tiergarten
U-Bahn Kurfürstenstraße
Tel 30 644 931 510
www.blainsouthern.com
Open 11am to 6pm,
closed Sunday and Monday

CONTEMPORARY ART

When the *Tagesspiegel* moved to new headquarters, it left its huge premises on Potsdamer Straße vacant, including its rear courtyard. Florent Tosin, who had just closed down his gallery, set up shop here first and kick-started the radical redevelopment of the site. Andreas Murkudis followed suit with his concept store, de nombreux galeristes dont

Blain|Southern, now a leading gallery with a second branch in London. They showcase such major artists as Lucian Freud, Mat Collishaw, Lawrence Weiner, Wim Wenders, Jannis Kounellis, Marius Bercea, Francesco Clemente, Yinka Shonibare and sculptor Lynn Chadwick.

CAMERA WORK

Kantstraße 149, Charlottenburg
S-Bahn Savignyplatz
Tel 30 310 0773, www.camerawork.de
Open 10am to 6pm,
closed Sunday and Monday

PHOTOGRAPHY

Steffi Schulze's art photography gallery has been operating since 1997 in a former workshop-cum-hangar tucked away in a courtyard. Retrospectives and themed exhibitions span the work both of well-established masters (Herbert List, Herb Ritts, Richard Avedon, Leni Riefenstahl) and contemporary talents such as Robert Polidori, Eugenio Recuenco, Tina Berning & Michelangelo Di Battista, Patrick Demarchelier, Ellen von Unwerth and young photographer Andreas Mühe, son of the much-missed Ulrich Mühe, star of the *The Lives of Others*. The gallery also sells classic and vintage prints. It has a collection of over 300 photographs, most of which belonged to the Kennedy family, which led to the creation of a museum called **THE KENNEDYS** (tel 030 2065 3570, www.thekennedys.de), initially located on Pariser Platz, but subsequently moved to the former Jewish girls' school refurbished by gallerist Michael Fuchs. Here Camera Work has also created a second exhibition space, **CAMERA WORK CONTEMPORARY (CWC)** (Auguststraße 11–13, Mitte, tel 030 240 486 614).

CAPITAIN PETZEL

Karl-Marx-Allee 45, Mitte
U-Bahn Schillingstraße, Strausbergerplatz
Tel 30 2408 8130, www.capitainpetzel.de
Open 11am to 6pm,
closed Sunday and Monday

CONTEMPORARY ART

The four pavilions with their blue-and-yellow tiled facades, built in 1964 on the Karl-Marx-Allee by Josef Kaiser and Walter Franek, had varying fortunes. One of them was converted into a bar and another into a medical supplies shop. Yet another is now a vast gallery with large windows run by Gisela Capitain from Cologne, sister of Jenny Capitain, famous New York-based fashion journalist, and Friedrich Petzel. During the time of the GDR, the building housed the Kunst im Heim, an exhibition space for the fine and applied arts from communist countries. To begin with, Capitain and Petzel provocatively showed American artists such as Seth Price and Troy Brauntuch. Today the gallery showcases the work of Andrea Bowers, Natalie Czech, Charline von Heyl and Diango Hernández.

COLLECTION REGARD

Steinstraße 12, Mitte
U-Bahn Weinmeisterstraße
Tel 30 8471 1947
www.collectionregard.de
Open Friday 2pm to 6pm
and by appointment

PHOTOGRAPHY

The Parisian collector Marc Barbey has a passion for forgotten German photographers, especially photojournalists who captured Berlin, such as Hein Gorny, who was the first to be allowed to shoot Berlin in ruins from the sky just after the war. Barbey now owns a unique archive collection of 800 prints and 16,000 negatives. In the his apartment gallery, he opens up his collection to the public every Friday (or by appointment), exhibiting pictures by Manfred Paul, Lotte Jacobi, Paul Almásy and Bruno Barbey. The latter, a Magnum photographer, is Marc Barbey's uncle.

CONTEMPORAY FINE ARTS

Grolmanstraße 32/33, Charlottenburg
U-Bahn Uhlandstraße, S-Bahn Savignyplatz
Tel 30 8877 7167, www.cfa-berlin.com
Open 11am to 6pm, closed Sunday

CURRENT ART

One of the classic galleries on the Berlin scene since 1992, this fine exhibition space, founded and managed by Bruno Brunnet and Nicole Hackert, shows and represents some big names – Georg Baselitz, Julian Schnabel, Juergen Teller, Raymond Pettibon, Sarah Lucas, Chris Ofili – and has an extra space to allow room for installations such as Marianne Vitale's *Fat City*, her boxers or her army of robots made from railway scrap. CFA is also present in Basel, Miami and Hong Kong, attracting a very wealthy clientele, though its staff are always happy to talk to art lovers and anyone wanting to find out more.

DUVE BERLIN

Gitschiner Straße 94/94a
(entrance D, floor 2), Kreuzberg
U-Bahn Prinzenstraße
Tel 30 77 902 302, www.duveberlin.com
Open 11am to 6pm, Saturday noon to 4pm,
closed Sunday and Monday

CONTEMPORARY ART

Next to the overground section of the U1 that runs directly along the canal is Alex Duve's two-room gallery. A charismatic and genial face on the contemporary art scene at fairs, he's always ready to chat about the latest artists he's showing. His space, on the first floor of a Kreuzberg courtyard, has often focused on contemporary painting, such as slick works from Evan Gruzis, or minimal canvases from Jens Einhorn, but the gallery is beginning to feature more installation and sculpture, such as the work of Debora Delmar Corp. and Marguerite Humeau, who has described herself as "an Indiana Jones in Google times".

ESTHER SCHIPPER

Potsdamer Straße 81e, Tiergarten
U-Bahn Kurfürstenstraße
Tel 30 374 433 133
www.estherschipper.com
Open 11am to 6pm,
closed Sunday and Monday

CONTEMPORARY ART

This is the gallery where every artist dreams of being shown. One of the finest private galleries in Berlin, it was originally located on Linienstraße before moving to the highly coveted Potsdamer Straße. Esther Schipper's international reach takes the gallery and its artists – among them Matti Braun, Ugo Rondinone, Pierre Huyghe, Liam Gillick, Angela Bulloch and Daniel Steegamnn Mangrané – to the biggest art fairs and most prestigious museums.

GALERIE ANSELM DREHER

Pfalzburger Straße 80, Wilmersdorf
U-Bahn Hohenzollernplatz, Spichernstraße
Tel 30 883 5249
www.galerie-anselm-dreher.com
Open 3pm to 6pm, Saturday 11am to 2pm,
closed Sunday and Monday

CONCEPTUAL ART

Everyone has exhibited here, from Panamarenko to Boltanski, Dan Flavin to Sol LeWitt. Ange Leccia, John M. Armleder, Jochen Gerz, Joseph Kosuth and Bertrand Lavier all made their Berlin debuts here. Since 1967, Anselm Dreher has been an important mover and shaker in the field of Conceptual Art. His small gallery is something of a hallowed temple now, currently showcasing Blinky Palermo, Heimo Zobernig, David Polzin and Karin Sander.

GALERIE MAX HETZLER

Goethestraße 2/3,
in the courtyard, Charlottenburg
S-Bahn Savignyplatz
Tel 30 346 497 850
www.maxhetzler.com
Open 11am to 6pm,
closed Sunday and Monday

CONTEMPORARY ART

For over forty years, Max Hetzler has been dividing his time between Paris and Berlin. Something of an adventurer, he once hung pictures in an old vegetable market on Zimmerstraße, and then in a huge former industrial area in Wedding, perfect for large-scale works. He has two galleries in Charlottenburg, but he's not really into gentrification – as you can see if you visit his gallery in a former post office building on Goethestraße. Names such as Yves Oppenheim, Thomas Struth, Jeff Koons, Rineke Dijkstra, Bridget Riley, Navid Nuur, Edmund de Waal and Günther Förg headline the exhibitions.

GALERIE NORDENHAKE

Lindenstraße 34, Kreuzberg
U-Bahn Kochstraße
Tel 30 206 1483, www.nordenhake.com
Open 11am to 6pm,
closed Sunday and Monday

SCANDINAVIAN ARTISTS

Sweden's Nordenhake gallery opened its Berlin outpost in 2007, in a fine space flooded with natural light. Founded in Malmö in 1973 and based in Stockholm since 1986, Nordenhake is a major player on the contemporary Nordic scene, promoting artists for the most part from Scandinavia, Poland and Iceland, including Miroslaw Balka, Esko Männikkö, Sirous Namazi, Jonas Dahlberg, Gunilla Klingberg and the Swiss Rémy Zaugg. A breath of fresh (Nordic) air.

GALERIE THOMAS SCHULTE

Charlottenstraße 24, Mitte
U-Bahn Stadtmitte
Tel 30 2060 8990
www.galeriethomasschulte.de
Open noon to 6pm and by appointment,
closed Sunday and Monday

CONTEMPORARY ART

Opened in 1989 by Thomas Schulte, this gallery focuses on tried and tested names such as Gordon Matta-Clark, Fabian Marcaccio, Idris Khan, Richard Deacon, Allan McCollum, Juan Uslé, Katharina Sieverding, Jacco Olivier and Robert Wilson. Since 2006, it has been located in a historic building, the Tuteur Haus, that has miraculously survived the ravages of the past century. In 2010, the gallery expanded into an adjoining space – the "corner space" – where the work of up-and-coming artists is exhibited.

GRIMMUSEUM

Fichtestraße 2, Kreuzberg
U-Bahn Südstern, Schönleinstraße
Tel 151 1241 2524, www.grimmuseum.com
Open 2pm to 6pm, closed Sunday to Tuesday

EXPERIMENTAL SPACE

Luise Grimm was a Berlin artist who died in 1991 at the age of ninety. Her old premises have been turned into a gallery that showcases emerging contemporary artists, as well as up-and-coming curators. Refreshing and unpredictable. .

GRUNDEMARK NILSSON

Lindenstraße 34, Kreuzberg
U-Bahn Kochstraße
Tel 30 8147 3709
www.grundemarknilsson.se
Open noon to 6pm and by appointment,
closed Sunday to Tuesday

SWEDISH PHOTOGRAPHY

This gallery is run by Dorothy Nilsson and specializes in Swedish photography, as well as leading exponents of Berlin photography. Check out Martina Hoogland Ivanow's ethnological work and the photos of J.H. Engström.

HELGA MARIE KLOSERFELDE EDITION

Potsdamer Straße 97, Tiergarten
U-Bahn Kurfürstenstraße
Tel 30 9700 5099
www.helgamariaklosterfelde.de
Open Wednesday to Saturday 11am to 6pm
and by appointment

EDITIONS, MULTIPLES

Based in Hamburg, and now in Berlin in a former shop whose old-fashioned decor has been retained, this gallery specializes in limited editions and multiples by artists like Joseph Kosuth, John Baldessari, Matt Mullican and Rosemarie Trockel. Some projects are particularly unusual, like the recent one created by Cécile B. Evans and Yuri Pattison titled *To Live and Work in Midcentury*. Inspired by the Eames' collaboration with IBM in 1964, it featured three signature chairs by Ray and Charles Eames reworked in transparent Plexiglas. Unique pieces, obviously. And visionary.

ISABELLA BORTOLOZZI GALERIE

Schöneberger Ufer 61, Tiergarten
U-Bahn Kurfürstenstraße
Tel 30 2639 7620
www.bortolozzi.com
Open noon to 6pm and by appointment,
closed Sunday and Monday

INTERNATIONAL CONTEMPORARY ART

The Italian gallery owner Isabella Bortolozzi works out of an apartment, which means making your way through the common areas of these residential buildings overlooking the south bank of the Landwehrkanal. There are other galleries in the nearby Potsdamer Straße, and the Kulturforum just across the bridge. In other words, you don't need to cross the city to the urban wastelands to find out about the international artists that Bortolozzi exhibits here in her home or at the Berlin Biennale (and also at the Serpentine Gallery in London and the Palais de Tokyo in Paris). These include her compatriot Andrea Branzi, who is very involved with the Berlin porcelain manufacturer KPM, the French painter Pierre Klossowski, the Belgian duo Jos de Gruyter & Harald Thys, Oscar Murillo and Wu Tsang.

JORDAN/SEYDOUX

Auguststraße 22, Mitte
U-Bahn Oranienburger Tor
Tel 30 51 73 65 06
www.jordan-seydoux.com
Open noon to 6pm and by appointment,
closed Sunday and Monday
PRINTS AND MULTIPLES

Despite the name, Jordan Seydoux is not a natural person. Or rather only halfway, as this gallery is a joint effort by Amélie Seydoux, a site graphic designer, and the Parisian gallery owner Bernard Jordan. Opened in May 2008, specialising in prints and multiples, their gallery is open to such diverse talents as Glen Baxter, Pol Bury, Gérard Traquandi, John Armleder, John Giorno, Tony Cragg and Baselitz, and it sometimes overflows into the street, as in the winter of 2010 with close-up projections of Bertrand Gadenne's owls and raptors, whose disturbing mobility transformed the street into a giant eagle's nest. Today, the gallery exhibits the work of Franz Badur, Nanne Meyer, Peter Saul, Françoise Petrovitch and Imi Knoebel in limited editions.

KICKEN BERLIN

Linienstraße 161a, Mitte
U-Bahn Rosenthaler Platz, Oranienburger Tor
Tel 30 2887 7882
www.kicken-gallery.com
Open 2pm to 6pm and by appointment,
closed Saturday to Monday
PHOTOGRAPHY

Without doubt Berlin's most important and influential photography gallery, Kicken was founded in Aachen, in 1974, by Rudolf Kicken and Wolfgang Schürmann, under the name Lichttropfen. It was renamed Kicken after a move to Cologne, and Schürmann's departure. Kicken moved to Berlin in 2000 and has become a venerable

institution, specializing in historic, modern and contemporary photography, with a special focus on German and Czech avant-garde photographers of the early 20th century, spanning Bauhaus, subjective and conceptual photography, fashion photography and photojournalism. In addition to its principal space, revamped by architect Jürgen Mayer H., the gallery offers two other exhibition modules in the form of private salons opening onto a brick courtyard, accessible by appointment. The historic collection is complemented by temporary exhibitions of new work by the likes of Dieter Appelt, Jitka Hanzlová, Richard Pare, Alfred Seiland and Charles Fréger. The authoritative catalogues are highly sought-after.

KÖNIG GALERIE

Dessauerstraße 6–7, Kreuzberg
U-Bahn Prinzenstraße
Tel 30 261 03 080
www.koeniggalerie.com
Open 11am to 6pm, closed Monday
CONTEMPORARY ART

Tatiana Trouvé, Micol Assaël, Helen Marten, Henning Bohl, Nathan Hylden, Alicja Kwade, Jeppe Hein – the artists represented by this eminent gallery are prominent figures on the international art scene. Johann König, who pursues an eclectic policy embracing all media and styles, is an important figure on the contemporary Berlin scene. He has been known to seal an event's success or failure simply by agreeing to take part, or not. His first Berlin gallery opened in 2002 on Rosa-Luxemburg-Platz, in the historic building by Hans Poelzig housing the Kino Babylon, but moved into a former industrial building on Dessauerstraße in 2006. Four years later he created a stir by annexing the church of St Agnes built in the 1960s, not far from the Martin-Gropius-Bau. The resulting space opened officially for Gallery Weekend in 2015 with a show of spectacular paintings from Katharina Grosse, which filled the nave with her vibrant, spray-painted canvases. The church, which covers several hundred square metres, has continued to showcase excellent work: from Ragnar Kjartansson's collaboration with rock music darlings The National to huge installations from the young French prodigy Camille Henrot. The Dessauerstraße location reopened in May 2016, confirming König's reign among Berlin galleries.

KUNSTSAELE
Bülowstraße 90, Schöneberg
U-Bahn Bülowstraße
Tel 30 8180 1868
www.kunstsaele.de
Open 11am to 6pm and by appointment,
closed Sunday to Tuesday
COLLECTIONS
When you're a collector, there's nothing better than opening your own space and sharing your treasures with the public. This is what Geraldine Michalke and Stefan Oehmen have done with their twin collections of contemporary art – the Bergmeier Collection for her, and the Oehmen for him – which are exhibited here between two events dedicated to "extra-collection" artists. Examples include "Mobile Cinema" by Romana Schmalisch and Robert Schlicht, and "Conceptual Space" by the photographer Martin Dammann. Sharing and exchanging space and people with the Aanant & Zoo gallery, the Kunstsaele is also located next door to the Salon Populaire, a collective that brainstorms art (www.salonpopulaire.de).

LORIS
Potsdamer Straße 65, Tiergarten
U-Bahn Kurfürstenstraße
S-Bahn Potsdamer Platz
Tel 30 275 95 579, www.lorisberlin.de
Open 2pm to 6pm, and by appointment,
closed Sunday to Wednesday
MULTIMEDIA COLLECTIVE
Potsdamer Straße is dedicated to art galleries and is organised in sections. The part running from the Landwehrkanal to the Lützowstraße is somewhat sinister, yet this is where Loris has set up his gallery in a banal building that could have been a laundrette or a Baltic travel agency. In this collective project created in 2007 by ten Berlin artists (Oliver Dignal, Paulina Gimpel, Ulrike Hannemann, Andy Heller, Ruth Hommelsheim, Oliver Krebs, Jan Lemitz, Anne Metzen, Pujan Shakupa and Nina Wiesnagrotzki), they can each exhibit work in photography, video, collage, installations, or even performances given the size of the place. Loris is open to all kinds of expression and collaboration and also publishes works of art in limited copies by cutting-edge printers. Recently it hung the strange work of Ulrika Hannemann who photographed the former presidential palace in Ho Chi Minh City designed by the architect Ngô Viet Thu, producing images that translated how the building had been abandoned using absurdist images of absence and censorship.

MEHDI CHOUAKRI
Fasanenstraße 61, Wilmersdorf
U-Bahn Spichernstraße
Tel 30 2839 1153
www.mehdi-chouakri.com
Open 11am to 6pm,
closed Sunday and Monday
CONTEMPORARY ART
Since starting out in Berlin in 1996, Mehdi Chouakri has had galleries in almost every part of the city. His first one was on Gipsstraße, in Mitte. The next one was buried under the arches of the S-Bahn station at Jannowitzbrücke, on the banks of the Spree. After that he made a symbolic move close to the Hamburger Bahnhof-Museum für Gegenwart, into part of the Edison Höfe, in Mitte, a former lightbulb factory. There he promoted the work of Sylvie Fleury, Luca Trevisani, Charlotte Posenenske, Claude Closky, Saâdane Afif, Peter Roehr and Hans-Peter Feldmann. He's now on the move again, seized by a desire to move West, and to achieve a double by simultaneously opening one

gallery on Fasanenplatz, in a former antique shop, and another on Mommsentraße, in Hans-Peter Jochum's old gallery. The ranks of longstanding artists have been joined by Philippe Decrauzat, N. Dash, Mathieu Mercier and Isabell Heimerdinger. A heavyweight, then, a major presence at the world's leading art fairs and working with the most exacting collectors. **Other location:** Bleibtreustraße 41, Charlottenburg

NEUGERRIEMSCHNEIDER

Linienstraße 155, Mitte
U-Bahn Oranienburger Tor
S-Bahn Oranienburger Straße
Tel 30 2887 7277
www.neugerriemschneider.com
Open 11am to 6pm,
closed Sunday and Monday
CONTEMPORARY ART
The gallery's visual identity, inscribed letter by letter in a series of coloured circles, is illegible. The website is far from expansive, simply inviting visitors to send an email for further information. A better sign. The real-life venue is where it's all at: owners Tim Neuger and Burkhard Riemschneider feature big hitters of the calibre of Olafur Eliasson, Tobias Rehberger, Jorge Pardo, Thaddeus Strode and Simon Starling. Needless to say, the gallery is a regular at Art Basel and other top international fairs.

PAVLOV'S DOG/ RAUM FÜR FOTOGRAFIE

Bergstraße 19, Mitte
S-Bahn Nordbahnhof
U-Bahn Rosenthaler Platz
Tel 30 5316 2978
www.pavlovsdog.org
Open 4pm to 8pm and by appointment,
closed Sunday to Wednesday
EXPERIMENTAL PHOTOGRAPHY
Presumably the name of this photo gallery alludes to the famous conditioned reflexes observed in Pavlov's dog experiments. In fact, it isn't that odd to link photography to these experiments, though they were

also carried out on cockroaches. The three terms of reflex, condition and repetition apply very appropriately to both psychology and photography, and the quartet led by Michael Biedowicz naturally has plenty of fun with them, as do their artists. Especially their next-door neighbour Sascha Weidner, together with Jonas Unger, Sergey Chilikov, Lea Golda Holterman, Philipp Dorl and Martin Klimas, who each have a not very Pavlovian personality and a decidedly unconditioned eye. Or do they?

PERES PROJECTS

Karl-Marx-Allee 82, Friedrichshain
U-Bahn Weberwiese, Strausberger Platz
Tel 30 2759 50 770
www.peresprojects.com
Open 11am to 6pm,
closed Saturday and Sunday
INTERNATIONAL CONTEMPORARY ART
Peres Projects, whose exhibition openings always cause a stampede, moved to this vast 500-square-metre space after making a name for itself in Mitte and Kreuzberg. Cuban gallerist Javier Peres's stable of artists includes painters David Ostrowski, Dorothy Iannone, Mark Flood and Alex Israel, whose work is showcased to great effect in this all-white former Soviet building. The exhibitions here are invariably worth checking out.

REITER BERLIN PROSPECT

Potsdamer Straße 81b, Tiergarten
U-Bahn Kurfürstenstraße
Tel 30 275 81397
www.reitergalleries.com
Open noon to 6pm and by appointment,
closed Sunday to Tuesday
CONTEMPORARY ART
Torsten Reiter has galleries in Leipzig and London but is a newcomer to the Mercator Höfe, where he has acquired a former apartment on the ground floor facing the Andreas Murkudis concept store. The small scale of his gallery helps concentrate the force of the works exhibited here, including

photos by Steffen Junghans, constructions by Guillaume Lachapelle and forms of violence by Sebastian Neeb. The same goes for *Don't Think About Death* by the Danish artist Dan Stockholm, but one of the highlights of recent times has been the exhibition of Berlin artist Sebastian Schrader's pure neo-Expressionist paintings – a powerfully dizzying vision of migrants, refugees and street outcasts.

ROBERT MORAT GALERIE

Linienstraße 107, Mitte
U-Bahn Rosenthaler Platz
Tel 30 252 09 358
www.robertmorat.de
Open noon to 6pm,
closed Sunday and Monday
PHOTOGRAPHY
Based in Hamburg but active in Berlin, a regular at Paris Photo and Unseen in Amsterdam, Robert Morat's gallery is a welcome addition to the world of contemporary and 20th-century photography. The focus here is on the elite of German and international art photography, some as permanent items and others exhibited during single or group shows. Don't miss it.

SALON DAHLMANN

Marburger Straße 3, Charlottenburg
U-Bahn Augsburgerstraße, Kurfürstendamm
Tel 30 2190 9850
www.salon-dahlmann.de
Open Saturday 11am to 4pm
and by appointment
APARTMENT GALLERY
The name refers to Hildegard Dahlmann, the former owner of this building bought by the Finn Timo Miettinen, who is based in Helsinki and CEO of the firm Ensto Oy Finland. Designed by Miettinen himself, an art and design collector, this "salon", which basically means a private apartment transformed into a gallery, is very popular in the city. Every Saturday afternoon (and by appointment), Miettinen exhibits part of his collection –

such as Gordon Matta-Clark, Dan Graham, Wolfgang Tillmans, Jeroen Jacobs, Luis Gordillo and Georg Baselitz – in a temporary exhibition, and also organizes concerts and performances and holds workshops and meetings. The light installation by Björn Dahlem in the entrance sets the tone, and in the courtyard there's a Hans Arp sculpture. It is decorated in the style of historic German and Finnish designs. This is yet another space and concept that is revitalizing West Berlin.

SPRÜTH MAGERS

Oranienburger Straße 18, Mitte
S-Bahn Oranienburger Straße
Tel 30 288 84030
www.spruethmagers.com
Open 11am to 6pm,
closed Sunday and Monday
CONTEMPORARY ART
Monika Sprüth started out in 1983 in Cologne, where she created a gallery intended to provide an antidote to the male-dominated scene at the time. She eventually joined forces with Philomene Magers in 1998 to create what is now one of the most influential galleries in the world, with an outpost in London and another on Los Angeles' "Miracle Mile", which opened in 2016. The focus is still on Conceptual artists, like Jenny Holzer, Barbara Kruger, Rosemarie Trockel and Cindy Sherman, many of whom have been on the books since the very beginning. These have now been supplemented by a vanguard of young, exciting names, such as Ryan Trecartin and Cyprien Gaillard. The gallery building, close to the New Synagogue on Oranienburger Straße, also houses the cultural media shop Image Movement.

TANYA LEIGHTON

Kurfürstenstraße 156 & 24–25, Tiergarten
U-Bahn Bülowstraße
Tel 30 22 16 07 770
www.tanyaleighton.com
Open 11am to 6pm,
closed Sunday and Monday
CRITICAL CONTEMPORARY ART

Founded in 2008, this contemporary art gallery is a hub for critical, international work that takes a cross-disciplinary approach to exhibitions. Critics, historians, filmmakers: the list of the gallery's collaborators for talks and artists' editions is impressive, from Pop artists Derek Boshier to *Frieze d/e* editor Pablo Larios. Leighton is known for her interest in Video work, as well as Performance, Minimalist and Conceptual art. Having expanded into another, more spacious address just across the street in 2015, the gallery's importance as a site of significant cultural exchange is on the rise.

WOESKE GALLERY

Mommsenstraße 35, Charlottenburg
S-Bahn Savignyplatz
Tel 30 5316 4864
www.woeskegallery.com
Open 11am to 7pm, Saturday until 2pm,
closed Sunday and Monday
FIGURATIVE ART

The lure of the former West once again. After Kreuzberg and their first gallery that opened in 2010 in an old factory on the banks of the Spree, Tillmann Woeske and Nadine Edelstein moved to Charlottenburg in 2013, joining the hardcore of gallery owners on Mommsenstraße. But they held on to their idea of a project space for young neo-figurative artists, such as Sebastian Mögelin, Roy Nachum, Feng Lu and Megan Ewert, whose tortured portraits are visibly influenced by Bacon. Between solo exhibitions, the Woeske puts on collective shows, such as the one by young artists trained at the New York Academy of Art.

MUSEUMS AND CULTURAL CENTRES

AKADEMIE DER KÜNSTE

Pariser Platz 4, Mitte
S-Bahn and U-Bahn Brandenburger Tor
Tel 30 200 571 000
www.adk.de
Open 10am to 10pm, closed Monday
FINE ARTS

The Academy of Arts is sandwiched between the Adlon Palace and DZ Bank, built in 2001 by Frank Gehry. It has stood here since 2005 on the site where Hitler's architect Albert Speer had installed his offices in 1937. One side gives onto Pariser Platz and the other to Behrenstraße, where you arrive directly in front of the Holocaust memorial. The venerable institute, founded in 1696, now occupies a building designed by Behnisch & Partners, where it organizes interesting temporary exhibitions always linked to the artistic history of the city and to the work of its most famous artists, such as Heinrich Zille and George Grosz.

ALTE NATIONALGALERIE

Museumsinsel, Bodestraße 1–3, Mitte
S-Bahn Hackescher Markt
U-Bahn Friedrichstraße
Tel 30 266 42 42 42
www.smb.museum
Open 10am to 6pm,
Thursday until 8pm, closed Monday
19TH-CENTURY ART

The Alte Nationalgalerie, built between 1865 and 1876 on the orders of Friedrich Wilhelm IV and designed by Friedrich August Stüler in an imposing Neoclassical style, was intimately bound up with the birth of the Second Reich. It was the first monument on Museumsinsel to be restored and used to house the works that had stayed in the East. The works conserved in the West, in the Schloss Charlottenburg, were later brought in to form one of the richest and most important collections of 19th-century art in the world. Highlights include paintings by Manet, Monet, Degas, and Cézanne, and an important group of works by Caspar David Friedrich.

ALTES MUSEUM

Museumsinsel, entrance via the Lustgarten,
Bodestraße 1–3, Mitte
S-Bahn Hackescher Markt
U-Bahn Friedrichstraße
Tel 30 266 424 242, www.smb.museum
Open 10am to 6pm,
Thursday until 8pm, closed Monday

GREEK AND ROMAN ART

Built by Karl Friedrich Schinkel in 1830, the aptly named "Old Museum" is the oldest in Berlin after the Gipsformerei. Burnt down in 1944, rebuilt exactly as it was in 1966, and reorganized after reunification, it is entirely devoted to collections of Greek and Roman art, now that the Egyptian collection has moved to the Neues Museum. Don't miss the display of Etruscan art. The restoration of the Greek rooms by the architects Hilmer & Sattler was completed in 2011. The rotunda, with its columns and statues, is magnificent.

BAUHAUS-ARCHIV MUSEUM FÜR GESTALTUNG BERLIN

Klingelhöferstraße 14, Tiergarten
U-Bahn Nollendorfplatz
Tel 30 254 0020, www.bauhaus.de
Open 10am to 5pm, closed Tuesday

HISTORY OF THE BAUHAUS

This design museum is housed in a late work by Walter Gropius, the founder of the Bauhaus. Initially designed in 1964 for Darmstadt, it was built in modified form in Berlin in 1976–79. Its distinctive silhouette is today one of Berlin's landmarks. Inside, the fascinating installation entitled "Weimar-Dessau-Berlin, 1919–1933" provides an overview of its history. In addition, there are temporary exhibitions, together with a library and archives that can be consulted by appointment, a store and a café with a terrace, all looking slightly the worse for wear, it must be said.

BERLINISCHE GALERIE

Alte Jakobstraße 124–128, Kreuzberg
U-Bahn Moritzplatz, Kochstraße
Tel 30 7890 2600
www.berlinischegalerie.de
Open 10am to 6pm, closed Tuesday

BERLIN ART

Here you have an overview of the whole of Berlin art and culture since the late 19th century, from caricature (Zille) to photography, architecture, painting, and all the currents and schools that go with them. Off Berlin's beaten tracks but close to the Museum of Jewish Art, the gallery has a collection that was put together in 1975 and was housed for twenty years in the Martin-Gropius-Bau. It moved into its current premises, designed by Jörg Fricke, in 2004. Artist Fritz Balthaus's installation in the forecourt, *Marked Space/Unmarked Space*, is a ground-level pointer to the spirit of the place. The interesting temporary exhibitions have covered such subjects as the Dada montages of Erwin Blumenfeld and the provocations of Klaus Staeck, and more recently, the artist Matthias Beckmann and the reconstruction of Berlin in the aftermath of the fall of the Wall. The Berlinische has also exhibited photos by Arno Fischer, Marianne Breslauer and Nan Goldin.

BOTANISCHER GARTEN UND BOTANISCHES MUSEUM

Königin-Luise-Straße 6–8, Steglitz
S-Bahn Botanischer Garten
U-Bahn Rathaus Steglitz
Tel 30 8385 0100, www.bgbm.de
Open daily, opening hours vary;
check the website

BOTANICAL

Sown across more than forty hectares in the heart of the leafy district of Dahlem, in western Berlin, lies one of the most famous botanical gardens in Europe, a symphony of magnificent plants and flowers. Displays range from the plants of the desert to, most impressive of all, the Tropenhaus, the largest tropical greenhouse in the world. There is also a museum and a specialized bookstore where you can learn about everything related to trees, flowers, mushrooms, and rare, exotic or local species. There are regular thematic temporary exhibitions.

BRÜCKE MUSEUM

Bussardsteig 9, Dahlem
Bus 115, Pücklerstraße stop
Tel 30 831 2029
www.bruecke-museum.de
Open 11am to 5pm, closed Tuesday
EXPRESSIONISM

This museum is devoted to the important Expressionist group Die Brücke, which was founded in 1905 in Dresden. It included Kirchner, Nolde, Bleyl and Schmidt-Rottluff. This museum in a Bauhaus-style building tucked away in leafy Dahlem houses an important collection of works by them. On the same site is the former studio of the Third Reich's favourite sculptor, Arno Breker, built in 1941 by Hans Freese. In 1967, the architect Werner Düttmann, strongly influenced by the Maeght Foundation in Saint-Paul-de-Vence, devised a flat, cubic building in modernist style that has since been overhauled to improve the galleries and lighting. As well as its permanent collection of Expressionist works, this museum organizes many temporary exhibitions and conferences often prompted by events in the arts world, such as the case of the forger Beltracchi.

C/O BERLIN

Amerika Haus,
Hardenbergstraße 22–24, Tiergarten
U-Bahn and S-Bahn Zoologischer Garten
Tel 30 2844 4160
www.co-berlin.org
Open daily 11am to 8pm
VISUAL ARTS

Tasked with organizing and showcasing major photography and visual arts events, C/O Forum has managed to take on a leading role in the world of professional photography in Berlin in the space of just

a few years. It was founded in 2000 by the photographer Stephan Erfurt, the designer Marc Naroska and the architect Ingo Pott, and took up residence inside the crumbling yet flamboyant old imperial post office at the corner of Oranienburger Straße and Tucholskystraße in the centre of Mitte. Built in 1875–81 and designed by Carl Schwatlo in a somewhat bureaucratic yellow-brick-and-coloured-mouldings vein, the latter was the postal administrative centre for the Third Reich, then for the GDR until the mid-1960s. After a peripatetic interlude, it has finally come to rest in the west, in the former Amerika Haus, a shutter click or two from the Helmut Newton Foundation, and not far from Camera Work, thereby creating a sort of Berlin photography cluster. Built in 1957 by architect Bruno Grimmek as part of the Interbau, the Amerika Haus, built to symbolize the post-war reconciliation between the United States and Germany, was for a long time the US cultural and information centre in Berlin. Robert Rauschenberg and Frank Lloyd Wright exhibited their work here, Kennedy and Nixon visited the place, and Berliners flocked there to see previews of new Hollywood films. The Amerika Haus was closed after the American Embassy opened on Pariser Platz, and the building itself was ceded to the city. It was restored and adapted to become the site for C/O, which opened in the autumn of 2014 with photo exhibitions both outside and in.

DAADGALERIE

Oranienstraße 161, Kreuzberg
U-Bahn Moritzplatz
Tel 30 698 07 607
www.daadgalerie.de
Open noon to 7pm, closed Monday
VISUAL ART, MUSIC

The Ford Foundation's showcase gallery has been active in Berlin since the 1960s and moved to this new site at the beginning of 2017. It was previously located on Zimmerstraße, near Checkpoint Charlie, where it exhibited artists such as Ben, Pisteletto and Kounellis. The new spaces were designed by architect Kuehn Malvezzi, and cover 500 square metres on two floors, including exhibition spaces for the visual arts and a concert studio for up to a hundred listeners.

DEUTSCHE KINEMATHEK – MUSEUM FÜR FILM UND FERNSEHEN

Potsdamer Straße 2, Tiergarten
S-Bahn and U-Bahn Potsdamer Platz
Tel 30 266 424 242
www.deutsche-kinemathek.de
Open 10am to 6pm,
Thursday until 8pm, closed Monday
CINEMA

One of the key parts of the brief for the reconstruction of Potsdamer Platz was that it should group together the head office of the Berlinale, the cinemas for the film festival, hotels to accommodate the stars and guests, the German film institute, the film library and the film museum. Installed on the bottom four floors of the Sony Center (designed by Helmut Jahn), the museum benefits from an ingenious, suggestive design by Hans Dieter Schaal, relying heavily on optical effects, which can be quite disorienting when, for example, you pass through the trompe-l'oeil set for *Metropolis*. All the great moments and makers of German cinema are here, from silent films up to Franka Potente, star of *Lola rennt*(*Run, Lola, Run*); films produced during the Weimar Republic (*Doctor Mabuse, Lulu, The Blue Angel, M*); Marlene Dietrich, whose famous theatre and cinema costumes, bequeathed by her daughter Maria Riva, are showcased with a flair worthy of Orson Welles; Leni Riefenstahl; the new stars of the post-war period (Gert Fröbe, Hildegard Knef and Angelica Domröse); and the provocative work of Fassbinder. A shocking evocation of the Nazi era is condensed into a metal room which might be a morgue, its walls lined with iron drawers which, when opened,

reveal photos or video extracts that cannot fail to horrify. In the basement, you can visit the multiplex **ARSENAL CINEMA** that screens promising candidates from the Berlinale, retrospectives of living filmmakers, old films and works from all over the world (tel 030 2695 5100, www.arsenal-berlin.de). The specialist bookshop has been replaced by the Dussmann museum shop, which is more fun and sells a wider range of goods (tel 30 202 52 512, www.dussmann.de).

DEUTSCHES HISTORISCHES MUSEUM

Unter den Linden 2, Mitte
S-Bahn Hackescher Markt
S-Bahn and U-Bahn Friedrichstraße
Tel 30 203 040, www.dhm.de
Open daily 10am to 6pm
HISTORY

The history of this museum is something of a long-running political saga. In 1985, Chancellor Helmut Kohl announced that the West German government would create a German national museum to coincide with the 750th anniversary of the city of Berlin. A site opposite the Reichstag was earmarked and Italian designer Aldo Rossi selected to design the new building. After the fall of the Wall, the project was revised to accommodate the museum of German history founded in 1952 by the communists on Unter den Linden, to be installed in the Zeughaus, a Baroque edifice that was used as an arsenal by the Prussian army in the early 18th century. The project to combine the two collections here was ratified in 1994, and Kohl himself selected the architect I.M. Pei for the refurbishment and enlargement of the Zeughaus, which closed in 1998. The Pei wing, which opened in 2003 with an exhibition on John F. Kennedy (now a separate museum), resembles a giant glass and pale stone semi-colon in the heart of a historic site. Luminous, airy and transparent, its glass stair-tower is reminiscent of the model for the Monument to the Third International by Russian Constructivist Vladimir Tatlin in 1919. In 2006, the Zeughaus reopened to the public with an excellent permanent display designed by Hermann Czech on the history of Germany from 1200 to the fall of the Wall. The DHM also houses a cinema, the **ZEUGHAUSKINO**, which shows films, documentaries and other visual documents on the history of Germany that you cannot find elsewhere, such as films from the former GDR and "unknown shots" of the city from the Berlin. Dokument series. The entrance to the cinema is on the right of the museum, by the Spree.

DEUTSCHES TECHNIKMUSEUM BERLIN
Trebbiner Straße 9, Kreuzberg
S-Bahn Anhalter Bahnhof
U-Bahn Möckernbrücke, Gleisdreieck
Tel 30 902 540, www.sdtb.de
Open 9am to 5:30pm, Saturday and
Sunday 10am to 6pm, closed Monday
SCIENCE AND TECHNOLOGY
Created in 1982 on a huge plot of land, the German Museum of Technology occupies several buildings, including the Spectrum (250 experiments and demonstrations of physical phenomena), the library and the archives. It is an extremely popular museum; a simple visit to the library can teach you almost everything you need to know about anything. Temporary exhibitions are organized regularly, like the one devoted to the construction of the U-Bahn, which added much to a fabulous historical panorama of German railways. Carriages, locomotives and impressive models are on display in the former roundhouse of the old Anhalter Bahnhof, built in 1841 and, until the beginning of the 20th century, the second-largest station in Europe. Bombed to rubble in 1945,

it was razed in 1959 to make space for this immense six-hectare park, where a stroll takes you past old forges, water- and windmills and abandoned train tracks. The new buildings are oriented towards the Tempelhofer Ufer and are crowned by a soaring silvery plane. They were designed by Helge Pitz and Ulrich Wolff and were opened in 2003. They house permanent installations devoted to Konrad Zuse, whose work in the 1930s helped pave the way for computers, and to textile, paper and printing technologies. The larger of the two also houses displays devoted to German aviation and maritime navigation. The former Oldtimer Depot has been overhauled and the old German cars have been joined by other forms of technology, including robots.

THE FEUERLE COLLECTION
Hallesches Ufer, 70, Kreuzberg
S-Bahn Anhalter Bahnhof
Tel 30 2579 2320
www.feuerlecollection.org
Guided tours by appointment Friday,
Saturday and Sunday
PRIVATE COLLECTION
After the Sammlung Boros, housed in the indestructible walls of Albert Speer's Reichsbahn Bunker, comes another private art collection, open to visitors by appointment only (with guides available), in another bunker, a few metres from the Spree. Semi-subterranean, this one was built in 1943 for telecommunications use. The collector Désiré Feuerle is originally from Stuttgart and used to own a gallery in Cologne. He chose this building to exhibit his collection of ancient Asian art and commissioned the architect John Pawson to convert it, no easy task since it's a solid concrete structure with

"*Berlin, it is obvious, aroused powerful emotions in everyone. It delighted most, terrified some, but left no one indifferent.*" Peter Gay, *Weimar Culture*, 1968

THE IMAGINARY MUSEUM

A selection of works reflecting the artistic richness and diversity of Berlin that would make great additions to your own private museum.

THE GEOMETRIC TAPESTRY (1926/1964) by Anni Albers at the **BAUHAUS-ARCHIV**, a textile work inspired by the stained glass created by Josef Albers (1926) and often used to illustrate the modernity of the period. www.bauhaus.de

KÄMPFE (1915), a woodcut in black, red and blue by Ernst Ludwig Kirchner, an artist who co-founded the Die Brücke group. It belongs to a series of illustrations for the fantastic tale by Adelbert von Chamisso entitled *Peter Schlemihls wundersame Geschichte* (The Miraculous Story of Peter Schlemihl). **BRÜCKE MUSEUM.** www.bruecke-museum.de

SYNTHETIC MUSICIAN (1921), a Cubist picture by Ivan Puni, known as Jean Pougny, a Russian artist who worked in Berlin by "exhibiting" himself in the Ku'damm as a sandwich man dressed in Cubist clothes. At the **BERLINISCHE GALERIE.** www.berlinischegalerie.de

THE ZINC JET FIGHTER PLANE (1989), part of Anselm Kiefer's work "Poppy and Memory" at the **HAMBURGER BAHNHOF.** Breathtaking after breaking the sound barrier. www.hamburgerbahnhof.de

GRAY DAY (1921) by George Grosz, showing a terrible Nazi Berlin somewhere between communist disappointment and capitalist inevitability. At the **NEUE NATIONALGALERIE.** www.neuenationalgalerie.de

THE PINK AND CREAM WEDDING SUIT (1946) created by fashion designer Uli Richter for the Berlin actress and singing star Hildegard Knef. It now hangs in the collection of the **LIPPENSTIFT-MUSEUM** created by makeup artist René Koch. www.rene-koch-berlin.de

THE ARMOURED "NEWTONMOBILE" (2000), designed by Giugiaro and offered to the photographer Helmut Newton and now "parked" in one of the rooms of the **HELMUT NEWTON FOUNDATION** amid his personal belongings, which include a Louis Vuitton bag with his initials HN and sheathed in copper. www.helmutnewton.com

THE MINIATURE MODERNIST AND POSTMODERN ROOMS for doll's houses in the **MUSEUM DER DINGE.** Minuscule wonders! www.museumderdinge.de

CHILD'S PLAY (1939), by Paul Klee, among the numerous masterpieces of the **BERGGRUEN COLLECTION.** www.smb.museum

GOTHIC CHURCH ON A ROCK BY THE SEA (1815), a breathtaking picture by Schinkel, who was also the greatest Prussian architect, here showing off his German Romanticism credentials. He has a complete room to himself in the **ALTE NATIONALGALERIE.** www.smb.museum

walls over two metres thick. The work completed, it opened to the public in November 2016. Désiré Feuerle's extraordinary, and slightly mad, vanity project is not without controversy – this is Berlin, after all. The visitor experience is beautifully presented. You are asked to leave all phones in the cloakroom, and to listen to the friendly and articulate guides. Immersed in a sensory experience heightened by music from the minimalist composer John Cage, one enters a world that is both dreamlike and brutalist. The exhibits, some extremely rare (dating back to the 7th century), some just wonderfully expressive, take you on a journey from Cambodia to China via Thailand and are shown with other, contemporary pieces. Stimulating, full of meaning, with sudden flashes of contemporary art (bondage photos by Nobuyoshi Araki), time paused: this is an exhilarating encounter.

GEDENKSTÄTTE BERLINER MAUER

Bernauer Straße 111, Mitte
S-Bahn Nordbahnhof
U-Bahn Bernauer Straße
Tel 30 467 986 666
www.berliner-mauer-gedenkstaette.de
Open 10am to 6pm, closed Monday, exhibitions and outdoor sites daily 8am to 10pm

BERLIN WALL MEMORIAL

As well as the 333 metres of the East Side Gallery painted by 106 artists from 21 countries and listed as a historic monument, and the very touristy **MUSEUM HAUS AM CHECKPOINT CHARLIE** that draws thousands of visitors, the place where you can find the most striking remains of the Berlin Wall is on Bernauer Straße starting at Brunnenstraße, where on the west side of the wall there used to be a very high stand for visitors, from where Wessies could helplessly wave to their cousins trapped in the East. Today, there is the **GEDENKSTÄTTE BERLINER MAUER** (Wall Memorial), consisting of

a monument in memory of the victims of divided Berlin, a documentation centre and the **KAPELLE DER VERSÖHNUNG** (Chapel of Reconciliation), a curious yet interesting wooden building designed in 1999 by Rudolf Reitermann and Peter Sassenroth on the site of the old church that was razed because it was located along the line of the Wall. In this regard, have a look at the foundations of the houses along this street that were also destroyed for the same reason, with a commentary of recollections from their occupants. Very poignant. The memorial was completed in August 2011 for the fiftieth anniversary of the building of the Wall.

GEMÄLDEGALERIE

Matthäikirchplatz, Tiergarten
S-Bahn and U-Bahn Potsdamer Platz
Tel 30 266 42 42 42
www.smb.museum
Open 10am to 6pm, Thursday until 8pm, closed Monday

EUROPEAN PAINTING

Intended as the final piece in the Kulturforum jigsaw, which includes Hans Scharoun's Philharmonie and Mies van der Rohe's Neue Nationalgalerie, this museum houses a superb collection of European paintings from the 13th to the 18th centuries (Botticelli, Dürer, Cranach, Tintoretto, Veronese, Bruegel, Holbein, Rembrandt, Vermeer, Rubens, Poussin), previously split between the Gemäldegalerie in the west and the Bode Museum in the east. The perfectly lit rooms provide an excellent setting for the 1,400 paintings and artworks on display. In 2013, Berlin approved proposals to build a new museum to house the 20th-century works that will sit between the Neue Nationalgalerie and the Philharmonie. Scheduled to open in 2022, it will combine works from the Gemäldegalerie with other gifts such as Heiner and Ulla Pietzsch's collection of Surrealist art.

GEORG-KOLBE-MUSEUM

Sensburger Allee 25, Charlottenburg
S-Bahn Heerstraße
Tel 30 304 2144
www.georg-kolbe-museum.de
Open 10am to 6pm, closed Monday

STUDIO, MUSEUM

The famous sculptor Kolbe lived and
worked here from 1929 until his death
in 1946. The simple, square, brown brick
villa with its adjoining studio is now
a museum dedicated to his memory and
his work. Once a member of the Berlin
Secession, Kolbe worked with Mies van
der Rohe, notably on the latter's famous
Barcelona pavilion of 1929, and left
a rich artistic legacy which, alas, was
largely destroyed before the war, when
his sculptures were melted down to help
pay for the war effort, and during it.
Fortunately, many survived, including
those which dot the flower garden.
The temporary exhibitions are always
linked to a specific period in his life, but
can also showcase new, promising talents
such as Thorsten Brinkmann. The museum
has a literary club, which organizes
readings and, from time to time, tactile
tours for the visually impaired.

GIPSFORMEREI

Sophie-Charlotten-Straße 17–18,
Charlottenburg
S-Bahn Westend
Tel 30 3267 6911
www.smb.museum/museen-und-
einrichtungen/gipsformerei
Open 9am to 4pm, Wednesday until 6pm,
closed Saturday and Sunday

SCULPTURE CASTS

Berlin's oldest museum institution
was founded in 1819 and centres around
a fabulous collection of more than
6,000 replicas. These were exhibited at
the end of the 19th century in an ad-hoc
building constructed to a design by
Johannes Merzenich. Although numerous
original works were destroyed in the course
of successive wars, most are represented

here by official reproductions. Some
have been used to "supply" the permanent
exhibition of casts of Greek, Roman and
Byzantine statues, which is in the nearby
ABGUSS-SAMMLUNG ANTIKER PLASTIK
(Schloßstraße 69b, Charlottenburg,
tel 030 342 4054) and where you can buy
perfect replicas. Nefertiti in the living room.

HAMBURGER BAHNHOF MUSEUM FÜR GEGENWART

Invalidenstraße 50–51, Tiergarten
S-Bahn Hauptbahnhof
U-Bahn Naturkundemuseum
Tel 30 266 424 242
www.smb.museum/en/museums-and-
institutions/hamburger-bahnhof/home.html
Open 10am to 6pm, Saturday and Sunday
from 11am, Thurday 10am to 8pm,
closed Monday

CONTEMPORARY ART

Opened with great fanfare in 1996 in the
former Hamburger station (built in 1847),
this museum displays European and
American art from the last twenty years
of the 20th century, exhibited in an
interior designed by Josef Paul Kleihues.
The permanent collection features works
by Roy Lichtenstein, Cy Twombly, Bill
Viola, Andy Warhol, Joseph Beuys, Anselm
Kiefer, Georg Baselitz, Keith Haring,
John Cage and Donald Judd, while shows
have featured the likes of Walter de Maria,
Sophie Calle, Manfred Pernice, Teresa
Hubbard, Wolfgang Tillmans, Alicia Wade,
Paul Pfeiffer and Carsten Höller.
The National Gallery Prize for Young Art
is shown here each year. Next door to
this temple to contemporary art is the
Rieckhalle, home to the celebrated Flick
collection since 2004; consisting of some
2,500 works of modern and contemporary
art, it was originally meant to be exhibited
in Zürich, in a building designed by
Dutch architect Rem Koolhaas. Friedrich-
Christian Flick was the great-nephew and
heir of the arms merchant Friedrich-Karl
Flick, who made his fortune as principal
arms supplier for the Third Reich.

The younger man was reluctant to open his archives to the public and refused to contribute to a foundation set up to compensate the victims of the Nazi war camps, a source of thousands of unwilling workers for his uncle's factories. His project for Zürich was greeted with indignation by the city's Jewish community and was rejected by the town councillors. So he offered to lend his remarkable collection, which includes works by Luc Tuymans, Pipilotti Rist and Bruce Nauman, to the city of Berlin. The project has been the subject of some controversy, but the millionaire businessman pledged to restore the former train shed made available to him for the purpose by Deutsche Bahn. Mission accomplished in 2011.

HAUS AM LÜTZOWPLATZ

Lützowplatz 9, Tiergarten
U-Bahn Nollendorfplatz
Tel 30 261 3805, www.hal-berlin.de
Open 11am to 6pm, closed Monday

CONTEMPORARY ART

This neo-Baroque home dating from around 1870 gives us a hint of what the neighbourhood was like during Berlin's imperial heyday. Partially destroyed in 1945, it was reconstructed in 1949 by the Berlin Artists' Society, which had temporarily established itself here. Ever since that year and the first exhibitions, the house has become a mandatory stop on any tour of the great Berlin galleries, reaching a glorious peak in the mid-1960s, when Asger Jorn, Vasarely, Dubuffet, De Kooning, Francis Bacon and Andy Warhol came here to work and exhibit. While the Wall was in existence, it was a kind of halfway house between East and West. In 2003, it was renovated and enlarged, though it still sticks to its pattern of six major annual shows featuring such pivotal artists as Elvira Bach, Dorothy Iannone, Emmett Williams (pioneer of the Fluxus movement), Horst Hussel, photographer Pico Risto, Antonio Paucar, Iris Kettner and Erik Niedling. At the rear

of the courtyard garden, which is a great setting for openings, an atelier is available for use by artists native to or living in Berlin, like the photographer and illustrator François Cadière. It is reached via a metal staircase designed in 1988 by Volkmar Haase.

HAUS AM WALDSEE

Argentinische Allee 30,
Zehlendorf, 18km south-west of Berlin
S-Bahn Mexikoplatz, U-Bahn Krumme Lanke
Tel 30 801 8935, www.hausamwaldsee.de
Open 11am to 6pm, closed Monday

INTERNATIONAL CONTEMPORARY ART

In the early 1920s, the legendary Haus Am Waldsee was the domain of the Berlin avant-garde: here, during the Weimar Republic, the in-crowd could discover such unexpected talents as Renée Sintenis, Hermann Blumenthal, Oskar Schlemmer, Max Ernst, Georges Braque, Georges Rouault and Picasso. After the Second World War it reopened, showing the same artists and plenty of others declared "degenerate" by the Nazis. Today this lakeside haven of greenery and tranquillity focuses on German and foreign artists living and working in Berlin, such as Olav Christopher Jenssen, Beate Gütschow and Norbert Bisky. It is part of the official Berlin Biennale circuit. The café, decorated in a pure Deutsche Werkstätte style, is very successful.

HAUS DER KULTUREN DER WELT

John-Foster-Dulles-Allee 10, Tiergarten
U-Bahn Bundestag
Tel 30 3978 70, www.hkw.de
Open daily 11am to 7pm,
exhibition closed Tuesday

ART CENTRE

Designed by the American architect Hugh A. Stubbins and donated by the US to the City of Berlin on the occasion of the Interbau 57 international architecture exhibition, this immense pavilion was instantly and lastingly baptized "the pregnant oyster" by the locals. It lies in the centre of the Tiergarten, by the Spree, where the house of Bettina von Arnim once stood, and resembles some architectural retro-futurist spaceship out of a Hollywood science-fiction extravaganza. Or, more modestly, perhaps a Jetsons cartoon. The temporary exhibitions that used to be organized here to initiate us to world cultures are now only sporadic. As a result, visitors come essentially to admire a stylistic vestige of an era that might have been revived by today's vintage mania – almost all of the furniture is from the 1950s, creating a time-warp feeling that you might be David Vincent in some deserted extraterrestrial airport. The intelligently stocked bookshop sells everything ever written about the building and an immense cafeteria overlooking the Spree offers a wonderful panorama of the new political Berlin, as well as an unbeatable view of the office of Chancellor Angela Merkel.

JAGDSCHLOSS GRUNEWALD

Hüttenweg 100, banks of the
Grunewald lake, Grunewald
Bus 115, Clayallee stop,
corner of Königin-Luise-Straße
Tel 30 813 3597, www.spsg.de
Open 10am to 6pm (April to October),
closed Monday Open Saturday and Sunday
10am to 4pm (November and December)
Closed in January and February

PAINTING AND FURNITURE
This lavish hunting lodge was built in 1542 for the Prince Elector of Brandenburg, Joachim II, who liked nothing better than joining in beats in the surrounding woods. After being modernized in the early 20th century for Emperor Wilhelm II, the building was converted into a museum in 1932, where you can now see beautiful Baroque and Biedermeier furniture, crockery, paintings and porcelain, while the local residents wait patiently for each Christmas to come around so they can attend Nativity concerts here.

JÜDISCHES MUSEUM

Lindenstraße 9–14, Kreuzberg
U-Bahn Hallesches Tor
Tel 30 2599 3300, www.jmberlin.de
Open 10am to 8pm, Monday until 10pm

HISTORY
The idea of establishing a Jewish museum was first mooted in 1971, when Berlin's Jewish community was celebrating its 300th anniversary. Opened in 2001, the Jüdisches Museum covers two centuries of Judeo-Germanic cultural and political history, with all the suffering that implies. The permanent exhibition is composed of collections of paintings and documents from the Jewish art collection of the Berlin Museum, together with archives and donations. For a long time, the Jüdisches Museum was located in the elegant Baroque building, built in 1735, which now serves as its entryway. The former headquarters of the Prussian Chamber, the building has been boldly extended by American architect Daniel Libeskind. Described by the architect as a "deconstructed Star of David", the edifice is as much a giant sculpture as a building. Sheathed in zinc and titanium, the building has three symbolic focal points, including the Garden of Exile, consisting of forty-nine concrete columns 6 metres high (the figure 7 being sacred in Judaism) crowned with willow oaks, and the Holocaust Tower, a huge cement coffin that is very moving.

KÄTHE-KOLLWITZ-MUSEUM

Fasanenstraße 24, Wilmersdorf
U-Bahn Uhlandstraße
Tel 30 882 52 10, www.kaethe-kollwitz.de
Open daily 11am to 6pm

GERMAN EXPRESSIONISM
Käthe Kollwitz (1867–1947), the quintessential Berlin artist, defined herself thus: "I've never worked coldly . . . but rather with my blood as it were. People who look at my work should feel that." The poignant, revolutionary, humanist work displayed here – more than 200 drawings,

engravings, lithographs and sculptures – powerfully bear witness to her engagement. Opened in 1986 by the art dealer Hans Pels-Leusden and based on his own collection, this museum is sited in one of four Grisebach houses built between 1871 and 1892, where there is also a Literaturhaus with a wonderful café. This is a paradoxical pantheon for Käthe Kollwitz, who lived in extreme poverty throughout her life in Prenzlauer Berg, where a square and a street are named after her, and was persecuted by the Nazis.

KINDL – CENTRE FOR CONTEMPORARY ART

Am Sudhaus 3, Neukölln
U-Bahn Rathaus Neukölln
Tel 30 8321 59 12 16
www.kindl-berlin.com
Open noon to 6pm,
closed Monday and Tuesday
CONTEMPORARY ART
A long abandoned brewery in Neukölln, the Kindl Brauerei was designed in 1913 by Hans Claus and Richard Schepke as an Expressionist cathedral, with a seven-storey bell-tower and a nave occupied by six enormous copper brewing tanks. The König Otto café has moved in, while in the basement the Rollberger micro-brewery is reviving the place's brewing history. Another development in this post-industrial space is the Kindl – Centre for Contemporary Art, created and managed by Burkhard Varnholt and Salome Grisard. They have converted the three machinery rooms and the boiler room into exhibition spaces, with their original mechanical beauty retained. Shows have included "Berlin Façades Volet I", featuring images of the city's architecture, and "Ruinen der Gegenwart" (Ruins of the Present Day), a multimedia, multi-disciplinary exhibition by Arata Isozaki, Gordon Matta-Clark, Dorothee Albrecht, Francis Alÿs and Clemens Botho Goldbach, among others.

KUNST-WERKE INSTITUTE FOR CONTEMPORARY ART

Institute for Contemporary Art,
Auguststraße 69, Mitte
S-Bahn Oranienburger Straße
Tel 30 243 4590
www.kw-berlin.de
Open 11am to 7pm,
Thursday until 9pm, closed Tuesday
CONTEMPORARY ART
This once-thriving 19th century margarine factory has been a regular hive of artistic activity since 1991, as well as hosting the Berlin Biennale, created by Klaus Biersenbach with the support of the Loto Stiftung Berlin. Now headed by Dutchman Krist Gruitjhuijsen, the KW is embarking on a new era with more exhibitions and collaborations with the many Berlin art institutions. After an inaugural exhibition devoted to the South African artist Ian Wilson, Gruitjhuijsen hinted that he might reopen the legendary Pogo Bar, once famous for its illegal techno parties in the basement. Enlarged in 1999 by Johanne Nalbach, this building has just been renovated with new access to the various spaces, which include a bookstore.

LIEBERMANN-VILLA AM WANNSEE

Colomierstraße 3, Steglitz/Zehlendorf,
28km south-west of Berlin
S-Bahn Wannsee
Tel 30 80 58 59 00
www.liebermann-villa.de
Open April to September 10am to 6pm,
Thursday, Sunday and holidays until 7pm,
October to March daily 11am to 5pm,
closed Tuesday
ARTIST'S HOUSE AND MUSEUM
The Berlin Impressionist painter Max Liebermann (1847–1935) loved being by the water. His holiday home stands on the shores of the Wannsee, and after being ostracized by the Nazi regime as a Jew, he spent every summer there until his death in 1935. It was designed by the architect Paul Otto Baumgarten and based

on a Hamburg villa on the banks of the Elbe that the painter admired. The garden was designed by Liebermann himself, with the help of his friend Alfred Lichtwark, director of the Kunsthalle in Hamburg. The villa was sold and converted into a hospital, but returned to Liebermann's daughter. Her heirs sold it again, to the city this time, which granted Deutschen Unterwasser-Club (a scuba diving club) permission to use it as a clubhouse. Now a listed historical monument, and a museum visited by over 80,000 people every year, this unique place is worth a visit for its lakeside views, its award-winning garden with its path lined with birch trees, its vegetable garden, its orchard and its countless volunteer gardeners. When the weather is fine, the café and terrace are a beautiful place for a breather (open only to those with an admission ticket). As you come out, take a look at the Villa Langenscheidt, an extraordinary 19th-century half-timbered house, which belongs to wealthy publishers.

LIPPENSTIFT-MUSEUM RENÉ KOCH

Helmstedter Straße 16, Wilmersdorf
U-Bahn Berliner Straße
Tel 30 854 2829
www.lippenstiftmuseum.de
Open by appointment 11am to 7pm,
closed Saturday to Tuesday

POWDER PUFFS AND LIPSTICK

A star of makeup and a lipstick VIP, René Koch is the most famous German makeup artist and a Berlin personality known for his dark glasses, velvet waistcoats, Louis Vuitton scarves and zest for life. This has brought him widespread media coverage, with long interviews in the print press, TV

shows and primetime charity shows, at which he will croon the odd ditty. As a beautician and make up designer for all the stars (and lady friends), including Marlene Dietrich during her famous German tour and Ingrid Caven, whom he has known for thirty-five years, Koch has also written books that sell like bottles of nail polish. Located since 1979 in Wilmersdorf, in a 1920s residential building, his beauty parlour was decorated in line with the times – white, gold and glass – and packed with mementos of these glamorous encounters, including hundreds of white cards on which they left a red kiss. You can find Mireille Mathieu, the actress Katrin Sass (*Good Bye Lenin!*), the American-Berlin singer Gayle Tufts, Juliette Gréco, Bonnie Tyler, Sydne Rome and even the sultry Romy Haag, with whom he shot a supah-trash film here in 1982 called *Plastik Fieber*, which looks like John Waters' *Polyester* directed by Max Ophuls. The effervescent René has also been collecting make-up and related items– posters, compacts, precious cases by Jansen, books, 45s, brushes, beauty lighters, evening bags, powder puffs, gadgets such as a Lip Talk sex-toy phone – for the past forty years. His collection was exhibited for the first time in 2009 at the Galeries Lafayette, and a year later in Dresden. The collection now forms the basis of his Lippenstift-Museum, with items presented in thematic displays: Marlene, transvestites, *La Cage aux Folles*, beauty in the GDR and Hildegard Knef, his idol. René Koch is present during visits and comments and tells stories with his enthusiastic smile. Visitors include students of beauty schools from as far afield as Hamburg and Moscow, as well as the knowledgeable or merely curious. Once a month, Koch teaches groups of blind people about powders and blushes, so there is a real heart beneath the glitter. In 2015, the Museum Schwules (Berlin's LGBT museum) organized a retrospective for his seventieth birthday.

MARTIN-GROPIUS-BAU

Niederkirchnerstraße 7, Kreuzberg
S-Bahn and U-Bahn Potsdamer Platz
Tel 30 254 860
www.gropiusbau.de
Open 10am to 7pm, closed Tuesday
TEMPORARY EXHIBITIONS

Built between 1877 and 1881 by the architect Martin Gropius (great-uncle of Walter Gropius, co-founder of the Bauhaus), this magnificent building housed the Museum of Fine Arts until World War II. A neighbour of the Gestapo headquarters, it was heavily damaged by Allied bombing in 1945. In 1978, it was rebuilt exactly as before. Until fairly recently, it housed the Berlinische Galerie (now elsewhere) and the Museum der Dinge (moved in 2007). It continues to host a rich programme of exciting photography exhibitions (Brassaï, Karl Valentin, Aleksandr Rodchenko, Man Ray, Richard Avedon, Robert Lebeck, F.C. Gundlach, Herlinde Koelbl, André Kertész, László Moholy-Nagy, Barbara Klemm). It has also hosted the "Istanbul-Modern-Berlin" exhibition and a Pierre Soulages retrospective and a travelling show devoted to David Bowie, also seen at the V & A in London, and the Grand Palais in Paris, but here expanded to include a section covering Bowie in Berlin.

MIES VAN DER ROHE HAUS

Oberseestraße 60, Alt-Hohenschönhausen
Tel 30 97 00 06 18
www.miesvanderrohehaus.de
Open 11am to 5pm, closed Monday
ARCHITECT'S HOUSE

Ludwig Mies van der Rohe (1886–1969), one of the 20th century's greatest architects, settled in Berlin in the early 1900s and started out by working for architect Peter Behrens and interior designer Bruno Paul. He set up his own agency in 1913 and built his first house in Potsdam, which can be seen today in its renovated state after years of use as the head office of the former East German Republic's Academy for Film. He also designed the Urbig house, where Churchill stayed during the Potsdam conference in 1945, and, in Berlin itself, several private homes, including this one commissioned by printer Karl Lemke. It is located in the outlying Hohenschönhausen neighbourhood (now in Lichtenberg) on the edge of a small artificial lake called the Obersee. Mies designed everything in it right down to the furniture, which is now on display at the Kunstgewerbemuseum. Occupied by Lemke and his wife until 1945, the house was requisitioned by the Red Army, which used it as a garage. From the 1960s until 1977, when it was listed as a protected building, it was used by police officers from the nearby Stasi headquarters. When the Berlin Wall fell, the Landhaus Lemke was rescued again through the efforts of a group of community-minded East Berliners. It was restored in 2002 and is now an unusual sort of museum, more interesting for its atmosphere and design than its setting. A visit on a winter's Sunday morning may not be the best time to enjoy the garden, but the view of the frozen lake and the snow-draped landscape is magical.

MUSEUM BERGGRUEN

Schloßstraße 1, Charlottenburg
U-Bahn Richard-Wagner-Platz
Tel 30 266 424 242
www.smb.museum
Open 10am to 6pm, Saturday and Sunday from 11am, closed Monday
MODERN ART

Heinz Berggruen was born in Berlin in 1914 and emigrated to the United States in 1936, not returning to his native city until 1945 – as an American GI. He then lived in Paris, where he opened a modern art gallery. A close friend of Picasso and Dora Maar, over a period of fifty years he assembled an exceptional collection, which included 100 Picassos and sixty Klees, as well as works by Matisse, Braque, Giacometti and Laurens. Heinz Berggruen initially lent his collection to Berlin, but in 2000 it was bought by Berlin's State Museums for a fraction of its market value. This remarkable collection now occupies the eighteen rooms of the Stülerbau pavilion, which is an annex of Schloss Charlottenburg. This great collector, who died in 2007, bequeathed another collection of some fifty paintings to his son, who donated them to the *Land* of Berlin. It was decided to enlarge the current museum by annexing the neighbouring building, from which it is separated by a garden. Now incorporating the Museum Scharf-Gestenberg and the Brohan-Museum, the Berggruen Collection forms a museum complex of the highest order.

MUSEUM DER DINGE

Oranienstraße 25, 3rd floor, Kreuzberg
U-Bahn Kottbusser Tor
Tel 30 9210 6311
www.museumderdinge.de
Open noon to 7pm,
closed Tuesday and Wednesday
EVERYDAY GERMAN DESIGN

This museum, once thought of as the basis for a future but hypothetical design museum, left the Martin-Gropius-Bau a few years ago to take over the third floor of a very ordinary building on bustling Oranienstraße, just above DIM. Once overseen by Andreas Murkudis, this decades-long collection of everyday objects is exhibited chronologically from the late 19th century up until the 1990s.
The objects are displayed on shelves and in well-lit showcases like wares in a shop, emphasizing the sheer accumulation of things. You can spend hours examining the toys, dishes, radios, toiletries, pens, groceries, wooden subway seats, model cars, scales, glasses, coffee pots, furniture,

buttons, glass objects, piggy banks, ashtrays and even the famous Frankfurt kitchen – evidence of the inventiveness of the interwar period when it came to the home. There is an exhibition space for contemporary design centred on upcycling, and the bookshop and gift shop are well worth climbing three flights of stairs for, as it is hard to work out how the lift works. The website is well designed and entertaining, and highlights a new object every month.

MUSEUM DER STILLE

Linienstraße 154a, Mitte
S-Bahn Oranienburger Straße
Tel 30 2789 1990
www.museum-der-stille.de
Open 2am to 7pm, closed Monday
MUSEUM OF SILENCE

In 1994, when Mitte was overwhelmed by reconstruction and renovation projects, the noise and disruption of the building work drove the Russian painter Nikolai Makarov into a stirring reflection on silence. This led to the creation of the Museum of Silence, a silent provocation aimed at countering the constant noise and a society caught up in ear-splitting acceleration. There's nothing on the street to indicate the presence of the museum. Just one red window and these words: Museum der Stille. Some people thought it was a museum for fans of silent cinema. Others paid no attention to it at all. Makarov exhibited his own work there, an expression in form and colour of this silence. In 2014, he asked a number of architects to produce ideas for places of silence, to give voice to the inaudible. Sergei Tchoban, Franco Stella, Stefan Braunfels, Max Dudler, among others, produced models of their ideas. Result: the Museum der Stille speaks sotto voce once more. To be visited quietly, please. Especially since admission is free.

MUSEUM FÜR FOTOGRAFIE UND HELMUT NEWTON STIFTUNG

Jebensstraße 2, Charlottenburg
U-Bahn Zoologischer Garten
Tel 30 3186 4856
www.helmutnewton.com
Open 11am to 7pm, closed Monday

PHOTOGRAPHY MUSEUM

Strangely located at the foot of the elevated train tracks of Zoo station, this rather unattractive former casino where Prussian officers used to come and relax was the place chosen by photographer Helmut Newton (it was the last building he had seen before fleeing Berlin by train in 1938) when he decided with his wife, June (alias Alice Springs), to donate his archives to the city of Berlin after Paris had turned its nose up. Following Newton's death in 2004 in Los Angeles at the age of ninety-three, it was his widow who opened this foundation. The thousand-odd pictures that make up the collection were presented in two temporary exhibitions, "Sex and Landscape" and "Us and Them", which became permanent. The museum reopened in June 2008 and includes exhibits such as Newton's Polaroids, while also showcasing new German photography. It features a reconstruction of Newton's studio apartment, along with his cameras, clothes, glasses and a weird car with Monte Carlo plates.

MUSEUM FÜR NATURKUNDE

Invalidenstraße 43, Mitte
U-Bahn Zinnowitzer Straße
Tel 30 2093 8591
www.naturkundemuseum-berlin.de
Open 9:30am to 6pm, Saturday and Sunday from 10am, closed Monday

NATURAL HISTORY

Built in 1889 by the architect August Tiede, this is the largest and richest natural history museum of its kind in Germany, with more than thirty million items. It was recently expanded with great success by Diener & Diener. Affiliated to the Humboldt University, the museum contains priceless collections, particularly strong in fossils and minerals. It has an outstanding programme of exhibitions devoted to topics such as the evolution of man or parasites. The place will fascinate children and is almost deserted during the week.

MUSIKINSTRUMENTEN-MUSEUM

Tiergartenstraße 1,
entrance on Ben-Gurion-Straße, Tiergarten
S-Bahn and U-Bahn Potsdamer Platz
Tel 30 2548 1178
www.sim.spk-berlin.de
Open 9am to 5pm, Thursday until 8pm, Saturday and Sunday from 10am, closed Monday

OLD MUSICAL INSTRUMENTS

The MIM is housed in a building designed by Hans Scharoun and is right next door to the Philharmonie. It forms part of the SIM, a research institute focused on the practical issues of musical performance. For example, how did Bach's music sound on the 18th-century instruments of his time? To answer such questions, they preserve and keep in working order nearly three thousand old instruments. They organize various period music events, including, every Saturday at noon precisely, a concert with something for everyone: a presentation and demonstration of the largest electric Wurlitzer theatre organ in Europe, with its four keyboards, 1,200 pipes, 200 registers and battery of percussion instruments.

NEUES MUSEUM

Museumsinsel, Bodestraße 1, Mitte
U-Bahn Friedrichstraße
S-Bahn Hackescher Markt
Tel 30 266 424 242
www.neues-museum.de
Open 10am to 6pm, Thursday until 8pm

PREHISTORY AND EGYPTIAN ART

The original building designed in 1855 by Friedrich August Stüler was seriously damaged during the war. For sixty years, it remained a ruin, open to wind and rain. Happily, it was restored, completed and healed by David Chipperfield (for which he won the Mies van der Rohe award in 2011), and reopened to the public in late 2009, crowning ten years of arduous work. The result is an architectural splendour that almost eclipses the wonders it holds, beginning with the world-famous bust of Nefertiti which, during the war, was hidden and preserved, like the rest of the Egyptian art collection and the German treasures, in the Eisenach salt mines. The New Museum combines in its reconstituted shell the Egyptian Museum, the Papyrus Collection, and the Museum of Prehistory. Simultaneously austere and grandiose, proudly showcasing vestiges of its glorious past, it takes your breath away the moment you enter, with its majestic double staircase and its dizzyingly high walls scraped down to the brick, revealing here and there fragments of the original bas-reliefs. You take that staircase to the first floor, where the Egyptian antiquities are presented at eye level in glass display cases set on granite-like concrete bases. The exquisite bust of Nefertiti, all the more spectacular in its toned-down surroundings, gazes out from a glass dome. On the floor, 19th-century mosaics amaze and enchant. On all sides, from the old passageway that led to the Altes Museum to the central glass ceiling that has replaced the bombed-out roof, the presentation is outstanding. Vestiges of the past include eleven bronze and terra-cotta statues by Otto Freundlich, Edwin Scharff and Marg Moll that were shown in 1937 in the Nazi exhibition of "degenerate art" and rediscovered when the U55 subway line was being dug out under the Rotes Rathaus (city hall). The Museum of Prehistory on the second floor is more didactic; children will love the fact that they are encouraged to touch things. The ground-floor bookstore will delight Egyptophiles.

PERGAMONMUSEUM

Museumsinsel, Am Kupfergraben 5, Mitte
S-Bahn Hackescher Markt,
S-Bahn and U-Bahn Friedrichstraße
Tel 30 266 424 242, www.smb.museum
Open 10am to 6pm, Thursday until midnight
ANCIENT ARCHITECTURE,
NEAR EASTERN ART

Built on the western part of Museumsinsel between 1910 and 1930 to plans by Alfred Messel and continued, on his death, by Ludwig Hoffmann, the Pergamon was the world's first museum devoted to the architecture of antiquity. It is named after the altar of the temple of Zeus at Pergamon, a miracle of the ancient world that entered its collection in 1886 and around which the building was constructed and later destroyed, along with some of its treasures, during the Second World War. In addition to its Greek and Roman collections, the Pergamon is home to the **MUSEUM FÜR ISLAMISCHE KUNST** (Museum of Islamic Art) and the **VORDERASIATISCHES MUSEUM** (Museum of the Ancient Near East), which owns the admirable Ishtar Gate from Babylon. Half of the museum, including the famous altar, will be closed to visitors until 2019, as a new entrance and reception centre for all the museums on the island are being built. The southern part, with its Babylonian treasures and the impressive market gate from Miletus, will stay open.

SAMMLUNG BOROS

Reinhardtstraße 20, Mitte
S-Bahn and U-Bahn Friedrichstraße
U-Bahn Oranienburger Tor
Tel 30 2759 4065
www.sammlung-boros.de
Open by appointment,
closed Monday to Wednesday
CONTEMPORARY ART BUNKER

Built in 1942 by Albert Speer during the Allied raids, the Reichsbahnbunker was intended to house railway employees. After the war it became a Soviet prison and then a warehouse for tropical fruit imported from Cuba by the government of the GDR. When the Wall fell, the building soon began a new role as a studio for hardcore techno and a place for fetish parties. Its fame was such that in 1995 it hosted the Sexperimenta event. But after a final techno party the following year, the bunker, totally indestructible, stood empty until its purchase in 2003 by the advertising executive and collector Christian Boros. The architect Jens Casper of Realarchitektur was commissioned to oversee its conversion. He removed some of the incredibly thick reinforced concrete walls, reducing the original 120 rooms to eighty and opening up some brutalist perspectives. The Boros family residence is a penthouse on the roof. Opened in 2008, the permanent exhibition is a spectacular feat of museum design, with each artist, from Olafur Eliasson to Tobias Rehberger and Kris Martin to Santiago Serra, contributing ideas on how their work should be displayed. There is nothing bland about this place: almost no natural light penetrates the two-metre-thick concrete walls, which still bear the marks of the building's original function. In front of one wide loophole window, Boros has provocatively placed a hospital bed with a dying figure on it. One of the rooms in the Best Western hotel right opposite looks straight into it, a view that might cause its occupants unease. Constantly at 14°C, its machinery still visible, with an entire arsenal of the anxiety-inducing elements still in place, the complex has nevertheless lost much of its pathos. The initial installation was replaced in 2012 with a new set of works that have been attacked by critics for their weakness. But the place is still worth seeing. The tour lasts ninety minutes in groups of fifteen and must be booked in advance.

SCHLOSS UND GARTEN SCHÖNHAUSEN

Tschaikowskistraße 1, Pankow
S-Bahn and U-Bahn Pankow
Tel 331 9694 200, www.spsg.de
Open 10am to 6pm, closed Monday;
November to March open 10am to 5pm,
closed Monday to Friday
PALACE

A stronghold of Queen Elizabeth Christine, wife of Frederick the Great, Schloss Schönhausen was one of the few historic royal residences not destroyed during the Second World War or razed by the communist regime after the war. This survivor therefore became the official home of the first president of the GDR, before being converted into a hostel for official guests of the socialist state. Indira Gandhi, Ho Chi Minh, Queen Beatrix of the Netherlands and Mikhail Gorbachev all slept here. These events have given the place great historical resonance and the entertaining and instructive museum here helps trace some of the unpredictable pathways of German political history. But you also discover, through a series of fascinating yet odd shortcuts, how the northern Rococo style morphed into comic modernity when the GDR tried to impose its own style in the early 1960s.

SCHLOSS UND PARK SANSSOUCI

Maulbeerallee, Potsdam,
25km south-west of Berlin
S-Bahn Potsdam Hauptbahnhof Train Park
Sanssouci, Charlottenhof
Tel 331 9694 200, www.spsg.de
Palace and park open all year,
follies April to October Tuesday to Sunday
ROYAL PALACES

Fed up with spending the whole year "in town", King Frederick II (the Great) had a pleasure palace worthy of his rank built in around 1742 as his summer residence in the rural tranquillity of Potsdam, just outside Berlin. He drew up plans, decided on the dimensions,

the number of rooms and the decor
and had it built by Georg Wenzeslaus
von Knobelsdorff, then the architect and
curator of the royal buildings. The
philosopher-king established his summer
quarters here as of 1747, decreeing
Sanssouci as a "palace without women",
after casting his own wife from his life and
bed long before by moving her to Schloss
Schönhausen and making no secret of his
homosexual inclinations. The palace is an
exemplary piece of Baroque architecture,
but twenty years later Frederick had
a second palace built, the Neues Palais,
on the western side of the park, to a design
by Johann Gottfried Bühring. The result
was a Rococo extravaganza. Intended
to demonstrate his absolute power to his
distinguished visitors, the building was
henceforth dubbed the Versailles of Berlin.
Sanssouci was later expanded and
restructured by his successors, especially in
the 19th century by Frederick William IV,
and then "extended" to include Schloss
Charlottenhof and the Roman baths built
by Schinkel, plus a huge park scattered
with follies and edifices ranging from the
Chinese Pavilion through to the Orangerie
and the waterworks shaped like a mosque.
Untouched by the ravages of the Second
World War, and preserved and pampered
against all odds by communist councillors
(Potsdam was in East Germany), Sanssouci
was eventually declared a World Heritage
site by UNESCO. The whole area is
now administered by the Foundation for
Prussian Palaces and Gardens of Berlin-
Brandenburg. You'll need more than a day
to visit it, especially in summer, when
the rich musical season is a leading cultural
event that attracts music-lovers from all
over the world.

SCHWULES MUSEUM

Lützowstraße 73, Tiergarten
U-Bahn Kurfürstenstraße
Tel 30 69599050
www.schwulesmuseum.de
Open 2pm to 6pm, Thursday until 8pm,
Saturday until 7pm, closed Tuesday

HISTORY OF SEXUALITY

When it was founded in 1984, Berlin's Gay
Museum, dedicated to telling the history
of the city's gay and lesbian community,
adopted for its name the pejorative term
Schwule ("fag"), so commonly used by
even the population in question that it has
passed into the language and is no longer
considered offensive. And there is certainly
nothing offensive in this museum,
which traces the story of the evolution
of a community from the 19th century up
to the present day, with its days of glory
under the Weimar Republic, its dark days
under the Nazis (the following era was
not much more favourable), and the
political struggle that led to emancipation
in the 1970s. The Schwules Museum
was originally an association formed by
Dr Andreas Sternweiler and was installed
for over a quarter of a century inside an old
Mehringdamm carpentry shop in Kreuzberg
until it was moved to the Tiergarten
in May 2013, during its twenty-fifth
anniversary year, thanks to a grant from
the municipality. The brand new saffron-
coloured building (the whole street is
undergoing urban renewal) has been
enhanced with smart architecture and an
interior design by the agency of Carsten
Wiewiorra, Anna Hopp and Guido
Schwark agency in Berlin. Inside, there are
several well-lit rooms offering a collection
built up from private bequests on
permanent display in chronological order,
while temporary exhibitions focus on
a given artist – for example the amazing
Sascha Schneider, king of homo-heroic-
erotic art from 1900 – or photographers
such as the South African activist
Zanele Muholi and her black lesbian
beauty queens. They also hold debates,

CITY STYLE

THE WILHELMINE OR GRÜNDERZEIT STYLE ("Founders' Epoch"), from 1871 to 1918. Opulent and extravagant, this architecture is characterized by heavily stuccoed facades with statues and columns decorating the piano nobile. Some examples in Kreuzberg and Schöneberg, some streets in Wilmersdorf and sections of the Ku'damm.

PUBLIC HEALTH AND INDUSTRIAL STYLES Housing industries (and their workers, whilst improving public health) were a major aspect of architecture from the late 19th century until the 1930s, ranging from Neo-Gothic to pure rationalism. The three main architects were Peter Behrens, August Endell and Hermann Blankenstein. Examples in Mitte, Prenzlauer Berg, Moabit and Kreuzberg.

JUGENDSTIL (OR ART NOUVEAU) replaced the Wilhelmine style at the turn of the 19th century. It is reflected in residential, commercial (large stores), institutional (ministries, banks) and hotel architecture. Found all over the city and well suited, from a structural point of view, to the advent of the Neoclassicism associated with the Weimar Republic, which was influenced by classical Greek architecture. Mainly visible in Charlottenburg, Wilmersdorf, Mitte and Steglitz-Zehlendorf.

MODERNISM – the Bauhaus and much more – was the supreme architectural movement in Berlin during the interwar period. All that remains today are the houses in Grunewald (listed), a few buildings in Wilmersdorf and Lichtenberg, and three really fine examples: the former Kino Universum and the building for the former Berliner Theater, designed by Erich Mendelsohn, and the former Shell headquarters on the banks of the Landwehrkanal, in Tiergarten, a masterpiece by Emil Fahrenkamp.

INTERNATIONAL MODERNISM was adopted in West Berlin in the 1950s to provide decent housing for Berliners. It was seen most clearly in the Interbau 57 project in Hansaviertel. Everything built subsequently in Tiergarten, on the Ku'damm, in Wilmersdorf and Schöneberg is "modern", but not particularly attractive. More remarkable: the buildings designed for the Kulturforum by Hans Scharoun.

PLATTENBAU was the solution found in the 1960s to poor housing in the East. The story goes that Erich Honecker used it as a propaganda tool to demonstrate how well people lived there. But the smart facades of P-Berg were simply illusions concealing some very substandard living conditions. A technique – prefabricated sections of reinforced concrete – became style. Symbol of the subsequent *Ostalgie*-trash culture, Plattenbau, found all over East Berlin, penetrated the West as well, disfiguring a large part of Wilmersdorf.

REUNIFICATION STYLE took many forms, visible in the reconstruction of Potsdamer Platz, the ministries and the new Chancellery, and the new central station (Hauptbahnhof). It expresses the status of the reunified country's political capital. Principal material: glass, an expression of transparency and democracy.

HOHENZOLLERNISM after the race to ultra-modernity, following the refurbishment of what was left of the historic buildings, the time has come for an imperial reconstitution, with the building of a perfect replica, controversial, naturally, of the Stadtschloss in Mitte. So Prussian style can once more be discussed in the city, that of a newly recovered grandeur.

meetings and book signings, and there's a small café and sparse bookshop for community outreach.

STASI MUSEUM

Ruschestraße 103, building 1, Lichtenberg
U-Bahn Magdalenenstraße
Tel 30 553 6854
www.stasimuseum.de
Open 10am to 6pm,
Saturday and Sunday from 11am
STASI MUSEUM

Seven decades of dark, unspeakable history, marked by Nazism, the destruction of the city, its division and a repressive communist government: in order to heal its wounds, Berlin reopens them, creating museums on the very sites where tragic and grim events took place. Visiting such places is invariably a disturbing and moving experience for visitors. Alongside innumerable memorials, including those commemorating the Holocaust, the Wall, and the failed attempt on Hitler's life in 1944 by Claus von Stauffenberg, there's one that is particularly chilling and that's the **GEDENKSTÄTTE BERLIN-HOHENSCHÖNHAUSEN** (Genslerstraße 66, Hohenschönhausen, tel 030 9860 8230) housed in the former Stasi prison in Hohenschönhausen, which graphically tells the story of how the victims of the repressive GDR regime were arrested, interrogated and confined. Only slightly less scary is the former Ministry of the Interior of the GDR in Lichtenberg, which has been transformed into a place of remembrance and research. The buildings have been left intact, with their original furniture, equipment and weapons, and were opened to the public in 1990, followed in 2012 by the office of Erich Mielke, the last head of the Stasi.

TCHOBAN FOUNDATION/ MUSEUM FÜR ARCHITEKTURZEICHNUNG

Christinenstrasße 18a, Prenzlauer Berg
U-Bahn Senefelderplatz
Tel 30 437 39 090
www.tchoban-foundation.de
Open 2pm to 7pm,
Saturday and Sunday 1pm to 5pm
ARCHITECTURAL DRAWINGS

Russia-born Sergej Tchoban worked in Moscow and Berlin, where he designed various buildings (Nhow hotel, AquaDom, Berolina Haus and Mall of Berlin, among others), and was twice selected to design the Russian pavilion at the Venice Biennale. He created his own foundation in 2009 and four years later opened this museum, transforming the former am Pfefferberg brewery into a multi-cultural centre. This stack of staggered concrete blocks covered with blue glass encompasses a library and a splendid exhibition space for architectural drawings, mostly Berlin-related. The same site includes **AEDES AM PFEFFERBERG** (www.aedes-arc.de), another key cultural institution dedicated to architecture which organizes exhibitions, debates and conferences at several Berlin sites.

ARCHITECTURE AND GARDENS

BOTANISCHER GARTEN UND BOTANISCHES MUSEUM

Königin-Luise-Straße 6–8, Steglitz
U-Bahn Rathaus Steglitz
S-Bahn Botanischer Garten
Tel 30 8385 0100, www.bgbm.de
Opening times vary, see website

BOTANICAL GARDEN
This is one of Europe's most famous botanical gardens. It covers 40 hectares in the heart of the green Dahlem neighbourhood, in west Berlin. It boasts magnificent landscapes dotted with interesting specimens. The collection includes desert plants, as well as tropical plants, housed in the Tropenhaus, one of the largest glasshouses in the world. The site includes a museum andspecialist bookshop wheer you can learn everything to do with trees, flowers, mushrooms and rare, exotic and local species. There are also regular temporary exhibitions.

INTERBAU

Hansaviertel, Tiergarten
S-Bahn Bellevue

MODERN ARCHITECTURE
As the Second World War came to an end, the victorious Allied powers occupied Berlin and divided up the former capital of the Reich between them. The Soviets kept the eastern half; the Americans, British and French shared the west. Each power managed its own sector, cleared its own acres of rubble – 75 million cubic metres between them – and rebuilt its own neighbourhoods. Some 40 percent of the city centre and 30 percent of the greater urban area lay in ruins. From 1947 to 1955, it was a case of drastic steps for drastic needs: slapping plaster onto whatever was left standing, smothering ornamented facades under a drab coat of yellow-brown roughcast. In what soon became the enclave of West Berlin, the new modernity

FLORA AND FAUNA

A truly green city, with 44% of its surface area occupied by forests, woods, parks and squares, not to mention the zoos, botanical gardens and private gardens, Berlin is home to an abundance of flora and fauna. Lined with 438,000 trees, an average of eighty specimens per kilometre, Berlin's streets are the world's greenest and shadiest (in summer). Top of the list are limes, of course, otherwise why would Unter den Linden – Under the Lime Trees – be called that, fragrance included? Next come maples, oaks, planes, sweet chestnuts, birches, black locusts and, a bit of a curiosity, carob trees, whose bean pods litter the pavement in strong winds, on Kantstraße for example. In the city centre, Charlottenburg-Wilmersdorf is the most wooded area, with most trees over forty years old. Further out, Pankow has much younger trees, planted in the last fifteen years. It's also said that there are over 2,500 centennial trees dotted around the city. Berlin is Europe's most species-rich capital. In addition to the zoo and domestic animals, some fifty species of mammals – boars, foxes, martens, racoons, rabbits – live wild in the city. The skies are populated by 180 species of birds, including falcons. In the waters of the city's rivers and lakes, pikeperch and trout spawn happily, with no known predators.

held sway, vertically and horizontally, as an open statement of what capitalism was able to deliver. The urbanization of the worst hit districts, such as Wilmersdorf and Tiergarten, and the new buildings lining the Ku'damm produced hideous results prompting comments from Berliners that the reconstruction architects did more damage to their city than the Allied air raids. In the mid-1950s, it was finally decided that West Berlin deserved better. That was the starting point of Interbau, an international architecture exhibition in which fifty-three architects from thirteen countries took part, including eighteen Berliners. Walter Gropius, Pierre Vago, Sep Ruf, Eugène Beaudouin, Egon Eiermann, Oscar Niemeyer – the aristocracy of architecture turned out in force. Thirty-six projects were actually built out of forty-five planned, all dotted around a leafy enclave called the Hansaviertel in the Tiergarten district and all had to meet the same basic requirement: to provide Berliners with new, modern, comfortable, immediately accessible housing in harmony with nature. You can see how well they succeeded by checking out the designs of Walter Gropius (Händelalle 3–9), Alvar Aalto (Klopstockstraße 30), Oscar Niemeyer (Altonaerstraße 4) and Paul Baumgarten (Altonaerstraße 1). The surrounding area is green, but there is little of interest to see.

ZOO BERLIN

Hardenbergplatz 8, Tiergarten
S-Bahn and U-Bahn Zoologischer Garten
Tel 30 25 4010, www.zoo-berlin.de
Open daily 9am to 6:30pm,
October to February until 4:30pm,
February to March until 6pm

HISTORIC ZOO

Berlin's oldest zoo, the Zoologischer Garten, opened in 1844 in a park designed by Peter Joseph Lenné. Its first guests were the 850 animals from the former royal menagerie, gifted to the city by King Frederick William IV of Prussia. But above all, it was the first zoo ever built in Germany. Its 35 hectares were soon divided up for the fanciful buildings in absurdly exotic styles commissioned by its then director, Heinrich Bodinus. He housed the antelopes and giraffes in an incredible pavilion topped with four minarets. The elephants were assigned an Indian style and ostriches an Egyptian one. Finally, in 1913, a fabulous three-storey aquarium was opened. Pagodas, temples, rotundas, glass palaces, even the famous entrance with its two elephants and their palanquin, all these buildings and the animals they housed were decimated during the Second World War. One of the few animals to survive, the hippo Knautschk, born in 1943, was the zoo's most famous resident for many years and a favourite with Berliners. He was followed by the panda Yan Yan, now sadly deceased, the gorilla Gigi and the polar bear Knut, hand-reared in the zoo. Restored, rebuilt, modernized, a model of its kind, the Zoo has been reunited with the

TIERPARK (Am Tierpark, 125, Lichtenberg, tel 030 515 310), set up in 1954 by the GDR authorities in the 160-hectare grounds of Schloss Friedrichsfelde; it has a famous collection of African elephants. The Zoo and the Tierpark between them house 2000 different species, with more than 20,000 animals, roaring, crawling, flying or just doing what animals do, from the amazing and funny orangutans to the crocodiles, fed every Monday afternoon at 3:30. Visited each year by almost three million human beings, the two zoos form a kind of vast VIP enclosure. All the animals are sponsored by individual Berliners.

CULTURAL PURSUITS WITH BARRIE KOSKY

In addition to being an avid and fast reader (he devours four to five books every ten days), Barrie Kosky listens to a lot of music, usually on the internet. Aside from the Komische Oper Berlin, he particularly likes the Hebbel, *"a beautiful little theatre with a wonderful soul"*. When it comes to museums, he regularly visits the Ägyptisches Museum, part of the Neues Museum, which was spectacularly restored by David Chipperfield. But the Komische Oper Berlin is the prime focus of his attention.

HAU – HEBBEL AM UFER
Stresemannstraße 29, Kreuzberg, tel 30 2590 0427, www.hebbel-am-ufer.de

KOMISCHE OPER BERLIN
Behrenstraße 55–57, Mitte, tel 30 4799 7400, www.komische-oper-berlin.de

NEUES MUSEUM
Museumsinsel, Bodestraße 1, Mitte, tel 30 266 424 242, www.neues-museum.de

THE SCENIC ROUTE
FOUR WALKING TOURS AROUND THE CITY

Although Berlin extends across a vast area, it is well suited for walking providing you are organized: you can't just go from one neighbourhood to another by switching pavements.

A green, flat city, the German capital is in a state of endless transformation. Wherever you might be – Kreuzberg, Schöneberg, Moabit, Mitte, Charlottenburg or Friedrichshain – you'll find that the city is rich in secrets, viewpoints, vistas, architectural treasures and new sights, offering endless thematic invitations to (re)discovery.

From parks, lakes and islands in the heart of the city to hip concept malls and a tour of new galleries, from Dahlem to Tiergarten and Peacock Island to Potsdamer Straße, currently in the throes of refurbishment, via the Berlin of David Bowie, these walks should be enjoyed at a leisurely pace so that you have time to take everything in.

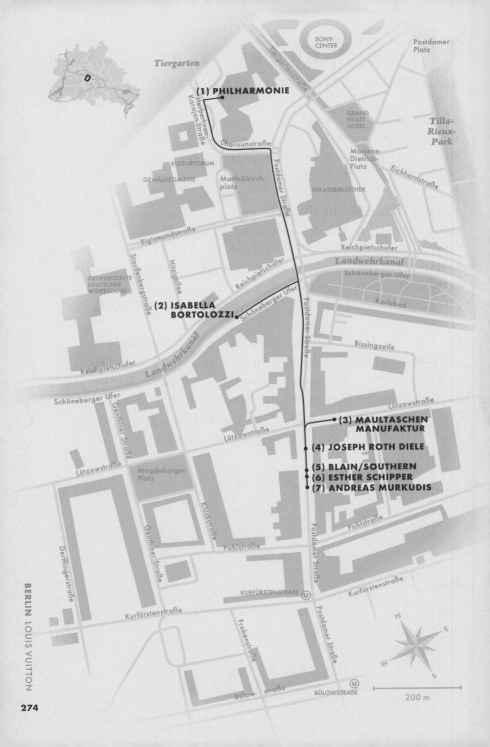

(1) PHILHARMONIE

(2) ISABELLA BORTOLOZZI

(3) MAULTASCHEN MANUFAKTUR

(4) JOSEPH ROTH DIELE

(5) BLAIN/SOUTHERN

(6) ESTHER SCHIPPER

(7) ANDREAS MURKUDIS

ART AND ARCHITECTURE
POTSDAMER PLATZ

Time: half a day

On the Schöneberg side of the Tiergarten, Potsdamer Platz boasts contemporary designs created by leading international architects such as Renzo Piano and Richard Rogers. It has become the symbolic square of a reunified, rebuilt Berlin. And the road leading from the centre of the square is a broad avenue heading – where else? – to Potsdam.

(1) PHILHARMONIE (Herbert-von-Karajan-Straße 1). Designed by Hans Scharoun in 1963, the Philharmonie is a spectacular building. Inside, guests take one of 2,200 seats, arranged in arcs, to listen to performances from the leading contemporary musicians. It is the centre of the Kulturforum, a space intended to be the cultural heart of Berlin, taking over the no-man's-land that lay here before the wall came down.

(2) ISABELLA BORTOLOZZI (Schöneberger Ufer 61). Art runs in the family for Bortolozzi, whose father collected 17th- and 18th-century art. In her ground-floor space here on Schöneberger Ufer 61, she presents works by contemporary instigators of the art word, such as Wu Tsang, Danh Vo and Oscar Murillo.

(3) MAULTASCHEN MANUFAKTUR (Lützowstraße 22). Home of the Maultaschen or Swabian ravioli, this unassuming little "factory" produces some of the best dumplings in Berlin. Buy them here to take home and prepare, or grab a small plate with a side of potato salad to go.

(4) JOSEPH ROTH DIELE (Potsdamer Straße 75). Named after Joseph Roth, the Austrian-Jewish journalist, best known for his 1927 essay *The Wandering Jews* that charted the Jewish diaspora, this café-restaurant serves classic German fare: Käsespatzle and Schnitzel. At lunchtime, the chequered floors and gingham tablecloths play host to locals, from art dealers to fashionistas.

(5) BLAIN|SOUTHERN (Potsdamer Straße 77–87). In the former HQ of the Tagesspiegel newspaper, it's all happening. At Blain|Southern, international artists such as Chiharu Shiota, Lynn Chadwick and Wim Wenders take over the vast space in the Berlin outpost of this London art gallery. In the same complex, Thomas Fischer and Guido W. Baudach are also worth stopping in on.

(6) ESTHER SCHIPPER (Schöneberger Ufer 65). Esther Schipper is one of the most important gallerists in Berlin. Having started in Cologne in 1989, she was one of the first to show artists such as Liam Gillick, Angela Bulloch and Philippe Parreno. In 2015, the gallery announced that it had acquired the Kreuzberg Johnen Galerie.

(7) ANDREAS MURKUDIS (Potsdamer Straße 77–87). When Murkudis moved out of Mitte in 2011, he asked architects Judith Haase and Pierre Jorge Gonzalez to design this imposing concept store, and in the process he created a new fashion hub on Potsdamer Straße. As much of a white cube as the galleries it shares a courtyard with, the space showcases objects and fashion with a minimal, avant-garde aesthetic.

(7) KUNSTHAUS DAHLEM

(8) BRÜCKE MUSEUM

Kreuzchensteig

Bussardsteig

Clayallee

Clayallee

Dohnenstieg

Am Hirschsprung

Finkenstraße

Starstraße

Finkenstraße

Dohnenstieg

Im Dol

Finkenpark

Im Dol

Königin-Luise-Straße

Vogelsang

Falkenried

Pacelliallee

Im Dol

Bernardottestraße

Am Hirschsprung

Drosselweg

Pacelliallee

Domäne Dahlem

Archivstraße

Koserstraße

Kaiser-Wilhelm-Platz

Bitterstraße

Thielallee

(6) DOMÄNE DAHLEM

Im Winkel

(1) DAHLEM-DORF

(5) LUISE DAHLEM

Königin-Luise-Straße

Edwin-Redslob-Straße

Peter-Lenné-Straße

Löhleinstraße

U DAHLEM-DORF

Brümmerstraße

Lansstraße

Otto-von-Simson-Straße

(3) MUSEEN DAHLEM

Thielallee

MUSEUM EUROPÄISCHER KULTUREN

ETHNOLOGISCHES MUSEUM

(2) FREIE UNIVERSITÄT

Habelschwerdter Allee

Arnimallee

Arnimallee

Fabeckstraße

Takustraße

Königin-Luise-Straße

Schwendenerstraße

Altensteinstraße

Altensteinstraße

Limonen-teich

(4) BOTANISCHER GARTEN UND BOTANISCHES MUSEUM

200 m

NATURE AND CULTURE
DAHLEM

Time: 1 day

Dahlem is a plush residential neighbourhood of luxurious villas in an all but rural setting south-west of Berlin. Even the U-Bahn station has a bucolic thatched roof. In addition to one of the world's finest botanical gardens, this rustic spot is home to Berlin's biggest university, a dozen research institutes and the city's largest museum, boasting a world-renowned collection of ethnological and non-European art. And there are even fields of grazing cattle.

(1) DAHLEM-DORF (Königin-Luise-Straße). The centre of Berlin, with its 1970s, tiled U-Bahn stations, feels a million miles away already. Dahlem's U-Bahn station, which serves the U3 line that goes all the way into the West of the city, was designed to look like a North German farmhouse by its architects F. and W. Hennings. A fitting welcome to the picture-postcard village.

(2) FREIE UNIVERSITÄT (Habelschwerdter Allee 45). One of the most prominent universities in Germany, FU provides teaching for over 34,000 students, who can be spotted all around the village. Founded in 1948 as a reaction against the academic restrictions of the Soviet sector's Humboldt University, it is now the largest public university in Berlin. The architectural gem here is the "Berlin Brain", designed by Norman Foster, which opened in 2005.

(3) MUSEEN DAHLEM (Lansstraße 8 or Arnimallee 25). Berlin's painting collection (Gemäldegalerie) was exiled here after the war, until 1998. The site now plays host to the Museum of European Cultures, as the Museum of Ethnology and the Museum of Asian Art prepare for relocation in at the beginning of 2017 to the future "new old" Stadtschloss, currently being rebuilt/reinvented in Mitte.

(4) BOTANISCHER GARTEN UND BOTANISCHES MUSEUM (Königin-Luise-Straße 6–8). The gardens and greenhouses of the city's botanical museum cover 43 hectares, with a magnificent collection of 22,000 plant species. The greenhouse of bamboo is particularly enchanting. Don't pass up the delightful Manufactum gardening boutique, stocked with chic tools and accessories.

(5) LUISE DAHLEM (Königin-Luise-Straße 40). This Dahlem institution is the perfect place to stop for some *Königsberger Klopse*, a classic burger, or, less traditionally, pizza with locally produced Brandenberg buffalo mozzarella. There's a garden for sunny days, and seven beers on tap.

(6) DOMÄNE DAHLEM (Königin-Luise-Straße 49). The ancient lands of the knights of Wilmersdorf have been cultivated for over 800 years and are now a living agricultural museum (Landgut und Museum). The modest Baroque manor dates from 1680, with outbuildings framing a quiet square, home to a Saturday morning organic market, a grocery store and a bistro.

(7) KUNSTHAUS DAHLEM (Käuzchensteig 8). The building was designed by Hans Freese as a studio space for the sculptor Arno Breker, one of the Third Reich's busiest sculptors. It's now a museum devoted to post-war German modernism, with an emphasis on sculpture supplemented by other art forms.

(8) BRÜCKE-MUSEUM (Bussardsteig 9). No, not a museum about bridges – this exhibition space is named after the first German modern art movement – Die Brücke, that was founded in 1905 by Karl Schmidt-Rottluff, Erich Heckel and Ernst Ludwig Kirchner. Today, its collection mostly focuses on German Expressionist painting.

KLADOW

(4) MEIEREI

Havel

Parschen-Kessel

Pfaueninsel

(5) KAVALIERSHAUS

(3) LAMABRUNNEN

Biberteich

VOLIERE

Wasservogelteich

KÜCHENBAU

(6) MASCHINENHAUS/FONTÄNE

(1) SCHLOSS PFAUENINSEL

FAHRHAUS

SCHWEIZERHAUS

FREGATTEN SCHUPPEN

(2) ROSENGARTEN

BADESTELLE

S-BAHN WANNSEE

KASTELLAN HAUS

Pfaueninselchaussee

Wannseeweg

(7) WIRTSHAUS ZUR PFAUENINSEL

Westlicher Düppeler Forst

Wannseeweg

Nikolskoer Weg

Pfaueninselchaussee

N
W   E
S

200 m

WATERSIDE TRAILS
ON PEACOCK ISLAND
(PFAUENINSEL)

Time: 1 day

Nestling in the romantic, lake-district landscape of the Wannsee, Peacock Island is a bucolic royal folly that seems to have stepped out of an antique painting. When the weather cooperates and the sun comes out, it's a minor miracle of nature, created by two generations of architects, landscape designers and gardeners who artfully invented a unique and harmonious world, purely for the pleasure of kings.

(1) SCHLOSS PFAUENINSEL [Nikolskoer Weg]. To visit the island, a 67-hectare nature reserve, take the ferry. Peacock Island Palace is a dazzling white castle boasting two towers linked by an iron walkway. Built between 1794 and 1797 by Frederick William II, who had bought the then undeveloped island as a place to relax and enjoy assignations with his mistress, the castle was designed in the Romantic style of fake ruins which was fashionable at that time. The palace is worth visiting between April and October for its exuberant, exotic, thematic, Neoclassical interiors which were all the rage during this period.

(2) ROSENGARTEN. Frederick William III commissioned the design of the park, including these English-style gardens, from the outstanding architects and landscape designers Peter Joseph Lenné, Johann August Eyserbeck and Ferdinand Fellmann, who created them in 1820. Like many other gardens, Peacock Island also has a botanical area, marked in this case by a majestic cedar of Lebanon.

(3) LAMABRUNNEN. The island was known as Peacock Island long before the Prussian rulers introduced these exotic birds to the place – but no one knows why. The peacocks you will see here today are descendants of those in the former royal menagerie that was built on the island. Various features, such as the LamaBrunnen and the Büffelteich (Buffalo Lake), a little further around the island, are reminders of the population of exotic animals that lived here before being transferred to the central Tiergarten zoo in 1842.

(4) MEIEREI. The designers of the island also managed to preserve the forest of 100-year-old oak trees to camouflage various essential "utilities", such as the a dairy farm hidden behind the artificial ruins of a faux medieval cloister in 1802.

(5) KAVALIERSHAUS. This unusual building was built between 1804 and 1824 by architect Karl Friedrich Schinkel in the middle of the island, behind the tall facade of a 15th-century patrician house brought over by boat from Danzig in 1824.

(6) MASCHINENHAUS/FONTÄNE. The gardens on the island required a regulated water supply: this steam engine powered the pump that distributed water across the island in clay pipes from 1822 onwards.

(7) WIRTSHAUS ZUR PFAUENINSEL (Pfaueninselschaussee 100, tel 805 22 25, www.pfaueninsel.de). This delightful beer garden is the perfect place to stop on your way off the island. Traditional German cuisine is also served, if you need something heartier. **PFAUENINSEL** S-Bahn Wannsee, bus 218, Pfaueninsel stop, then ferry, www.spsg.de

(8) REICHSTAG
Platz der
Republik
Pariser
Platz

BRANDENBURGER
TOR

(7) HANSA
TONSTUDIOS

(5) ZOOLOGISCHER
GARTEN

(6) PARIS BAR

(4) KADEWE

(2) CAFÉ ANDERES UFER
(1) HAUPTSTRAßE 155

(3) DEKO-BEHRENDT

← GRUNEWALD

IN THE FOOTSTEPS OF DAVID BOWIE

Time: 1 day

In 1976, in the grip of an existential crisis, David Bowie moved to West Berlin, that surreal fragmentary city, cut off from the rest of the western world. Bowie never concealed his admiration for German Expressionist cinema and films such as *M* and *Metropolis*. The catalyst for his departure was a meeting with the author of *Goodbye to Berlin*, Christopher Isherwood. After a brief stay at the Schlosshotel in Grunewald, Bowie rented an apartment at Hauptstraße 155 in Schönefeld, which he shared for a time with Iggy Pop, who became his accomplice as he explored the exciting Berlin scene of the period.

(1) HAUPTSTRAßE 155. Bowie occupied six rooms on the first floor of this late Wilhelmine-style apartment block, paying a ridiculously low rent. This is where distraught Berliners came to pay their respects to the musical legend, after his death in 2016, filling the street with a vigil of candles, flowers, written messages and photographs. A commemorative plaque stands outside, made of €3,400 worth of bone china.

(2) CAFÉ ANDERES UFER (Hauptstraße 157). Berlin's first gay bar, its name is now **NEUES UFER**. Bowie was a regular here, and the bar still celebrates the association without ostentation.

(3) DEKO BEHRENDT (Hauptstraße 18). This amazing costume, party-goods and make-up store, seems to be a reminder of Bowie's album *Diamond Dogs*. Searching for a muse, Bowie set his sights on Romy Haag, the flamboyant, transsexual Berlin superstar who ran her own cabaret, and founded **CHEZ ROMY HAAG** (Fuggerstraße 33), in Schöneberg's gay district, frequented then by the Rolling Stones and Freddie Mercury, among others. Today it's a gay cruising bar, the Connection Club, where you'd be hard put to find any false eyelashes. The black facade has become a shrine.

(4) KADEWE (Tauentzienstraße 21-24). Not far off, Bowie used to plunder the shelves of the food hall filling his fridge before Iggy Pop raided it again – just one symptom of their ongoing quarrels.

(5) ZOOLOGISCHER GARTEN (Hardenbergstraße). The film about Christiane F. is set around this station, which Bowie stars in and created the soundtrack for.

(6) PARIS BAR (Kantstraße 152). Bowie regularly took inspiration from the artists in this old salon-style restaurant during his time living in Berlin.

(7) HANSA TONSTUDIO (Köthener Straße 38). These legendary studios were located right next to the Berlin Wall and were where Bowie recorded the three wonderful albums in his "Berlin trilogy" – *Low*, *Heroes* and *Lodger*. Here, your best guide has to be Thilo Schmied (www.musictours-berlin.de), born and brought up in East Berlin, he is brimming with info and enthusiasm.

(8) REICHSTAG (Friedrich-Ebert-Platz 1). Bowie gave an open-air concert in front of the ruins of the Reichstag on 6 June 1987. With the amps on full blast, pointing towards the East, and thousands of young East Germans on the other side of the Wall, Bowie's provocative rendition of *Space Oddity* managed to reduce the East German authorities to silence.

LOUIS VUITTON'S GUIDE FOR TRAVELLERS

Travellers are not ordinary people. Curious, cultivated and demanding, they know that a journey is never insignificant. Such adventures can be fascinating, but also disastrous. We rarely travel luggage-free. Suitcases, bags and trunks accompany the globetrotter on long journeys, while the business traveller is never without a bolster bag containing a fresh outfit, nor a briefcase into which he or she has slipped a good read. We always put something of ourselves in our bags. Everything that touches on our personal world is there and needs to be well protected.

Cities, countries, people, landscapes, monuments, lifestyles, cultures – even on short trips, the traveller is driven by curiosity and a desire for new discoveries. A similar spirit guides his reading. Art, literature, images, stories – he wants to be transported far, far away. Ever since it was founded in 1854, Louis Vuitton has been in tune with the desires and aspirations of those who travel, whether physically or mentally. Today, it continues to help them fulfil their expectations, their wishes and their dreams.

THE ART OF PACKING

BACK IN THE DAY

Before going it alone and founding his own House, Louis Vuitton was a trunk maker and packer to the French court. For not only did he craft trunks that were as light as they were tough, but he was himself responsible for carefully packing his clients' effects in these chests, using a tried and tested procedure. Today, while the containers are no longer quite the same, the spirit is identical: practicality, lightness, comfort – everything that has been stored in the baggage must come out in perfect condition.

HOW TO PACK YOUR CLOTHES

Folding, rolling, turning down collars, slip-casing suits, stuffing shoes with tissue paper, doing up every second button – nothing is left to chance and nothing is improvised. Properly understood, packing is an art in which each item of clothing is folded and stored in a particular way.

SHOES

1. Put shoe trees in men's shoes.
2. Fill women's shoes with tissue paper.
3. Slip each shoe into its own pouch.

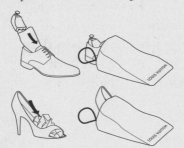

JEANS

1. Lay the jeans flat, legs apart, seams facing outwards, pockets face down.
2. Place one leg over the other.
3. Fold the jeans two or three times, or roll them up.

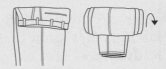

FINE SWEATER

1. Lay the fine sweater flat, neck at the top. Fold the sleeves inwards.
2. Roll it up from collar to base.
3. If necessary, roll it again, from left to right.

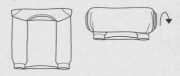

SHIRT

1. Raise the shirt collar in order to protect it.
2. Fasten every second button.
3. Fold it in two in the classic way, lengthways, with the collar visible and the sleeves folded behind.
4. Place one shirt over another, "head to toe", in order to avoid unwanted creases.

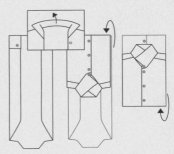

DELICATE DRESS

1. Place a t-shirt face down on the dress.
2. Fold the sides of the dress over the t-shirt.
3. Carefully fold the dress in three, starting at the top.

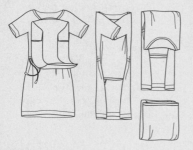

JACKET

1. First, raise and flatten the collar.
2. Fold in each sleeve, leaving the shoulders straight.
3. Carefully fold the jacket to fit the length of the bag.

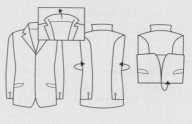

SKIRT SUIT

1. Fold the skirt in two vertically.
2. Raise and flatten the jacket collar.
3. Place the skirt inside the jacket.
4. Button up the jacket to protect the skirt.

MAN'S SUIT

1. Lay the trousers flat, the legs folded in the usual way.
2. Pass the outer leg of the trousers through the hanger. Fold it in two over the inner leg.
3. Pass the inner leg through the same hanger, fold it in the same way, towards the trouser waist.
4. Place the jacket on the hanger.
5. Put the complete suit in its bag.

TEXTILES, TIES AND BELTS

Roll up ties and belts, also scarves, which should be tightly rolled.

THE TEN ICONS OF TRAVEL

The history of the House of Louis Vuitton is measured out in landmark creations. These are hard-wired into the brand's genes and are part of the collective memory of luggage.

WARDROBE

The quintessence of hard-sided luggage, the wardrobes are the ultimate example of a practical form becoming a cult object. These legendary trunks were invented in 1875 to allow travellers to carry all their effects in a single container, a matchlessly robust combination of wooden structure and coated leather or canvas exterior. The two parts of this prodigious wardrobe-trunk have a hanging space on one side and drawers on the other. The woman's model has racks for hanging long dresses, while some of the drawers are spacious enough to hold voluminous hats. Even today, demanding travellers refuse to do without this accessory, which ensures that their clothes and accessories will remain perfectly safe and organized during their journey. Other advantages include the unpickable lock, and the fact that each client has a unique, single key for all his or her Louis Vuitton bags. And, finally, there's the pleasure of finding your mobile wardrobe at each destination. Travellers who travel lighter use these wardrobes as the centrepiece of their living space, setting the trunk in the hall, lounge or bedroom.

STEAMER BAG

Created in 1901, the Steamer Bag was originally one of those extra bags in canvas and leather offered with the trunk, made simply as an elegant receptacle for the personal laundry worn by travellers during a long ocean crossing. Hence its name. As for its nickname, "the inviolable", this was due to its reassuring reputation for never divulging those personal details, thanks to a highly sophisticated locking system. Tough, thanks to its hard-edged rectangular base, and exceptionally capacious, its versatility as a container made this complementary baggage a permanent favourite. Like the Keepall, the Steamer Bag benefited from the invention of the supple Monogram canvas in 1959, establishing itself as an item of luggage in its own right. Entirely hand-sewn, this bag still requires fifteen hours of crafting in the workshop.

KEEPALL

For many years, travellers who ordered a trunk or hard-sided luggage from Louis Vuitton were offered auxiliary bags in canvas with leather straps. One was the Keepall, designed in 1930. It is the ancestor of all the bolster-shaped duffel bags which, with changing lifestyles and means of transport, have become separate items in their own right. The invention of the supple Monogram canvas in 1959 made the Keepall the perfect answer to the demands of New Wave stars. A treasured personal signature, it was ideal for a weekend dash to Saint Tropez or Deauville at the wheel of a sports car. This spirit of freedom emanates from the films shot at the time on the beach at Pampelonne – ah, those sublime blond actresses! – or in the Saint-Germain-des-Prés of Jean-Luc Godard, François Truffaut and Jacques Rivette.

SPEEDY

Archetype of the versatile soft bag, the Speedy was conceived in the 1930s. Its extremely simple, generous form, easily identifiable for those familiar with its older brother, the Keepall, immediately established itself as the obvious partner of modern travel, where its lightness and versatility were a key advantage. In the 1960s, a new size was created for Audrey Hepburn. An easygoing city bag, it became one of the prime accessories of the modern woman. It plays a role in several histories – the history of Louis Vuitton, of course, but also within movies and fashion.

NOÉ

Designed in 1932 by Gaston-Louis Vuitton, grandson of Louis, when a champagne producer asked him to devise a robust but elegant bag capable of carrying five bottles of champagne (four upright and one in the middle, top-down), the Noé has become one of the House's cult objects. It too benefited from the invention of supple canvas, becoming a favourite of free, active women for whom distinction is a given. Today, the proportions have been modified and the bag is available in several sizes and finishes. Popular with female clients worldwide, the Noé is one of the great Louis Vuitton classics.

ALMA

The Alma was inspired by the Squire Bag, which was designed in 1934, and one of its first enthusiasts was an illustrious fashion designer. Reinvented in 1992, this pure Art Deco form naturally became a Louis Vuitton emblem, with its combination of roominess and obvious elegance. The quintessential multipurpose city bag comes in a range of sizes and materials and its design is constantly reworked through artist collaborations and following seasonal runway shows.

NEVERFULL

Resolutely contemporary, the Neverfull has been living up to its name since 2007. Its striped lining recalls the finest luggage of yesteryear, but this tote offers far more than mere history: it is superbly functional. Its slim, vegetable-tanned leather handles make the Neverfull tough enough for any occasion, and it is light and supple. Printed in Palm Beach or Porto Cervo colours, covered in Stephen Sprouse roses or awash with Yayoi Kusama waves, the Neverfull is perfect for the beach or the city and will carry back the best memories of either. Forever.

ICON OF ICONS
MONOGRAM CANVAS

The Monogram canvas was designed by Georges Vuitton in 1896. Initially conceived to thwart the fakers who copied striped and chequered canvases, it soon became the house symbol. At once bold and harmonious, the motif has always been utterly modern. LV, the initials of the house, are simply intertwined so that they remain perfectly visible, and three stylized flowers worked in different themes and variations mirror these. The elegance and restraint of these repeated ornaments create an image of graphic perfection, which is underscored by the positioning of the motifs.

PORTE-DOCUMENTS VOYAGE

Like the Steamer Bag and the Keepall, the Porte-Documents Voyage was one of the auxiliary bags offered with the hard-sided trunks. It was used for keeping travel pillows, but has now been diverted from this original function and, clad in Épi leather, as here, or Monogram canvas,

its new function, greatly appreciated by business travellers, is to carry documents, dossiers, papers and notes, which emerge without a crease or dog-ear from their journey. Neither a satchel nor a briefcase, the Porte-Documents Voyage is a sure way of keeping pages from scattering.

ALZER

The suitcase's traditional appearance masks a deceptively spacious, robust interior. The Alzer is like a chest, or even a strong box, with its reinforced locks, separate compartment and inner straps. A reassuring holder of treasured clothes that must be impeccable on arrival, its dimensions are ideal for optimum storage of everything you need when travelling for a few days. Its Monogram canvas exterior lends itself to personalization, helping to make this protective case unique, the must-have for refined travellers with a sense of what's best about tradition.

HORIZON

The Maison Louis Vuitton has called on renowned designer Marc Newson to create the luggage of the future. A great traveller himself, Newson designed Horizon with his own travel needs and experiences in mind. He used the most sophisticated technologies and materials available to make a superlative suitcase that is ultra-light, ultra-resistant and ultra-easy to handle. It has miniature wheels, moves silently and rotates 360 degrees. Its telescoping trolley handle is on the outside of the case, providing extra space inside and a flat interior surface for ease of packing. Equipped with accessories and storage pockets, it is sealed with a clever lightweight aluminium zipper. It took almost eighteen months to develop this "smart" suitcase, a technological marvel that can even be connected to other devices. Available in two sizes, with a choice of several surface styles, the perfectly elegant Horizon suitcase demonstrates once again Louis Vuitton's constant concern for innovation.

LOUIS VUITTON: AN OPEN BOOK

Books have always played
a special role in the history
of Louis Vuitton. The literary
adventure begun by Gaston-Louis
continues today with several
authoritative series.

AN ENLIGHTENED BIBLIOPHILE

Gaston-Louis Vuitton (1883–1970),
the founder's grandson, was a great lover
of art books and literature. The founder of
three bibliophile clubs, he corresponded
with publishers, illustrators and authors,
cultivating privileged relations with
many writer-travellers. These unique
bonds are reflected in the documents and
objects kept in the House archives,
such as Ernest Hemingway's bookshelf-
trunk, which still contained handwritten
notebooks, and the desk-trunk of Savorgnan
de Brazza, the hidden compartment of
which housed a top-secret report.

RENEWING THE LITERARY TRADITION

Today, the House of Louis Vuitton has its
own publications, with three travel-related
collections.

THE CITY GUIDES

Eagerly awaited every year, acclaimed
by opinion leaders, they capture
with glorious subjectivity the essence of
urban experience in an up-to-the-minute
selection of addresses, from the latest
designer hotel to a gourmet restaurant,
from the hottest fashion designer
to the best organic market, from a
photography gallery to a secret museum,
from a refined spa to a late-night watering
hole, or a surprising antiques dealer
to a maker of scrumptious chocolate.
Their mix of fascinating insider
information covers every aspect of
metropolitan life. This expert local
knowledge is made even more vivid by
the viewpoints of distinguished residents.

THE TRAVEL BOOKS

First published in 2013, this collection
revisits the travel notebook collection.
Louis Vuitton asked artists, illustrators,
graphic designers, painters and *mangaka*
to produce images that sum up their
vision of a city or country they don't
know, or know only slightly, in 120 original
plates. The Japanese Jirô Taniguchi
goes into exile in Venice, the Belgian
Brecht Evens arrives in Paris, the Frenchman
Jean-Philippe Delhomme sketches
New York, the Chinese Liu Xiaodong
flies to South Africa, the Arctic is captured
by the Irishman Blaise Drummond and
Mexico is charted by Nicolas de Crécy.

Colourful, personal and packed with
detail, this collection handsomely
combines Louis Vuitton's various initiatives
in art and publishing.

VOYAGER AVEC...

This collection, prized by literature lovers, comprises over thirty titles in which excerpts from the works of distinguished writers offer fresh perspectives on travel. The collection has invited readers to "travel with" Marcel Proust, Le Corbusier, Joseph Conrad, Nicolas Bouvier and Friedrich Nietzsche. This collection, published in French, is illustrated.

FASHION EYE

Each book in this photography series, launched in 2016, focuses on one location seen through the lens of a fashion photographer. Some places are well-known, others less so. There are famous photographers – some living, others long gone – and emerging talents. Paris by Jeanloup Sieff, Shanghai by Wing Shya, New York by Saul Leiter, California by Kourtney Roy, British Columbia by Sølve Sundsbø, Monte Carlo by Helmut Newton and Miami by Guy Bourdin. Some works are from the archives, others are contemporary shots. This is travel photography at its aesthetic best, a welcome return to the genre.

ART BOOKS

Louis Vuitton also collaborates on the publication of lavish books about the House and its heritage distributed worldwide. Co-edition titles include *Louis Vuitton: Art, Fashion and Architecture*, *Louis Vuitton City Bags: A Natural History*, *Louis Vuitton Fashion Photography* and *Volez Voguez Voyagez – Louis Vuitton* with Rizzoli, New York; *Louis Vuitton: The Birth of Modern Luxury* with Éditions de La Martinière; *I've just arrived in Paris* and *For Friends* with Steidl; *Louis Vuitton: The Spirit of Travel* with Éditions Flammarion; *Cabinet of Wonders: The Gaston-Louis Vuitton Collections* with Thames and Hudson and *World Tour* with Éditions Xavier Barral.

Limited, numbered artists' editions are also available, such as those by photographer

Jean Larivière and illustrator Ruben Toledo, echoing their creations for the House. Furthermore, in 2012, Louis Vuitton celebrated its savoir-faire and the art of travel by offering the House's first app for iPad, *Louis Vuitton: 100 Legendary Trunks*, conceived in association with Éditions de La Martinière, who edited the paper version.

THE ART OF WRITING

Moving forward from an outstanding heritage, Louis Vuitton journeys through the world of writing. Writing instruments, exclusive inks, crystal inkwells, writing kits, collector's trunks and boxes, as well as stationery, make up a highly symbolic art of writing which reinforces links with the House's history, as embodied in rare historic objects, and enables its clients to encounter some remarkable artists and artisans.

TRAVELLERS' BOOKSTORES

This tradition of the book initiated by Gaston-Louis Vuitton nearly a hundred years ago is now maintained and spread throughout the world. Several Maison Louis Vuitton have their own bookstore where Louis Vuitton publications are offered alongside a careful, pertinent selection of books on art, fashion, design and travel, helping to complete and enrich the heritage of knowledge, art and culture.

LOUIS VUITTON TIMELINE

1854
Louis Vuitton opens his first store at 4, rue Neuve-des-Capucines, Paris, and develops his first trunk, covered with grey Trianon canvas.

1859
Louis Vuitton moves his production workshops to Asnières, by the Seine, west of Paris.

1880
The newly married Georges Vuitton becomes co-director of the House with his father.

1883
Birth of Gaston-Louis Vuitton, son of Georges and Joséphine Vuitton.

1885
Opening of a Louis Vuitton store at 289 Oxford Street, in the heart of London. Four years later it moves to 454 Strand.

1888
Creation of the Damier canvas. For the first time in the history of the House, the words "Marque L. Vuitton déposée" appear on the canvas.

1890
Creation of the patented unpickable and individualized tumbler lock.

1892
Death of Louis Vuitton, aged 71.
Georges Vuitton works on his book *Le Voyage depuis les temps les plus reculés jusqu'à nos jours*, which would be published in 1894 and earns him the rank of Officier d'Académie.

1896
Creation of the Monogram canvas.

1905
Among other items, Pierre Savorgnan de Brazza orders two large bed-trunks from Louis Vuitton.

1914
Louis Vuitton opens the world's biggest store of travel items at 70, avenue des Champs-Élysées.

1920
A passionate collector and reader, Gaston-Louis Vuitton publishes *Voyage iconographique autour de ma malle*.

1923
The workshops in Asnières prepare 150 objects for Citroën's "Croisière Noire" African expedition.

1930
Launch of the Keepall soft bag.

1931
After the Croisière Noire, the House equips the Citroën Croisière Jaune (to China) and takes part in the Exposition Coloniale Internationale in Paris, where the Modernist Louis Vuitton Pavilion is entirely designed by Gaston-Louis Vuitton.

1959
Development of a new technique for coating the Monogram canvas, which will enable the conception of the whole soft baggage range and assure its success.

1978
Opening of the first Japanese stores in Tokyo and Osaka.

1983
Launch of the Louis Vuitton Cup, the winner of which challenges for the America's Cup. First edition at Newport, Rhode Island.

1985
Launch of the Épi leather line, now a House classic.

1992
Opening of the first store in China, in Beijing.

1996
Centenary of Monogram canvas.

1998

Louis Vuitton steps into the world of fashion with its debut ready-to-wear collection by Artistic Director Marc Jacobs.

2001

Creation of the Monogram Graffiti canvas, designed by Marc Jacobs in collaboration with American artist Stephen Sprouse.

2003

Launch of the Monogram Multicolore line, designed in collaboration with Japanese artist Takashi Murakami.

2004

Louis Vuitton celebrates its 150th birthday by opening the Maison Louis Vuitton on New York's Fifth Avenue.

2005

Opening of the Maison Louis Vuitton at 101, Avenue des Champs-Élysées, the brand's biggest store anywhere in the world, with interior architecture by Peter Marino.

2008

Collaboration between the American artist Richard Prince and Marc Jacobs for the spring-summer women's ready-to-wear collection. Launch of the Louis Vuitton Sofia Coppola collection of leather goods.

2010

Louis Vuitton takes part in Expo 2010 in Shanghai. "Voyage en capitale, Louis Vuitton et Paris": exhibition at the Musée Carnavalet in Paris.

2011

Opening of the Maison Louis Vuitton Marina Bay in Singapore, and of the first Australian Maison in Sydney. "Louis Vuitton. Voyages", an exhibition at the National Museum of China, Beijing.

2012

Louis Vuitton partners Japanese artist Yayoi Kusama in a series of artistic projects and products sporting her signature dots. "Louis Vuitton Marc Jacobs" exhibition at the Musée des Arts Décoratifs, Paris.

2013

The House collaborates with French artist Daniel Buren on the advertising campaign and store windows for its spring/summer women's ready-to-wear collection.

2014

The first Louis Vuitton ready-to-wear collection by Artistic Director Nicolas Ghesquière. Opening of the Fondation Louis Vuitton, designed by architect Frank Gehry. Celebration of the Monogram by Frank Gehry, Rei Kawakubo, Karl Lagerfeld, Christian Louboutin, Marc Newson and Cindy Sherman.

2015

Opening of the exhibition space adjoining the Louis Vuitton family home in Asnières-sur-Seine. Exhibition *Volez Voguez Voyagez – Louis Vuitton* at the Grand Palais, Paris.

2016

Louis Vuitton joins up with Unicef to help children in peril. Launch of Les Parfums Louis Vuitton

2017

Launch of the Masters collection, a series of bags and accessories created in collaboration with the New York artist Jeff Koons which revisits the emblematic works of the great masters of art.

INDEX BY NEIGHBOURHOOD

M./Mme/Mlle

....

....

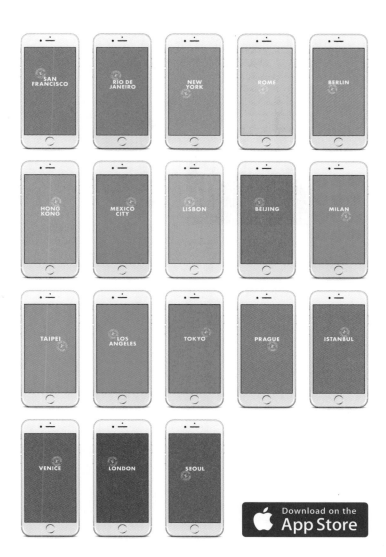

LOUIS VUITTON **CITY GUIDE**

LOUIS VUITTON **CITY GUIDE**

AUTHORS, PHOTOGRAPHERS AND EDITORIAL TEAM

AUTHOR

Pierre Léonforte

Pierre Léonforte is a journalist who divides his time between France and Italy. He works with the magazines *AD*, *Marie Claire Maison*, the review *Schnock* and *Air France Magazine*. He has also been editor-in-chief of the Louis Vuitton City Guide, which he helped create. He has written several books, including *L'Art de vivre à Marseille, Jean-Paul Hévin : Délices de Chocolat* (Flammarion), *Paris des Hommes* (Minerva), *Room Service* (Tatami) and *Louis Vuitton : 100 Malles de Légende* (La Martinière). He is also the author of the weekly column "Concierge Masqué" on the French *Vanity Fair* website.

PHOTOGRAPHY

Tendance floue

Founded in 1991, Tendance floue (literally, a tendency to be out of focus) is a group of thirteen photographers who have created a collective with the aim of working together to open up new perspectives and diversify the ways that contemporary photography can represent the world. In addition to their personal work, these photographers nurture their collective photographic research by comparing images, assemblages and combinations, their pooled results giving rise to completely new material. Involved in the press, publishing, exhibitions, screenings, collection prints, and corporate and institutional marketing, this collective is open to everything, embracing all the different media of contemporary photography. Berlin is brought into focus by Tendance floue photographer Patrick Tournebœuf. www.tendancefloue.net

Patrick Tournebœuf

Patrick Tournebœuf photographs people through what they leave behind, the spaces they embrace and sometimes abandon. In 2000, he travelled around seaside resorts in the off-season to create part of his series *Nulle part* (Nowhere). By modelling time, his work on the Berlin Wall *La Cicatrice* (The scar) was able to take a new fix on forgetful memory. Today he continues his search into photographic memory, photographing French heritage sites for his series *Monumental*.

PRESIDENT
Michael Burke

EDITORIAL DIRECTOR
Julien Guerrier

MANAGING EDITOR
Marie-Hélène Brunet-Lhoste

EDITORIAL CONSULTANT
Pierre Léonforte

**MANAGING EDITOR
ENGLISH EDITION**
Nicola Mitchell

COPY EDITOR
Bernard Wooding

EDITORIAL ASSISTANT
Erin Conroy

ARTISTIC DIRECTION
Lords of Design™:
Frédéric Bortolotti
Frédérique Stietel

LAYOUT ARTISTS
Marie Barbelet
Catherine Riand

MAPS
EdiCarto

PRINT PRODUCTION
Desgrandchamps:
Karine Rejon Midas
François Ollivier

THANKS
To everyone who has helped
with this edition, in particular:
Audrey Belescot, Nicolas
Bussière, Rosita Fanelli,
Édith Jarboua, Anja Kaehny,
Matthias Lenz, Florence
Lesché, Chantal Muller,
Anthony Vessot,
Valérie Viscardi
And also: Sangeeta
Berkelmann, Patrick
Hellmann, Johanna Schirm.

We decline all responsibility
with regard to any errors or
omissions that have occurred
despite the careful editing and
proofreading of the guide.

19th edition of the collection

Published by
Louis Vuitton Malletier
Louis Vuitton City Guide
2, Rue du Pont-Neuf
75001 Paris
cityguide@frvuitton.com
www.louisvuitton.com

A limited corporation with a
board of directors and capital
of €21,119,700
318 571 064 RCS Paris
APE: 514S
TVA: FR 43 318 571 064

The Louis Vuitton City Guide
is a collective work published
by Louis Vuitton Malletier.
It is produced by authors,
illustrators, layout artists,
copy editors, translators
and proofreaders working
in collaboration with
the company BETC, under
the direction of the company
Louis Vuitton Malletier and
its President and Editorial
Director.

The Louis Vuitton City Guide
is printed on Primalux 65g
FSC made with pulp
from sustainable forests.
It is set in the Futura
typeface designed by
Paul Renner in 1932,
digitalized and distributed
by URW++ (Germany),
and in the Arno Pro typeface
designed by Robert Slimbach
in 2007 for Adobe (US).

R08386